HEARING AND DOING

HEARING AND DOING

Philosophical Essays Dedicated to H. EVAN RUNNER

Edited by
John Kraay
and
Anthony Tol

Wedge Publishing Foundation
Toronto - Canada

ISBN 0-88906-105-X
Printed in the United States of America.

Contents

Dedication

The essays in this book are dedicated to H. Evan Runner, professor of philosophy at Calvin College, Grand Rapids, Michigan. They were composed to mark the joint occasion of his sixtieth birthday on January 28, 1976, and his twenty-fifth year of teaching at Calvin.

Volumes such as this one generally contain contributions written by colleagues who explore the implications or antecedents of the honored person's thought or offer critical evaluations of his major publications. This volume is not like that. The essays in it are written by former students, most of whom are not widely known authors and some of whom are just at the beginning of their academic career. Each essayist chose to remain within his or her specialty, impressed with the fact that the substance of Dr. Runner's teaching has important implications for every field of study.

The contributors to this book belong to the large number of students whom Dr. Runner challenged in the pursuit of Christian thought and action. Dr. Runner addressed his students with great spiritual conviction and deep religious meaning in a wide philosophical context. He gave stimulating "perspectives" courses in Christian philosophy, an innovative interpretation of classical thought, and a probing discussion of pivotal problems in modern philosophy. In order to help us understand that philosophy is but one of the expressions of the underlying religious forces in the culture of the West, Dr. Runner organized the Groen van Prinsterer Society—popularly known as the "Groen Club"—at Calvin College, where we were confronted with the crucial questions that face our society. Here we learned how seemingly immediate "issues of the day" are in the final analysis shaped and sustained by the spiritual forces at work in our culture. Perhaps most importantly, the rich personal contact with Dr. Runner, which often entailed an inordinate assault on his time (but never his patience), has had a lasting influence on many of us. Numerous tales can be told about how Dr. Runner's spontaneous and illuminating guidance helped us take the first faltering steps in the bewildering world of scholarship, pointing a path through its labyrinth of opinions and positions.

In these ways Dr. Runner *won us over* to a commitment. He impressed upon us the centrally Biblical conviction that *life is religion*, that life in its most concrete and direct actuality derives its meaning from the creational situation of God *speaking* and man *responding*. Religion is the dynamics of our individual and communal life in which our words, our work, and our actions in the world receive direction and focus.

To us, his students, this understanding of the Biblical meaning of religion was revealing in itself and liberating in its manifold implications. Most of us, initially, could do no better than to let religion rule in private affairs, as engendered by individualistic forms of Protestantism. But many of us also sensed that the claim of the gospel could not be ignored in the public concerns of society. Yet, how can one respond to this claim and meaningfully meet the problems of the economic order, of social justice, of political action, and of science's "value-free" domination when all around us religion is reduced to the confines of personal piety? In such areas men think they are autonomous and are masters of their own destiny. Dr. Runner taught that these areas, as part and parcel of creaturely life, are channels of service in which we are to effectuate the responsibilities to which we are called as God's stewards. We were taught to see how Biblical religion frees us for such cultural and intellectual responsibilities. Biblical religion dispels the illusion of autonomy. Biblical religion—hearing and doing the Word—lets life come into its own because it brings every dimension and concern into a perspective in which tasks and responsibilities arise.

Because Dr. Runner was thetical, he could also be critical, especially toward pragmatism, a dominant spiritual force in North America. William James, in his influential series of lectures entitled *The Varieties of Religious Experience*, has defined religion as "the feelings, acts, and experiences of individual men in their solitude, so far as they apprehend themselves to stand in relation to whatever they may consider the divine." To Dr. Runner, this definition would only vindicate the subjectivistic, private kind of affair that religion has come to be in America. James's words give a rather definite expression to the American temper on religion and implicitly contain the problems of the American way of life. Contrary to their intended effects, they pave the way for a disruptive polytheism and are disquieting in their uncritical, pragmatistic legitimization of only that religion which "works" in the arena of public life, the arena in which religious and communal desires are transformed into intelligent, workable choices. The Humanism behind pragmatism, itself of a much deeper religious nature than individual feelings and experiences, remains unnoticed and is not accounted for. Pragmatism stands in the very broad historical line which considers man and mankind as autonomous, as capable of himself creating order in his own house. In the light of today's vast scientific and non-scientific forces, in which man's communal opinions and desires are manipulated almost at will, we see, first, how this pragmatistic Humanism, with its public workability, is impotent in the face of manipulative machinations; secondly, how the hidden persuaders are not unpragmatic in that they do prove their workability, though enforced; and thirdly, how the pragmatistic, autonomous ordering of life, especially in the hands of the hidden persuaders, becomes a revealing nihilism. Should we be surprised to see that this way of life is considered meaningless by so many people today?

Surrounded by such lack of meaning, students, too, are adrift, ready to embrace any reactionary or revolutionary program of action, ready to lose themselves in ritual or illusion. But Dr. Runner showed his students a better way. A full decade before the Humanistic counterculture of the sixties, he articulated a radically Biblical critique of our pragmatic society. He broadened conversion to include intellectual renewal. He introduced his students to the tradition of the Reformation as it had been continued in the Netherlands, reappropriated since the days of the *Réveil* (in the mid-nineteenth century) by such men as Guillaume Groen van Prinsterer and Abraham Kuyper, and developed philosophically in our century by D. H. T. Vollenhoven, Herman Dooyeweerd, and those around them. A wealth of Scripturally directed learning, predicated on the conviction that the Word of God is radically and intensely relevant for the whole of life, was opened up to us, inviting us to listen to the Word and to respond in kind, not in slavish repetition of that tradition's time-bound terminology, but in discernment of the ordering principle at work in it.

Dr. Runner's outreach was not limited to the Calvin College setting. He has also given guidance to several Christian action movements in the United States and Canada. His prophetic leadership in the Association for the Advancement of Christian Scholarship, since its inception in the mid-fifties, laid the foundation for the establishment of the Institute for Christian Studies in Toronto. In his publications he unfailingly pointed to the way of Christian discipleship, of hearing and doing the Word, in a critical period of Anglo-Saxon culture.

This book is a small token of profound appreciation. All the contributors were, at some time, Dr. Runner's students at Calvin College. It was especially there that one could partake of his memorable and incisive teaching. In dedicating these essays to H. Evan Runner, it is the hope of each contributor that at least some of their teacher's emphases are recognizable in this book.

On behalf of the contributors

John Kraay
Anthony Tol

Free University of Amsterdam,
Summer 1979.

Introduction

This book is the result of an idea launched by the present editors of providing a gift to Dr. Runner in the form of a *Festschrift* written by former students. The response was overwhelming. Glenn Andreas, one of Dr. Runner's closest friends, and Paul Schrotenboer, secretary of the Reformed Ecumenical Synod, enthusiastically joined us, together with Bernard Zylstra of the Institute for Christian Studies and Harry Van Dyke of the Free University of Amsterdam, to form a committee for this purpose. It was a festive moment indeed when Glenn Andreas was able to present to Dr. Runner on his sixtieth birthday the gift of the manuscripts in rough form. Upon the appearance of this publication the editors wish to express their sincere thanks to the members of the committee for the advice and encouragement they gave and for the work they have done.

The essays in this book have been arranged in terms of a spectrum which begins with concrete, twentieth-century directional concerns and ends with specific, scientific topics. The spectrum may be broadly partitioned into five categories, sufficiently distinct to serve as organizing layout for the summarizing discussion here.

The first group of essays deals with *current political and social approaches to problems.*

Hendrik Hart presents an engaging discussion of the spirit of positivism and its influence on political views in societies that are supposedly non-totalitarian. He suggests that the spirit of positivism may well invite totalitarianism, even in democratically liberal and intellectual climates. Finding this a real possibility, he confronts it with the claims of the gospel.

Bernard Zylstra reviews the thought of the democratic liberal Daniel Bell, who has come to doubt the modernistic, liberalistic idea of progress.

Zylstra assesses this neoconservative, reactionary criticism of modernism which, he holds, has itself not become sufficiently free from deeply ingrained traits of modernity.

Edward A. Langerak takes a hard look at the idea and ideal of freedom. He reviews numerous approaches to various definitions of freedom and finds all of them wanting in some essential way. He concludes that any substantially adequate definition of freedom as idea engages and appeals to ideals which, in turn, refer ultimately to what a human being is and should be.

The second group of essays is concerned with very direct matters pertaining to Scripture and the *Biblical-religious light* it sheds on various areas.

James H. Olthuis works toward what he calls a "certitudinal" hermeneutic of Scripture. Rather than following the traditional methods of either letting the Bible speak to supposedly virginal minds or letting Scripture say only that which conforms to one's own presuppositions, he seeks to understand the Bible out of a pre-understanding that is itself ground true to the pistical nature of Scriptural texts.

Hugh Cook finds in Thoreau's use of literary imagery many references to the King James Bible. He argues that Thoreau's intention is not to promote a deeper acquaintance with the Bible and its meaning, but rather to give literary expression to his own dualistic Transcendentalism.

Arnold H. De Graaff discusses monistic and dualistic views of man; neither type can be considered Biblical. In terms of a confessional understanding of man and life, De Graaff approaches the anthropological problem of man's spiritual unity in its relation to the diversity of man's functions. After rejecting traditional models for ways of handling this problem, he formulates the contours of an alternative model, from which he draws some implications for psychotherapy.

The third and fourth groups of essays are historically oriented. The first of these concerns, in some sense, the mind of *medieval scholasticism* and its peculiarly problematic way of formulating the relation between faith and reason.

Wendy Elgersma Helleman traces in Augustine's early educational theories the influence of his growing Biblical understanding of the meaning of education. But she also finds a notion of corporality and incorporality lingering throughout this development which leans on Greek ontology instead of expressing a Biblical confession, and which remained influential for many subsequent centuries.

Peter J. Steen investigates the theme of the relation between time and eternity and finds intrinsic connections between this theme and the medieval, scholastic theo-ontological speculation concerning God's being. He notes also many points of influence and similarity within the Protestant traditions of thought.

John Van Dyk gives a summarizing impression of the theologically influential work of Peter Lombard's *Sentences*. Admitting its theological importance, he argues that the work should also be considered in terms of its significance for medieval philosophy.

John C. Vander Stelt shows how the relation between faith and reason, as inherited from scholasticism, leads to an inconsistent empiricism in the theological thinking of Archibald Alexander, as the latter combines scholasticism with an uncritical use of the presuppositions and concepts of Scottish Common Sense philosophy.

The second group of historically oriented articles concerns modern philosophical history and is directed to post-Kantian and post-Hegelian *German philosophical thought*.

Henry Vander Goot explains and criticizes Schleiermacher's view of religion, which he had formulated so as to be acceptable to the despisers of religion among the Humanistic culturalists of his day. The focal problems within Schleiermacher's view of the relation between religion and culture, argues Vander Goot, are not without influence upon the modern study of the philosophy of religion, hermeneutics, comparative religions, and the theology of culture.

Theodore Plantinga looks at Dilthey's historical work and distinguishes his approach, which emphasizes the personal element in philosophy, from that of the earlier Hegel and the later Nicolai Hartmann. His claim that Dilthey does allow for a standard of truth independent of historical origin makes problematic the usual historicistic interpretation of Dilthey's historical work.

John Kraay focuses on the central thrust of Heidegger's well-known "Kant book." His argument that Heidegger, while seeking to do full justice to Kant's basic insight, attempts to dig deeper than Kant did in founding philosophy offers an alternative to interpretations in which this book is either viewed as a mere illustration of *Sein und Zeit* or is taken as a violent usurpation of Kant for Heidegger's own purpose.

The last group of essays contains *systematic reflection* on distinct topics of scientific foundational import.

Albert M. Wolters focuses on D. H. T. Vollenhoven's "problem-historical method" for understanding and writing the history of philosophy. He seeks to demonstrate that in Vollenhoven's own brief accounts of the method it remains unclear how the problems, when logically formulated, retain a historical character, and whether matters distinctly historical are sufficiently treated as problems. In evaluating Vollenhoven's work, he draws on analogies with French structuralism.

Calvin G. Seerveld offers a global view of the sort of questions any science of aesthetics must deal with. In his account of the meaning of aesthetics he brings to bear a new characterization, different from his former analyses, when he centers aesthetic meaning on "allusiveness." He contrasts this, among other things, with the waning tradition of Beauty.

Anthony Tol seeks to discern what the meaning of number is in the process of counting and what is required for the concept of number as treated in arithmetic and number theory. In his results he shows intuitionistic and logicistic approaches to be defectively one-sided, and he argues that the very general feature he calls "numerosity" may give a focal unity to the different demands upon number in counting and as concept.

The essays that include a bibliography have italicized numbers where references are made to sources. The sources are listed with corresponding numbers at the end of each such essay.

It is a great pleasure for us to be able to incorporate a substantial extract of interviews with Dr. Runner. With the present *Festschrift* in mind, Al Wolters and Harry Van Dyke conceived the idea of asking Dr. Runner to recount some important periods in his life. Each spent a day with him and recorded what was said. In a mixture of incisive subtlety and uninhibited spontaneity, Dr. Runner reminisced about the course of his life, dwelling on crucial periods and etching in details and contours. Having agreed to publication, he made a special effort to illuminate the background, development, and mainsprings of his career, in a way that is characteristically his own. Thus, as was hoped, the printed interview turned out to be well suited both to suggest something of his personal charm and to document the way in which native talent, evangelical fervor, and thorough training could make him the unforgettable teacher he has come to be.

The interview tapes were worked out by Harry van Dyke, who, in deference to Dr. Runner's flow of words, has (regretfully) managed to remove all traces of the interviewers' leading questions. He also selected pertinent quotations from Dr. Runner's publications. The final result, authorized by Dr. Runner, appears at the end of this volume.

The Central Interfaculty of the Free University of Amsterdam has been of real help in making this international venture practicable. In this connection a special word of thanks is due to Jacob H. Santema, director of its Philosophical Institute, for his ready cooperation with respect to technical facilities. Henny van Geffen Mes, one of the Institute's assistants, greatly helped in preparing the typescripts. John Hultink, one of Dr. Runner's former students, offered his services in the production of the book. Theodore Plantinga advised in the make-up of the book. Finally, Wedge Publishing Foundation cooperated in arranging the necessary financial subsidy for this venture.

J.K.
A.T.

Struggle for a New Direction

HENDRIK HART

Introduction

The influence of philosophical positivism on the day-to-day course of affairs in the enterprise of scholarship has been so vast that Radnitzky (in *Contemporary Schools of Metascience*) estimates its drag effect on different traditions to have been not less than "causing the delay of other approaches by about half a century" (p. 382). What is meant by positivism here must be very widely and generally understood. Kolakowski's use of the term (in *The Alienation of Reason*) comes close. He takes it to be an anti-philosophical philosophy about what is to count as valid knowledge, where valid means phenomenal, nominalist, factual and scientific.

I take positivism to have its roots in the Greek conviction that true knowledge is to be characterized as primarily rational-logical in kind. When these roots in the last century gave rise to a movement characterized by anti-metaphysical, objectivist, value-neutral, empiricist, natural-scientist attitudes, positivism was born. Thus, the term is used in this essay in a wide, though not indefinite, sense. Kant also used it in this sense—the positive as the given, the observed, the scientific—and he inspired its introduction as name for a movement by Comte and Spencer.

In this wide sense, positivism may have a number of characteristics such that no single positivist will entirely accept all of them and that none of them is found in all positivists. It may even have characteristics that seem mutually exclusive, such as nominalism and determinism.

In the opinion of many, positivism is now no longer a viable option. In philosophy this is becoming increasingly evident. In the philosophy of science this is shown in the work of people like Apel, Feyerabend, Grene, Habermas, Hanson, Hempel, Kuhn, Laszlo, Polanyi, Popper, Radnitzky, and Toulmin, while splendid work in the psychology of thinking, observation and perception has been done by such scholars as Buytendijk, Köhler, Lorenz, Maslow, Piaget, and Merleau-Ponty. They have established that the simplistic views of thinking and observation entertained by empiricists, positivists and behaviorists are grossly inadequate.

Yet, the spirit of positivism has very deep roots. And even in philosophy, the overriding quest for rigor, for logical exactness, for scientific respectability, is far from dead. In the various scholarly disciplines it would seem that it is in the prime of its life. Philosophic convictions take long to root, but perhaps even longer to die.

Even though positivism as a movement arose in protest against speculative metaphysics and unfounded dogmatism and attempted to put analysis on a scientific basis, it certainly inherited notions of science, knowledge, experience, etc. that had their own roots and historical background in the very metaphysical systems that were now suspect. And it must be seriously asked whether the critics of positivism do not in principle retain the metaphysical roots that gave rise to it.

As a matter of fact, many of these critics only seem to desert the more strictly scientistic notion of rigid empirical verification, through sense observation, of theories with a physicalistic bent. However, they retain notions such as that philosophy is a formal-logical analysis of concepts, that truth is a logical matter, that epistemology is necessarily vague, that all analysis must be rigorous, etc. They may also remain convinced that true knowledge is primarily rational, that the best knowledge is scientific, or hold similar beliefs. The term *positivism* in this exploration will also refer to critics of positivism who entertain these thoughts.

So long as a scientistic spirit remains, the wisdom of the universities will stay harnessed in statistical correlations, the use of immense quantities of energy will be dispersed in detailistic research, the larger questions of human interest will continue to escape the fine mesh of logical and symbolic rigor, and the results of theoretical analysis will have been so designed as to be of little use in coming to grips with the fundamental issues that today threaten to undermine 2000 years of Western civilization. In this context we find Radnitzky stating a general relationship of some significance: "Positivistic social science is the only one a totalitarian society can use and *tolerate*" (p. 329). I would like to comment in this essay on that sentence.

Radnitzky adds a lengthy footnote to this sentence. In it he comments a bit more extensively on what he means by totalitarianism. He declares that the main character of the totalitarian outlook is its functional dissolution of individuality into society at large. He then goes on to say that we also find tendencies toward anti-liberal, anti-intellectual and anti-pluralistic attitudes. Elsewhere he typifies the closed-mindedness of such a society as "a world full of violent creeds, rash opinions and the imperious commands of little ignorant men with great authority" (p. 339).

Now, Radnitzky appears to have noted this sort of problem primarily in the Fascism of the Right and the Communism of the Left. However, is it true that the authoritarian ignoramus with his fear of the liberal, pluralistic and intellectual mind is found primarily in a Fascist or Communist context? And is totalitarianism reserved only for them? As Radnitzky points out, totalitarian states exclusively tend to tolerate positivist social science. But shouldn't we, furthermore, investigate whether the reverse is true as well, namely, that the spirit of positivism invites totalitarianism in any climate, even the democratically liberal and intellectual climate?

This essay cannot possibly pretend to be a report of careful research into this possibility. But it can attempt to point out certain relationships that seem obvious and can stimulate such research. We are only now coming into a period in which everything that positivism had declared to be either irrelevant or unscientific is increasingly being regarded as lying near the core of authentic research. Consequently, many research programs will have to be initiated by the stimulus of intuitively sensed relations of significance. Later, during the actual course of research, these surmised relations will undoubtedly be better understood and better formulated. But until then, our statements will have to be "feelers" of the sort that positivists would dismiss as vague.

Accordingly, I will begin by giving just a few possible grounds for my question, after which I will try to indicate possible relationships that can be investigated in the future.

Grounds for suspicion

For a Christian scholar, these questions are of peculiar significance. The record of Christianity in ameliorating social conditions seriously deformed by sin is not a particularly proud one. The main traditions in Christianity tend to be conservatistic. Consequently, God has often been left, historically, with no alternative other than to use non-Christian traditions to expose these social conditions as evil. It is frequently only after such exposure that Christians join the bandwagon. And late is better than never. However, another tradition has by then likely taken the initiative. It is probably already working on a solution while the Christians are still exposing the ills.

Today we seem to be living in exactly that kind of a situation. All over the world there is a growing tendency to undermine the strength of traditional destroyers such as capitalism and materialism, authoritarianism and paternalism, nationalism and individualism, absolutism and conservatism. Some of the solutions seem to have a built-in resistance to Christianity, such as Communism, libertarianism, anarchy, and revolution. People espousing these solutions usually are not open to the gospel, while Christians (after initial flirtations) sooner or later discover the fundamental and irreconcilable differences.

But other tendencies (foreign to the gospel) that replace the recognized evils may easily escape attention, especially in a period of enthusiastic Christian resistance to being behind the times. It is exactly in this sort of time, therefore, that the Christian community should try to find a healthy, critical attitude toward the new ways. Those with whom we share a certain critical evaluation are not necessarily those who offer us solutions that we can share. And it is for this reason that I am asking my question. In this context the question can also be formulated as follows: Are there conditions that will foster a totalitarianism of the liberal spirit?

But now the more specific grounds for my question. In a brochure of 1967, entitled *The Democratic Way of Death*, I tried to indicate that the elevation of the political method of democracy to a communal way of life leads to the absolutization of the community in such a way that a plurality of conviction is not publicly tolerable. Thus, North American society tends, insofar as the main tradition is concerned, to be so committed to the "democratic way of life" that it exhibits totalitarian characteristics. Where the state becomes the guardian of one way of life only, the whole culture risks the danger of totalitarian trends. And this does not only happen in the U.S.S.R. or in South Africa.

Such is very clearly the case, for example, in the state-sponsored schools in both the U.S. and Canada. Though the society of these countries is clearly pluralistic, the schools primarily educate for "citizenship" and in so doing enforce not only one way of life but also a state-sanctioned denial of true, public convictional plurality. Though the U.S. certainly styles itself the bulwark of true freedom and democracy, it is not sufficiently aware of these unfree forces, even though it is quick to notice the presence of trends in South Africa that are similar in principle. In this context it is perhaps understandable that the same U.S., which is noted for its love of freedom, is also the home of powerful undercurrents of anti-intellectualism and anti-liberalism—the two other characteristics of totalitarianism mentioned by Radnitzky. Yet, in spite of these tendencies, no serious and responsible analysis of the U.S. can come to the conclusion that what we have here is, pure and simple, either Communism or Fascism.

Other examples can be mentioned. Thus there seems to be very little critical depth on the part of the liberal tradition that now so strongly puts pressure on certain regimes (at the painful exclusion of others) in Latin America and Southern Africa. For, while we can well sympathize with the exposure of dreadful injustices in these parts, one must wonder about the spiritual and foundational awareness of leaders who seem to remain blind to the fact that what can be called a political technique (democracy) tends to become totalitarian (its very opposite) when preached as a way of life.

And what of the question we may need to ask ourselves about "one man, one vote" democracy: Is it really the only way, and, if not the only, then the best under all circumstances? Is the ballot box a significant place today? Could it be that voter apathy has good grounds? In addition one wonders whether much critical analysis has gone into the heavy stress on the need of each citizen to own property. Is there a correlation between that view and capitalism? Is it truly impossible to be one's proper self without having property in the sense of owning land? Many are the leaders in our enlightened West who appear to be seeing these two as the sole source of true liberty, justice and happiness.

Why is it that democracy is never critically evaluated in democratic communities? Why does not the thought suggest itself that today (when Humanism is dissolving, when immaturity and irresponsibility are rising) the democratic "one man, one vote" way is antiquated and conservatistic? Are there relationships between atomistic, empiricistic positivism and "one man, one vote" democracy? John Locke has played an important role in the rise of both, and his works may well provide clues to the answers to these kinds of questions. Has the West shown the rest of the world that whenever you give a person a dollar and a vote, you will have a happy person? Or that no person can be happy without them?

Still another complex of questions arises. There can be little doubt that Radnitzky is right in seeing closed societies full of violence, rashness, pomp, and pseudo-authority. But only the blindest prejudice could deny that these same characteristics are found in quarters other than the ones he mentions. Violence is a popular article also outside of Communist and Fascist communities; ignorance and lack of vision are evident in the behavior of many a Western parliamentarian; and the dictatorial action of many who "liberally" protest authoritarianism is oppressive. Violence is combatted with violence. Justice is so absolutized and torn from its context that it often produces severe hardship. Again one might ask: Is the positivist self-characterization of "most critical" so non-*self*-critical that it produces forces that are blind, imperialist, totalitarian, dictatorial, authoritarian, repressive, unfree, solipsist, absolutistic? (See Polanyi: *Personal Knowledge*, pp. 219, 268, 323.)

These are just some of the problems which any observer of the contemporary scene in so-called liberal and democratic communities can easily perceive. They point to phenomena that clash with the professed aims and purposes of those communities. Why are they there? Is it because through the influence of the universities, in which future leaders are trained only to objectively manipulate logical relationships uncritically, the leadership of these communities is saturated with the spirit of positivism? And is it for this reason also that the coming generation of sensitive young people is idealistic without being self-critical?

These people realize that in the service of seeking justice one must be willing to suffer injustice. Do they also see that in that service one must not commit injustice or even lack in mercy? They realize that suffering injustice by letting injustice continue is masochism and cowardice; indeed, it promotes injustice. But do they see that the oppressed cannot be liberated through the oppression of the oppressor? Forces of oppression are best known by the oppressed and hardly at all by the oppressor. But does this mean that they should teach oppressors their vice by experience? Is oppression a virtue when directed at oppressors?

It is at this point that I would launch my intuition that positivism tends to promote totalitarianism. If my intuition is correct, it would not only be true that there are definite signs of totalitarianism in some of our most cherished liberal, intellectual, pluralistic traditions, it might also be possible to indicate definite grounds suitable for the breeding of such tendencies.

Not-so-liberal positivism

Democracy as a significantly public way of dealing with fundamental issues of public justice in society is particularly meaningful if that society harbors very deep and important differences. Consequently, the more important democracy becomes, the more important it will be to respect the pluralistic character of such a society. In that kind of society it is exactly the so-called liberal mind which is historically the champion of freedom for all traditions found among its people. And seeing the immense pressures that come from the competitive struggle between the different traditions as they strive to influence their culture, there is great need for an intellectual tradition. By the latter is meant a tradition of critical self-reflection alive within the society, to protect it from hidden dogmas that could threaten to upset the delicate balance. Thus, the liberal-democratic intellectually-critical pluralistic mind intends to keep a society open, to guard it from a traditionalistic tyranny of any kind.

The greatest danger for such a mind is that it sees itself, contradictorily, as the only viable tradition for a *modern* society. A modern society *is* pluralist. It must be capable of harboring within itself the most profoundly differing convictional communities. Consequently, the liberal tradition can only be one of the traditions. All must be self-critical; all must leave room for the others. Influence can only be via channels acceptable by all.

The state, as the guardian and promotor of public justice for all on an equal basis and of the well-being of the whole public, must jealously guard public freedom—if necessary, through legislation. No segment of society must be dominated by one group only. Schools, industry, commerce, and especially the state itself must be pluralistically open. A political party may be one in mind; the state must have room for all. A particular school may be unified in its aims; the national system must be open for many aims. And the government must protect all and make room for all and seek the public good of all. At the same time, every tradition will necessarily see itself as the only true way for society to develop. All ultimate convictions have a total *outlook,* a total claim. But none may adopt a totalitarian *strategy*.

It can be argued and documented that democracy, instead of being regarded as a method to arrive at viable decisions in a society that must guard the integrity of its pluralism, has been taken to be a "way of life" in North America. This means that instead of preserving the plurality of "ways of life" originally found, democracy has tended to become the way to unify that society into one community. Pluralism became a doctrine referring to private opinion, but it was democratically ousted from the public forum. State propaganda and state-sponsored education established the democratic way of "the American Way of Life" as the official doctrine of public life. The varied national mosaic was straightjacketed by a pattern of acceptability that functioned as a civic religion.

At the same time, dogmatic positivism (in the wide sense defined by Radnitzky and thus including logical empiricism, the analytic school, linguistic analysis, behaviorism, pragmatism, etc.) became the only respectable doctrine at the universities. The two forces possibly combined into one direction; any vote is as good as any other, and so is any fact. Thus—lack of depth, lack of seeing the proper character of relationships, lack of awareness of the reality of wholes. Living becomes the simple technique of scientifically manipulating the simple elements of which all is composed (votes, sensations, atoms, etc.). Meanwhile, the total claims of ways of life tend to become secularized into totalitarianisms.

The crucial question to be asked in this context is: What happened to the liberal mind? At this point, with democracy tending to become totalitarian democratism and pluralism threatening to degenerate into lip service to genuine openness, the critical mind was more necessary than ever—especially when "the American Way" tended to become captured by authoritarian, capitalistic, conservatistic traditions of the Right.

At this time the liberal mind was falling prey to not-so-liberal positivism. The latter, being in principle uncritical and establishmentarian, made it very difficult for minds in its grasp to come to grips with truly basic issues. For these issues are such as not to lend themselves to the technicistic manipulations of logically rigorous methods, let alone to be approached with them at the exclusion of other methods. Self-critical, radical and resourceful reflection is foreign to this kind of tradition. A worldview that banks on what is observable has little room for norms, ideals, or desirable situations not now evident. All that is observable is what is now there.

Thus, even though the liberal mentality did not disappear, it was no longer integrally related to the mindset fostered in the academy. Basic presuppositions went underground either to disappear (pluralism) or to return in the garb of uncritically assumed dogma (democratism). A dogmatism that includes among its beliefs the conviction that it is itself in principle undogmatic will not quickly be recognized as a dogmatism by its own adherents—a characteristic not necessarily found in all dogmatisms.

European attempts to come to grips with the threatening situation in academia and in society at large, such as existentialism or phenomenology, went unheeded as irrelevant (!) and inexact. (The fate of Herman Dooyeweerd in Reformed Christian circles is not unrelated to this; the main barrier was not that his followers proclaimed their approach to be the only one but that they challenged a tradition which had entrenched itself as the only possible one.) The academy, being traditionally the place where the mind is formed, did not allow minds to deal academically with fundamental issues.

This may explain why the present attitude of the liberal traditions toward the immense problems of Southern Africa and Latin America on the one hand shows such a curious mixture of true concern for justice and freedom (its old sensitivities), while on the other hand its uncritically assumed dogmas are not really confronted but serve as the apparently obvious basis for explaining why the statistics do mean what they mean. This may also help us understand why the younger idealistic mindset (liberal or neo-Marxist) is so full of irrational and contradictory attitudes. On the one hand, no form of politics must be regarded as crime (political prisoners must always be freed); on the other, all rightist politics is criminal. On the one hand, all life is sacred and no war justified; on the other, the unborn child may be killed in the war for the preservation and instant gratification of every desire of individuals now living.

How, in such a situation, do totalitarian tendencies enter into a liberal democratic, pluralistic and intellectually respectable society or into those segments of such a society which respect these traditions? I think what happens in this situation is that social processes tend toward the "doughnut effect." This means that in a truly multiple field of convictions of a basic character, the result of democratically trying to force an artificial unity (communication in which finally the only content of the messages is the process) will be a weak mass of indistinguishable facts of the same color built around a hollow center. The emptiness arises as a result of the following. Society agrees that "N" must be at its basis. But "N" must be so conceived that it is agreeable to all. Whatever is finally left of "N" is just "N," that is, a mere symbol standing for no thing.

A hollow center in such a society needs to be filled. No society can continue to exist or function effectively without a clear vision of its generally agreed fundamental aims and purposes. But what will these be?

There are various possibilities. One is that the most powerful group (money, propaganda, votes) simply occupies the center by means of such things as power plays, voter manipulation, or moralistic intimidation, declaring that since it got there democratically, its ways are society's chosen ways. The liberal mind educated in the positivistic (anti-liberal) academy will have little to offer by way of resistance, since the positivistic ways, in the first place, favor the power of the materially technically slanted trends and, in the second place, mask the real meaning of what is happening. What I am trying to say here usually escapes detection by this kind of mind.

In this climate the corporate mind of big business or big government or big education can enter the center and begin to manipulate society. But that is not all. The dogmatic totalitarianism of big money and technical expertise will soon offend the still living sensitivities of the liberal tradition. The latter, though no longer critically resourceful, will still start to challenge those who illegally occupy the center and will receive the aid of all who either blatantly or intuitively have experienced the oppressive effects of democratism. The fire of opposition will undoubtedly be fed by the leftover convictions of liberal traditions that are still preached but are no longer being critically developed—freedom and individual autonomy.

A younger generation dogmatically raised on notions of freedom and autonomy in the context of a repressive society will eagerly fight for its freedoms but will not know what to do with them. The meaning of communal responsibility is foreign to its young members. If that generation continues to be fed at the academies by the positivistic spirit, it will celebrate the freedoms won by protest against oppression with oppressive individualism in the guise of civil libertarianism. And many of the protestors often have, for various (good and bad) reasons, no really formative cultural power. Thus they often resort to violent take-overs and, once in a position of responsibility, to dictatorial procedures.

The results are then as odious as the former situation was. Since the meaning of freedom has not been given positive content (impossible in an academy given to rigorous objectivism), every rule, every standard, every form of authority, and every call to responsibility will be experienced as unfree and as an assault on autonomy. There are no resources for coming to grips with problems. Above all, there is no tradition of radical self-criticism and exposure of assumptions.

In spite of the fact that these thoughts bear all the symptoms of simplistic superficiality and tendentious generality, I am convinced that serious attention to these possible relationships (which will undoubtedly result in much more than mere refinement of the above claims and may well yield contrary conclusions) is necessary if we are to confront the burning social problems of our day, both in the Old and New West (Europe and North America) and in the rising Third World (Africa and South America), in a truly helpful manner. Recent experiences in the latter have taught me two things. One is that we must continue to expose, oppose and overcome the reactionary forces of capitalism, materialism, authoritarianism, paternalism, conservatism, bourgeois culture, nationalism, etc. The other is that neither Communism nor neo-Marxist socialism nor traditional liberalism have a genuine solution to the Third World problem, and in many cases it must be doubted whether there is genuine concern to help—or at least there is such an overwhelming lack of appreciation for socio-cultural context conditions, for group-psychological factors and for historical background, coupled with a lack of principled, orderly and committed reflection, that much of the help offered is counterproductive.

Perspective

Am I now asking for a completely negative attitude toward modern movements of liberation and toward those forces that in our world expose injustice and oppression? Such is decidedly not the case. Both Marxism and neo-Marxism have pointed out real bastions of unrighteousness institutionalized in Western civilization. And liberalism correctly criticizes the absolutisms of the Right. We can but sympathize with their outcry. And in order to enable the victims of these distortions to understand clearly just where we stand, we must be open about our support for the exposure.

But we need to be just as open about the origin of our own convictions and about the way we are called to walk in obedience to the gospel. We are ever to guard against falling into the trap of choosing sides in a confrontation that is of the world's own making. And I am not forgetting here that the church has often been part of that world. Just as we can show solidarity with the oppressed, so we can show awareness of our own background in sin by not being too haughty about our relationship to those who historically happen to be stuck in a more antiquated form of evil. Besides, is the oppressor less in need of the redemption of the gospel than the oppressed?

What I am trying to suggest is that in the battles of this world, the Christian cannot avoid a position which must seem peculiar to all sides. For, although the gospel can identify with every human need, it does not accept any solution except its own. To give shape to that solution is ever a monumental task. It requires taking a radical position as well as showing historical and pedagogical sensitivity. It requires a critical mind (especially self-critical) set in the context of sympathetic understanding.

By this I do not advocate the kind of balance and wisdom suggested by the ever careful attitudes of those who are afraid to upset, offend, or even overturn any tradition at all. What I am trying to remember is that all of us are still very much of this earth, whereas the Kingdom of God is not of this earth at all. This difficult relationship is complicated by the fact that the Kingdom, while not of this earth, is earthly—which will have to be made evident on this earth. And the evidence will have to come via the visibility of God's redemptive work in Christ, which only becomes visible via what has been redeemed. And whatever has been redeemed will in this dispensation never manifest itself except in the midst of and alongside of unredeemed factors. All of these tensions and dualities run right through our lives.

Thus we must erect pockets of righteousness in our lives—signposts of the coming Kingdom of God which is here already, spiritually isolated from this earth and spiritually close to all of created reality. We must not count on respect from the world for our security, though we shall have to be so secure in this world that it will wish to search for the source of such peace. We shall have to reject every form of conforming to this world, including those attractive forms in terms of which so much evil is coming to light these days. But the rejection cannot take the form of belligerence. Rather, it must take the form of sympathetic, critical guidance and of alternative ways of being in this world.

Can such a delicate position be given concrete shape in the lives of those who have been called to the task of scholarship? Can the theorist who takes God's attitude toward this world in Jesus Christ seriously make a contribution to this world? Will the *total* claim of the gospel find a meaningful position in this world in which the *totalitarian* claims of Fascist and Communist regimes are counteracted by a liberal tradition which unknowingly has its own *totalitarian* tendencies? This problem is increased by the inner necessity of science to strive for universality. If positivism and totalitarianism reinforce one another, may there be a form of scholarship that serves the cause of the gospel?

A role for scholarship

It seems to me that one of the approaches delayed by positivism is that of a Christian attitude toward theorizing such as was developed at the Free University in Amsterdam. Its founder, Abraham Kuyper, worked in a tradition which, via John Calvin, goes as far back as St. Augustine. This tradition received philosophic concretization in the work of a community of scholars variously known as Amsterdam school, Dooyeweerdians, cosmonomians, etc. Long before the current assault on positivism took hold in various quarters, this tradition, on its own, had developed a critique of positivism which was long repudiated but which is today being vindicated from many angles. Within that approach, work has been done on the relation between pluralism and totalitarianism and also on the relation between theory and the rest of humanity and the cosmos—work that could be of help to us today. Since the most significant introduction of this approach into North America came at the hand of H. Evan Runner, it is appropriate in this essay to outline briefly what help could be expected from it in our currently critical situation.

The following points seem to me to merit our attention specifically. One is that in this tradition, work has been done on the relation between, on the one hand, the necessarily total claim of any ultimate conviction over all that seems to be governed by such a claim and, on the other hand, the need for recognizing that such a claim can in fact never expect to play a totalitarian role within the society of those who clearly exhibit a plurality of convictions. It seems to me that this tradition can contribute worthwhile material from its finding that communities are necessarily homogeneous and total in their fundamental convictional unity, whereas in a pluralistic society room can nevertheless be made for more than one such community in a fundamental recognition of the integrity of each—and not by letting the peculiarities of each function only in a restricted area.

In addition, this tradition has reflected fruitfully on the possibility of fundamental convictional invariance while yet maintaining a critical openness toward one's own basic position. Consequently, a contribution can be made to the debate on the relation between truly rejectionable dogmatism, on the one hand, and self-critical maintenance of fundamental positions, on the other, without sacrificing the bearing of such an irreducible plurality on the common task of science.

A third contribution can be made by this tradition in the area of reflection on the relation between theorizing and all non-theoretical dimensions of cosmic existence. It becomes increasingly clear today that the interaction between science and whatever else there is in the world is not fully appreciated. This tradition has been aware of this kind of relationship in a fundamentally appreciative way and has analyzed the structure of it in detail.

Finally, more needs to be done in our day about looking into the inner structure of science in all of its forms, so that its actual structural limits will become known. Such reflection has been an integral part of this tradition since its inception. Questions such as what should and can be accomplished by the theoretical mind and what it should or cannot be expected to do (by itself or others) are important today.

There is every reason to expect that because of the peculiar position of this tradition, contributions can be made that are not likely to be forthcoming from other quarters—contributions that can in principle be expected to come only from this tradition. Radnitzky is almost certainly right in seeing that the role played by the academic community in our world is of great consequence. Whether or not this community can learn the lesson of unavoidable convictional plurality will doubtless be a factor in the possible contribution it can make. Today it seems that the academy is becoming more "open" than it has been in the last generation or two. But it is not yet clear that scholars are aware of the religious nature of all ultimate convictions. (Is this why Polanyi is not fully accepted?) And it is still less clear that Christians will be tolerated when making their contribution openly, with integrity, relevantly, and respected by their peers of other traditions. This is no doubt due partly to the exclusive claim of the gospel and partly also to the general lack of an existing Christian tradition in this area. But neither of these grounds is sufficient for Christians not to join hands in an effort to be operative in academia in a way motivated by the gospel.

Consequently, it seems to me that the immediate future for the community of scholars that now operates in North America as a result of Runner's influence should lie in a concentrated assault on these questions in the area of philosophy and theory of science, and in an attempt to test and experiment with the result of such work in other areas of science. That assault will be the more effective when the findings about convictional integrity, coupled with a sense of historical relativity, with a willingness to engage in self-critique, with an awareness of integration with the other dimensions of experience, and with an admission of the limits of science, will not only be lucidly set forth but will in the first place be permeated by the implications of these findings themselves.

June 1975

Daniel Bell's Neoconservative Critique of Modernity*

BERNARD ZYLSTRA

In this essay I plan to present an analysis of Daniel Bell's *The Cultural Contradictions of Capitalism*, published early in 1976.[1] In the Preface of this book, Bell writes, "I deal with culture, especially the idea of modernity, and with the problems of managing a complex polity when the values of the society stress unrestrained appetite. The contradictions I see in contemporary capitalism derive from the unraveling of the threads which once held the culture and the economy together, and from the influence of the hedonism which has become the prevailing value in our society." We are clearly confronted in this book with a diagnosis of crucial problems present in every industrialized nation in the Western world.

Daniel Bell is a professor of sociology at Harvard University. He is the author of a number of distinguished books, notably *The End of Ideology* (1960) and *The Coming of Post-Industrial Society* (1973), whose very titles sum up significant debates in social and political thought. He is a member of the American intelligentsia, and in the past was a fervent proponent of the democratic liberalism of the welfare state. The first striking phenomenon of this book is that its author indeed is a member of the "liberal establishment" in the United States. For this book is essentially a critique of modern culture. Such critiques have been numerous—from Rousseau, through Marx, Spengler, the counterculture of the sixties, to the neomarxism of Herbert Marcuse and the Frankfurt School—but they have hardly ever appeared from the side of progressive liberalism. This is not surprising, since liberalism, in both its classic laissez-faire and its contemporary welfare-

*This article was first published in *Christian Scholar's Review*, Vol. 7, No. 4 (1978), pp. 337-55.

state versions, has looked upon the history of the Western nations as essentially a history of *progress* in the affairs of men. Moreover, liberalism has generally considered capitalism as the most efficient economic instrument of this progress, even if it was readily acknowledged—especially since the days of Keynes—that the separation between the economy and the state should not be interpreted as strictly as in the early generations of the industrial revolution. Moreover, American liberals have looked upon the United States as the vanguard of world progress. Until recently the great majority of them accepted the "American destiny" as articulated by George Washington in a letter to Lafayette: "We have sown a seed of Liberty and Union that will germinate over the whole earth. Some day the United States of Europe will be constituted, modelled after the United States of America. The United States will be the legislator of all nations."[2] Bell's book is important because it expresses a doubt about this "progressive" view of history. And the basis for this doubt lies in what Bell sees embodied in what he calls the cultural contradictions of (American) capitalism. He believes that we are coming to a watershed in Western society, that we are witnessing the end of the bourgeois idea as well as the end of the creative impulse of modernism.

Bell is not the only democratic liberal who has come to this conclusion. There is, at least in the United States, a widening stream of "neoconservatism" consisting mainly of liberals who are questioning some of their early enthusiastic notions of progress. Robert Nisbet of Columbia University and Nathan Glazer, also of Harvard, are representatives of this new trend.[3] An analysis of the ideas of Daniel Bell, who in the past has often been a formulator of trends, if not a trend-setter, is therefore eminently rewarding. In order to come to grips with his argument, we will have to focus on his conception of society and the nature of man, his assessment of the impact of modernity and religion on bourgeois culture, and his remedy for the tensions of our era.

Tensions between social realms

Bell presents his critique of our culture as a sociologist, and in the extensive Introduction he spells out what he means by *society*. He rejects the holistic notion of society as a structurally integrated whole, internally unified by some inner principle such as Hegel's *Geist* or Marx's mode of production. Instead, he writes, at least modern society is not integral but disjunctive. It can best be analyzed by thinking of it as an uneasy amalgam of three distinct realms: the *social structure*, the *polity*, and the *culture*. "These are not congruent with one another and have different rhythms of change; they follow different norms which legitimate different, and even contrasting, types of behavior" (10). This *three-realm* approach to the nature of society affords Bell the first opportunity of locating contradictions in society: they are discordances between these realms. Although we will later see that the basic source of contradiction must not be sought in the tension between social realms, it is important to understand how Bell describes them, since their distinction as well as their relationship provide the structure for his analysis and his therapy.

In each of the three realms Bell distinguishes between axial principle and axial structure. By the former he means the *energizing principle* that is a primary mode or logic of a social realm; by the latter he has in mind the *organizing frame* around which the institutions of a social realm are built.[4] The concept of an axial or energizing principle is comparable to Herman Dooyeweerd's theory of a leading or qualifying function of a social structure, and the concept of an axial or organizing structure is somewhat parallel to Dooyeweerd's notion of a foundational function.[5] In the light of these basic distinctions, Bell describes the three social realms.

The *social structure* comprises the economy, technology, and the occupational system. In modern society its axial principle is economizing or functional rationality. Its axial structure is bureaucracy and hierarchy. Its measure of value is utility, and its principle of change is increase in productivity.

The *polity* regulates the distribution of power and adjudicates the conflicting claims and demands of individuals and groups. In this realm, which is generally described as "the state," the axial principle is legitimacy, which, in a democracy, brings with it the implicit condition of the idea of equality, that all men are to have an equal voice in the consent of the governed. The axial structure of the polity is that of representation or participation. Political decisions are as a rule not made by technocratic rationality but by bargaining or by law.

The third realm of society, that of *culture*, is the most prominent in Bell's analysis. Following Ernst Cassirer, he describes culture as the arena of expressive symbolism and meanings:

> . . . those efforts, in painting, poetry, and fiction, or within the religious forms of litany, liturgy, and ritual, which seek to explore and express the meanings of human existence in some imaginative form. The *modalities* of culture are few, and they derive from the existential situations which confront all human beings, through all times, in the nature of consciousness: how one meets death, the nature of tragedy and the character of heroism, the definition of loyalty and obligation, the redemption of the soul, the meaning of love and of sacrifice, the understanding of compassion, the tension between an animal and a human nature, the claims of instinct and restraint. Historically, therefore, culture has been fused with religion (12).

At this point already, a few crucial matters call for comment. It is an advantage of Bell's sociology that he has rejected the holism and organicism of nineteenth century social thought. But it should be noted that he looks upon these three realms as divisions of *society*, at least "analytically."[6] Society ties these realms together. The *primal given* in Bell's theory is not religion, history or nature, but society. Everything is secondary with respect to this primal. Moreover, from a socio-structural point of view, these three realms embrace whatever is socially existent. Is this really the case? I think Bell is on the right track with his structural distinction between the socio-economic order and the polity; it does justice to a given complexity and is "empirically testable"—which is the criterion posited over against the holistic conceptions (7). But, in my view, the realm of culture does not meet that criterion since it is "holistic" in its own way with respect to everything that does not belong to the socio-economy or the polity: it comprises the "modalities" of art, loyalty, love, instinct and restraint, cognition, belief and religion. These facets of human existence exist empirically, but not within one distinct realm, as Bell suggests. I suspect that he is aware of this weakness in his analysis since, though he refers to the axial *principle* of the realm of culture (self-expression), nowhere does he point out what the axial *structure* of this realm is. Genuine empirical sociological analysis would, of course, have to do that. But the respective modalities of culture as mentioned in the foregoing quotation are so diverse that they cannot possibly exhibit a common axial structure. Furthermore, what Bell describes as the axial or energizing principle of the realm of modern culture—the expression, realization, fulfillment and remaking of the "self"—is definitely not confined to this realm but is operative also in the socio-economy and the polity. One reason for this confusion in Bell's basic sociological distinctions is the inclusion of religion within a social realm. We will have an opportunity later to note that Bell has a relatively high view of religion; that, as a matter of fact, an alternative to the contradictions of capitalism cannot be found without a renewal of religion. Nevertheless, from his functional sociological perspective, religion is considered a modality of culture. This is an inversion of the real state of affairs: culture, as well as the socio-economy and the polity, is a modality of religion. For religion is the spiritual direction of man's existence—of the human "self"—in every realm.[7]

At any rate, for Bell this particular distinction between the three realms, and the content he ascribes to each, are crucially important, for they afford him an opportunity to locate the contradictions that are the object of his concern in this book. "It is the discordances between these realms which are responsible for the various contradictions within society" (10). To begin with, the discordances are caused by different rhythms or principles of change within the three realms. For example, in the enlargement of an economic enterprise, specialization and structural differentiation are responses to the change in scale. Bell seems to imply that this change in rhythm in the economic sphere is not a major cause of the contradictions of capitalism. His major concern is the change in the realm of culture, especially the change brought about by the syncretism of *modern* culture, which mingles strange gods, jumbles various arts, and merges religions detached from their histories. "Modern culture is defined by this extraordinary freedom to ransack the world storehouse and to engorge any and every style it comes upon. Such freedom comes from the fact that the axial principle of modern culture is the expression and remaking of the 'self' in order to achieve self-realization and self-fulfillment. And in its search, there is a denial of any limits or boundaries to experience. It is a reaching out for all experience; nothing is forbidden, all is to be explored" (13f). It is the *modernity* of culture that leads to the disjunction of realms:

> Within this framework, one can discern the structural sources of tension in the society: between a social structure (primarily techno-economic) which is bureaucratic and hierarchical, and a polity which believes, formally, in equality and participation; between a social structure that is organized fundamentally in terms of roles and specialization, and a culture which is concerned with the enhancement and fulfillment of the self and the "whole" person. In these contradictions, one perceives many of the latent social conflicts that have been expressed ideologically as alienation, depersonalization, the attack on authority, and the like. In these adversary relations, one sees the disjunction of realms (14).

The dual nature of man and the role of religion

However, there is more to the matter. The contradictions of our society are a result not only of tensions between realms. There must be an underlying common source.[8] For society, in the final analysis, is a reflection of the (religious) nature of man. And the nature of man, in turn, mirrors the structure of reality as a whole. Sociology, anthropology and ontology are thus interdependent disciplines. The interdependence between social theory and a theory of human nature is frequently acknowledged. This is true of Plato and Hobbes, of Hegel and Laski,[9] and also of Daniel Bell. Here we are faced with a peculiar difficulty, which Bell shares with the main trends in contemporary social thought: since society—and not nature—is his primal given, he does not like to speak of human *nature*, since that term implies "that human beings have some fixed properties" (162n). Bell rejects the notion of fixed human properties, since that would render the "remaking" of man impossible. He will speak of "human character" and the "human condition," which is a condition of "biological and sociological nurturing" (163). This nurturing requires a pliability in the "nature" of man so that the remaking of the self—within limits (282)—is possible.[10]

Nevertheless, occasionally Bell will refer to "the double nature of man" (cf. 277). That *double nature*, at least in the history of Western consciousness, has entailed a constant "tension between the rational and the nonrational, between reason and will, between reason and instinct, as the driving forces of man" (50). There are thus disjunctions not only "between the social structure and the culture but also between the modes of cognitive and emotive expression" (92). In view of this, Bell relates the contradictions of contemporary capitalism to the entire history of the West. "In the history of Western society, there has always been a dialectic of release and restraint. The idea of release goes back to the Dionysiac festivals, Bacchanalian revels, saturnalias, the Gnostic sects of the first and second centuries and the subterranean threads unraveled since; or to the examples in biblical legend and history of Sodom and Gomorrah or the Babylonian episodes" (156).

Bell is of the opinion that the contradictions in our society at least in part are a result of the fact that the subterranean demands for release of human experience have come to the surface in modernism, which climaxed in the countercultural hedonism of the sixties. But how did Western civilization prevent the Dionysiac outbursts before the onslaught of modernism? How did we in the past keep this double nature of man in check? Here Bell pays tribute to the role of the great historic religions in Western culture. They were forces of restraint against the revels of release. Religion, in Bell's view, has performed two main functions. First, religion has guarded *order*. For example, in the Old Testament we find an emphasis on law and "a fear of human nature unchecked: an association of release with lust, sexual competitiveness, violence, and murder. The fear is the fear of the demonic—the frenzied ecstasy (ex-stasis) of leaving one's body and crossing the boundaries of sin." Religion has sought to defuse the demonic by expressing it in emblematic terms: the symbolic sacrifice in the Old Testament or the ritual sacrifice of Jesus on the cross. And, second, religion has provided *continuity with the past*. The authority of the religious prophet was always located in the past, and thus prophecy became a basis for denying the validity of antinomian progressive revelation. In this way the accepted criteria of the past limited the range of human experience in the present. Moreover, the realm of culture, when fused with this restraining function of religion, had a criterion for judging the present on the basis of the past; culture, therefore, provided a continuity of past and present through tradition. "In these two ways, religion undergirded almost all of historic Western culture" (157). Religion, in

Bell's view, is thus clearly a conservative force within culture. It is on the side of reason against instinctual emotion and passion; on the side of order against anarchy; on the side of asceticism against hedonism; on the side of the past against the future.

Modernism and the self

Bell links the rise of modernity to the decline of religion. For 2000 years in the history of the West, rational judgment was considered superior to passion, instinct and will. Reason's superiority in the anthropological hierarchy was destroyed by *modernism*. Since the rise, development, and exhaustion of modernism are central to the main argument in Bell's book, it is imperative to look carefully at his delineation of this concept. In many ways Bell's reflections here are extremely helpful; in other ways, I think, they obscure the issue.

Perhaps the most dominant factor in Bell's description of modernism is the inversion of the classical, rationalist view of man: the primacy of reason has given way to the primacy of instinct. Modernism inverts the classical hierarchy. "It is the triumph of the spirited, of the will" (50). And it thus issues in the above-mentioned disjunction between the modes of cognition and the modes of emotive expression. There is a measure of ambiguity in Bell's discussion about the birth of modernism. At times he refers especially to the nineteenth century, since the shift to release coincided with the breakup of religious authority (19). At other times he will, like Eric Voegelin and Leo Strauss,[11] point to Hobbes as one source of modernism. "The secular Hobbesianism fed the mainsprings of modernity, the ravenous hunger for unlimited experience" (81). He also finds a source of the modern temper in a line which runs from Bacon through Comte and Hegel to Marx, in which science is the main means of man's control over nature and thus the avenue of man's move from the "kingdom of necessity" to the "kingdom of freedom" (151).[12]

This indeed brings us closer both to the source and nature of modernity. But we should realize that we will have to go back further than the seventeenth century, and that much more is involved in modernity than a shift in the appreciation of the respective positions of reason and emotion in human personality. Rationality and contemplation are not more authentically *human* than emotion and sensation, as Bell—along with the "classical" and "neoclassical" rationalists—suggests (cf. 111). To be sure, the destruction of the given hierarchy of modes in human personality is a trait in the radicalization process of modernism.[13] But this radicalization cannot be effectively checked by balancing the rational over against the nonrational. For the desire for "unlimited experience" in modernism can be pursued by the intellect as well as by the passion. An anthropological delineation of the features of modernity will therefore have to focus not merely on the hierarchy of the modes of experience but also, and more pointedly, on the very conception of the human self which engages in the experience, either intellectually or emotionally or in any other way.

Bell realizes this, and at a particular point when he describes "the fundamental assumption of modernity," he no longer speaks in the first place about tensions between realms or a triumph of passion over reason but about the "new man" who wants to fashion his own existence in complete autonomy.

> The fundamental assumption of modernity, the thread that has run through Western civilization since the sixteenth century, is that the social unit of society is not the group, the guild, the tribe, or the city, but the person. The Western ideal was the autonomous man who, in becoming self-determining, would achieve freedom (16).

In this very context, Bell relates this fundamental assumption to the notion of the individual conscience as the source of judgment, which supposedly is a "striking result of the Reformation." He should have pursued his historical analysis in order to find the roots of modernity in the pre-Reformation Renaissance, if not already in certain late-medieval trends.[14] But with respect to the content of modernity's view of man as *autonomous self-determination*, Bell is on the right track. Nevertheless, his interpretation of the modern view of man as "a radical change in the meaning of the individual from a being to a self" (18) is not entirely adequate. For the notion of man as a *self*, created in the image of God, is part of the Christian heritage, and is a presupposition of modernity's secular notion of the self as its own law: the *autos* as the *nomos*. This complexity in interpretation brings to the fore an exceedingly significant question in the understanding and in the supersession of modernism. Is modernism a rejection of classical antiquity, of Christianity, or both? Did not Christianity, in its own way, repudiate at least a good part of classical antiquity? If so, is there not a continuity between the Christian religion and modernity?[15] Or is it possible that modernity, in rejecting revelation, revived basic conceptions of classical philosophy and culture? It is certainly true that the early humanism of the fifteenth century was characterized by an intense interest in classical art, literature, and philosophy. Or, finally, should we look upon modernism as a radical break with the *entirety* of Western tradition—Greco-Roman as well as Judeo-Christian?

Bell does not discuss this complex question of interpretation, but he seems to opt for the last suggestion, at least with respect to the question of man as a self. Classical philosophy, he writes, thought of beings that had a *nature*, and therefore a *common quality* in which the lower is derived from the higher, in which there was thus a hierarchy of virtue.

> But in the modern consciousness, there is not a common being but a *self*, and the concern of this self is with its individual *authenticity*, its unique, irreducible character free of the contrivances and conventions, the masks and hypocrisies, the distortions of the self by society. This concern with the authentic self makes the motive and not the action—the impact of the self, not the moral consequence to society—the source of ethical and aesthetic judgments (19).

Quite clearly, in Bell's view, this change from a being to a self implies a repudiation of classical philosophy. He calls this change one of the *sociological* "crossovers" in the history of bourgeois society which radically transformed both the cultural and the economic realms. But this occurred in the context of the repudiation of religion or—to use Bell's words—the sociological crossover from religion to secular culture. This drastically affected the way in which expressive conduct is handled in modern society, for the traditional function of religion—restraining the demonic in the dual nature of man—now became a function of secular culture. Instead of taming the demonic, secular culture accepted it, reveled in it, and glorified it as a source of creativity. In its demand for the autonomy of the esthetic, modernism supported the broader idea that experience in and of itself is of supreme value, that everything was to be explored, that anything was to be permitted. "In the legitimation of action, the pendulum had swung to the side of release, away from restraint." Modernism has thus been the great seducer. "Its power derived from the idolatry of the self" (19).

All of this brings with it that peculiar trait of modernity: *rejection* and *negation*. Bell cites Irving Howe,[16] who suggests that the modern can be defined in terms of what it is not, as an "inclusive negative" (46). Modernism is a revolt. It is a revolt against the past, against order, against ordering principles, against limits, against rationality, against organization. In the vacuum thus established, modernism posits the immediate experience of the self as the source of judgment; it demands the direct presentness, the simultaneity and immediacy, of experience. It insists on "the absolute imperiousness of the self, of man as the 'self-infinitizing' creature who is impelled to search for the beyond" (47). This "beyond" is no longer the realm of divine transcendence in relation to which human existence acquires meaning. Such a transcendence would eliminate the possibility of self-infinitizing. Rather, the "beyond" is the future, which is—I am now using my own words—an intra-mundane, immanent extension of the absolute present, a future in which man can realize "the desire, and the growing ability, to master nature and to make of oneself what one can, and even, in discarding old roots, to remake oneself altogether" (16).

In other words, what is fundamentally at stake in modernity is the impulse of man the creature to become a creator, to displace creaturely finitude with the prerogatives and the attributes of the creator. Bell himself does not employ this terminology, probably because the most fundamental distinction between different types of "beings"—the one between Creator and creature—does not belong to his socio-ontology. But he is quite aware of the radical and revolutionary implications of modernism entirely cut loose from the (covenantal) bond of religion. In referring to Marx's conception of the final stage of history as the move from the realm of necessity to the realm of freedom, he writes: "The 'end of history,' thus, would signal the triumph of man over all constraints and his achievement of the total mastery of nature and the self" (151).

Modernism, Puritanism, and bourgeois society

Bell's critique of modernity pertains particularly to its expressions in the realm of culture. The substance of Part One of his book, notably the chapters entitled "The Disjunction of Cultural Discourse" and "The Sensibility of the Sixties" (85-145), deals almost entirely with cultural modernism as "a search for the heightening of experience in all dimensions" (118) and with the exhaustion of modernism as a creative cultural force in our time (144f). Bell's earlier book, *The End of Ideology*, had as its subtitle "On the Exhaustion of Political Ideas in the Fifties." From a more immediate context, his present book could have been given the subtitle "On the Exhaustion of Cultural Modernism in the Sixties."

Bell argues that the creativity of modernism came to a climax and an end in the countercultural lifestyle and art of the sixties, with its unrestrained display of violence and cruelty, sexual perversity, its noise, its anti-intellectual attack on content, its elimination of the boundary between art and life, and its indiscriminate substitution of any "happening" for authentic esthetic experience (122). In all of this, Bell believes, modernism revealed itself as exhausted, empty, and bankrupt within the realm of culture.

But what, then, is the relation between modernity and the other two realms of society—the techno-economic structure and the polity? In a certain sense, one can say that Bell wants to defend the development and change within the economy and the state, as if these are not responsible for the cultural contradictions of capitalism, as if the unrestrained hedonism in the realm of culture is the main reason for the tensions in the productive and the political sectors of society. Bell knows that this is not correct, since at least the development in the economic realm has also been highly influenced by modernism. This is the thread I want to follow in order to depict the fabric Bell weaves from it.

The fundamental assumption of modernity expressed itself not only in the culture but also in the economy, in the rise of the bourgeois entrepreneur. "Freed from the ascriptive ties of the traditional world, with its fixed status and checks on acquisition, he seeks his fortune by remaking the economic world. Free movement of goods and money and individual economic and social mobility become the ideal. At its extreme, laissez-faire becomes 'rampant individualism' " (16). Citing Marx's paean to the bourgeoisie in *The Communist Manifesto*, Bell readily acknowledges that the cultural as well as the economic impulse were aspects of the same surge of modernity in radically opening up the Western world. But then he immediately speaks of the extraordinary paradox that each impulse quickly became highly conscious of the other, feared the other, and sought to destroy it.

> What is striking is that while bourgeois society introduced a radical individualism in economics, and a willingness to tear up all traditional social relations in the process, the bourgeois class feared the radical experimental individualism of modernism in the culture. Conversely, the radical experimentalists in the culture, from Baudelaire to Rimbaud to Alfred Jarry, were willing to explore all dimensions of experience, yet fiercely hated bourgeois life (18).

Bell then immediately adds: "The history of this sociological puzzle, how this antagonism came about, is still to be written."[17] He does not pretend to write this history, but he does offer an explanation of this antagonism. His *fundamental thesis* is that capitalism, and with it bourgeois society, is the offspring not only of modernism but also of Puritanism. "In historical retrospect, bourgeois society had a double source, and a double fate. The one current was a Puritan, Whig capitalism, in which the emphasis was not just on economic activity but on the formation of *character* (sobriety, probity, work as a calling). The other was a secular Hobbesianism, a radical individualism which saw man as unlimited in appetite, which was restrained in politics by a sovereign but ran fully free in economics and culture" (80).

We are thus confronted with a reformulation of the classical Weber thesis concerning the origin and development of capitalism. Here Bell depicts a concrete instance of the ordering and restraining role of religion in society. "In the early development of capitalism, the unrestrained economic impulse was held in check by Puritan restraint and the Protestant ethic" (21). The Puritans came to North America in the seventeenth century in order to live the life of the spirit and to control the passions of the body. Their communities were ruled by a rational moral zeal. "The core of Puritanism, once the theological husks are stripped away, was an intense moral zeal for the regulation of everyday conduct, not because the Puritans were harsh or prurient, but because they had founded their community as a covenant in which all individuals were in compact with each other . . . . One's own sins imperiled not just oneself but the group" (59). This communal moral and religious zeal provided a basis for social order, precisely in the economic expansion of the vast North American continent, because it controlled the passions of the individuals by the triumph of reason and religion. It provided an incentive for the immense amount of work that had to be done because of its stress on calling. And it offered a motive for restraint in the satisfaction of material wants because of its innerworldly asceticism. The resultant energy of the Puritans "built an industrial civilization" (82).

This explanatory hypothesis has several advantages for Bell. First of all, it fits his general thesis about the restraining role of religion in society. Secondly, and more importantly, it gives him an opportunity to distinguish between modernism and capitalism and to put the major share of the blame for the contradictions of the latter upon the former. Contrary to the impression which the title of the book gives, Bell in effect is a proponent of capitalism and a critic of modernism—although, as we will see later, only a moderate critic. This is already evident in the relatively neutral definition of capitalism which he presents at the beginning of his argument: "Capitalism is an economic-cultural system, organized economically around the institution of property and the production of commodities and based culturally in the fact that exchange relations, that of buying and selling, have permeated most of the society" (14). This definition is far too broad because systems organized around property and production and based on buying and selling have been part of the history of the human race ever since barter and trade were introduced. Moreover, this definition is imprecise because it disregards inherent elements of the capitalist system such as: the monetization of land, labor, resources, and commodities; the acquisitive purpose of property relations; the need for capital accumulation; and the application of science to production and marketing by means of industrial technology. To put the matter differently: *Bell does not sufficiently realize that capitalism itself is one of the most outstanding expressions of the Promethean surge of modernity*. This is a basic weakness in his entire argument.

The third advantage of the Weberian hypothesis is its implicit positive interpretation of the Protestant ethic and the Puritan religion. Bell views these as the "transcendental tie" of bourgeois society which provide it with a set of ultimate meanings in its character structure, its work, and its culture. Without *this* transcendental tie, he believes, only hedonism remains. This is not the place to discuss extensively the intricate question of "religion and the rise of capitalism," but a few comments are in order. Bell indeed suggests that "the Protestant ethic was undermined not by modernism but by capitalism itself. The greatest single engine in the destruction of the Protestant ethic was the invention of the installment plan, or instant credit" (21). But if that is the case, the question immediately arises whether the spirituality of the Puritan religion and of the Protestant ethic was indeed genuinely *transcendent*. If it had been, would it not have effectively rejected the dangers entailed in this technique of installment buying and in the consensus on "the moral verity of material abundance" (75)?

A responsible answer to that question requires that we begin by making a number of distinctions within that amorphous phenomenon described by the terms *Protestant ethic* and *Puritan religion*. There is not one *single* ethic bequeathed to us by the Protestant Reformation. Rather, it inspired a variety of ethical systems: Lutheran, Reformed, Anabaptist, Anglican, Puritan, Pietist, etc. Moreover, though the word *Puritanism* covers a much narrower field, nonetheless it pertains to a wide variety of religious movements in sixteenth and seventeenth century England and North America. In addition, it is essential to distinguish between the reformation endeavors of Luther and Calvin, on the one hand, and the types of spirituality defended in the Protestant communities of the seventeenth century, on the other. Finally, with reference to the question at hand—the relation between religion and capitalism—the hypothesis must be considered that certain types of spirituality, developed in the context of the Christian religion since the early Middle Ages, were transitional links to post-Christian modernity. This hypothesis can be formulated more precisely with respect to a variety of trends in the Christian church. In connection with Puritanism, one might put it this way: The anthropocentric focus in certain trends of late Puritanism on the striving of the individual human will in the acquisition of soul salvation entails a spirituality and a concomitant ethic parallel with modernity's pursuit of happiness.

I would like to suggest a tentative illustration of this hypothesis. Eric Voegelin, in an extensive analysis of modernity's development in the eighteenth century, has introduced the term *intramundane religiousness*, which he describes as follows: "In the conflict with the Christian tradition the new religiousness expresses itself through the inversion of the direction in which the *realissimum* of existence is to be sought. The new attitude had become visible by the time of Hobbes when the orientation toward a *summum bonum* was replaced by the flight from the *summum malum* of death in the civil war."[18] I think it can be argued that John Bunyan's *The Pilgrim's Progress* (1678) represents this "new religiousness" in a "Christian" setting. Bunyan's religiousness is not the spirituality of the classical *participatio dei*, nor the *imitatio Christi* of Thomas à Kempis, nor Calvin's *soli deo gloria*. Rather, his religiousness is primarily conditioned by the striving of the individual human will to flee the *summum malum* of eternal damnation. This is evident in the very first words which the Pilgrim addresses to his wife and children before he sets out on his pilgrimage:

> I am for certain informed that this our city will be burned with fire from heaven, in which fearful overthrow both myself, with thee, my wife, and you, my sweet babes, shall miserably come to ruin; except (the which, yet I see not) some way of escape can be found, whereby we may be delivered.[19]

Here the Christian religion is viewed as a way to escape the pain of hell and to acquire the pleasure of heaven. Here we see a reinterpretation of the Christian religion in terms of modernity's ethic of the pain-pleasure calculus.[20] This reinterpretation does not necessarily entail the elimination of every vestige of a transcendental spirituality directed to the service of the Creator—in which service lies the meaning of man's earthly existence. But this religious pain-pleasure calculus is one source of the secular, materialist pain-pleasure calculus of bourgeois ethics. The progress of Bunyan's pilgrim is a Puritan precursor of Daniel Defoe's *Robinson Crusoe* (1719), whose solitary pursuit focuses on the acquisition of property and material security.[21]

It is the great merit of John Locke that he managed to formulate a political theory in which the striving of modernity for material security—the substitute for Christian spirituality—could be attained in an orderly, conservative manner. He accomplished this by a "balanced" recognition of the parallel human interests in the acquisition of soul salvation and in the acquisition of material property, and by redefining the societal role of church and state in terms of the protection of these respective interests in a voluntaristic, individualistic manner. In his view, "Government has no other end but the preservation of Property,"[22] and "The only business of the church is the salvation of souls."[23] Locke realized that the latter entails an ethic. "The end of a religious society . . . is the public worship of God and, by means thereof, the acquisition of eternal life. All discipline ought therefore to tend to that end, and all ecclesiastical laws to be thereunto confined."[24] Locke is quite aware that, by and large, the "Puritan" ethic required by the pursuit of soul salvation is conducive to social order. If it is not, the interest of the commonwealth prevails. Tawney's assessment of the "Triumph of the Economic Virtues" in the setting of late Puritanism is to the point here. He writes:

> Plunged in the cleansing waters of later Puritanism, the qualities which less enlightened ages had denounced as social vices emerged as economic vir-

> tues. They emerged as moral virtues as well. For the world exists not to be enjoyed, but to be conquered. Only its conqueror deserves the name of Christian. For such a philosophy the question "What shall it profit a man?" carries no sting. In winning the world, he wins the salvation of his own soul as well.[25]

In this light, I think, it is more appropriate to interpret late Puritanism as *one source of the conservative wing of modernism* than as an alternative to modernism or as a "transcendental tie" of capitalism. Within the movement of modernity, as in many civilizational movements, there is a conservative trend, a radical trend, and a middle-of-the-road liberal trend. *Conservatism* and *radicalism* are dialectical components of the same spirit that has been the dominant force in Western civilization. The former may be conducive to economic asceticism, with delayed gratification as a built-in source of capital accumulation; the latter may be conducive to hedonism, with its demands for instant enjoyment as the built-in source of inflation. The former may be protective of the given social order at a particular moment of modernism's historical concretization, while the latter may be drastically innovative in the search for new experiences. The former may seem to be more rational, since order and rationality have often been considered equivalences in the history of Western thought; the latter may seem to be more irrational, sensual and material, since at that level of human existence "innovation" in experience is more readily attained. The various trends "to the right" within modernism have indeed often channeled its radical expressions within "feasible" limits. And conservatism has thus frequently been an effort to stabilize the impact of modernism at a specific level of civilizational disarray. In this light, liberalism is radical in the eyes of conservatism but conservative in the eyes of the radical, especially when liberalism does not dare follow the "left" in its never-ending demands for change and innovation.

Daniel Bell himself admits this in the discussion of the counterculture of the sixties. Liberalism had for decades defended personal freedom in art and imagination, in politics and culture. But it hesitated when it was confronted with the demands for the same personal freedom in new areas of experience, such as "sex" and "drugs." Yet, Bell writes, "liberalism finds itself uneasy in trying to say why. It approves the basic permissiveness, but cannot with any certainty define the bounds. And this is its dilemma. In culture, as well as in politics, liberalism is now up against the wall" (79).

Religion as utopia

Faced with this dilemma, is there a way out? At this point we are confronted with a fascinating phenomenon in the dialectical unfolding of the spirit of modernism. In principle modernism has rejected both natural law[26] and divine revelation as sources of norms for human action. However, faced with the dilemma of change or stability at the level of action, the adherents of modernism will often appeal to religion or natural rights in defense of either progressivism or conservatism to add ideological weight to their position. In this light we can interpret the repeated eclipses and revivals of the natural law tradition in the modern age, [27] both in defense of stability and change.[28] Similarly, modernists not only of the right but also of the left[29] have appealed to religion to add weight to their position. Bell rejects the appeal to nature—as he finds it in Leo Strauss[30]—but accepts the appeal to religion.

> What, then, are the guides to human conduct? They cannot be in nature, for nature is only a set of physical constraints at one extreme and existential questions at the other, between which man threads his way without any maps. It cannot be history, for history has no *telos* but is only instrumental, the expansion of man's powers over nature. There is, then, the unfashionable, traditional answer: religion, not as a social "projection" of man into an external emblem, but as a transcendental conception that is outside man, yet relates man to something beyond himself (166).

Here Bell's analysis is at once both profound and shallow. For though he hopes that "some religious answer surely will be forthcoming," that we may indeed witness a "new reformation" (168f), he does not go beyond these largely formal statements. *Precisely at this critical point of the spiritual vacuum of modernity, he reveals himself to be a victim of modernity.* For Bell does not have faith. His real difficulty is to ascertain—echoing Max Weber[31]—"who is God and who is the Devil" (169). Bell realizes the need for a utopia, and religion functions excellently to furnish utopias. However, as he wrote in the conclusion to *The End of Ideology*, the ladder to that utopia, to the City of Heaven, can no longer be a "faith ladder"; it must be an empirical one.[32] Since the criterion of empiricalness with reference to the spiritual core of human existence stems directly from modernity, it is evident that Bell's utopia—a religion without faith—cannot serve as an alternative to the excesses of modernism. It can at best stem the tide during the seventies after the radicality of the sixties—in America, but not in Europe.

The fiscal dilemma

The best evidence for this internal critique of Bell's book is its second part, where an attempt is made to delineate a public philosophy for the third realm of society, the polity or the state. There is no structural connection between Bell's appeal to religion, with which the first part begins and ends, and the solution offered in the second part. It will not take long to make this clear.

Without the Puritan ethic to restrain us, Bell argues, *wants* have replaced *needs* in our society: ". . . the engine which began to drive the socio-economic system (in its Soviet Communist as well as its Western bourgeois form) has been the prodigal idea of private wants and unlimited ends" (224). In the past, private wants were served by the *market*, and common needs by the *public household*. Today this is no longer the case. There is a shift in the basic allocative power in our society from the market to the public household. The latter is now called upon not only to fill common needs but also the private, material wants. For this reason the polity has developed into what is generally referred to as the welfare state. In view of this, Bell argues, the key political problem of our time is that of fiscal sociology: *who gets what, when, and where*? The sociological dilemma with which Bell is concerned in this book takes on the form of a *fiscal dilemma* in the area of the state. Here Bell is heavily dependent upon an early essay of Joseph Schumpeter, who described this dilemma as follows:

> The fiscal capacity of the state has its limits not only in the sense in which this is self-evident and which would be valid also for a socialist community, but in a much narrower and, for the tax state, more painful sense. If the will of the people demands higher and higher public expenditures, if more and more means are used for purposes for which private individuals have not produced them, if more and more power stands behind this will, and if finally all parts of the people are gripped by entirely new ideas about private property and the forms of life—then the tax state will have run its course and society will have to depend on other motive forces for its economy than self-interest. This limit, and with it the crisis which the tax state could not survive, can certainly be reached. Without doubt, the tax state *can* collapse (232).[33]

In view of this fiscal dilemma, the theme of Bell's book—the cultural contradictions of capitalism—receives a new and urgent shape, not only in typically "capitalist" countries but in all industrial and industrializing societies in which the state has taken a directive role. It is again the ancient problem of asceticism and hedonism: "Each state has to balance the calculation of capital accumulation (and the restriction of consumption) against the social needs and demands of the population" (231). In other words, can we today find a substitute for the restraining role which religion played in the past? It is crucial to note that Bell, in the second part of his book, is no longer searching for an answer in terms of a renewal of religion. The problem is largely confined to a political horizon. Collectivist societies do not experience a great deal of difficulty here, since they can impose restraints supported by ideology or terror or both (231). But what of the Western democracies? The fact that as yet no large democratic society has learned to cope effectively with inflation (due mainly to an increase in private demands), says Bell, is an indication that we are facing a severe crisis: How are we to discover a "balance" between private vices and public interests? (236).

The public household

Bell thinks he has found a solution. In the normal run of the argument in books of this kind, we would expect a defense of socialism. But Bell does not look in this direction: ". . . the death of socialism is the unrealized political fact of this century" (245). Instead, quite suddenly, not old-time religion but old-fashioned liberalism is proposed as the therapy for the contradictions of capitalism. We have just seen how earlier in the argument liberalism was described as basically permissive, unable to define bounds, and hence up against the wall (79). But now, at the end of the book, liberalism brings people together in social harmony: "The foundation of any liberal society is the willingness of all groups to compromise private ends for the public interest" (245). In order to arrive at this liberal compromise, Bell is forced to pick and choose from the smorgasbord of modernist appeal. He rejects *economic liberalism* which has become, in corporate structure, economic oligopoly and, in the pursuit of private wants, a hedonism that is destructive of social needs.[34] He wants to retain *political liberalism*, with its concern for individual differences and liberty.

> The two can be sundered. We can reject the pursuit of bourgeois wants, as lacking a moral foundation for society, and insist on the necessity of public goods. Yet we need political liberalism to assure the individual of protection from coercive powers and, within appropriate spheres, of rewards for his own efforts and merits. And the arbiter of both cannot be the market—which has to be seen as a mechanism, not a principle of justice—but instead must be the public household (277).

Bell acknowledges that this reaffirmed liberalism requires a standard, a norm for the *salus publica*—in Aristotle's words, "the good condition of human beings." Here we come to the heart of the matter. Without benefit of insight into human nature, without the blessing of divine revelation, what can Bell say about the content of that good condition? What is the supra-arbitrary law by which the positive legal order of the public household is to be judged? Earlier we saw that Bell was searching for religion without faith. Now we see him searching for liberty without law (that is, a law established *for* the human will; Bell will, of course, defend the need for a law established *by* the human will). For with reference to the question whether there is a normative law that establishes the contours of liberty, Bell retraces his steps once more and asserts that *liberalism* and *relativism* go hand in hand. He quotes from Isaiah Berlin's *Four Essays on Liberty*: "The notion that there must exist final objective answers to normative questions . . . seems to me invalid" (279). Normative questions may indeed be asked, but normative answers cannot be given. Bell is able to ask profound questions about the cultural contradictions of capitalism, but he is not able to answer them. These contradictions are a reflection of the tension between private vices and public interests. Liberalism cannot resolve this tension. Bell admits that liberalism simply accepts this tension (279). *For this tension is inherent in the human condition.* "One, then, necessarily lives in the tension between the particular and the universal, and accepts that painful double bind of necessity" (171). In the final analysis, the contradictions within society are reflections of the dual nature of man, and this, in turn, mirrors a tension in the way the cosmos hangs together. A reconciliation between these opposites is not within man's reach. But out of all the alternatives open to us, liberalism can best teach us to cope with this tension, with these contradictions. For one thing, the bicentennial celebration of the United States of America has reminded us that the founding fathers bequeathed to us the mechanisms of compromise in the representative institutions and the mechanisms of adjudication in the courts, especially the Supreme Court, which is "unique in the acceptance by the entire polity of its rule as the normative arbiter" (280).

These mechanisms, Bell admits, important though they are, are not enough. There must be a common will in the nation. But that brings us back to the need for a *given* foundation, "a prior condition— the need for some transcendent tie to bind individuals sufficiently for them to make, when necessary, the necessary sacrifices of self-interest" (281). We have now reached the last page of Bell's book. *What is that transcendent tie?* In the past, it was provided by great rulers, great doctrines, great destinies. Today these do not exist, and if they did they would not suffice. What glimmer of hope can Bell's liberalism afford us? It is a glimmer purified by trial and defeat. For in trial and defeat

> . . . a virtue emerges: the possibility of a self-conscious maturity (which the stoics called the tragic sense of life) that dispenses with charismatic leaders,

> ideological doctrines, and manifest destinies, and which seeks to redefine one's self and one's liberal society on the only basis it can survive. This basis must be created by conjoining three actions: the reaffirmation of our past . . . ; recognition of the limits of resources and the priority of needs, individual and social, over unlimited appetite and wants; and agreement upon a condition of equity which gives all persons a sense of fairness and inclusion in the society . . . .
>
> This would be a kind of social compact . . . . Within limits, men can remake themselves and society, but the knowledge of power must coexist with the knowledge of its limits (281f).

A virtue *emerges*: *self-conscious* maturity to *redefine* one's *self*. Men can *remake* themselves, within limits. We have how come full circle. The crisis of our time, Bell has argued for nearly 300 pages, is the crisis of modernity, of man's self-determination to establish the virtues and limits of his own experience—of modernity, where man's freedom is his essence.[35] Bell shudders when he sees the radical consequences of modernity in the libidinous, Bacchanalian practices of the counterculture, its literature, its art. He wants to limit the limitless hedonism of our wasteland. But he does not know why there should be limits. All he can do is make an appeal to liberalism, itself one of the threads in the fabric of modernity, so that he can arrive at "conservative conclusions" (p. xii) needed to stabilize the path of modernity at the present level of cultural chaos and confusion.[36]

Daniel Bell's reaffirmation of liberalism functions as a neo-conservatism in the cultural and political developments of the seventies. It is the intellectual parallel of Jimmy Carter's presidency.[37] This neoconservatism is not an authentic spiritual quest for the normative transcendent sources of political authority, social order, and cultural standards. Neoconservatism remains confined within the immanent horizon of modernity. Beyond that horizon lies the source of justice and equity, personhood and harmony, loyalty and love.

Notes

1. Daniel Bell, *The Cultural Contradictions of Capitalism* (New York: Basic Books, 1976). The numbers between parentheses in the text refer to pages in the book.

2. Cited by Eric Voegelin, *From Enlightenment to Revolution* (Durham, North Carolina: Duke University Press, 1975), pp. 181f.

3. Cf. Robert Nisbet, *Twilight of Authority* (New York: Oxford University Press, 1975); Nathan Glazer, *Affirmative Discrimination* (New York: Basic Books, 1976).

4. For a discussion of these distinctions, see Daniel Bell, *The Coming of Post-Industrial Society: A Venture in Social Forecasting* (New York: Basic Books, 1973), pp. 9-12.

5. Cf. H. Dooyeweerd, "Grondproblemen der wijsgerige sociologie," in *Verkenningen in de wijsbegeerte, de sociologie en de rechtsgeschiedenis* (Amsterdam: Buijten & Schipperheijn, 1962), pp. 67-146; L. Kalsbeek, *Contours of a Christian Philosophy: An Introduction to Herman Dooyeweerd's Thought* (Toronto: Wedge; Amsterdam: Buijten & Schipperheijn, 1975), pp. 196-259.

6. Bell's basic sociological concepts are parallel with Max Weber's ideal types. "In the contemporary philosophy of science, *nomen* [*sic!*] are not merely names but concepts, or prisms. A conceptual schema selects particular attributes from a complex reality and groups these under a common rubric in order to discern similarities and differences. As a logical ordering device, a conceptual scheme is not true or false but either useful or not" (Bell, *The Coming of Post-Industrial Society*, p. 9).

7. See the statement by Paul Tillich: "In this situation, without a home, without a place in which to dwell, religion suddenly realizes that it does not need such a place, that it does not need to seek for a home. It is at home everywhere, namely, in the depth of all functions of man's spiritual life. Religion is the dimension of depth in all of them. Religion is the aspect of depth in the totality of the human spirit." *Theology of Culture* (New York: Oxford University Press, 1959), p. 7.

8. In *The Coming of Post-Industrial Society* (p. 314n), Bell formulates the matter in this way: "Though the changes in culture and social structure derive from a common source, the contrasting demands or impulses in each realm clearly impose an agonizing tension whose consequences (are) important . . . for locating crucial strains in the society."

9. Cf. B. Zylstra, *From Pluralism to Collectivism: The Development of Harold Laski's Political Thought* (Assen, The Netherlands: Van Gorcum; New York: Humanities Press, 1968), pp. 44f and 96f, and the literature cited there.

10. In his discussion of "nature," Bell refers to the argument between Leo Strauss and Alexander Kojève in Leo Strauss, *On Tyranny* (New York: Free Press, 1963), but overlooks the important analysis of this argument by George Grant in *Technology and Empire: Perspectives on North America* (Toronto: House of Anansi, 1969), pp. 79-109.

11. See Eric Voegelin, *The New Science of Politics* (Chicago: University of Chicago Press, 1952), pp. 152f and 178f; Leo Strauss, *Natural Right and History* (Chicago: University of Chicago Press, 1950), pp. 166-202.

12. Bell traces the development of the idea of man as the controller of nature from the end of the fifteenth century through Marx in his essay "Technology, Nature, and Society," in Saul Bellow *et al.*, *Technology and the Frontiers of Knowledge* (Garden City, New York: Doubleday, 1975), pp. 39-49. Marx's discussion of the "two kingdoms" or realms can be found in *Capital* (New York: International Publishers, 1967), Vol. 3, p. 820. For a brief treatment of the dialectical relation between these realms, see B. Zylstra, "Karl Marx: Radical Humanist," *Vanguard*, December 1973, pp. 9-14; and Johan van der Hoeven, *Karl Marx: The Roots of His Thought* (Toronto: Wedge, 1976), pp. 83-6.

13. See Eric Voegelin's statement: "The rapid descent from reason through technical and planning intellect, to the economic, psychological and biological levels of human nature, as the dominants in the image of man, is a strong contrast to the imposing stability of the Christian anthropology through eighteen centuries. Once the transcendental anchorage is surrendered, the descent from the rational to the animal nature, so it seems, is inevitable." *From Enlightenment to Revolution*, p. 13. Cf. also Hannah Arendt, *The Human Condition* (New York: Doubleday Anchor Books, 1959), pp. 110-17. Here it should be noted that the Bible does not speak in terms of the primacy of "reason" over against the nonrational, as if sin had its source in the latter. Sin has its source in the heart of man, which, as the center of the self, directs both "reason" and "passion."

14. For the late-medieval setting in Joachim of Flora, see Eric Voegelin, *The New Science of Politics*, pp. 110f; and Voegelin, *Science, Politics and Gnosticism* (Chicago: Henry

Regnery, 1968), pp. 92f. For the Renaissance background of the notion of self-determination, notably in Pico della Mirandola, see Nicholas Lobkowicz, *Theory and Practice: History of a Concept from Aristotle to Marx* (Notre Dame & London: University of Notre Dame Press, 1967), pp. 134f. See also D. H. T. Vollenhoven, "Christendom en humanisme van middeleeuwen tot Reformatie," in *Philosophia reformata*, Vol. 11 (1946), pp. 101-40; and K. J. Popma, "Humanisme en Renaissance," in *Philosophia reformata*, Vol. 33 (1968), pp. 167-83.

15. George Grant poses the question "as to the connection between the religion of western Europe and the dynamic civilization which first arose there" (*Technology and Empire*, p. 106). See also Grant, *Time as History* (Toronto: Canadian Broadcasting Corporation, 1969/1971), pp. 21ff. I have discussed Grant's penetrating analysis of this problem and his view of modernity as rooted in the primacy of the will (which he ultimately relates to the sovereign will of God the Creator) in "Philosophy, Revelation, and Modernity: Crossroads in the Thought of George Grant" in Larry Schmidt, ed., *George Grant in Process* (Toronto: Anansi, 1978), pp. 148-57.

16. Irving Howe, ed., *The Idea of the Modern in Literature and the Arts* (New York: Horizon Press, 1967), p. 13. For the theme of "negation" in Hegel and Marx, see Herbert Marcuse, *Reason and Revolution* (New York: Oxford University Press, 1941); for parallel trends in modern art and literature, see William Barrett, *Time of Need* (New York: Harper and Row, 1973); and H. R. Rookmaaker, *Modern Art and the Death of a Culture* (London and Downers Grove, Illinois: Inter-Varsity Press, 1970).

17. Bell does not refer to books like R. H. Tawney, *Religion and the Rise of Capitalism* (New York: Harcourt, Brace & Co., 1926); Harold J. Laski, *The Rise of European Liberalism* (London: George Allen & Unwin, 1936); Karl Polanyi, *The Great Transformation* (Boston: Beacon Press, 1957); Christopher Hill, *Puritanism and Revolution* (London: Martin Secker & Warburg, 1958); and C. B. MacPherson, *The Political Theory of Possessive Individualism* (New York: Oxford University Press, 1962).

18. Eric Voegelin, *From Enlightenment to Revolution*, p. 69.

19. John Bunyan, *The Pilgrim's Progress* (New York: Airmont, 1969), p. 17. The theme of the negation of the world is announced in the full title: *The Pilgrim's Progress from this World to that which is to Come*. Voegelin interprets this as a Gnostic modification of the Christian idea of perfection. See *Science, Politics and Gnosticism*, pp. 88f.

20. See Hannah Arendt, *The Human Condition*, pp. 278-86; Eric Voegelin, *From Enlightenment to Revolution*, especially pp. 52-73.

21. Cf. Christopher Dawson, *The Dividing of Christendom* (New York: Sheed and Ward, 1965), pp. 256f.

22. John Locke, *Two Treatises of Government*, edited by Peter Lasslett (New York: Cambridge University Press, 1960), 2nd treatise, par. 94 (p. 373).

23. John Locke, *A Letter Concerning Toleration* (Indianapolis: Bobbs-Merrill, 1950), p. 36. For a brief discussion of the individualization of salvation, see B. Zylstra, "Thy Word Our Life," in *Will All the King's Men?* (Toronto: Wedge, 1972), pp. 153-221, especially pp. 196-201.

24. Locke, *A Letter Concerning Toleration*, p. 22.

25. R. H. Tawney, *Religion and the Rise of Capitalism* (New York: The New American Library, Mentor edition, 1947), p. 206.

26. Cf. Leo Strauss, *Natural Right and History* (1950).

27. See Arnold Brecht, *Political Theory* (Princeton: Princeton University Press, 1959), pp. 138-42; H. J. Hommes, *Een nieuwe herleving van het natuurrecht* (Zwolle: Tjeenk Willink, 1961).

28. Harold Laski explained the constant rebirth of a theory of natural law as a repeated expression of discontent with the existing order. See his *Authority in the Modern State* (New Haven: Yale University Press, 1919), p. 113.

29. See Roger Garaudy, *Marxism in the Twentieth Century* (New York: Charles Scribner's Sons, 1970), especially "Marxism and Religion," pp. 106-63.

30. See note 10 *supra* and Bell's arguments on pp. 162f and 171.

31. See especially Weber's speeches "Politics as a Vocation" and "Science as a Vocation," in H. H. Gerth and C. Wright Mills, eds., *From Max Weber: Essays in Sociology* (New York: Oxford University Press, 1946), pp. 77-156. Weber's point of departure was "the one fundamental fact, that so long as life remains immanent and is interpreted in its own terms, it knows only of an unceasing struggle of the(se) gods with one another" (p. 152). By "god" or "demon" Weber has in mind the fundamental "object" of one's allegiance.

32. The passage reads as follows: "There is now, more than ever, some need for utopia, in the sense that men need—as they have always needed—some vision of their potential, some manner of fusing passion with intelligence. Yet the ladder to the City of Heaven can no longer be a 'faith ladder,' but an empirical one: a utopia has to specify *where* one wants to go, *how* to get there, the costs of the enterprise, and some realization of, and justification for the determination of *who* is to pay." *The End of Ideology: On the Exhaustion of Political Ideas in the Fifties* (New York: The Free Press, 1960), p. 405.

33. The quotation is from Joseph Schumpeter, "The Crisis of the Tax State," originally published in German in 1918, reprinted in English in W. F. Stolper and R. A. Musgrave, eds., *International Economic Papers*, No. 4 (New York: MacMillan, 1954, pp. 5-38), at p. 24.

34. In practice, of course, hedonism in the modern age—the universal pursuit of material abundance, supported by the economic and political structures—is not easily abandoned. Hannah Arendt comments perceptively about this difficulty: "A hundred years after Marx we know the fallacy of this reasoning; the spare time of the *animal laborans* is never spent in anything but consumption, and the more time left to him, the greedier and more craving his appetites." *The Human Condition*, p. 115. Charles Taylor confirms this. "The drive to consumption is therefore no adventitious fad, no product of clever manipulation. It will not be easy to contain. It is tied up with the economic self-image of modern society, and this in turn is linked to a set of powerfully entrenched conceptions of what the value of human life consists in." Charles Taylor, "The Agony of Economic Man," in Laurier LaPierre *et al.*, eds., *Essays on the Left: Essays in Honour of T. C. Douglas* (Toronto: McClelland & Stewart, 1971), p. 232.

35. This terminology is George Grant's. See his discussion of this notion of freedom in connection with the developments of modern technology in "The Computer Does not Impose on Us the Ways it Should be Used," in Abraham Rotstein, ed., *Beyond Industrial Growth* (Toronto: University of Toronto Press, 1976), pp. 117-31.

36. For a discussion of the response of liberalism to the spiritual crisis of the West, see Eric Voegelin, *From Enlightenment to Revolution*, pp. 143f, where August Comte's intramundane eschatology is compared with Emil Littré's liberalism, that "peculiar mixture of destructiveness and conservatism." Voegelin's analysis of liberalism in Western culture is comparable to the interpretation of the nineteenth century Christian historian and statesman, Guillaume Groen van Prinsterer. For a partial translation of the latter's classic *Ongeloof en revolutie* (1847), see *Unbelief and Revolution*, Lecture XI and Lestures VIII & IX, edited and translated by Harry Van Dyke (Amsterdam: The Groen van Prinsterer Fund, 1973 and 1975 resp.). See B. Zylstra, "Voegelin on Unbelief and Revolution," in *Antirevolutionaire staatkunde*, Vol. 46, No. 5/6 (May-June 1976), pp. 155-65.

37. For a discussion of the politicocultural place of America within the spectrum of Western civilization, see B. Zylstra, "Modernity and the American Empire," in *International Reformed Bulletin*, first/second quarter 1977, pp. 3-19.

Freedom: Idea and Ideal

EDWARD A. LANGERAK

Freedom seems easier to die for than to define. When nations destroy each other while shouting the battle cry of freedom, we conclude that they often have different ideas of what freedom is. One aim of this essay is to show that imbedded in these different ideas of freedom are different ideals—differing values linked ultimately to disputes over what a human being is and should be.[1] The second aim is to accomplish the first aim by means of a broad but concise and integrated survey of what I believe are the central debates about freedom. While the scope of the essay is ambitious, the goal is modest; it does not include providing a new definition of freedom, arguing for a specific view of human nature, or advocating a particular value system. The goal is to show how these latter issues are integrated and to provide a framework for both relating and distinguishing them. My motivation for this goal is my belief that generally these issues are integrated without the proper distinctions, producing results that are confusing and sometimes dangerous.

The strategy is to begin with an initial question concerning freedom, a question involving a hypothesis that constitutes perhaps the most common view of freedom. We will then consider a number of objections to this view—objections that provide either amendments or alternatives to it. Toward the end we will consider a formula that provides the best *idea* of freedom, but which implies that the more basic issue is freedom as an *ideal*.

I

Suppose that, as a matter of fact, nobody intentionally prevents or pressures you from doing whatever you want to do. Are you free?

Before we examine the surprising variety of negative answers, we should note that many people, perhaps most, are inclined to respond affirmatively. They would say that the hypothetical situation, unfortunately, never occurs, but that if it did, that would be the highest degree of freedom anyone could have. The rationale for this response goes back to the beginning of an important strand in modern Western thought. Thomas Hobbes, reflecting on the possibility and character of society, stated in 1651 the essence of the above concept of freedom. His view became a formative influence in the development of European liberalism:

> LIBERTY, or FREEDOME, signifieth (properly) the absence of Opposition; (by Opposition, I mean external Impediments of motion) . . . . And according to this proper, and generally received meaning of the word, *A* FREE-MAN *is he, that in those things, which by his strength and wit he is able to do, is not hindred to doe what he has a will to (19*: 161).

This view of freedom is at the heart of John Stuart Mill's influential essay entitled *On Liberty (32)*, although Mill went further than Hobbes by insisting that freedom is the absence of certain kinds of coercion or pressure, and not just the absence of "impediments of motion." Hobbes had claimed that "Feare, and Liberty are consistent . . . so a man sometimes pays his debt, only for *feare* of Imprisonment, which because no body hindred him from detaining, was the action of a man at *liberty*" (*19*: 163). Mill on the other hand, rightly saw that such a claim could be appealed to by a "big brother" government using every kind of coercion to pressure persons to behave in prescribed ways, since Hobbes' claim would enable it to say that it is not interfering with their freedom. Therefore Mill insisted that threats of imprisonment and other coercive pressures are also infringements on freedom. And freedom so understood remains the type of freedom defended by European liberalism and most American conservatives. F. A. Hayek, for example, begins his impressive book *The Constitution of Liberty* by claiming that freedom is

> The state in which a man is not subject to coercion by the arbitrary will of another or others . . . . In this sense "freedom" refers solely to a relation of men to other men and the only infringement on it is coercion by men (*16*: 11-12).

This is also the view inspiring Milton Friedman's *Capitalism and Freedom,* and is the "negative freedom" defended by Isaiah Berlin in his influential inaugural lecture on "Two Concepts of Freedom."[2] When freedom so defined (hereafter referred to as "negative freedom") ranks high in your value system, you will find yourself defending economic and social policies that minimize government regulation and involvement, and you will have a tendency to envy the "rugged individualism" that characterized nineteenth century capitalism.

Of course, one could claim that negative freedom is the correct *definition* of freedom, while disagreeing that it is an important *value*, insisting, for example, that economic security and happiness are higher values. We shall see that one must avoid confusing an attack on the proposition that negative freedom is the proper *idea* of freedom with an attack on the proposition that negative freedom is an important *ideal*. We will see that some socialists, who have a low opinion of the value of negative freedom by itself, agree with conservatives, who have a high opinion of it, that it is the correct idea of freedom.

One conceptual difficulty with defining freedom negatively has to do with defining the "coercion" or, more broadly, the "pressure" by others that infringes on freedom. If I point a loaded pistol at you and say: "Your billfold or your life," you still, in a significant sense, have a free choice, a choice you would not have were I physically to overpower you and simply take your billfold. (The availability of this choice was illustrated by the comedian who replied: "Let me think a minute.") We saw that Hobbes even implied that you *freely* give me your billfold. Mill, Hayek and Berlin, on the other hand, would insist that your choice was coerced, and therefore your freedom was severely impinged on. Obviously the definition of coercion is an important part of defining freedom negatively.

Hayek defines coercion as: ". . . such control of the environment or circumstances of a person by another that, in order to avoid greater evil, he is forced to act not according to a coherent plan of his own but to serve the ends of another" (*16:* 20-1). This is a relatively clear definition, but when interpreted narrowly it does not seem to cover all cases in which pressure by one person impinges on the freedom of another. Consider a case in which I do not control the circumstances that have made you desperate but I take advantage of them to pressure you to change your mind about something. Through no fault of mine you are starving, and I offer you a delicious stew if you give up your inheritance. It seems clear that I have applied the kind of pressure that interfered with your freedom, and that you did not *freely* give up your inheritance. Indeed, this observation stimulates some people to argue that the early labor movement, which reduced the ability of employers to take advantage of the desperate straits of employees, increased rather than decreased freedom in the labor market.

One might reply that we are interpreting Hayek's definition too narrowly; my offer of the stew is the control of your circumstances that constitutes coercion. But if we take this route, the extension of "coercion" threatens to become so broad as to include any kind of influence I have on you. Let us say you are very fond of me and need my respect and affection. Knowing this, I threaten to hate and scorn you unless you give up your inheritance. Here I have taken advantage of a psychological need rather than a physical one, but otherwise the example is analogous to the earlier one. If this is coercion, then any conditional offer I make that would fulfill one of your needs is coercive. From this consequence, it is only a small step to argue that bribes to greedy people, and persuasive arguments to gullible people, are coercive.[3] Obviously this would be a much broader notion of coercion than Hayek intended, since it would make negative freedom almost non-existent, available only to persons unaffected by others.

Therefore, apart from the objections examined below, the definition of negative freedom is infected with the difficulty involved in defining coercion, namely, the difficulty of defining it either too narrowly or too broadly.[4] This fact reduces its usefulness as the basic notion of freedom.

II

One alternative conception of freedom claims that the "as a matter of fact" phrase in our definition of negative freedom reveals a fundamental misunderstanding of the essence of freedom. Freedom, it claims, is a matter of *feeling* free, of the absence of *perceived* restraints,[5] and therefore your freedom depends on whether you *believe* someone or something is preventing or pressuring you from doing what you want to do. If in fact you are not being pressured but you believe you are, then you are not free; if in fact you are being pressured but you do not believe you are, then you are free.

This position, which I will call the "feeling view" of freedom, has been developed in a number of different ways, some of which overlap views that we will examine below. For now we will note that this view, usually defined by those critical of it, derives its plausibility from the fact that persons live in cultures, that cultures have structures, and that these structures generally include a multitude of rules, constraints, tabus, and accepted wisdom (see Dorothy Lee, *3*: 61-73; see also *29*). To feel free is to have a sense of harmony with this cultural structure, to perceive it as "enabling" rather than as constraining:

> . . . to the extent that the adherents of a culture conform to, and are satisfied with, their traditional institutions, they feel free and are not aware,

> for the most part, of any significant restraints. It is only upon consciousness of other cultures and critical comparison with their systems of liberties that dissatisfaction tends to arise and complaints are made of coercion and tyranny. There is some truth, therefore, in Franz Boas' attempt to define cultural freedom in subjective terms as the feeling of harmony with one's culture. Ignorance is bliss and does promote the feeling of contentment and freedom . . . (Bidney, *3*: 23).

To state the "feeling free" position in this way is, of course, to reveal its weakness; it tends to confuse freedom with contentment.[6]

One specific and important way that a culture can shape an individual is by teaching him what he "really" is. My feeling free, then, becomes a matter of my acting in harmony with that aspect of myself that my culture has taught me to perceive as my "true" self. Thus the ancient Greeks felt free when they acted in harmony with their reason, because they perceived humans as essentially rational animals. They felt unfree when their emotions and passions got the better of them, while the Romantics, on the other hand, felt free only when acting in harmony with their emotions. Some existentialists, such as the early Sartre, using "existence preceeds essence" as a slogan, rejected any sense of self-identity, whether culturally inculcated or not (though one might wonder whether this rejection itself was not culturally inspired). This position runs the risk of reducing the feeling of freedom to that of arbitrariness, much as Dostoevsky's Underground Man, a person without any sense of self-identity, confuses an "absolutely free choice" with completely unfettered whim and caprice.[7]

Suppose we reduce freedom to "feeling free" and agree that my feeling free depends on my acting in harmony with that aspect of myself that I have accepted as my "true" self. Then the extent to which I identify myself as an individual atom, as being separate from others in my society rather than as part of a social organism—to that extent I will feel free only when acting individualistically. The Greeks thought that the collective life was prior to the individual, and that a person was truly human only as one part of a social organism. Obviously they could feel free while acting for the welfare and happiness of the entire *polis*. Americans, influenced by the individualism of Hobbes, Locke and others, tend to feel free only when acting on their own. Social critics have suggested that in the context of their emphasis on freedom, this individualism has created unique problems for American society.[8]

One might challenge the accuracy of the above historical generalizations, but it should be clear that reducing freedom to "feeling free," apart from confusing freedom and contentment, does not escape the basic issue of what a human being is and should be. In a later context we will see philosophers using this fact to argue for a rather dangerous view of freedom.

III

Two other objections to our initial hypothesis about freedom argue that its implications for lack of freedom are too narrow. First of all, why should we restrict "prevention" to *somebody*, when many of the obstacles to our freedom derive from our own deficiencies and our natural environment? I am not free to swim across the Atlantic Ocean—not because someone is preventing me but because my own weakness, combined with its size, prevents me. We often think of the technological conquest of natural barriers and the increase in human power and knowledge as making mankind *freer* than before. If so, the former natural barriers and the former weakness and ignorance would seem to have been restrictions on freedom, even if they were not the result of some person's or group's action. But if we move in the direction of thinking that all internal and external barriers are restrictions on freedom, we seem to make the notion of unfreedom so broad as to become uninteresting.

At this point some thinkers distinguish between kinds of freedom. Perhaps in some broad sense of freedom, any barrier is a restriction on freedom, but they are interested in *political* and *social* freedom:

> If I say that I am unable to jump more than ten feet in the air, or cannot read because I am blind, or cannot understand the darker pages of Hegel, it would be eccentric to say that I am to that degree enslaved or coerced. Coercion implies the deliberate interference of other human beings within the area in which I could otherwise act. You lack political liberty only if you are prevented from attaining a goal by human beings (*2*: 122).[9]

This seems a wise move to make, as long as we remember what kind of freedom we are discussing. But now a second, more serious, difficulty arises, one that is related to the use of "deliberate" by Berlin, and to our use of "intentional" in our initial hypothesis.

The negative freedom view limits the realm of political and social unfreedom to those barriers deliberately or intentionally erected. However, human actions, especially when institutionalized in social and economic structures, have *consequences* that are *not intended.* Frequently these consequences can be either foreseen or later inferred to be the inevitable result of the actions that did not intend them. For example, suppose that the choice of an economic system that allows the unrestricted accumulation and use of capital results in the poverty of many and the wealth of a few. Those successfully insisting on such a system would be causing any lack of freedom inherent in the resultant poverty, although it would never cross their liberally-educated minds to intend such a thing. Herein lies the motivation for the Marxist critique of capitalistic freedom: the freedom of a few is purchased with the slavery of many, not because the few intend that but because the capitalist economic and social structure has inevitable results—results which impinge on the ability of the working class to do as they want. (Some neo-Marxists, such as Marcuse, stress that the social structure can also have an insidious effect on the wants of the oppressed, often causing them to be willing partners in their own slavery.)

To the extent that these results are recognized as the unintended consequences of structures that are intended, and to the extent that the structures, and thereby the results, are modifiable, it seems that we should refer to them as restrictions on political and social freedom (see *9*:9). Even here, however, we will need some concept of what a human being essentially is and should be. Otherwise we will extend the notion of "lack of freedom" too far, since not all modifiable results that affect human wants are impingements on freedom. The fact that the economic structure does not allow everyone to go to the graduate school or hospital of his first choice should not be thought of as a restriction on freedom if the latter phrase is to retain any meaning. However, if the economic structure forces a segment of the population to forego any education or medical care at all (e.g. the children of migrant workers), this result is an inexcusable restriction on freedom. The implicit criterion seems to be a view of what is needed to be fully human; graduate education at Princeton or a team of Mayo Clinic surgeons is not needed, but basic medical care, and enough education to become something other than Edwin Markham's "Man with the Hoe,"[10] is.

To spell out the criterion would involve us in the basic issues of normative anthropology. Therefore the above objections, while forcing only an amendment rather than a rejection of our initial hypothesis, underscore the fact that attempting a definition even of mere negative freedom requires a view of what human nature is and should be.

IV

Consider our initial definition. It hypothesizes that freedom resides in nobody's coercing you from doing whatever you want. What is the source of those wants? This question leads to another set of issues regarding freedom. First, some "hard determinists" point out that if the source of the wanting is external to you, if everything you want is completely a function of temporally prior states of affairs, then you cannot be free, even if nothing prevents you from doing what you cannot avoid wanting to do.

This is a serious issue, but it lies outside the scope of this essay. Even a determinist like Jonathan Edwards, in distinguishing between "being compelled" and "being determined," accepted the sort of concept of freedom that we are discussing,[11] so the problems we are raising would be problems for him. Hence I do not believe this essay is committed one way or the other on the issue of determinism.

A second problem related to the source of wants is more relevant to our concerns. If you are the source of your wants, and if freedom consists in not being hindered in doing what you want, you have two rather different options in maintaining and increasing your freedom. The obvious one is to overcome the obstacles; the less obvious one is to overcome your wants. While this latter way is associated with Eastern philosophy, with the Buddha's teaching that one achieves liberation by ridding oneself of desires, it is also an undercurrent in Western thought. The Stoic philosopher Epictetus, for example, taught that "freedom is not procured by a full enjoyment of what is desired, but by controlling the desire" (*8*: 282). His reasoning was that my wants are one of the few things completely in my control; therefore, since my freedom is a function of my wants, it is completely in my control. Thus Epictetus claims that although he is a slave, he is freer than his master. Under this theory, a person locked in a prison cell becomes free as soon as he ceases wanting to get out.

This objection forces a revision in the definition of negative freedom, as Berlin realized after he published his essay (*2*: xxxviii). We must define negative freedom not with respect to *actual* wants but with respect to *possible* wants. Thus a person is free to the extent that nobody interferes with what he *might* want to do, not just with what he actually wants to do. This revision is more consistent with our intuitions concerning freedom—freedom is a function of what one could do and not just of what one in fact does.

However, this revision raises an interesting question: Why should we worry about what we *could* want instead of just what we *do* want? If a dictator makes his subjects satisfied, so that they do not want to do other than what he commands, is anything valuable missing? This question forces us to realize that as we sharpen up the definition of negative freedom, the issue of what it *means* may be closely related to, but is not identical with, the issue of where it *ranks* in our hierarchy of values. Epictetus and the Buddha could grant Berlin his definition of freedom and claim that they are on to something more worthwhile—bliss. So again the problem of the relationship between the definition of freedom and the value of freedom is raised.

V

A rich tradition of thinking about freedom, a tradition with many different strands, asserts that it is first and foremost the *character* of your wants that makes you free, and that lack of coercion is insufficient, indeed, irrelevant for freedom. One strand, largely stimulated by theological beliefs, claims that freedom consists in *spiritual* freedom, and that it is a gift of God. St. Paul taught that: "Where the spirit of the Lord is, there is freedom" (II Cor. 3:17), and many theologians have taken this as their clue to both the definition and the evaluation of freedom. Often their thinking takes on a dualistic character, as they allow that there may be another kind of freedom that the world strives for, but that the latter is worthless next to spiritual freedom. Martin Luther's essay on "Christian Liberty" distinguishes between man's spiritual nature and his bodily nature, and, equating the latter with the "flesh" or "outward man," observes with St. Paul that the flesh and the spirit lust against each other. Christian liberty is strictly a matter of the spirit:

> It is evident that no external thing, whatsoever it be, has any influence whatever in producing Christian righteousness or liberty, nor in producing unrighteousness or bondage. A simple argument will furnish the proof. What can it profit the soul if the body fare well, be free and active, eat, drink, and do as it pleases? For in these things even the most godless slaves of all the vices fare well. On the other hand, how will ill health or imprisonment or hunger or thirst or any external misfortune hurt the soul? With these things even the most godly men are afflicted, and those who because of a clear conscience are most free. None of these things touch either the liberty or the bondage of the soul (*26*: 174-5).

Clearly here we have an entirely different kind of freedom from our initial hypothesis. The "spiritual freedom" view makes a sharp distinction between freedom and licence. *Both* of them are a type of bondage: license is bondage to vice, and freedom is bondage to God's will. When Christians sing: "Make me a captive, Lord, and then I shall be free; My heart will freely move, when Thou hast wrought its chain," they are not thinking of freedom as the *absence* of unwelcomed restraints but as the presence of welcomed ones. Thus freedom is associated with goodness, and unfreedom with vice. And this spiritual freedom, or goodness, is often thought of as a gift of God—not as something achieved by works.[12]

The doctrine of "spiritual freedom" challenges us to become clear about what we mean by *self*-determination. If freedom involves self-determination, our initial hypotheses attempted to specify what must be absent (coercion) for self-determination, and a later view will attempt to specify what must be present (power). But the "spiritual freedom" view forces us to face the question what is meant by the *self*. If my true self is something completely different from my body, then Luther seems right in insisting that even if freedom does involve self-determination, bodily coercion or the lack of it is irrelevant to my freedom.

Of course, the body/spirit dualism is not unique to theological thinkers. For example, secular poets in prison occasionally find the inner resources to assert that the enslavement of their body is irrelevant to their freedom: "Eternal Spirit of the chainless Mind! / Brightest in dungeons, Liberty! Thou art . . . ."[13] But it is the rationalists, such as Spinoza and Kant, who were most successful in integrating their doctrine of freedom with their dualistic view of human nature, as well as with their value system. Believing reason to be the higher part of human nature, and believing that the laws of reason include the moral law, they found freedom in obedience to the laws of reason. Kant stressed that since these laws were dictated by a person's own reason, that is, were self-legislated, submission to them is compatible with complete autonomy.

Understanding this concept of rational freedom requires attending to the relationship between freedom and law. Rational freedom is not freedom *from* law but freedom *through* law. Freedom understood solely as the absence of coercion tends to view laws as an impingement on freedom, though this impingement can sometimes be justified. (Mill, for example, thought that the infringement by law on freedom was justified to protect others.) With John Locke we find an important shift; he defined freedom as *including* laws, rather than viewing laws as (sometimes justified) infringement on freedom:

> For law, in its true notion, is not so much the limitation as the direction of a free and intelligent agent to his proper interest . . . that ill deserves the name of confinement which hedges us in only from bogs and precipices. So that however it may be mistaken, the end of law is not to abolish or restrain, but to preserve and enlarge freedom (*25*: 101-2).

We can easily see both the attractiveness and the danger of this move. The danger is that it tends to confuse justified coercion with the absence of coercion; we will see that this confusion easily justifies totalitarianism in the name of freedom. The attractiveness is that justified laws protect our freedom, not only from the violence of others ("freedom for the pike is death for the minnows"), but also from our own stupidity. The latter protection is charmingly illustrated by an anecdote about John Ruskin. As a toddler he once reached for a whistling tea kettle. His nurse tried to prevent him, but his mother told the nurse to allow him to touch it. That, he said, was his first lesson in the meaning of freedom.

If obedience to nursery laws and civil laws can enhance freedom, it would seem that obedience to rational, moral laws would be the very essence of freedom. This is precisely the claim made by Kant:

> Hence freedom of will, although it is not the property of conforming to laws of nature, is not for this reason lawless: it must rather be a causality conforming to immutable laws, though of a special kind . . . [namely] the categorical imperative and the principle of morality. Thus a free will and a will under moral laws are one and the same (*21*: 114).[14]

Kant thought that a person's lower, sensuous impulses were constantly in battle with his reason, and that therefore true freedom was the result of the most rigorous moral effort.

Thus we see that a dualistic view of human nature, combined with either some theological beliefs or a rationalistic value system (or both), produces a concept of freedom at odds with the lack-of-coercion concept.

There are related, important ways of integrating a concept of rational freedom into a value-laden view of human nature. Most of them make heavy use of the premise that freedom is through law, rather than from law. We noted the dangerous ambiguity of this premise. It could be interpreted as the claim that obedience to laws enables us to give up certain freedoms (e.g. the freedom to harm others or to touch hot tea kettles) in order to obtain other, more important freedoms (e.g. the freedom from being harmed). But the premise can also be interpreted as the claim that obedience to law *is* freedom, and is all there is to freedom. In certain value-laden contexts, this claim may be enlightening. But we should examine one tragic way this claim was developed, a development that begins with Rousseau, continues through Hegel and Bosanquet, and ends with Fascism.

Rousseau struggled with the following problem: a free person must live in society; society requires laws; therefore a free person must conform to laws. "But it may be asked how a man can be free and yet forced to conform to the will of others" (*39*: 95). His answer involves a useful distinction between different levels of willing. Suppose I want to cure myself of a cold, and I mistakenly believe that taking a sauna will do it, when, in fact, a sauna will make it worse. If you prevent me from taking a sauna, you will prevent me from doing what I will, but not from what I really want. Likewise, thought Rousseau, if society had a criterion for determining what really will enhance my freedom, it could make me conform to that criterion without actually impinging on my freedom; it would, paradoxically, force me to be free. Rousseau argued that this criterion was the "general will," and that "the general will is found by counting the votes."

> When, therefore, the motion which I opposed carried, it only proves to me that I was mistaken, and that what I believed to be the general will was not

> so. If my particular opinion had prevailed, I should have done what I was not willing to do, and, consequently, I should not have been in a state of freedom (*39*: 96).

Obviously, such a doctrine would create enough mischief even in a thoroughly fair democracy. When used by Hegelians, real trouble was bound to arise. Following Kant, Hegel derided the "utter immaturity" of thinking that freedom consisted in arbitrariness or in "the ability to do what we please" (*17*: 27). Seemingly in agreement with Kant, he defined freedom in terms of duty: "Thus duty is not a restriction on freedom, but only on freedom in the abstract, i.e. on unfreedom. Duty is the attainment of our essence, the winning of *positive* freedom" (*17*: 259-60). However, Hegel rejected Kant's view of what duty is, and thereby had a different view of what it is to attain our essence. The character and implications of this shift are dramatically seen in Bernard Bosanquet's defense and development of Hegel.

Bosanquet's first step was to claim that there is more to self-determination than mere absence of constraint: ". . . the condition of man as to being himself is fundamentally affected not only by the power to do what he likes without constraint, but by the nature of what he likes to do" (*4*: 128). Thus what he called the "self *par excellence*" may demand obedience to something different from "yourself as you are" (*4*: 131-4). So the second step was Rousseau's distinction between different levels of willing: ". . . what we will is not always what would satisfy our want" (*4*: 136). And what would satisfy our real *wants* is our *real* or *rational* will, which is satisfied by any institution that serves the needs of the self *par excellence*: "Any system of institutions which represents to us, on the whole, the conditions essential to affirming such a will, in objects of action such as to constitute a tolerably complete life, has an imperative claim upon our loyalty and obedience as the embodiment of our liberty" (*4*: 139). The third step was the fatal one: the institution that represents the real or rational will was, following Rousseau, identified with the State (*4*: 139). To make this identification "less paradoxical to the English mind," Bosanquet hastened to add that the State is not just a "political fabric"; it includes all institutions by which life is shaped, from the family, to the trade, to the church and university. It is "the structure which gives life and meaning to the political whole . . . the State, in this sense, is, above all things, not a number of persons, but a working conception of life" (*4*: 140-1).

After relating freedom to the "higher self" and identifying the latter with this broad, nebulous, Hegelian notion of the State, Bosanquet's final step was drawing the conclusion that the State is justified in using coercion to carry out its purposes, including that of molding the higher self:

> The State, as the operative criticism of all institutions, is necessarily force; and in the last resort, it is the only recognized and justified force . . . . We make a great mistake in thinking of the force exercised by the State as limited to the restraint of disorderly persons by the police and the punishment of intentional lawbreakers. The State is the fly-wheel of our life. Its system is constantly reminding us of duties, from sanitation to the incidents of trusteeship, which we have not the least desire to neglect, but which we are either too ignorant or too indolent to carry out apart from instruction and authoritative suggestion (*4*: 141-2).

The State thus acts as an authoritative "extension of our own minds," that is, as an extension of our higher self. Bosanquet did not hesitate to point out that therefore the State is justified in forcing our private selves to conform to our higher self:

> Thus it is that we can speak, without a contradiction, of being forced to be free. It is possible for us to acquiesce, as rational beings, in a law and order which on the whole makes for the possibility of asserting our true or universal selves, at the very moment when this law and order is constraining our particular private wills in a way which we resent, or even condemn (*4*: 118-19).[15]

This is Orwellian Newspeak—"Freedom is Slavery." Rousseau, at least, controlled the dimensions of state action through majority vote. But the Hegelians rightly noticed that there is little correlation between majority vote and the dictates of the rational, higher self. So if freedom has to do with the latter, citizens may have to be enslaved in order to be free.

Bosanquet's own motives for this doctrine were of the highest character, but the doctrine was easily used by those whose goals were not noble. In an early defense of Fascism (in the prestigious American journal *Foreign Affairs*), the neo-Hegelian Fascist Giovanni Gentile argued that Fascism solved the conflict between freedom and authority: "For freedom can exist only within the State, and the State means authority" (*12*: 303). This authority is absolute; it "does not bargain, it does not surrender any portion of its field to other moral or religious principles which may interfere with the individual conscience" (*12*: 304). One might think that this view sacrifices all democratic freedoms, but Gentile argued the opposite:

> The Fascist State, on the contrary, is a people's state, and, as such, the democratic State *par excellence* . . . . Its formation therefore is the formation of a consciousness of it in individuals, in the masses. Hence the need of the Party, and of all the instruments of propaganda and education which Fascism uses to make the thought and will of the *Duce* the thought and will of the masses (*12*: 302-3).

The State and the individual are one. Therefore the State carries out the will of the citizens; this is ensured because the State sees to it that its policies become the desire of the citizens. Why not work the other way around, letting the desires of the citizens become the policies of the State (which is what we ordinarily think of as the democratic way)? Because this "liberal" or "individualistic" way is based on a fundamental misunderstanding of freedom, as Gentile's colleague Mario Palmieri stated:

> Two radically different conceptions of Liberty are thus in conflict, and there is no hope that the abyss which separates them can ever be bridged. In the Fascist conception, to be free, means to be no more a slave to one's own passions, ambitions, or desires; means to be free to will what is true, and good, and just, at all times, in all cases; means, in other words, to realize here in this world the true mission of man . . . . But it is a fact, a conclusively true historical fact, that the ordinary human being *does not know* how to use his freedom . . . . According to Fascism, a true, a great spiritual life cannot take place unless the State has risen to a position of pre-eminence in the world of man . . . . As Giovanni Gentile says: ". . . The maximum of liberty coincides with the maximum strength of the State" (*36*: 376-7).

Thus value-laden concepts of freedom, human nature, the State, and their relationships produced a sweetly reasonable argument for tyranny. What went wrong? The first important step was the identification of freedom with goodness and with the activity of the higher part of the self. If we rule out this step, we also rule out Luther's and Kant's ideas of true freedom. I think there is much to be said for making this move, and in the next section we will discuss a formula that maintains the distinction between freedom defined as self-determination, on the one hand, and the proper use of this freedom, on the other. However, I will suggest that we still cannot avoid the value-laden issue of what "true freedom" is.

The second important step was the division of human nature into lower and higher parts, and an identification of that higher part. Luther identified the latter with the spirit that obeys God; Kant identified it with reason; and the Hegelians and Fascists identified it with the State. The former are definitely to be preferred; identification of goodness with any human institution is a most tragic form of idolatry.[16] But all radical divisions of human nature end up blurring the line between freedom and bondage. We need an *integral* view of human nature, in which free self-determination is not the victory of one part over another part but is the expression of the whole person. Erich Fromm, for one, has argued for this:

> . . . the realization of the self is accomplished . . . by the realization of man's total personality, by the active expression of his emotional and intellectual

> potentialities . . . . In other words, *positive freedom consists in the spontaneous activity of the total, integrated personality* (*11*: 258).

The thinkers who argue that freedom should be defined as spiritual or rational freedom are right in not hesitating to relate normative anthropology (views of what human nature is and should be) to their understanding of freedom and self-determination. However, their non-integrative view of human nature and their imprecise way of relating the definitional and the evaluative aspects can be wrong to the point of becoming dangerous.

VI

Perhaps the strongest challenge to conceiving of freedom as simply the absence of coercion involves the claim that freedom implies the power to achieve one's wants, not merely the lack of restraints. Since Berlin's article, this latter view has usually been referred to as the concept of "positive freedom." The claim is that you are not really free to do something, e.g. educate your children or start your own business, unless you have the *means* to do so. Without the means to do something, you at most are free to *try* to do it.

This way of thinking is part of the nineteenth century revision of liberal individualism and was defended by some of the same people who brought us Bosanquet's view of freedom. These idealists claimed that human nature is fundamentally social, and that freedom involves power, namely, the power to do what is worthwhile. Bosanquet's teacher, T. H. Green, when discussing whether a laborer has the same freedom of contract as the employer, underscored all of these elements.

> When we speak of freedom as something to be so highly prized, we mean a positive power or capacity of doing or enjoying something worth doing or enjoying, and that, too, something that we do or enjoy in common with others . . . . When we measure the progress of a society by its growth in freedom, we measure it . . . by the greater power on the part of the citizens as a body to make the most and best of themselves(*14*: 51-2).

We saw how this way of relating freedom, power, the social character of human nature, and a view of what is worthwhile can be developed into an argument for tyranny in the name of freedom. Perhaps for this reason some liberals are very chary of any concept of positive freedom. Berlin emphasizes the tendency of defenders of positive freedom to talk about the "true self" and to coerce people into behaving as they *ought* to behave. He argues that therefore we should think of freedom as simply negative freedom, and the lack of power to do what one wants as, not the lack of freedom, but the inability to use the freedom that one has (*2*: 124-5; see also *44*: 153). To avoid muddled thinking, he says, we must admit that in some situations, power, equality, justice, and other values are to be preferred to freedom, but one should not sacrifice freedom to obtain these other values and then call it an increase in freedom. One should call it what it is—a trade-off of freedom for other things, things perhaps more valuable.[17]

Berlin is supported, on a conceptual level, by the conservative economist and philosopher F. A. Hayek, who thinks that no confusions about freedom are " . . . as dangerous as its confusion with a third use of the word . . . the use of 'liberty' to describe the physical 'ability to do what I want', the power to satisfy our wishes, or the extent of the choice of alternatives open to us" (*16*: 16).

> Only since this confusion was deliberately fostered as part of the socialist argument has it become dangerous. Once this identification of freedom with power is admitted, there is no limit to the sophisms by which the attractions of the word "liberty" can be used to support measures which destroy individual liberty, no end to the tricks by which people can be exhorted in the name of liberty to give up their liberty (*16*: 16).

Surprisingly, the well-known socialist Harold Laski agrees with Hayek and Berlin about the definition of liberty, and his agreement involved an explicit change of mind. In a book first published in 1930, he took note of the Hegelian misuse of positive freedom: "In the whole history of political philosophy there is nothing more subtle than the skill with which the idealist school has turned the flank on the classic antithesis between liberty and authority" (22: 39). Perhaps for this reason, in 1930 he added a note to a book first published in 1925, stating his change of mind:

> In 1925 I thought that liberty could most usefully be regarded as more than a negative thing. I am now convinced that this was a mistake, and that the old view of it as an absence of restraint can alone safeguard the personality of the citizen (*23*: prefatory note).

Laski did not change his mind about socialism, however, and he completely disagrees with Hayek about its actual relationship to freedom. He maintains that although economic security is not itself liberty, it is a condition without which liberty is never effective. Thus socialism is "inescapably connected with freedom," but the economic power it equitably distributes is a condition for using freedom, rather than a part of freedom itself (*22*: 34-7).

Thus, several thinkers who disagree about the relative value of freedom and power agree that freedom should not be defined as including power. I believe that this definitional distinction between freedom and power is misguided to the extent that it is motivated by the desire to avoid Hegelian sorts of misuse of the concept of freedom. Berlin's problem is that he defines much more than power into the notion of positive freedom; he builds the entire idealist anthropology and value system into it.[18] But the simple claim that "to be free to do something, you must be able to do it" does not entail the value-laden dualism that Bosanquet used. Even T. H. Green, whose own definition of freedom included, as we saw, most of the doctrines appealed to by Bosanquet, admits that merely defining freedom to include power does not commit one to the Hegelian use of the term:

> All that is so implied is that a man should have power to do what he wills or prefers. No reference is made to the nature of the will or preference, of the object willed or preferred; whereas according to the usage of freedom in the doctrines we have just been considering, it is not constituted by the mere fact of acting upon preference, but depends wholly on the nature of the preference, upon the kind of object willed or preferred (*14*: 84).

We saw that it was the latter move that allowed for forcing one to be free, not the mere inclusion of "power" in "freedom."

Although simply defining freedom as including power does not lead to Fascism, Hayek is right in assuming that it can strengthen the socialist argument. It does so in two ways. First, it motivates a society that is committed to equality of freedom[19] to commit itself to a somewhat equal distribution of resources, including economic and educational resources. It is access to these resources that gives one the power to make his choices effective; hence, without access to them one is not free to make his choices effective. This point is insisted on by Robert Dahl, who observes that in 1956 one half of one percent of Americans owned one quarter of the wealth in the country: "extreme inequalities in income such as now exist in the United States mean extreme inequalities in capacity to make personal choices effective, and hence extreme inequalities in individual freedom" (*7*: 113-14).[20] We should note that since many political constitutions guarantee the right of freedom, if not equal freedom, the move to include power within freedom implies that the least advantaged persons in society may argue for a more equitable distribution of resources as a matter of their constitutional *right*. However, if power is something distinct from freedom, and something not guaranteed as a right, the least advantaged would have to appeal to charity or *noblesse oblige*. Thus it is not surprising that those concerned with redistributing the primary social goods of a society tend to reject Berlin's suggestion that clarity would be enhanced if they admitted that they want to exchange freedom for other social goods. Thinking of freedom as including power enables them to argue for what is *due* the least advantaged, rather than for what would be benevolent. Such thinking can argue on constitutional grounds for high inheritance taxes, genuinely graduated income taxes, and social control of the basic means of production and education. Of course, to avoid defeating their own purpose, such steps would have to avoid making the distribution of power, and thereby freedom, even more unequal—a stubborn fact that implies the avoidance of arbitrary and huge bureaucracies.

The second way that including power within the definition of freedom strengthens the argument for socialism relates to Hayek's complaint that: ". . . with the help of this equivocation the notion of collective power over circumstances has been substituted for that of individual liberty" (*16*: 16). If power has to do with being able to obtain the results one wants, then it is clear that frequently an organized group can have collective power with respect to issues that an individual cannot have individual power over.[21] Often these issues are those that are central to human happiness and welfare—issues such as control over nature, mining of fuels, and controlling pollution and the use of resources. One individual has little or no power over whether America has clean lakes and rivers, but voters can have collective power over it. As the world becomes more populated, resources become more scarce, pollution becomes more abundant, individual power over many important issues declines, and only organized groups that involve regulatory agencies can have power over them.[22]

However, as Hayek notes, usually one obtains participation in collective power only at the price of individual power and freedom. To have collective power over a fine transportation system, we lose individual power over a portion of our income (the taxes that pay for the transportation system). To have collective power with respect to keeping the environment clean, we lose individual power to pollute as we see fit. To have collective power over keeping farmlands in production, we lose individual power with respect to plotting out farmland and selling it for residences. In general, socialism encourages the acquisition of social power, even at the price of reduced individual power.[23]

Whether you welcome the trade-offs implicit in socialism depends to a large extent on your view of human nature. Is it fundamentally social, or is each man an island? Is society basically an archipelago of islands (with bridges), or a continent, an organism? The socialist answer is clear; their problem is to avoid the Fascist error of collapsing their commitment to an organic view of society into a commitment to a particular political institution. Hayek and Berlin do well to warn them of this danger.

But I believe the latter are wrong in trying to avoid this danger by defining freedom purely negatively. Hayek is wrong in saying: "Whether or not I am my own master and can follow my own choice and whether the possibilities from which I must choose are many or few are two entirely different questions" (*16*: 17). As we saw, if your choice is between starving and giving up your inheritance, you may be your own master in doing the latter, but you are not as free as you would be if other alternatives were open to you. And having other alternatives open to you means more than your being permitted to attempt them; it means your having the possibility of carrying them out, your having power with respect to them.

This point can be seen even from the perspective of Berlin and Hayek, as Hayek himself suspected when he warned that one can easily move from defining freedom negatively to interpreting it as involving power (*16*: 17). This move has become popular in current social philosophy. Maurice Cranston (*6*: 3) points out that "I am free" is analogous to "I am prepared" or "I am resolved," and is not analogous to "I am hungry." The first three propositions, unlike the last, are incomplete; you wonder what I am prepared for, resolved to do, or free from. In other words, freedom is *relational,* and sentences using the word *free* communicate most clearly when they are of the triadic form "x is free from y to do (or be, or have) z."[24] Freedom involves a person's being free *from* something *for* something. One of the things I can be free from is coercion, but I can also be free from desperate straits, from stupidity, from poverty, and from weakness. If one were to restrict the range of the variables by restricting freedom, or a type of freedom, to lack of deliberate coercion, that type of freedom would always be a quadratic relationship: "w is free from x controlled by y to do z." But, as we saw, such a restriction does not do justice to our intuitions about freedom.

Without any restriction on the variables, the above formula allows the broadest possible interpretation of freedom. Joel Feinberg points out that there are four categories of restraints that we can be free from:

> There are *internal positive constraints* such as headaches, obsessive thoughts, and compulsive desires; *internal negative constraints* such as ignorance, weakness, and deficiencies in talent or skill; external positive *constraints* such as barred windows, locked doors, and pointed bayonets; and *external negative constraints* such as lack of money, lack of transportation, and lack of weapons. Freedom from a negative constraint is the absence of an absence, and therefore the presence of some condition that permits a given kind of doing. When the presence of such a condition is external to a person, it is usually called an opportunity, and when internal, an ability (*9*: 13).[25]

With this broad an understanding of freedom, there is no Dostoevskian conflict between freedom and security;[26] security is a type of freedom. This point did not escape the English liberals, such as Jeremy Bentham: ". . . *security* is a word, in which, in most cases, I find an advantageous substitute for [liberty]: *security* against misdeeds by public functionaries: *security* against misdeeds by foreign adversaries—as the case may be" (*1*: 41-2).[27] Security can be thought of as including the temporal dimension of freedom, the probability over time of the enjoyment of things one values, including specific types of freedom (*1*: 66). Thus security is freedom from various ills, including anxiety and fear.

Of course even Mussolini made the trains run on time, giving people the security of freedom from an upset schedule. Therefore we must notice that security involves a trade-off of freedoms. Freedom from starvation in China was purchased at the price of certain freedoms that seem to rank higher in the value systems of many Americans than in the value system of the Chinese. This suggests that a debate over which society is freer should not be construed as a debate over the *concept* of freedom; it is a debate over a value ranking of specific freedoms. If you value security from any societal interference more than security from the risk of poverty and starvation (either for yourself or others), you will think of socialists as advocating slavery. Socialists, then, should not attack your definition of freedom but your value ranking of freedoms, which is probably inspired by your individualistic view of human nature. So Berlin, Hayek, and even Laski should not insist that socialism involves a trade-off of freedom for other values but should see it as a trade-off of some freedoms for other ones.

This way of distinguishing the idea of freedom from the issue which freedoms are ideal helps us understand the debate on the question whether freedom is an intrinsic value or an instrumental one. The utilitarians defended freedom as the means to another value, namely, happiness. You need not be a hedonist, however, to view freedom as an instrumental value; you can view it as the means to enjoy other rights, perhaps inalienable rights ("natural rights"), of which the pursuit of happiness is only one. The rationalists, of course, had the sort of concept of freedom that led them to view it as an intrinsic value, perhaps the highest ranking intrinsic value. The solution is to realize that the idea of freedom is very broad, that some freedoms may be intrinsic values, others instrumental values, some have a high ranking, others a lower ranking. Your decision about which are intrinsic, as well as which are ideal, will depend on your view of human nature and your value system.

VII

Freedom as *idea*, then, is a matter of conceptual analysis. But our analysis led us to such a broad idea of freedom that we see that the really interesting issues surrounding freedom have to do with which freedoms are *ideal.* What Luther and Kant defined as the only freedom, namely, the freedom from vice that enables us to use our other freedoms properly, rationally, or in a godly way, is a high ideal. But it is not the only one. When we ask "What is *true* freedom?" or "Who is the truly free person?" or "Which society is freer?" we begin the debate not so much over the idea of freedom as over which freedoms are ideals, and how they rank with one another. Liberals such as John Rawls, for example, should be interpreted as claiming that there is a set of freedoms that rank so high that they should never be traded off for other freedoms (*38*: 61-3). Now the issue of which freedoms ought to be most highly ranked is, as suggested earlier, largely the issue of what is required to be truly human, a normative issue that I believe is ultimately a basic religious question.

Notes

1. This essay, then is a modest attempt to do what Prof. Runner always did so well in my encounters with him: he uncovered basic value, ontological, and religious issues in what first seemed to be merely a difference in definitions.

2. "I am normally said to be free to the degree to which no man or body of men interferes with my activity" (*2*: 122).

3. Christian Bay says that a person's freedom includes ". . . the *incentive* to give expression to what is in him . . ." (*1*: 15). If so, it would seem that when my bribes and arguments influence you to change your mind, I am impinging on your freedom.

4. I realize that further argument is required to substantiate this point. For a discussion of the complexities of the notion of coercion, see Robert Nozick (*34*: 440ff). Even if one arrives at a coherent concept of coercion, a defender of negative freedom must show how it fits into a definition of freedom. To gloss over some of these difficulties, I have used the vague term "pressure" in the initial hypothesis.

5. Bay (*1*: 88) uses this phrase to define social freedom, though his idea of overall freedom is much broader.

6. One might think that in a value-pluralistic society such as the United States, there would be no pervasive sense of harmony with any cultural structure and therefore no danger of confusing freedom with acceptance of the cultural restraints. But social critics from Alexis De Tocqueville to Herbert Marcuse have warned otherwise. In 1835, in *Democracy in America* (New York: The New American Library, 1936, p. 117), De Tocqueville claimed that American democracy tended toward a conformity that exchanged the substance of freedom for its feeling: "The authority of a king is physical, and controls the actions of men without subduing their will. But the majority possesses a power which is physical and moral at the same time, which acts upon the will as much as upon the actions, and represses not only all contest, but all controversy . . . . I know of no country in which there is so little independence of mind and real freedom of discussion as in America." And Marcuse (*30*) insists that through advertising, propaganda, and the internalization of cultural "wisdom," Americans are still in a "voluntary servitude." Erich Fromm argues that it is more than a purely American malaise: ". . . modern man lives under the illusion that he knows what he wants, while he actually wants what he is *supposed* to want" (*11*: 252).

7. While The Underground Man, who diagnosed himself as "sick," rejoices in this arbitrariness, Jean-Paul Sartre finds this feeling of arbitrary freedom to be one of anguish: "It follows that my freedom is the unique foundation of values and that *nothing*, absolutely nothing, justifies me in adopting this or that particular value, this or that particular scale of values. As a being by whom values exist, I am unjustifiable. My freedom is anguished at being the foundation of values while itself without foundation . . . . Nothing can ensure me against myself, cut off from the world and from my essence by this nothingness which I *am*. I have to realize the meaning of the world and of my essence; I make my decision concerning them—without justification and without excuse" (*41*: 46-8). Since we distinguish between the concept of freedom and views of its value, it should not be surprising that the same concept elicits completely different emotions.

8. For example, Philip Slater (42) has suggested that human nature is and should be basically social, and that the overemphasis on individualism has pushed American culture to the breaking point.

9. Berlin, in a footnote, quotes Helvetius: "The free man is the man who is not in irons, nor imprisoned in a gaol, or terrorized like a slave by the fear of imprisonment . . . it is not lack of freedom not to fly like an eagle or swim like a whale." Berlin's position is consistent with the view that if geneticists were deliberately to produce individuals with various strengths and weaknesses (e.g. strong, unintelligent, contented factory workers), the latter's freedom would be impinged on. Though the deficiency might be thought to be "internal," it would be deliberately caused by another.

10. Markham's well-known poem seeks to impress on us our responsibility for unintentionally dehumanizing another: "Stolid and stunned, a brother to the ox . . . / Through this dread shape humanity betrayed . . . / Is this the handiwork you give to God, / This monstrous thing distorted and soul-quencht?"

11. *Freedom of the Will*, ed. Paul Ramsey (New Haven: Yale University Press, 1957), p. 163: "The plain and obvious meaning of the words 'freedom' and 'liberty,' in common speech, is power, opportunity, or advantage, that anyone has, to do as he pleases. Or, in other words, his being free from hindrance or impediment in the way of doing, or conducting in any respect, as he wills."

12. This point is accepted by Catholic philosophers who also think within a dualistic framework. See Jacques Maritain (*31*). Other thinkers see the achievement of spiritual freedom as a disciplined cooperation with God's grace. Perhaps no novelist has explored the issues of freedom more sensitively than Fyodor Dostoevsky. In *The Brothers Karamazov* (trans. Constance Garnett; New York: The New American Library, 1957), he seems to accept a dualistic view of human nature in which freedom is attained by conquering the lower nature, which he identifies with self-centeredness (pp. 35-6). He has Father Zossima explain the road to spiritual freedom, which involves self-imposed discipline as well as God's grace: "The world has proclaimed the reign of freedom, especially of late, but what do we see in this freedom? Nothing but slavery and self-destruction! For the world says: 'You have desires and so satisfy them, for you have the same rights as the most rich and powerful' . . . . Interpreting freedom as the multiplication and rapid satisfaction of desires, men distort their own nature . . . no wonder that instead of gaining freedom men have sunk into slavery . . . . The monastic way is very different. Obedience, fasting and prayer are laughed at, yet only through them lies the way to real, true freedom. I cut off my superfluous and unnecessary desires, I subdue my proud and wanton will and chastise it with obedience, and with God's help I attain freedom of spirit and with it spiritual joy" (pp. 289-90).

13. George Gordon, Lord Byron: "Sonnet on Chillon." See also Richard Lovelace: "To Althea, From Prison."

14. See also Spinoza (*43*: 276): "Whatever be the social state a man finds himself in, he may be free. For certainly a man is free, insofar as he is led by reason."

15. In fairness to Bosanquet, we should note that he limits state force with a doctrine of human rights (p. 189), though he has a disconcerting tendency to identify human rights with just those claims recognized by society and enforced by the State (p. 192).

16. The insight that human nature is fundamentally social, which is shared by many perceptive thinkers, does not, of course, imply that human nature is to be identified with a particular political institution.

17. In *A Theory of Justice*, John Rawls, who says he wishes to avoid the definitional debate about negative and positive freedom, sometimes seems to imply that freedom involves power (*38*: 202), but for practical purposes he seems to agree with Berlin: "The inability to take advantage of one's rights and opportunities as a result of poverty and ignorance, and a lack of means generally, is sometimes counted among the constraints definitive of liberty. I shall not, however, say this, but rather I shall think of these things as affecting the worth of liberty, the value to individuals of the rights that the first principle defines" (*38*: 204). Rawls also seems to imply that, in general, one ought not trade off liberty to acquire the other goods that would increase the worth of liberty (*38*: 61-3).

18. A similar point is convincingly argued by C. B. Macpherson (*28*: ch. V). In this thoughtful book, Macpherson points out at least three different senses of Berlin's "positive freedom" and shows that Berlin came close to defining power into "negative freedom" (p. 104).

19. Felix Oppenheim has correctly stated that the aim of democracy is not so much the *increase* in freedom as the more *equal distribution* of it. The total amount of freedom may be very high in a dictatorship; it is just that a few have most of it and most have little of it (*35*: 206).

20. See P. H. Partridge: "There is, then, this connection between freedom and power: When there is conflict between individuals and groups for possession or control of scarce means and conditions of action, control over means is a condition of the availability of alternatives, and hence of choice and freedom. It follows, therefore, that when men have unequal power, this will often mean that they will also be unequal with respect to the freedom they enjoy . . ." (*37*: 22).

21. For an excellent discussion of the concept of power and the distinction between individual power and collective power, see Alvin Goldman (*13*).

22. This fact, combined with the next, bodes ill for individualism, as many social commentators have been maintaining. See, for example, Garrett Hardin (*15*); Barry Commoner (*5*); and Robert Heilbroner (*18*). All three of these writers predict much more social control over individual action as a necessary condition for human survival. Individuals will sacrifice individual power and freedom not just to obtain greater (collective) power but also to retain past freedoms, such as the freedom to live and to do so in a minimally decent environment.

23. Already in 1935, the socialist Harold Laski admitted that individualism is reduced in this trade-off: "The individual who seeks self-realization finds himself confronted by a network of protective relationships which restrain him at every turn. Trade unions, professional and employers' associations, statutory controls of every kind, limit his power of choice by standardizing the manner of his effort. He has to adjust himself to an atmosphere in which there is hardly an aspect of his life not suffused at least partially with social regulation. To do anything he must be one with other men; for it is only by union with his fellows that he can hope to make an impact upon his environment" (*24*: 53).

24. That freedom is a triadic relation is the main point of Gerald MacCallum's article (*27*). One should admit that this interpretation of freedom is more of a formula than a definition. Indeed, the word *free* in the formula is not even defined. The formula makes explicit the possible dimensions of freedom rather than its essence.

25. Feinberg correctly notes that not every absence that constitutes lack of ability or opportunity should be thought of as a negative constraint. If my inability to fly like an eagle

means I am unfree, then the notion of unfreedom becomes so broad as to be uninteresting. We must have, he says, some "norm of expectancy of propriety" such that a significant deviation from it constitutes constraint. Obviously, spelling out this norm would involve us in the issue of what a "normal" human being is and should be.

26. See *The Brothers Karamazov*, in which the Grand Inquisitor asserts that Christ was mistaken in giving people freedom instead of the security of bread. We saw, however, that Father Zossima's freedom could be thought of as the security of obedience.

27. See Baron De Montesquieu (*33*: 151): "The political liberty of the subject is a tranquility of mind arising from the opinion each person has of his safety."

Bibliography

1. BAY, Chr., *The Structure of Freedom*; Stanford: University Press, 1958.

2. BERLIN, I., *Four Essays on Liberty*; Oxford: University Press, 1969.

3. BIDNEY, D. (ed.), *The Concept of Freedom in Anthropology*; The Hague: Mouton, 1963.

4. BOSANQUET, B., *The Philosophical Theory of the State*; London: Macmillan, 1951.

5. COMMONER, B., *The Closing Circle*; New York: Alfred Knopf, 1971.

6. CRANSTON, M., *Freedom*; New York: Basic Books, 1954.

7. DAHL, R., *After the Revolution?* New Haven: Yale University Press, 1970.

8. EPICTETUS, *Discourses*, trans. Th. Higginson; Roslyn: Walter J. Black, 1944.

9. FEINBERG, J., *Social Philosophy*; Englewood Cliffs: Prentice Hall, 1973.

10. FRIEDMAN, M., *Capitalism and Freedom*; Chicago: University Press, 1962.

11. FROMM, E., *Escape from Freedom*; New York: Holt, Rinehart and Winston, 1941.

12. GENTILE, G., "The Philosophic Basis of Fascism," in: *Foreign Affairs*, 6 (1928).

13. GOLDMAN, A., "Toward a Theory of Social Power," in: *Philosophical Studies*, 23 (1972), pp. 221-68.

14. GREEN, T. H., *The Political Theory of T. H. Green*, ed. J. R. Rodman; New York: Appleton-Century-Crofts, 1964.

15. HARDIN, G., "The Tragedy of the Commons," in: *Science*, December 13, 1968.

16. HAYEK, F. A., *The Constitution of Liberty*; Chicago: University Press, 1960.

17. HEGEL, G. F., *Philosophy of Right*, trans. T. M. Knox; Oxford: University Press, 1957.

18. HEILBRONER, R., *An Inquiry into the Human Prospect*; New York: Norton, 1974.

19. HOBBES, Th., *Leviathan*; Oxford: Clarendon Press, 1909.

20. HOLMES, O. W., "The Path of the Law," in: *Collected Legal Papers*; New York: Harcourt and Brace, 1921.

21. KANT, I., *Groundwork of the Metaphysic of Morals*, trans. H. J. Paton; New York: Harper and Row, 1964.

22. LASKI, H., *Liberty in the Modern State*; New York: Viking Press, 1959.

23 ——. *A Grammar of Politics*; New Haven: Yale University Press, 1930.

24 ——. "Liberty," in: *Freedom: Its History, Nature, and Varieties*, ed. Robert E. Dewey and James A. Gould; New York: Macmillan, 1970.

25. LOCKE, John, *The Second Treatise on Civil Government*, in: *John Locke on Politics and Education*; Roslyn: Walter J. Black, 1947.

26. LUTHER, M., "Christian Liberty," in: *Freedom: Its History, Nature, and Varieties*, ed. Robert E. Dewey and James A. Gould; New York: Macmillan, 1970.

27. MacCALLUM, G., "Negative and Positive Freedom," in: *The Philosophical Review*, LXXVI (1967), pp. 312-34.

28. MACPHERSON, C. B., *Democratic Theory: Essays in Retrieval*; Oxford: Clarendon Press, 1973.

29. MALINOWSKI, B., *Freedom and Civilization*; Bloomington: Indiana University Press, 1944, 1960.

30. MARCUSE, H., *An Essay on Liberation*; Boston: Beacon Press, 1969.

31. MARITAIN, J., "The Conquest of Freedom," in: *Freedom: Its Meaning*, ed. Ruth Nanda Ashen; New York: Harcourt Brace, 1940, pp. 631-44.

32. MILL, J. S., *On Liberty*; New York: Library of Liberal Arts, Bobbs-Merrill, 1956.

33. MONTESQUIEU DE, *The Spirit of Laws*, trans. Thomas Nugent; New York: Hafner, 1949.

34. NOZICK, R., "Coercion," in: *Philosophy, Science, and Method: Essays in Honor of Ernest Nagel*, ed. Morgenbesser *et al.*; New York: St. Martin's Press, 1969, pp. 440-72.

35. OPPENHEIM, F., *Dimensions of Freedom*; New York: St. Martin's Press, 1961.

36. PALMIERI, M., *The Philosophy of Fascism*, in: *Communism, Fascism, and Democracy*, ed. Carl Cohen; New York: Random House, 1962.

37. PARTRIDGE, P. H., "Freedom," in: *Encyclopedia of Philosophy*, III, ed. Paul Edwards; New York: Macmillan and Free Press, 1967.

38. RAWLS, J., *A Theory of Justice*; Cambridge: Harvard University Press, 1971.

39. ROUSSEAU, J. J., *The Social Contract*, trans. Charles Frankel; New York: Hafner, 1947.

40. SABINE, G. H., *A History of Political Theory*; New York: Holt, Rinehart and Winston, 1961.

41. SARTRE, J. P., *Being and Nothingness*; New York: Washington Square Press, 1966.

42. SLATER. Ph., *The Pursuit of Loneliness*; Boston: Beacon Press, 1970.

43. SPINOZA, B., *A Theologico-Political Treatise*, trans. R. H. M. Elwes; Ann Arbor: Edwards Brothers, 1942.

44. WEINSTEIN, W. L., "The Concept of Liberty in Nineteenth Century English Political Thought," in: *Political Studies*, 8 (1965).

Towards a Certitudinal Hermeneutic

JAMES H. OLTHUIS

The question of methodology—what method or methods commend themselves as legitimate ways of interpreting Scripture—is high on the theological agenda of our time. No one who seeks to deepen his understanding of the Scriptures can escape this question and the cluster of basic issues which surrounds it. There is simply no alternative. Interpretation is a human activity. And to do is to do in a certain *way*, to follow a certain method. Even when we are not explicitly aware of the method or are unable to articulate its rationale, a method is used, a way is walked, "glasses" are worn in interpretation.

The necessity to *interpret* the Scriptures has always been admitted. The Jewish rabbis developed their own ways. The Church Fathers and the scholars of medieval Catholicism were diligent in elucidating various senses of Scripture. In restoring the Scriptures to a position of centrality, the sixteenth century Reformers realized that they must give guidance in helping understand its true meaning.[1] Indeed, Calvin promises that his Institutes "will be a kind of key opening up to all the children of God a right and ready access to the understanding of the sacred volume."[2]

However, in the last 200 years following the age of Enlightenment, modern Evangelicals have increasingly shied away from hermeneutic concerns.[3] Since the historical-critical method (a legacy of Protestant liberalism), was often employed to undermine the special authoritative character of the Scriptures as the Word of God, since hermeneutics under the pull of Heidegger became for many an existentialistic understanding of the world and an all-or-nothing search for meaning—in general, since hermeneutics became too often a cloak for the denial of Scripture, Evangelicals have been on the defensive, apprehensive about admitting difficulties in Bible interpretation and timid about making the fullest possible use of historical, archaeological, literary, and linguistic data in their exegesis. In fact, confronted with the likes of Barth, Bultmann, Tillich, Fuchs, and Ebeling, many today come near to saying that the Bible really needs no interpreting; we need simply to read and re-read it. In actual fact, this tendency to simply quote rather than explain, coupled with a dogmatic zeal which discourages questions, covers over and sidesteps the real problems of exegesis. It is less than honest to proceed on the assumption that while others "interpret" (and by implication mishandle the Scriptures), we simply "read" (and by implication rightly understand the Word of life). It is only self-deception to believe that if one's approach to Scripture is pious and reverent enough, no problems remain. Avoidance of the critical questions for fear of arbitrariness in selecting a method or for fear of the liberal stigma solves nothing. It is only self-defeating, ironically giving credence to the baneful myth that intellectual respectability and the Christian faith are incompatible.

Proper use of the Scriptures

Fortunately, there are hopeful signs within the Evangelical church. In the present context, two matters stand out. There is a growing recognition that belief in the authority of the Scriptures as the Word of God does not involve a romanticizing or compromising of its creatureliness. The Bible is the Word of God. Here no tinkering or tampering is permitted. Yet the Bible is the inscripturated Word of God; it is the Word of God in the words of man. Even as it is totally God's Word, fully reliable and fully trustworthy, it is fully creaturely.

Secondly, there is a growing awareness that although a Biblical doctrine of Scripture can only develop in believing submission to the Scriptures as Canon, a simple affirmation of Scriptural authority guarantees neither a true doctrine of Scripture nor a true interpretation of Scripture.

Relating the two concerns: if we ignore the creatureliness of the Scriptures (and of its interpreters) and operate with a docetic view of the Scriptures (and of its interpreters), we remove the Scriptures from life and obscure the working out of their authority in our lives. Biblical authority, we are beginning to appreciate, is empty—mere lip service—unless we know how to understand what the Bible means. A high view of Scripture, Evangelical theology is discovering, does not exclude its adherents from full involvement in a critical study of the Bible, but rather commits them to it.[4]

In coming to this awareness, we are only recovering an insight which the prince of Reformation exegetes, John Calvin, had clearly seen. In his commentary on II Timothy 3:16, he explained that the Scriptures are the comprehensive equipment for the man of God, fitting him fully for all branches of work, only when they are properly used.[5] Here too—in the crucial matter of interpretation of Scripture—we are to work out our salvation with fear and trembling.

Proper use of the Scriptures is a tall order. It requires the full and proper functioning of human subjectivity rather than its suspension or bracketing. Letting the Scriptures speak for themselves does not mean attempting to put aside all methods, all pre-understandings, and simply allowing Scripture to impress itself upon our open and empty minds in *tabula rasa* fashion *à la* John Locke. Rather, it calls for a conscious and concerted exercise of our full abilities and talents to use the proper method and have the proper pre-understanding. For in the measure that the glasses we wear are not ground true to the Scriptures, in that measure the full thrust, range and scope of God's Word for life is obscured, limited and distorted.

Proper use of the Scriptures thus demands, to begin with, an awareness of the nature of the Scriptures as the Word of God. It is the specific structural contours of the Scriptures as a creaturely book, as the Word of God written, that will be the central concern of this essay.

Evangelicals are of one mind in confessing the authority of the Scriptures for all of life. The troublesome questions emerge when the principle of authority is put into practice: *How* is it authoritative? Nearly everyone agrees that the Bible is not a compendium of all possible knowledge. There is a significant consensus that the Scriptures are not a textbook for the various sciences. There is, however, less agreement not only as to *whether* the Scriptures are a manual for counselling, family, marriage, art, business, and school, but also as to *how* the Scriptures perform this handbook function.

I suggest that lack of sufficient precision in delineating the specific kind and nature of the Scriptural text has thwarted us in understanding how the Scriptures speak authoritatively to all of life. Only careful attention to the unique structural focus and makeup of the Scriptures will prevent us from mistaking and manhandling them in terms of fanciful theories and will increasingly enable us to interpret the Scriptures on their own terms. Only then is it possible to understand how the Scriptures speak normatively in all of life.

The problem

While acknowledging that "Scripture's absolute authority does not apply comprehensively to all spheres of life" and that "there are limits . . . to Scripture's authority," Geoffrey Bromiley, in one of the most forthright

Evangelical articles on this subject in recent years, concludes that the "range of biblical authority is no less comprehensive than absolute."[6] How he attempts to say both without contradiction is perhaps best intimated when he explains that "to this degree Scripture at its own level and in its own dimensions has a vital bearing even in things which are technically decided according to other authorities." But how? And it is just this question of "own level" and "own dimensions" which remains vague and murky. "The Scripture enjoys full and absolute authority in its own proper sphere, the sphere of the self-revelation of God." But, since this sphere is the "big one of God's relation to man," nothing can be excluded. The question returns with urgency: How? How does Scriptural authority work itself out in relation to the various life-zones?

Today a burgeoning group of scholars in the Evangelical church at large are attempting to cut the Gordian knot by declaring that the Scriptures possess full authority in what they intend to teach, and that what they intend to teach is salvation from sin and redemption to life in Jesus Christ. The Bible is a redemptive book, throwing light on all of life from its perspective of creation, fall, redemption, and the second coming. Now, all this is certainly true, but does it substantially advance the discussion? Granted that the Scriptures are redemptive in nature, content and intention, how does that help spell out and work out their authority for all the diverse areas of life? The important question returns unanswered: How? In what fashion, manner or way?

Some read the redemptive focus of the Scriptures as implying a direct relation to man's soul or heart and only an indirect and secondary relation to man's body and culture. At worst such talk leads to a complete divorce of the Scriptures and bodily, societal life; at best such a view still weakens the Biblical mandate to develop a lifestyle in accordance with the Gospel.

Other Christians, convinced that salvation is for all of life, treat the Scriptures as a divinely programmed computer. Their efforts border on frustration because the Scriptures contain few references to many modern problems. In any case, living by the Scriptures devolves into a haphazard you-pick-this-I-choose-that-affair.

In this essay I will present a proposal designed to set out the contours of a developing position in regard to Scripture which shows real promise of being a "third way," in order to invite collegial interchange, discussion, correction, and advance.

A special kind of book

The Scriptures come to us in inscripturated or written form. They are a book, and must be interpreted as such. To treat them as something other than a book, e.g. as a stone or a chair, is, of course, manifestly absurd. They are what they are—*biblia*.

But more must be said to do them justice. (And I am not at this point referring to their status as Word of God.) Indispensable to proper interpretation is awareness of the *kind* of book or text that the Scriptures are. Although this assertion, too, appears rather self-evident, its implications are often overlooked, ignored or mitigated; that is to say, although the lingual nature of the Scriptures is essential and foundational, the dominant, intentional or qualifying focus of the text is more than and other than lingual.

This is true, it would seem, of any text except dictionaries, and perhaps grammars. And only when the text is judged in terms of its structural intention, in terms of the type of questions it sets out to answer as a certain kind of text, can interpreters avoid violating the text. Thus, although the lingual is necessary for a text to be a text, it is not by itself sufficient. Of overriding significance in reading—even in finally judging linguistic considerations themselves—a telephone directory, a social registry, a love poem, a judicial verdict, a scientific argument, a diary, a sermon, a novel, Hansard, Emily Post, or whatever, is insight into their structural specificity.

A dictionary is only properly used in terms of the fact that it is a dictionary. To fault a phone directory for not being a social register is to violate its nature as phone book. If it was a social registry, it could not be a phone book. To judge *Popular Mechanics* according to the same criteria as *Time* is to fail to pay attention to their differing purposes. Each text must be allowed its own integrity. Failure to do this violates the text and leads to inappropriate questions.

Documents read differently when their interpreters have differing interests and criteria. Indeed, the vantage point, angle or special interest brought to a text shapes the questions to be asked of the text. When the structural governing or qualifying focus of a text is ignored, there is no overriding criterion (except one's own interests) to guide the interpretation. Asking questions without considering the governing focus of the text places the relevance as well as the legitimacy and appropriateness of the questions, no matter how legitimate in themselves, in doubt. Asking inappropriate questions does violence to the text by forcing the text in the interpreter's mold, rather than allowing the text to reveal itself in terms of its own specific way.

In literary criticism these things are taken quite seriously. They apply equally to the Scriptures.

A "sacred" book

Hermeneutically, it is only when we are straight as to the qualifying focus or macro-purpose of the Scriptures that we will be able to read the Word of God written as it intends to be read. The traditional description of the Bible as a "sacred," "spiritual," or "religious" book in part served that purpose. C. S. Lewis, for example, had a discerning eye for the special character of the Scriptures when he declared that "those who read the Bible as literature do not read the Bible."[7] It is, he continues, "not merely a sacred book, but a book so remorselessly and continuously sacred that it does not invite, it excludes or repels, the merely aesthetic approach." He obviously does not intend to deny that the Bible contains literature. But since "most of its component parts were written, and all of them were brought together, for a purely religious purpose," it can be read "as literature only as a *tour de force*. You are cutting the wood against the grain, using the tool for a purpose it was not intended to serve. It demands incessantly to be taken on its own terms."

In reminding us that for William Tyndale the "literal sense is itself the spiritual sense, coming from God and leading to Him," James Packer argues for the necessity of taking the "proper, natural sense of each passage (i.e., the intended sense of the writer) . . . as fundamental." Only in this fashion can we "respect the literary categories of the Scripture, and take seriously the historical character of what the Bible says."[8]

The Bible, to repeat Lewis' poignant phrase, "demands incessantly to be taken on its own terms." The question remains as to how best to describe those terms. It is at this juncture that talk of the "natural," literal sense of the Scriptures as being the spiritual or religious requires further structural specification. What does it mean that the "spiritual" is "natural" to the Scriptures?

That the Scriptures as the Word of God are the Word of the Spirit is true but unhelpful in this context, since we are seeking to determine the specific nature of the Scriptures as a creaturely book. In fact, since the terms *spiritual* and *religious* are often considered synonymous with pious, holy, numinous, mystical, supernatural, and the like, they are more misleading than helpful. Regarding the Scriptures as a religious book employing a peculiar religious language in contrast to or in some curious admixture with ordinary language generally involves consigning it to a special otherworldly realm of spirituality and grace in greater or lesser tension with creation and nature.[9]

However, it is precisely such partitioning into a sacred and a secular area of reality which must be overcome if we are to make headway in our hermeneutical efforts. The difficulties for interpretation caused by such a dualism are myriad and ultimately insurmountable. If we—at the beginning—conceive of the Scriptures as a "religious" or "spiritual" word to the heart supplementary to or even over against the ordinary, "natural," creational word to the body, it becomes problematic to integrally relate the two.[10]

The irony of such a dualism is as tragic as it is real. For after once reading this bifurcation into the Scriptures themselves, it is only possible in various makeshift ways to relate the two realms and interpret the Scriptures relevantly for life—choosing exemplary moral examples, winnowing out moral maxims or eternal truths, attempting by logical implication to determine God's will for us today, leaving by and large most of the Scriptures as incidental packing.

A book of certainty

It is at this point that I propose to talk of the Scriptures as a book of certainty,[11] as the Word of God in certitudinal focus. In other words, the Scriptures belong to that category or classification of books that have as their governing focus ultimates or end-questions.[12] The overriding, preeminent concern of this type of literature is the terminal matter of certainty. It can deal with any subject matter—and usually does—but its manner and mode of treatment evinces its overriding design to strengthen confession, to engender belief, and to promote hope. In contrast to scientific treatises, political tracts, cultural histories, marriage handbooks, and the like—all of which may or may not deal at points with matters of certainty in terms of their specific macro-purposes—"sacred" writings have the question of commitment, certainty, confession, and hope as their primary focus and macro-purpose. They speak to political life, but are not a political treatise. They speak to and about buying and selling, but are not a discourse on stewardship or thrift as such. They speak to the family, but they are not to be characterized as a handbook for family life. They speak to all the diverse affairs of life in their own unique structural way—the certitudinal.

It is no doubt possible to study the rule of the kings of Israel, as recorded in Scripture, from a political viewpoint. The economic policies and the psychic makeup of their planners can be scrutinized. The books can and should be studied in terms of their literary composition and linguistic peculiarities, not to speak of their *Sitz im Leben*. But, so my argument runs, all of these treatments, no matter how legitimate in themselves, would misfire, doing an injustice both to the topic under consideration and the Scriptures, if the certitudinal focus of the Scriptures were ignored.

Since neither the political, economic, psychic, or lingual are independent themes in Scripture, they can only rightly be treated when their certitudinal coloring is acknowledged. A certitudinal reading of the Scriptures is primary. Only after the overriding structural focus of the Scriptures is fully taken into account can we properly determine what the Scriptures tell us about the various other dimensions of life. Anything short of this basic procedure short-circuits and calls into question the validity of any exegesis. To approach the Scriptures as if their governing focus were economic, political, moral, or whatever is to overlook the avowed cardinal intention of the Scriptures to reveal God's Word to us in terms of the creaturely need for certainty.

Tone-deafness

Failure to see that the Scriptures as a book have this unique structural focus leads to a tone-deafness or arbitrariness in regard to the various issues at stake. Commentators can then, with impunity, pick this or that as the major concern (or besetting weakness) of the Scriptures.

If we fail to take seriously the structural, certitudinal focus of the Scriptures, we may be unhappy about the fact that certain critics approach the gospels as in the first place biographies of Jesus, or the books of Samuel and Kings as basically cultural history, and then fault the Scriptures on these terms, but we would have no real argument. Likewise, a myopic reading of the Scriptures as a scientific classification of flora and fauna or as a kind of *Poor Richard's Almanac* or a handbook for literature or a paradigm for logical argument of a political platform could not in principle be faulted.

We can protest that these and other ways do injustice to the text, that such use of Scripture is misleading and even perverse at times, tearing the fabric of Scripture, shredding it into remnants—only a few of which are salvageable—at the behest of particular biases, but unless our protest is based on the structural focus of the text itself, it is finally a matter of our word against their word. It comes down to a matter of subjective preference, and the critics have as much right to their opinion as we do to ours.

In summary, it is my thesis that attention to the certitudinal focus of the Scriptures allows us to take the Scriptures on their own terms and provides a criterion for disqualifying as illegitimate all readings which ignore its certitudinal focus. The certitudinal qualifies but does not limit the range and scope of the Scriptures; it channels rather than obstructs; it clarifies instead of mystifying the Scriptural address to all of life. Faced with human rebellion and sin, God chose to reveal His will anew in Jesus Christ and in special written form in the Scriptures. I am suggesting that the certitudinal is the specific creaturely avenue that God made use of in giving us the Scriptures. It remains to unpack in more detail the meaning and possible implications of this suggestion.

The universal need for certainty

This view of Scripture begins from the Scriptural teaching that there is an integral unity to life—"out of the heart are all the issues of life"—and simultaneously a rich pluriformity—God created each thing "after its own kind." The unity of the human calling and of creation rests on the unity of the Word of God. At the same time, creation and the human task in creation have many sides corresponding to the multidimensional character of the Word of God for life. "Fear God, and keep his commandments; for this is the whole . . . of man" (Eccl. 12:13).[13]

In experience we learn that the whole array of things, events and persons which together make up the creation all function in diverse ways and are experienced in these modes. We experience a thing alone, in pairs, in umpteens; as heavy, light, small, large; as fast, slow; as alive, dead; as sensitive, insensitive; as distinct, indistinct; as clear, obscure; as formed, unformed; as stolen, borrowed, owned; as cheap, expensive, and so on. In every one of the creational ways, man has a responsibility and concomitantly a need.

Mankind is faced with the claim to be truthful and live up to the promises he makes. Justice is to be meted out fairly. Stewardship of our resources and time is a pressing need. There is the call to express ourselves clearly and logically. We are called to exercise dignity in our social relations; we are to be sensitive and caring to one another. Physically and organically we need to take care of ourselves. Being human means responding to these various God-ordained claims.

However, there is at least one other dimension to human life, and it is this dimension which is crucial to our discussion. Man by definition is also a creature that seeks certainty. The human need for certainty, the universal search for ultimate meaning and final validation, the unavoidable nature of belief all testify to the reality of a depth-dimension to creation which we call the certitudinal.[14]

The necessity of believing in God or a pseudo-God is given with creation. Man must believe in something or someone, and it is in terms of this "certainty" that he lives his life. He cannot exist without clinging to "something" as the source and goal of his life. For the most part, modern men make gods out of themselves or the works of their hand, just as people in earlier times worshiped the forces of nature. In any case, the quest for the certainty that life is worth living is as inescapably human as thinking and feeling.

Belief is as natural as speech, confession as creaturely as digestion, commitment as human as contentment. The reality of the certitudinal is perhaps most tragically illustrated in the lives of those who believe there is no God. Paradoxically, they must answer the question of certainty even though their hearts are closed to the Giver of certainty. Man cannot but believe—even if it is in futility. Man cannot but commit himself—even if it is to meaninglessness. For it is the "god" confessed that gives unity to life. When there is a plethora of such gods, there is no real unity of self or of community. To be a self is to have a god; to have one god is to have a life of one piece; to have the one true God is to have a whole life of meaning and truth.

A certitudinal way of talking is not an extra-ordinary way, an additional, dispensable, committed way of looking at things for those who like it or are so disposed, for those who are religious fanatics. It is one of the ordinary ways of experiencing life which willy-nilly, consciously or unconsciously, everyone actualizes. It is not a super-natural *donum superadditum* or an irrational, mystic mode; it is the depth-level or grounding dimension of ordinary experience. This dimension, involving the ultimates of life, is experienced as the depth-dimension of creation, as the level of meaning which supervenes upon, interpenetrates, and is mediated through the various other levels of meaning which it presupposes and with which it coheres. It performs two key functions in human life, opening up (or closing down) life to that which is beyond the creaturely, and integrating (or dis-integrating) daily life in terms of that to which life is opened up.

The depth character of the certitudinal and its unique leading role in relation to all other dimensions is reflected in this state of affairs. What is confessed as surety in life is the dynamic which leads, grounds and guides one in all his activities. This dynamic functions either to open up life, leading to the Kingdom of God, or to close it down, leading to the kingdom of darkness. And it is man's confessional response worked out in views of life and systems of beliefs which leads and integrates all his other equally spiritual responses. This interrelation of responses is of utmost importance. All the other kinds of activities demonstrate the genuineness and sincerity of confession or show up its pretense and duplicity. For instance, whether or not acts of justice are realities in a person's life will indicate whether or not his commitment to justice is only dissimulation and lip service or veracious and *bona fide*.

The certitudinal is the most complicated level of life in that it explicitly and in the deepest possible way reveals or gets at the heart of existence. And since this certitudinal feature belongs to the structural makeup of every human activity, regardless of its specificity as, for instance, painting, judging, or thinking, every human act invites the doer to deepen its meaning (or admit its lack of roots) by answering the question of certainty: In whose strength, to whose honor, in the service of what priority do you do this?

Keeping troth, meting out justice, teaching, banking—in short, every human activity lacks surety, confidence and stability until the *credo* or certainty question has been answered. Full integrity and integration of personal life occurs only when the various sides of life are ordered, interrelated and deepened by one's belief. In this way the priorities of personal and communal existence are sorted out.

The whole man is spirit

The important leading and integrating role of belief must be stressed. At the same time, it is equally important for us not to lose sight of the fact that belief is only one way in which man reveals the direction of his life. There are other ways: out of the heart are *all* the issues of life. Man not only believes; as a person, that is, in his *heart*, he is a troth-keeper or troth-breaker, greedy or generous, informed or uninformed, healthy or unhealthy as a total person. The whole man is spirit, that is, responsible to walk before the Lord in obedience in all his comings and goings. Every act is whole-hearted; that is to say, every dimension of his existence is spiritual, involving his relation to God and his dependence upon God. All his creaturely ways of functioning, it is crucial to maintain, are not only expressive of, but make up and constitute his spirituality. To say anything less is an open invitation to dualism.

Consequently, no matter whether certain human acts have an economic focus, or whether others are qualified ethically, aesthetically or certitudinally (as, for example, prayer, worship, confession, taking Communion), all are Spirit of God directed or evil-spirited. The difference in structuration and pattern among the various kinds of acts reflects only the many different possible creaturely ways of revealing the allegiance of the human heart. Certitudinal(ly qualified) activities, by definition, that is, by the very structure of the certitudinal way of functioning, reveal heart allegiance in their own unique way: by confession of what is taken to be rock-bottom certainty. Thus, although the certitudinal dimension is not any more or less spiritual than all the other dimensions of life, it has its own uniqueness in that it explicitly invokes answers to the ultimate questions of life. Via the certitudinal, the ultimates in terms of which all of life is meaningful or meaningless are confessed, believed and paid homage.

The need to distinguish heart and certitudinal dimension

The recognition that confession of certainty is only one dimension of life implies, as we have already noticed, that belief is to be distinguished from the heart, the centeredness, the root-unity of man.

The failure on the part of philosophy and theology in general to make that distinction undermines, in my opinion, any effort, no matter how well-intended and gallant, to maintain that all of life is religion (service of God). If the distinction between heart (as the root-unity of man's total functioning) and belief (as one way of functioning) is not made, the belief dimension is wrongly identified with or considered exhaustive of man's spirituality. To act as if the belief-dimension is the heart and that it defines the spirituality of man involves opting for a fatal dualism of natural and supernatural which de-spiritualizes all the other so-called "natural" sides of man, splits creation in two, and destroys the unity of personhood. Or else one adopts a precarious monism which spiritualizes and mystifies all of existence and violates the creational integrity and relative independence of the non-certitudinal dimensions of life and is saddled with all the attendant contrasting tensions between higher and lower that are necessary to account for diversity.[15]

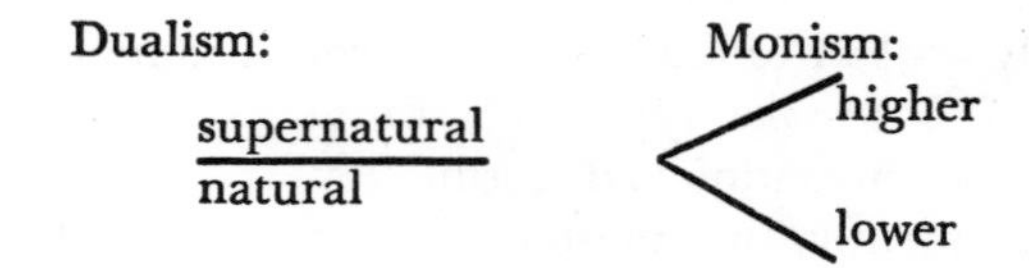

Either way—whether the heart or soul identified with the certitudinal dimension is dualistically elevated above the rest of creational life, or whether the certitudinal dimension blown up to be the heart, usually fixated on some other dimension,[16] is monistically considered the origin and root of all the other creational dimensions—the problems multiply and, I believe, are insurmountable.

The matter is extremely complex and requires much detailed investigation. If the heart is considered to be the higher or "spiritual" dimension in relation to all the other natural sides of life, faith becomes essentially a *donum supperadditum* which will always bear an extrinsic, external relation to the structures of human life. Redemption, all intentions notwithstanding, tends to become "other-worldly." On the other hand, if the certitudinal loses its structural specificity and is absorbed in some other dimension, faith can be no more than the built-in inexorable surge which is the nature of reality, and the call to belief and self-surrender is suspended. Rather than a radical change in direction from disobedience to obedience requiring God's sovereign grace, the call from sin to life is then essentially the exhortation to increased self-actualization of powers already inherent in the uni-directional cosmos.

Put more simply, in both cases it is imposible to do justice to both the universal, creaturely need to believe and the antithesis between Christian and non-Christian faith. Emphasizing one feature inevitably leads to minimizing or distorting the other. Monistically oriented Christians, despite the best of intentions, develop positions which, stressing man's responsibility, tend to obscure the grace of God; dualistically oriented Christians emphasize the Christian faith but are unable to give proper attention to its structural connections to the universal need to believe.[17]

It is thus completely understandable that most Evangelical Christians, concerned to maintain the absoluteness of Christianity, have a preference for dualistic positions and generally regard with suspicion studies in what is today known as the phenomenology of religion. Nor is it surprising that thinkers who have pioneered in that field have been "liberals" in regard to the Christian faith, with an affinity to monistic conceptions.[18]

At the same time, the deep gulf between the spiritual and the natural inherent in dualistic positions helps explain not only why conservatives play down the concerns of society but also why, even if the desire is present, they are unable to develop an intrinsically Christian approach to life. Correspondingly, the fact that social gospel or culturally optimistic positions native to monistic conceptions have little which marks them as distinctively Christian fits the pattern once again.

Distinguishing the centeredness of man in his heart from the belief-dimension of this centeredness allows one to consider all of life as spiritual ("from the heart") without absolutizing belief. At the same time, it is possible to take non-Christian religion seriously without denying its basic directional difference with Christian faith.

It was necessary to investigate at some length the nature of the certitudinal dimension (and its relation to and distinction from the heart) because I believe it to be the key enabling us, methodologically and in principle, to understand how the Scriptures speak relevantly and authoritatively to all of modern life. It remains, of course, to test the thesis continually in book-by-book, chapter-by-chapter exegesis and, in turn, to refine the thesis in its particulars.

The Scriptures in certitudinal focus

In the remainder of this paper, a number of hermeneutic implications of understanding the Scriptures to be the Word of God in certitudinal focus will be suggested and briefly explored. The Scriptures, I am saying, concentrate on revealing to us God in Jesus Christ through the Spirit as the Creator and Redeemer of life and, in terms of that certainty, a vision of what creation is, who we are, and how we can live lives of obedience as men and women of God. The Scriptures urge us to surrender our lives to the Lord and place before us the Direction of obedience. They unfold for mankind the vision of Christ's Kingdom and the necessity of confessing His name to live in that Kingdom. The Scriptures lay down the main lines of a confessional insight which is to guide our day-to-day activities. They tell us who we are (God's servants), where we are (in a creation in the grip of His Word), where we are going (in Christ to the final perfection of the already-dawning Kingdom), and what our task is (obedient gardeners, agents of the reconciliation). The Scriptures, as a book focusing on all of life in terms of ultimates, lay out for mankind the depth-meaning, the ground-lines, the overarching perspective of the Word of God.

Certitudinal discourse

In proclaiming their message, the Scriptures employ language which, by its very nature, is suited to the task—certitudinal discourse. The word *discourse* is used advisedly because it emphasizes the larger literary unit which bears the meaning. Individual words, even sentences or entire units, can be taken up in various contexts in different ways. As a whole and in each of its component parts, Scriptural discourse is certitudinal(ly qualified) discourse.

The structural specifics of certitudinal discourse remain to be traced out in detail.[19] A number of features, however, stand out. First and foremost, certitudinal discourse is not an admixture of mythical elements and ordinary language. It is "ordinary" language with a specific focus.[20] The certitudinal as the depth-level dimension calls for depth-level discourse. Such discourse has a cumulative, telescopic, perspectival, no if's or but's quality. It captures the whole of a situation in terms of its depth-meaning, even though that situation can legitimately be described in all kinds of other ways.

Typically it employs words and sentences that have their primary meaning on another level and opens them up and stretches their meaning to its creaturely limits. For example, father-son and husband-wife ethical discourse is often used to describe the covenant relation between God and man. Again, God is portrayed as a refuge, a rock or shepherd, and heaven in its opened-up certitudinal meaning is shalom, while the sea is turbulence.[21]

The Bible, it is generally agreed today, has a "distinct" approach. There is far less agreement as to what this distinctness in fact is. A large segment of the Biblical Theology movement very early identified this peculiar perspective as the Hebrew mentality and contrasted this more or less explicitly with the Greek thought patterns. Seminarians were counseled to "think Hebraic" and to abandon Athens for Jerusalem. James Barr has criticized, with good reason, the idea that the Hebrew language is special and inherently suited for expressing Biblical concepts.

This debate, exemplified in the interchange between Barr and Thorlief Boman,[22] falls into place through introduction of the certitudinal feature. The Biblical Theology movement had hold of the certitudinal flavor and character of Biblical discourse. However, instead of understanding that certitudinal discourse is possible and occurs no matter what language is spoken, they read the certitudinal into the semantic structure of Hebrew itself. Although opponents of the Biblical Theology movement were right in insisting that normal Hebrew and Greek were used in the Scriptures, they have tended to overlook the fact that *Scriptural* Hebrew and Greek discourse has certitudinal focus.

Hierarchical complementarity

The fact that meaning is contextual implies that it is first necessary to check the standpoint or focus from which the statement is made before judging a statement's validity or supposed contradiction with other statements. D. M. MacKay has astutely pointed out that although a mathematician and an engineer give different accounts of the behavior of a computer, one talking about the order of equations, the other about currents in transistors, both accounts are equally valid when considered from their own viewpoint. At the same time he has shown that the levels of description in such a case form a hierarchy: if anything mathematically significant is going on, the electronic transactions must be describable; if anything electronic is going on, thermodynamic transactions must be describable. In neither case is the converse true. Each standpoint has its own exclusiveness: "To opt for a mathematical scheme of explanation is to undertake to play that particular game through to the end without introducing electronic categories into that game, and conversely."[23]

Following this model, which has striking similarities to my own, MacKay suggests that scientific and theistic statements are "hierarchically complementary." "Nothing," he says, "could be more naturally explicable than the food supply of birds," yet Matthew 6:26 reads: "Consider the fowl of the air . . . your heavenly father feedeth them." MacKay believes that what is meant by such claims is "that when we have finished giving our natural account of these processes, there remains a complementary and equally necessary story to be told, in terms of their significance for the standpoint of their creator, in whose creative activity alone they had their being." Not only must the language of certitude be treated as the language of certitude and not as the language of science, of art or of history, such language can only be adequate or inadequate in terms of its own specific structure or "logic."

By that criterion it becomes obvious that much criticism of the Scriptures is illegitimate and beside the point because it mistakes the nature of the Scriptural account.

"God gave us a daughter"

The Scriptures speak "God gave us a daughter" language. Having a child is a troth affair involving intercourse between husband and wife. Such an event can be looked at from consideration of the biotic-physical, psychic and economic aspects involved. But the Scriptures, in the midst of their talk about all these matters, know only the confessional focus. "God gave us a daughter" expresses confessionally the meaning of having a child. It does not deny any of the other aspects involved; they are subsumed in the depth-level certitudinal focus. Thus it is perfectly natural that Luke records Elisabeth's reaction to her pregnancy: "The Lord has done this for me" (Luke 1:25).

There is nothing obscurantist about this, as if the Bible presents a baby-in-the-cabbage or stork-in-the-sky theory of birth in order to avoid the physical and sexual. Nor is Elisabeth adding some religious meaning to a physical fact. It is perfectly true, factual and real. She is saying that since the Lord's Word holds for this area of life too, obedience to His Word brings blessing. In the final analysis, He has done it. And just as in the case of birth announcements, the Scripture presents all kinds of other details, but they are only properly understood in certitudinal focus. Again, Boaz pleads that the Lord recompense Ruth—and then Boaz goes ahead and redeems her (Ruth 2:12). Thus, time and again the Scriptures reveal that obedient human activities are God's activities. "Except the Lord builds the house, they labor in vain that build it" (Ps. 127). To modern ears that appears downright ridiculous, and even believers tend to shrug their shoulders and put off such statements as simply evidence of ancient mythology or at best metaphor.

Unbelievers do, of course, build houses that stand. In fact, unbelievers have generally shown themselves superior in cultural pursuits. "No matter," says the psalmist, and with him the Christian: "Unless the house is built by those who confess that their strength is in the Lord, it is finally without meaning and worth." This does not mean that it will not physically stand—it well might—but work not done in the name of the

Lord or dedicated to His glory is not what it ought to be and is thus, in the final analysis, judged to be without weight (glory).

The writers of Scripture, with certitudinal intention, selected various incidents, sayings, and facts and strung them together by their confessional threads. For example, the migration of Naomi and Abimelech to Moab is not simply dealt with as an economic-political matter, although it certainly was that.[24] Rather, the confessional meaning of this migration (turning their backs on the inheritance of the Lord and turning to those detestable people of Moab) is at issue. The meeting of Orpah and Ruth with Naomi is not recounted to praise Ruth's fidelity to her mother-in-law and to rebuke Orpah's infidelity but to point out that Ruth's choice for Naomi was a choice for the God of Naomi. The conquest of Jericho is not described simply as a military campaign—which it was. Its *certitudinal* meaning is accentuated. Jericho will be and shall remain a sign, a confessional sign for all to see, a sign that Israel finds its strength in the Lord and not in its (military) might. The four gospels, as is now being generally recognized, order their materials and employ detail in different ways in accordance with a variety of certitudinal themes—even Mark, which was long considered to be merely a "factual," "historical" account.[25]

Certitudinal history

Talk of the certitudinal opens the way to a constructive hypothesis in regard to the nettlesome question of Scripture and history.[26] History in the Scriptures is certitudinal(ly qualified) history. It is no more or less historical than economic, political, or general cultural histories. But just as these kinds of histories have their own distinct focus, as do histories of music and art, sport and recreation, certitudinal history is written with a distinctive focus. In fact, certitudinal history reports what happened in its depth-meaning; it is depth-level historiography, recounting not only in physical, psychic, economic, or whatever terms but in terms of the root meanings and ultimate questions of life.

Luke sets out to write a history of "all that Jesus began both to do and to teach," not to simply give a biography of Christ or a travelogue, so that Theophilus "might know the certainty of the things he has been taught." The writer of Kings, much to the chagrin of modern critics, says very little about Solomon's extensive building program; rather, because of the special meaning of the temple for Israel, he chooses to deal with the building of just the temple—in profuse detail. Omri, who by all cultural accounts was a far more significant king than his son Ahab, is given but a few verses. Ahab, by contrast, is described in a flourish of detail because in his reign the people of Israel hit a new low in disobedience to Yahweh.

Certitudinal-grammatical-historical exegesis

The crucial role that the certitudinal dynamics occupy in regard to Scriptural exegesis leads me to question whether either the historico-critical method of the higher critics or the traditional grammatical-historical method of the lower critics is adequate. Neither method, I would judge, has sufficiently in purview the distinctive structural focus which gives contours to Biblical revelation. Evangelicals have sensed this shortcoming and thus end up talking of theological-grammatical-historical exegesis. But as is all too common in regard to the term *theological*, its meaning is far from clear.[27] Here, too, I suspect that at least two kinds of matter are intended. Often it seems to mean True, Canonic, Biblically-attuned interpretation; at other times it seems to point to a special *kind* of exegesis as distinct from legal or political, a type of exegesis which deals with God, with the sacraments, with matters of certainty.

I am suggesting that we would do well to talk of a *certitudinal*-grammatical-historical exegesis which, as the case may be, can be Biblical or unbiblical in nature. The development of such a confessional or certitudinal hermeneutic would, among other things, cause us not only to take more seriously the fact that the Scriptural focus is neither primarily grammatical nor historical in nature but would enable us to argue more cogently that an ideologically pure, neutral historical method is an impossibility.

Authoritative for all of life

Scripture deals with all of life, but its creaturely focus is the certitudinally opened-up or deepened meaning of events, acts, etc. Scripture tells us nothing outside of this focus. Scripture tells us, for example, about the duty of children to parents—in fact, we can learn much about such matters from the Scriptures.[28] But that is not the full focus. Obedience to parents is talked of in a confessionally deepened way so that it becomes clear that such duties are only finally and fully to be judged meaningful or meaningless in the light of heart obedience or disobedience to Christ. In its basic thrust, that is what certitudinal focus is all about. The Scriptures never tire of reminding us that whatever we do, we must do it in the name of the Lord. In terms of the depth focus of the Scriptures, love of husbands and wives is only obedience when experienced in the Lord. Or negatively—and the Pharisees stand before us as glaring reminders—not doing certain things because the law prohibits them is of no avail unless done in surrender and commitment to the Giver of the Law.

The *focus* is not primarily on the ethical, economic or some other type of response but first of all on the certitudinal. Only when the confessional response meets God's mark do the other responses qualify as the fruits of faith.

But this is not to say that the *emphasis* is always on the certitudinal. For the confessional response, if obedient, leads of itself to works of justice and mercy. In this way the Scriptures emphasize all of life, taking advantage of the uniqueness of the certitudinal dimension. Along these lines both a social activist reading (which plays down the central role of belief) and a myopic spiritualist reading (which emphasizes belief to the detriment of the rest of life) can be overcome and avoided.

Although neither a handbook for morals, construction, farming, or business nor a textbook for the various sciences, the Scriptures are immediately relevant to all these concerns. The Scriptures re-proclaim the entire Word of God. Via their certainty focus, they have total and full authority with a range as wide as creation. Belief fostered and nourished by the Scriptures will integrate human life in obedience to God's good order for life.

Only in the certainty found in Christ and revealed in Scripture can mankind move surely and freely in God's creation. In the knowledge that God's Word holds for all of life, men and women are empowered in the Spirit to further search out His will for life in all its dimensions and in all situations. The experience of *shalom* will spread and deepen as humanity grows in awareness of and obedience to His many-sided demands for life.

"Creation is maintained by your rulings; all things are your servants" (Ps. 119:91). Indeed, the Scriptures are inspired of God and are profitable for use in teaching, refuting error, for guiding people's lives, and teaching them to be bold (II Tim. 3:16).

Notes

1. For the history of hermeneutics, cf. F. W. Farrar, *History of Interpretation* (Grand Rapids: Eerdmans, 1961); James Barr, *Old and New in Interpretation* (New York: Harper and Row, 1966); E. C. Blackman, *Biblical Interpretation* (Philadelphia: Westminster Press, 1957).

2. John Calvin, *Institutes of the Christian Religion* (Grand Rapids: Eerdmans, 1953), I, p. 23, "Preface to French Edition," 1545.

3. For modern hermeneutics, cf. James M. Robinson and John B. Cobb, Jr. (eds.) *The New Hermeneutic* (New York: Harper and Row, 1964); Carl Braaten, *History and Hermeneutics* (Philadelphia: Westminster Press, 1966); Richard E. Palmer, *Hermeneutics* (Evanston: Northwestern University Press, 1969); Gerhard Ebeling, *Word and Faith* (Philadelphia: Fortress Press, 1963); Hans-Georg Gadamer, *Truth and Method* (New York: Seabury Press, 1975): Wolfhart Pannenberg, "Hermeneutic and Universal History," in: *Basic Questions in Theology* (Philadelphia: Fortress Press, 1970), I, pp. 96-137; S. U. Zuidema, "Hermeneutics in Contemporary Theology," in: *Communication and Confrontation* (Toron-

to: Wedge, 1972), pp. 347-77. David H. Kelsey, *The Uses of Scripture in Recent Theology* (Philadelphia: Fortress Press, 1975), is must reading.

4. For example, M. G. Kline, *The Structure of Biblical Authority* (Grand Rapids: Eerdmans, 1972); James Packer, "Hermeneutics and Biblical Authority," in *Churchman*, 81, 1967, pp. 7-21.

5. John Calvin, *Commentaries on the Epistles to Timothy, Titus and Philemon* (Grand Rapids: Eerdmans, 1948), pp. 249-50.

6. Geoffrey W. Bromiley, "The Inspiration and Authority of Scripture," in: *Eternity*, August 1970, pp. 12-20. Quotations from page 20. Reprint from *Holman Family Reference Bible* (Philadelphia: Lippincott Co., 1970).

7. C. S. Lewis, *The Literary Impact of the Authorized Version* (Philadelphia: Fortress Press, 1963), pp. 32-3.

8. James Packer, *"Fundamentalism" and the Word of God* (Grand Rapids: Eerdmans, 1956), pp. 102-5.

9. Ninian Smart, in *The Phenomenon of Religion* (Toronto: Macmillan, 1973), p. 112, calls the "line between sacred and secular" the "hidden sentiment behind quite a lot of contemporary discussions in the philosophy of religion."

10. Cf. "Must the Church become Secular?" in: *Out of Concern for the Church* (Toronto, Wedge, 1970), pp. 107-25. There I discussed various types of two-realm theories in Christianity. Cf. also H. Richard Niebuhr's *Christ and Culture* (New York: Harper and Row, 1956).

11. For Christians, of course, *the* book of certainty.

12. In the near future I intend to pursue in detail the similarities and differences between my talk of certitudinal discourse and current discussion of "end statements" in lingual analyst circles. Cf. Donald Evans, *The Logic of Self-Involvement* (London: SCM Press, 1963); John Hick (ed.), *Faith and the Philosophers* (New York: St. Martin's Press, 1964); and *Talk of God: Royal Institute of Philosophy Lectures*, Volume II, 1967-68 (Toronto: Macmillan, 1969). Theologically, David Tracy employs the notion of "limit language" to illuminate the grounding dimension of experience. Cf. his *Blessed Rage for Order* (New York: Seabury Press, 1975).

13. The last phrase of this verse is most often translated "the whole duty of man." However, the word *duty* is not in the Hebrew text. I have deleted it because it obscures the Biblical teaching that obedience to God's commands is not simply a duty which man has but the mark and definition of his very existence as man.

14. Cf. Herman Dooyeweerd, *A New Critique of Theoretical Thought* (Philadelphia: Presbyterian and Reformed, 1969), II, pp. 291-330, for a discussion of what he calls the "pistical" aspect, and Harry Fernhout's "Man, Faith and Religion" (unpublished master's thesis, Institute for Christian Studies, Toronto, 1975), for a sympathetic critique of his views. Since faith designates the obedient direction of man in his heart and in all his actions, it seems unnecessarily confusing to also talk of faith as only one aspect, the "pistical." I prefer to talk of the "certitudinal" or "confessional" dimension of reality. Related to this and instructive are Mircea Eliade's intensive and extensive investigations of the universality of religion. One could well begin with his *The Sacred and the Profane* (New York: Harcourt Brace Jovanovich, 1968).

15. Cf. Calvin Seerveld's "Biblical Wisdom underneath Vollenhoven's Categories for Philosophical Historiography" in: *The Idea of a Christian Philosophy*, ed. H. Dooyeweerd (Toronto, Wedge, 1973), pp. 136-7.

16. The structural dynamics of absolutization are explainable in terms of man's need for certainty. Not every non-Christian, however, develops a certitudinal*ism*. Generally speaking, the certitudinal fixates on some other creaturely dimension and absolutizes it.

17. For a discussion of this struggle in the work of Kuyper, Bavinck and Dooyeweerd, see Fernhout's thesis. Cf. note 14.

18. One need only mention the names of Mircea Eliade, Paul Tillich, Raymond Panikkar, and Ninian Smart. For a good introduction to this area of study, cf. Joseph Bettis (ed.), *Phenomenology of Religion: Eight Modern Descriptions of the Essence of Religion* (New York: Harper and Row, 1969). Cf. also G. van der Leeuw, *Religion in Essence and Manifestation* (New York: Harper and Row, 1963); E. Evans Pritchard, *Theories of Primitive Religions* (Oxford: Clarendon Press, 1965); Joachim Wach, *Types of Religious Experience, Christian and Non-Christian* (Chicago: University of Chicago Press, 1951).

19. Cf. Donald Sinnema, "The Uniqueness of Certitudinal Discourse, with Special Reference to the Language of Scripture" (stenciled paper, Institute for Christian Studies, Toronto, 1975). For general discussion of "religious" language, see Ian T. Ramsey, *Religious Language* (Toronto: Macmillan, 1957); Frederick Ferré, *Language, Logic and God* (New York: Harper and Row, 1961); J. Hutchinson, *Language and Faith* (Philadelphia: Westminster, 1963).

20. Cf. Smart, *op. cit.*, p. 113.

21. Cf. Donald Sinnema, "The Biblical World Picture: Heaven, Earth and Sea" (unpublished paper, Institute for Christian Studies, Toronto, 1972).

22. James Barr, *The Semantics of Biblical Language* (New York; Oxford University Press, 1961); and T. Boman, *Hebrew Thought Compared with Greek* (New York: Norton, 1960).

23. D. M. MacKay, " 'Complementarity' in Scientific and Theological Thinking," in: *Zygon*, IX, September 1974, pp. 225-44, quotations from pages 231 and 236. Cf. also his *Clockwork Image* (London: InterVarsity Press, 1974). Unfortunately, MacKay's account still suggests that "theistic" statements are from the "standpoint" of God, rather than completely natural, *depth-level* statements.

24. Harry VanderVelde, "A Study of the Book of Ruth" (stenciled paper, Institute for Christian Studies, Toronto, 1972).

25. For example, W. H. Lane, *The Gospel According to Mark* (Grand Rapids: Eerdmans, 1974).

26. For the current discussion of history in Old Testament studies, see John Bright, *Early Israel in Recent History Writing* (London: SCM Press, 1956), and for opposite views in the Alt-Noth tradition, M. Weippert, *The Settlement of the Israelite Tribes in Palestine* (London: SCM Press, 1971).

27. Cf. Gordon J. Spykman, "A Confessional Hermeneutic," in: *RES Theological Bulletin*, I, December 1973, pp. 1-14.

28. For a treatment of Scriptural references to marriage and family, see my *I Pledge You My Troth* (New York: Harper and Row, 1975).

Thoreau and the King James Bible

HUGH COOK

"I desire to speak somewhere *without* bounds . . . for I am convinced that I cannot exaggerate enough even to lay the foundation of a true expression," says Thoreau near the conclusion of *Walden*.[1] This partly flippant, yet serious statement has relevance also in a discussion of Thoreau's use of the King James Bible. In *A Week on the Concord and Merrimack Rivers,* Thoreau states that he is fond of reading "the Scriptures of the several nations," although he claims that he is less familiar with the Hebrew Scriptures than with those of the "Hindoos," the Chinese, and the Persians, for he has come to the Scriptures of the Hebrews last.[2] The reader who is familiar with the life of Thoreau, however, recognizes this as an exaggerated, tongue-in-cheek statement, for Thoreau had been taught the Bible since early in his life.

Although critics are aware of Thoreau's obvious acquaintance with the King James Bible and the numerous allusions he makes to it in his prose, very little exact study of this facet of Thoreau's writings has been made; the resulting statements are often valid but too general.[3] A more precise study of Thoreau's prose style is necessary.

In his incisive introduction to *Walden,* Charles R. Anderson asserts that the book has often been interpreted as nothing more than either natural history or social criticism, and that neither approach succeeds in discovering the meaning of *Walden* as a *work of art. Walden* is the work of a *poet,* Anderson claims; it is a *literary* work.

If Anderson's structural analysis is correct, which seems to me the case, his insight provides the proper approach to *Walden,* for rather than separating content from form, it permits us to see that the book's Transcendental framework or worldview is expressed through a number of literary devices, such as comic exaggeration, parody, word play, aphorism, satirical anecdote, metaphor, and symbol. Correspondingly, this article attempts to demonstrate that a crucial component in the array of literary devices used by Thoreau to give aesthetic form to his Transcendentalism is his stylistic use of the King James Bible.

This means that an understanding of Thoreau's use of the King James Bible is central to an understanding of *Walden*. Not only is the Bible a rich source for devices such as ironic exaggeration, comic wit, and parody (important elements of Thoreau's prose style), but the Bible also proves to be the origin for a rich pattern of metaphor that lies at the heart of the book's symbolism.

Thoreau uses Biblical allusion to suggest the religious purity of the soul that has stripped itself of society's encumbrances, as well as the redemptive character of that soul's harmony with nature—two key Transcendental tenets. For that reason Thoreau's use of the Bible lies at the heart of the book's meaning.

That Thoreau repeatedly quotes the Bible not to lend divine authority to his ideas but for literary, stylistic reasons bound up with his presentation of a Transcendentalist worldview becomes more clear when one understands his attitude toward the Bible. Therefore, before examining *Walden*, we would do well to trace briefly the development of that attitude.

Thoreau's personal library contained six Bibles and one Greek New Testament, most of which were gifts early in his life from his maiden aunts.[4] Thoreau's earliest training in the Bible was received at the Concord public grammar school, where he undertook rote learning of the Bible, Shakespeare, Bunyan, and Johnson. During his stay at Harvard, his study of the Bible consisted of two terms of theology (a study of Paley, Butler, and the New Testament) with Professor Henry Ware.[5]

Thoreau's first references to the Bible during his Harvard years suggest youthful acceptance. This is illustrated by a passage in one of his college essays written in 1835, entitled "Simplicity of Style": "The most sublime and noblest precepts may be conveyed in a plain and simple strain. The Scriptures afford abundant proof of this. What images can be more natural, what sentiments of greater weight and at the same time more noble and exalted than those with which they abound?"[6] Early in his academic career, then, Thoreau was attracted by both the imagery and the content of the Bible.

The literary appeal of the imagery was to stay; appreciation for the content, however, soon waned. In an essay of 1836 on the effect of storytelling, Thoreau writes: "The same passion for the novel (somewhat modified, to be sure), that is manifested in our early days, leads us, in after-life, when the sprightliness and credulity of youth have given way to the reserve and skepticism of manhood, to the more serious, though scarcely less wonderful annals of the world,"[7] and exactly that process seems to have happened to Thoreau in his appreciation for the Bible. Academic skepticism sets in, and by 1837 evidences of Thoreau's early heterodoxy and nonconformity begin to appear: "With by far the greater part of mankind religion is a habit; or rather, habit is religion. However paradoxical it may seem, it appears to me that to reject *religion* is the first step towards moral excellence."[8]

Upon his graduation from Harvard in 1837, Thoreau's rejection of the Bible and the Christian faith seems already to have been formed, yet he was not able to erase totally his fascination for the Bible. Happily returning to his hometown, Thoreau enters the following parody of Psalm 137 in his class book: "If I forget thee, O Concord, let my right hand forget her cunning."[9] *Walden* is later to be full of the same wit.

Thoreau was one of those who rebel against early indoctrination. He states in *A Week*: "The New Testament is an invaluable book, though I confess to having been slightly prejudiced against it in my very early days by the church and the Sabbath school, so that it seemed, before I read it, to be the yellowest book in the catalogue" (p. 89). The *Journal* also gives evidence of this early rebellion, for Thoreau's aunts, the same ones who gave the young man Bibles early in life, were somewhat critical of him for not reading any theological literature while having plenty of time to observe frogs (V, p. 58). Thoreau remained critical of the church and of organized religion throughout his life.

This critical attitude is manifested in Thoreau's attitude toward the Scriptures, for rarely does he speak favorably of the Bible without including in the same sentence the sacred writings of the Hindus, the Chinese, and the Persians. All are to be considered "the Scriptures of men," or "the Scriptures of mankind." As Thoreau says in *Walden*: "Most men do not know that any nation but the Hebrews have had a scripture" (p. 174). The historicity of the Bible Thoreau also calls into question: he calls the Adam and Eve account a "fable."

Moreover, Thoreau asserts that the Old Testament is deficient, for it speaks only of Hebrew culture and climes, and not of New England. The New Testament, Thoreau feels, is too recent a book to receive the approval of being called a Scripture. As a matter of fact, there is evidence in Thoreau's writings that he did not consider the Old and New Testaments integral parts of one Bible, for he often uses the word *Scripture* to refer to the Old Testament, and the word *Bible* to the New Testament; rarely does Thoreau refer to the Old and New Testaments together.

Thoreau's rejection of the Bible's authority is based largely on his belief that it is not rooted enough in the real world, by which he means the physical realm, and that it deals too much with man's spiritual life at the expense of the physical. Thoreau's reading of the Bible, and therefore also his terminology, presupposes a dualistic world-and-life view. In *A Week* he says: "Yet the New Testament treats man and man's so-called spiritual affairs too exclusively, and is too constantly moral and personal" (p. 92). For that reason, in the same work, Thoreau calls the Bible "a sort of a castle in the air" (p. 90). As a matter of fact, this same propensity for other-worldliness Thoreau sees also in Christ, for of Him Thoreau states: "He taught mankind imperfectly how to live; his thoughts were all directed towards another world."[10]

A Week further expresses Thoreau's belief that God should be experienced concretely and should not be written about theologically, abstractly. "The wisest man preaches no doctrines; he has no scheme; he sees no rafter, not even a cobweb, against the heavens. It is a clear sky" (p. 88). The only way to approach God is *through* nature: "There is more religion in men's science than there is science in their religion" (p. 98). The passages in the "Sunday" chapter of *A Week* which speak of the Bible, religion, and Jesus Christ clearly show that Thoreau believes that religion should not be based on abstract theological doctrines; our understanding of God should instead be founded upon that which we can apprehend in concrete reality—a belief consistent with Thoreau's intent to achieve mystic union with the One *through* nature.

It is probable that Thoreau accuses the Bible and the teachings of Jesus Christ of being too spiritual and otherworldly also because much of nineteenth century Christianity in America was exactly that. That Thoreau should accuse others of otherworldliness becomes ironic, however, when we note that he himself stresses instead the natural realm—a view based on exactly the same dualism. In other words, Thoreau is not demanding a whole new clock—he is merely attempting to swing the old pendulum the other way. It is this otherworldliness, in any case, that Thoreau is against in *A Week* when he complains that certain people have their scheme of the universe all cut and dried, including notions of Father, Son and Holy Ghost. "But," says Thoreau, "in all my wanderings, I never came across the least vestige of authority for these things. They have not left so distinct a trace as the delicate flower of a remote geological period on the coal in my grate" (pp. 87-8).

Thoreau expresses the same sentiment in a letter to Isaiah T. Williams, dated September 8, 1841:

> If any soul look abroad even today it will not find any word which does it more justice than the New Testament, — yet if it be faithful enough it will have experience of a revelation fresher and directer than that, which will make that to be only the best tradition. The strains of a more heroic faith vibrate through the week days and the fields than through the Sabbath and the Church. To shut the ears to the immediate voice of God, and to prefer to know him by report will be the only sin.[11]

If the Bible has no authority for Thoreau because he considers it too spiritual and because it deals only with Hebrew culture and not enough with the New England situation, it is no wonder that he should feel compelled to write *Walden* and call it "*my* New Testament," and spice it throughout with Biblical allusions in order to give it religious significance.

In one of the few passages in *A Week* in which Thoreau speaks favorably of the New Testament, he cites a number of texts which, when taken out of context, could, in a distorted way, anticipate his Transcendental purpose in *Walden*. Thoreau quotes texts such as the following:

> Seek first the Kingdom of heaven.
>
> Lay not up for yourselves treasures on earth.
>
> If thou wilt be perfect, go and sell that thou hast, and give to the poor, and thou shalt have treasure in heaven.
>
> For what is a man profited, if he shall gain the whole world, and lose his own soul?

Finally, giving a decidedly Transcendental, Emersonian interpretation of the divinity of man and the limitless possibility of the individual self, Thoreau quotes: "Verily I say unto you, if ye have faith as a grain of mustard seed, ye shall say unto this mountain, Remove hence to yonder place, and it shall move; and nothing shall be impossible unto you" (pp. 91-2). Given the Transcendental distortion, one could easily imagine the last text above in an Emerson essay like *Nature*, something akin to "Build, therefore, your own world."

Now, the foregoing is not intended to be sorrowful tongue-clucking over Thoreau's lack of orthodoxy; rather, it provides a framework, a context for our examination of Thoreau's use of the Bible in *Walden*.[12] As stated earlier, this use begins with ironic exaggeration, comic wit, and parody.

Ironic exaggeration was one of Thoreau's favorite strategies. Not only are many individual examples to be found in *Walden*, in a sense the whole book is, as Thoreau admits, an exaggeration. Thoreau uses the Bible to contribute to this facet of his book. Statements such as "if he should live to the age of Methuselah" and "as old as Adam" strike the modern reader as trite, but Thoreau's comic exaggeration is much fresher when he describes Concord's volunteer fire department rushing out "like true idealists, rejecting the evidence of their senses," to Breed's hut, set afire by mischievous boys. At first the crew thinks to throw the whole frog pond onto the fire, but nothing can be done but let the fire burn, for it has advanced too far. As the crew engages in conversation, they discuss previous great conflagrations, one of which (Bascom's shop) was so large that, Thoreau says, "we could turn that last and threatened universal one into another flood" (p. 785).

Thoreau's comic wit also appears when he says of a certain parson who spends too much time hunting that "such a one might make a good shepherd's dog, but is far from being the Good Shepherd" (p. 761). In another instance, describing a cold winter's walk over the railroad causeway, Thoreau says, tongue-in-cheek: "I encountered many a blustering and nipping wind, for nowhere has it freer play; and when the frost had smitten me on one cheek, heathen as I was, I turned to it the other also" (p. 788). In another clever parody, Thoreau tells of the prudent landlord coming to the pond in January to cut ice to cool his summer drink. Thoreau calls it "impressively, even pathetically wise, to foresee the heat and thirst of July now in January — wearing a thick coat and mittens! — when so many things are not provided for. It may be that he lays up no treasures in this world which will cool his summer drink in the next" (pp. 802-3).

Comic parody appears frequently in *Walden*. In his first letter to the Corinthians, Paul urges the Christians there to be sober in speech: "Be not deceived: evil communications corrupt good manners." But Thoreau uses this text to describe his feeling toward the church service of his day: "Our manners have been corrupted by communication with the saints" (p. 688). And just in case the reader missed the point, Thoreau follows that sentence with another parody, this time of the Shorter Catechism of *The New England Primer*: "Our hymn-books resound with a melodious cursing of God and enduring him forever."

The Bible contributes significantly also toward much of the concrete imagery Thoreau uses, helping to create a colorful prose style. A few examples will serve to illustrate:

> I think that I speak within bounds when I say that, though the birds of the air have their nests, and the foxes their holes, and the savages their wigwams, in modern civilized society not more than half the families own a shelter (p. 662).

> It is not necessary that a man should earn his living by the sweat of his brow, unless he sweats easier than I do (p. 684).

> After all, the man whose horse trots a mile a minute does not carry the most important messages; he is not an evangelist, nor does he come round eating locusts and wild honey (p. 674).

Since *Walden* is to be seen as a poetic work, "two strategies of language, wit and metaphor, serve Thoreau as the negative and positive means of his quest," says Anderson.[13] We have seen briefly how Thoreau employs the Bible as a source for his wit, especially comic exaggeration and parody. We must see that much of Thoreau's use of metaphor also finds its origin in the Bible, particularly the central metaphor for the key symbol of the book—Walden Pond.

A number of passages in *Walden* celebrate the purity of the pond as its most important symbolic feature:

> Like the water, the Walden ice, seen near at hand, has a green tint, but at a distance is beautifully blue, and you can easily tell it from the white ice of the river or the merely greenish ice of some ponds, a quarter of a mile off. Sometimes one of these cakes slips from the ice-man's sled into the village street, and lies there for a week like a great emerald (p. 804).

Whether Thoreau's comparison of the ice to precious stones—here and in other passages—is a reference to "the pearl of great price" is uncertain, but that Thoreau sees the pond as a substitute for the traditional Christian view of salvation is evident, for immediately after the passage quoted above he states: ". . . as often as I looked out I was reminded of the . . . parable of the sower" (p. 804). In a striking metaphor, then, the water of Walden Pond, Thoreau's symbol of perfection, is harvested and sent to all nations, so that Thoreau can say: ". . . the sweltering inhabitants of Charleston, and New Orleans, of Madras and Bombay and Calcutta, drink at my well" (p. 805). This last statement is a clear reference to Christ's words to the Samaritan woman at the well,[14] a reference which lies at the very center of *Walden's* religious symbolism, and which is reinforced by Thoreau's statement in the same chapter: "Heaven is under our feet as well as over our heads" (p. 797). In other words, for Christ's "living water" Thoreau would substitute the water of Walden Pond, symbol of the clear Transcendental self:

> It is no dream of mine,
> To ornament a line:
> I cannot come nearer to God and Heaven
> Than I live to Walden even (p. 751).

If *Walden* is to be seen, then, as the poetic account of a spiritual, religious quest, one can understand Thoreau's intent with this central religious metaphor. A number of other expressions of it occur throughout the book, of which we quote two:

> To anticipate, not the sunrise and the dawn merely, but, if possible, Nature herself! How many mornings, summer and winter, before yet any neighbor was stirring about his business, have I been about mine! . . . though I never

> caught much, and that, manna-wise, would dissolve again in the sun (p. 655).

> It convinces me that Earth is still in her swaddling clothes, and stretches forth baby fingers on every side (p. 810).

Obviously this is religious language, in harmony with Thoreau's central religious purpose. What the reader catches are images of spiritual rebirth, of renewal—images which recur throughout the "Spring" chapter. In another passage Thoreau states:

> We should be blessed if we lived in the present always, and took advantage of every accident that befell us, like the grass which confesses the influence of the slightest dew that falls on it . . . . In a pleasant spring morning all man's sins are forgiven. Such a day is a truce to vice. While such a sun holds out to burn, the vilest sinner may return . . . the sun shines bright and warm this first spring morning, recreating the world . . . . You see some innocent fair shoots preparing to burst from his gnarled rind and try another year's life, tender and fresh as the youngest plant. Even he has entered into the joy of his Lord (p. 813).

Thoreau's idea here of a correspondence between the natural and moral realms finds further expression throughout *Walden.* The statement "in a pleasant spring morning all man's sins are forgiven" is a notion more Transcendental than Biblical, of course; the striking metaphor at the end of the passage, however, comes from Matthew 25, which recounts the familiar parable of the talents. "Enter thou into the joy of thy Lord" is told the faithful servants. Thoreau's point here, then, is clear: he who is faithful over little—that is, takes advantage of every opportunity nature offers—will receive a spiritual reward. The quasi-Biblical language is used by Thoreau in the presentation of a rather heterodox view of the path to salvation.

The brightness of morning assumes religious significance in another passage in the "Spring" chapter. Thoreau describes a valley and woods ". . . bathed in so pure and bright a light as would have waked the dead, if they had been slumbering in their graves, as some suppose. There needs no stronger proof of immortality. All things must live in such a light. O Death, where is thy sting? O Grave, where was thy victory, then?" (pp. 814-15).

This same chapter is a poetic description of the symbolic importance of spring as the season of rebirth. Winter has signaled the death of Thoreau's former way of life, and spring is the harbinger of reawakening, of spiritual rebirth. In one of the book's key passages, Thoreau states:

"Walden was dead and is alive again" (p. 812). The Bible source for this metaphor is the parable of the prodigal son, a parable of rebirth, and Thoreau makes allusion to it to give the season of spring at Walden religious significance. Again, this rebirth comes not in the traditional Christian sense but comes to the person who has brought himself into harmony with the natural order.

Walden is Thoreau's account of his quest for this harmony with nature. That the water of Walden Pond assumes symbolic religious significance is captured in Thoreau's statement: "I got up early and bathed in the pond; that was a religious exercise, and one of the best things which I did."[15] This morning ritual becomes Thoreau's attempt to cleanse himself and take on the pond's purity; it is, as Thoreau states, a "religious exercise"—in short, a *baptism*. In the traditional Christian sense, baptism is a sign and seal of forgiveness of sin, a cleansing based on Christ's atoning sacrifice. Thoreau's baptism, however, is a total immersion in Walden Pond, an intimate communion with the tides of nature in a pantheistic, Transcendental sense. Therein lies the essential meaning of the book, and its essential difference with a Christian position.

In conclusion, *Walden* is a poetic creation in search of spiritual truth, and for that reason Thoreau uses the Bible negatively as a source of wit and positively as a source of metaphor. Perhaps an irony contained in this topic is that Thoreau, in order to lend religious significance to his book, should endeavor to do so by alluding to a book whose religious validity he himself had rejected long before.

Notes

1. *Walden*, reproduced in *American Literary Masters*, Charles R. Anderson, ed. (New York: Holt, Rinehart and Winston, Inc., 1965), p. 819. Subsequent references to *Walden* will cite parenthetically the page numbers as they appear in this Anderson edition.

2. *A Week on the Concord and Merrimack Rivers* (Boston: Houghton, Mifflin and Co., 1893), p. 90.

3. Allison Ensor's article "Thoreau and the Bible—Preliminary Consideration," in: *The Emersonian Society Quarterly*, 33 (1963), pp. 65-70, locates many of the Biblical allusions but does not attempt to place them in a larger literary context.

4. Walter Hardin, *Thoreau's Library* (Charlottesville: University of Virginia Press, 1957), pp. 13, 33-4.

5. Kenneth Walter Cameron, "Chronology of Thoreau's Harvard Years," in: *Emerson Society Quarterly*, XV (1959), p. 18.

6. F. B. Sanborn, *Henry David Thoreau* (Boston: Houghton, Mifflin and Co., 1883), p. 156.

7. Sanborn, p. 158.

8. Sanborn, p. 163.

9. Robert Spiller, et al, *Literary History of the United States*, third edition (New York: The Macmillan Co., 1963), p. 391.

10. *A Week*, p. 93. Moreover, Christ fails to meet the Transcendental standard of self-reliance, for Thoreau states: "Even Christ, we fear, had his scheme, his conformity to tradition, which slightly vitiates his teaching" (*A Week*, p. 88). At best, Christ can be considered a good man, on the level of Homer, Socrates, and Shakespeare.

11. Walter Harding and Carl Bode, eds., *The Correspondence of Henry David Thoreau* (Washington Square: New York University Press, 1958), p. 52.

12. We might note that Thoreau refers to the Bible at least 45 times in *Walden*: 35 references quote specific texts, six allude to stories or characters in Genesis, and four talk of the Bible as a whole. That Thoreau's knowledge of the Bible was extensive is illustrated by the broad range of books to which he refers in *Walden*.

13. Anderson, p. 628.

14. John 4:5-42, a chapter which speaks not only of the well and living water but also of the sower and reaper image.

15. Anderson, p. 694.

Towards a New Anthropological Model[1]

ARNOLD H. DE GRAAFF

> "Test the spirits to see whether they are of God . . ." (I John 4:1-6).
>
> "God gave us the ministry of reconciliation . . . so we are ambassadors for Christ . . ." (II Cor. 5:11-21).

Introduction

During the last decades there has been a rediscovery, particularly by biblical theologians, of the Scriptures' message concerning the unity of man. In my own (Dutch Reformed) tradition, G. C. Berkouwer's study *Man: The Image of God* is a good example of this rediscovery. Reflecting many Biblical theological studies (Eichrodt, Robinson, etc.) on the Old and New Testament view of man, Berkouwer concludes:

> We may say without much fear of contradiction that the most striking thing in the Biblical portrayal of man lies in this, that it never asks attention for man in himself, but demands our fullest attention for man in his relation to God. We can doubtless characterize this portrayal as a religious one.
>
> This point of view is so central and dominant for the Word of God that it never gives us a neutral independent analysis of man in order to inform us as to the components and structure of humanness in itself.
>
> Man without this relation cannot exist, he is a phantom, a creation of abstracting thought, which is no longer conscious of the relationships, the basic actuality, of humanness, which concerns itself with that which can never exist: man in himself, in isolation. This man, now, in the impossibility of his being isolated and independent, is the whole man.[2]

From out of this understanding of the Biblical proclamation concerning the whole man in relation to God, Berkouwer comes to reject as pseudo-problems all the questions surrounding the (dualistic) dichotomistic and trichotomistic theories of man and the theories concerning the origin of the soul—creationism versus traducianism. He concludes that whenever the Scriptures use a specific term to refer to man, like *heart, soul, spirit, mind, flesh, body, inner man, outer man*, they always refer to the whole man looked at from a particular point of view.[3] This rediscovery of the whole man, in the unity of his various dimensions inseparably related to God, could be demonstrated from many sources, reflecting several theological traditions.

At this point, however, I want to call attention to a strange phenomenon. Once this rediscovery has been made and a theologian or philosopher attempts to conceptualize and systematize this Scriptural emphasis on unity, he is likely to take recourse to a traditional dualistic or monistic model, thereby jeopardizing his newly gained insights. Berkouwer and Dooyeweerd, to limit myself in examples to my own immediate background, after having emphasized so strongly the unity of man and the centeredness of all of man's functions in his heart, introduce a new tension and ambiguity in their theoretical constructs. Berkouwer repeatedly distinguishes the way theology studies man from the way anthropology and the other special disciplines investigate human nature. In doing so he creates the impression that some kind of objective, abstract study of man is possible after all—or at least that man can be studied, however incompletely or partially, apart from his relation to God.[4] When all is said and done, there is still a separation or tension between man's spirituality and his functionality. Somehow, man's relation to God does not completely permeate and totally characterize his nature in Berkouwer's conception. Dooyeweerd's distinction between the supra-temporal heart and the temporal modes within which man functions leads to a similar ambiguity and tension.[5] Against their own intention, which we want to honor fully, these theories again, to some degree, separate man's relation to God from his creaturely functioning. In this kind of dualism (of a structuralist monarchian type; see below) man's spiritual nature is no longer integrally related to his functionality. Apparently there is no model available that can do justice to the spiritual unity of man, enabling us to conceptualize the religious nature and motivation of all of man's behavior.

In this essay we shall examine in some detail the reasons for the lack of a Biblically founded, theoretical model by focusing on the main features of the typical, traditional anthropological conceptions available to us. In the process the contours of an alternative model will become evident, together with some of the implications for psychotherapy.

Man's religious nature and calling

When we look at the array of traditional models available to us, we may wonder why none of them are able to do justice to man's spiritual unity in the diversity of his functioning. To understand this matter, we must turn for a moment to the Biblical view of man.

Man, the Scriptures reveal to us, is created by God. As a creature he is dependent upon his Maker. This dependency is a part of his created nature. Not being self-sufficient, he cannot but entrust himself to someone or something beyond himself. Made in God's image, man is called to mirror his Lord's perfections. This call, too, is part of his created nature. He is *made* to respond to the Word of his Lord and to do His will in life. In one way or another—in an obedient or a sinful way—man *must* respond to God's revelation of His will for creation, and God holds man accountable for his response (Rom. 1). To be dependent upon his Creator and to respond to the Word of his Lord is man's joy and peace, for this is the way God made him. At the same time, by entrusting himself, by responding, and by imaging his Lord, man brings praise and glory to his Maker, whose will is being done.[6]

Since man is created as a religious creature, he is "incurably" religious. *All* people put their trust in someone or something. They must necessarily surrender themselves to a higher power. Thus there are no people who are irreligious.[7] Religion is a universal phenomenon, because God created man as a religious creature.[8] Having turned his back on his Creator and Lord, sinful man is forever driven on to search for a new resting place. He cannot help himself. Making one part of creation after another into his god, lost man enslaves himself. When man fixes his heart upon a dimension of God's good creation, it turns into a demonic power which distorts life. Disillusioned, broken, disintegrated, man turns away and starts his search for a resting place and ultimate certainty all over again. Rooted in the center of his being, in his heart or soul, is the urge to surrender himself to a higher power and, thus, to have a frame of reference for his life. Man cannot live without a god, but it is only the true God of heaven and earth who can satisfy the desire of his heart, and it is only *His* will for life that can bring integration, wholeness and peace.

According to the Scriptures, man is never man without God, even in his disobedience. Entrusting, believing, confessing, integrating is *constitutive* of his human nature. In view of this fact, the Scriptures never talk about man apart from his relationship and response to God and His Word. To talk about man apart from his believing would be to talk about an abstraction, something non-existent. For man *is* a religious creature.

This view of man as created to respond to the Word of his Lord from out of the center of his being is the first *confessional* given of a Biblically founded, theoretical model of man. In contrast, however, it also means that any theory that does not take its starting point in God's revelation cannot do justice to the spiritual relation of man to God in all his functioning. Such a theory must of necessity absolutize and deify one of man's functions and thus create a tension or separation between the absolutized function(s) and the rest of man's functions. As a result, all non-Christian anthropological theories are bound to be either dualistic, maintaining a separation between higher and lower functions, or monistic, maintaining a tension between the contrasting functions of the bifurcation of the original unity.

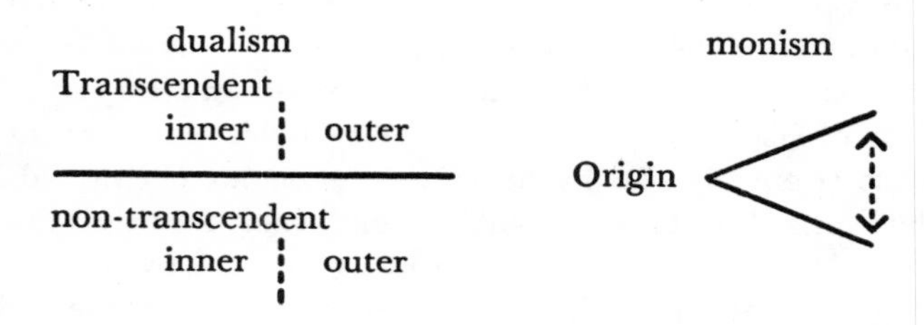

Confessional visions and ways of life

Before we turn to the traditional models, a further point must be made about the religious dynamic and direction of the traditional theories concerning man. The available theories are not merely analytical constructs. Rather, they are the theoretical outcome of communally held confessional views of man that serve as the religious basis and frame of reference for the models. To grasp this point more clearly, we must turn for a moment to man's confessing.

What man believes in his heart, he confesses with his mouth (Rom. 10). By confessing, man, in a unique manner, gives expression to his religious nature. When man confesses, he says: "Here I stand, I can do nothing else; this is my ultimate certainty and hope; beyond this there is nothing else; and this is what gives meaning to my life." For the Christian, his confession is a *response* to God's revelation in Jesus Christ worked in his heart by the Holy Spirit.[9]

In one way or another, obediently or disobediently, all men give expression to what lives in their hearts. Some people are very conscious of the vision of life that drives them and can articulate their deepest convictions in a clear "world-and-life view." Often such people give expression to what lives in the hearts of many people. All people, however, whether they are consciously aware of it or not, are in the grip of some worldview or confessional vision that motivates their activities, as becomes evident in their lives. Man cannot but give expression to his heart commitment. Even if he denies holding to any faith, his worldview, his life philosophy, his beliefs, or his values betray him, pointing to his religious nature.

Since man is created neighborly, his confessional response is always a communal response. Man exists in relation. Views of life, therefore, are always shared views, driving *groups* of people. Different people are in the grip of a common spirit; they are personally committed to a common vision of life. Men, living and working together in interdependence, respond to the Word of the Lord for life in obedience or disobedience.

All cultural manifestations are directed by and come about through a people's confession about life. Political activities, legal, economic and social activities, marriage, family, and child rearing practices are all expressions of a confessionally led way of life. Thus, each culture presents a coherent, meaningful pattern that finds its unity in the dominant vision of life. Within each cultural community there are different movements which compete in the formation of a society. Each such movement ". . . has its own principle of authority, its own principle of socio-cultural organization, its own core peoplehood, its own version of the 'enemy,' its own typical modes of institutionalization, and other characteristics."[10]

The worldview of a particular faith-community drives and shapes every aspect of its cultural activities, including its scientific activities. As scientists develop their theories, they either consciously seek to give an account of the religious starting point of their investigations, or they subconsciously work from out of a certain vision of life, as becomes evident in their writings.[11] Scientists are first of all believers. The facts they discover are humanly known facts, and that means facts seen and understood from out of a particular vision of life. Their belief in God or a pseudo-god is beyond verification or falsification. In fact, their belief serves as the ultimate validation of their theorizing and verifying. To understand and properly evaluate theories of man, therefore, it is necessary to focus on the underlying confessional view of man that has been given theoretical expression. All anthropological models are basically the theoretical outcome of different beliefs about human nature. In this respect Christian theories of man do not differ from non-Christian models. Both kinds of theories are rooted in certain beliefs about man, be it radically opposing beliefs.

The search for a criterion

When we now turn our attention to the existing theories of man, whether developed in the context of philosophical anthropology, theological anthropology, or theories of personality, we are confronted by a bewildering range of conceptions. How shall we find a criterion for comparing and evaluating these theoretical models? Many have tried to find such a criterion in the field of logic and language analysis, or in more general standards of science.[12] Others have found a criterion in an evolutionistic view of the unfolding of science.[13]

However, all such criteria already presuppose a certain confessional vision of life and man, seeking ultimate certainty in logical and lingual clarification, or in the evolutionary process. Finding himself in basic disagreement with such beliefs, the Christian scholar is confronted with this question: What criteria can I use to compare and evaluate other theories? Is there a universal standard, or am I doomed to some kind of eclecticism?

It is my thesis that to be valid, such a standard must be based on God's revelation. Only God's order for creation, including human nature, can provide us with the frame of reference for evaluating the models of others and for conceptualizing an alternative model that is based on the Biblical view of man.

The Scriptures, by the power of the Holy Spirit, open our eyes again to discern God's "general" revelation. God's order for creation, described in Genesis 1 and 2 and reaffirmed in Jesus Christ, the Word Incarnate (Col. 1), provides the cosmic context for interpreting the existing anthropological theories and for developing an alternative model.[14] If a person does not accept God's revelation as the norm for his life, he is bound to find the origin of the norms *for* life and the meaning *in* life within the creation, deifying one of its dimensions. For man cannot escape the Word of God which holds the creation in its grip and which daily impinges upon him. Human activity, including scientific activity, therefore, must be evaluated in terms of a person's response to the Word of God as it structures creation, whether he acknowledges and seeks to obey it, or whether he denies God's Word, absolutizing a part of creation instead and thereby distorting life.

Thus, when we want to evaluate a particular anthropological model, there are two questions we can ask: (1) What fundamental structural dimension(s) is the theorist responding to? (2) What place does he give to this (these) dimension(s) in his confessional view of man?

God's order for creation

Theoretically conceived, the Word of God seems to structure the creation, including man, in the following fundamental ways: (1) directionality, (2) modality, (3) temporality, (4) typicality, (5) configuration or structuration.

Directionality has reference to the religious or spiritual nature of all of life. It indicates that all things point beyond themselves to the Creator and that nothing in the creation is self-sufficient. All creatures, each according to its kind, respond as subjects to the Word of the Lord for their existence. Man, too, is a dependent creature. In the spiritual direction of his life, it becomes evident to whom he is committed—to God or to a pseudo-god.

Modality has reference to the irreducible, unique ways in which the creation, including man, functions. Thus man functions, to mention just a few modes, in a sensitive, cognitive, social, physical, and confessional way. None of these ways of being define man. Being sensitive, for example, is only one of the ways people are. All these diverse ways of being find their unity and direction in man's heart or soul or spirit.

Temporality has reference to the beginning, the development, the periodicity, the duration, and the ending of all things. Man, too, is a temporal creature. He is born, goes through certain developmental stages, and dies. Man's temporality is another constitutive dimension of his nature. Through sin, man's temporality has become an awesome curse, which is lifted only in and through the resurrected Christ who gives us the hope of life unending and of a new body on a new earth.

Typicality has reference to the classification of things. We find kingdoms or realms of creatures, each with its major subgroups. Mankind, too, is typically diversified. Man is either male or female, belongs to one race or another, manifests certain nationality characteristics, and shows a rich variety of personality types.

Configuration or structuration has reference to the peculiar modal pattern concrete things manifest. In man it allows us to recognize the different kinds of activities in which he engages. Although the whole man responds in each activity, each activity has a peculiar focus. Each human activity seems to be founded and qualified in a particular way.

These categories are intended as tentative working constructs to focus our attention on the basic ways in which the creation and man seem to be constructed.

If man does not acknowledge God and His revelation, he is bound to seek his basis and certainly in one of these fundamental dimensions of creation. This absolutizing of a creational dimension is reflected in the traditional anthropological models that have come down to us over the centuries and that are present today.

Typical models of man

To the dimension of modality man has responded by making one or more aspects the origin and law for everything else. Thus, we find *monistic* and *dualistic* conceptions, in which the physical, the cognitive, the social, the aesthetic, or some other mode of human functioning is absolutized. In *both* types of conceptions, man is divided in two parts, either a higher and lower, or a bifurcation of the original unity in two contrasting parts (in tension, interacting, running parallel, or one of them dominant).

The temporal side of creation is responded to either by absolutizing becoming, change and process, or by absolutizing the enduring structures of things in spite of change. Thus, we find *geneticistic* and *structuralistic* conceptions. Geneticistic thinkers tend to be monists, and structuralistic thinkers tend to be dualists.

The combination of these two kinds of responses to modality and temporality seems to be able to account for most traditional anthropological models, both past and present. During a lifetime of special philosophical-anthropological investigation, Professor D. H. T. Vollenhoven of the Free University of Amsterdam has demonstrated how the same basic models of man keep reappearing in the history of thought.[15] In view of the basic dimensions of creation to which all men must respond, this fact does not surprise us, for there are only so many irreducible dimensions that man can fix his heart on and absolutize.

These structural schemes have great heuristic value for understanding the pattern and coherence of a person's thought. They allow us to do greater justice to and gain a more accurate view of an author's position. Most important of all, they enable us to incorporate new insights into the structure of man from different scholars without taking over their religious framework. Only some detailed studies of particular anthropologists and psychologists can demonstrate this point. For now, let me just give a few tentative examples.

At present, it is my working hypothesis that Freud can be understood better if the model of man underlying his writings (after 1920, during the last phase of his development) is seen as a geneticistic dualism, which is a very deterministic, pessimistic and difficult position to maintain. In the light of this model, his confessional view of man stands out very clearly: man instinctively annihilates himself via the road of copulation; such is man's destiny, the remorseless law of nature, sublime Necessity, and not just chance; at least, it is comforting to think so.[16]

Having seen his religious basis, many Christians are inclined to stop at this point.[17] However, there is more to Freud's conception than his distorting belief about human nature. He, too, had to respond to God's order for creation. Being a careful observer, Freud noticed many regularities in man's (mal)functioning that were not seen clearly before him or not recognized at all. After our religious evaluation, therefore, we must go on to ask what creational states of affairs Freud uncovered and pointed to, however much mistaking or distorting their meaning. In this "distilling," an awareness of his anthropological model can be both our safeguard (what we need to distil from) and an aid in seeing the significance of his observations (the structural states of affairs he encountered).

When we do, we shall learn much about what happens when fundamental sexual and aggressive feelings are suppressed out of emotional anxiety; how fundamental these feelings are to all our functioning; and how the lack of integration of these feelings tends to distort all our conscious activities, giving rise to different kinds of defense mechanisms. In our own model of emotional malfunctioning, we, too, shall have to account for these phenomena. We need to be utterly critical of the religious spirit that permeates the traditional anthropologies. At the same time, we must be completely open to what we can learn about God's order for creation from other investigators and practitioners, and in so doing, we will gather the building stones for a truly alternative model rooted in God's revelation.

To give one more example of this last point, from Jung we must learn what we should have learned long ago, that even on a sensitive level man cannot but respond to the ultimate dimensions of life and the universal structures holding for man (life, death, birth, male, female, father, mother, old age, etc.). From a Christian perspective, this means that in all his functioning, also in his sensitive functioning, man responds as a spiritual creature, sensitive to the presence of God's Word in the world. This sensitive awareness, too, alongside the other kinds of awareness of the order of creation, is a call, a call to hear and do the Word of the Lord and live. While we learn from Jung, however, in spite of his geneticistic monism of a parallelistic kind, we must utterly reject his gospel for mankind, namely, that the process of individuation is the one way to gain peace with oneself and harmony with the world.[18]

Space prevents us from acknowledging the contributions made by Rogers, Skinner, Frankl, Maslow, and many others. Indeed, to do justice to the structure of the thinking of any one of these psychologists and to ferret out the structural states of affairs they have struggled with would require a separate study of the views of each one of them.

Christian use of existing models?

At this point we need to return for a moment to an issue raised in the introduction. Again and again it appears that as Christian scholars, we are inclined to accommodate our Biblically sensitive insights to non-Christian thought patterns, often in spite of ourselves.

In the introduction I referred to the attempts of Berkouwer and Dooyeweerd to do justice to the spiritual unity and centeredness of man's creaturely functioning. Although I fully endorse and want to honor their intention, the theoretical constructs they make use of frustrate that intention. Having tried for several years to work with Dooyeweerd's anthropological model in the field of psychology and psychotherapy, I am very conscious of how his model ultimately stood in the way of a more complete integration of the Christian faith and psychology. His model could not make plain how in man's psychic functioning his religious nature expresses itself. The relation between man's heart or soul and his sensitive way of functioning remained vague, if not problematic. This vagueness must be attributed directly to his monarchian tendencies, as a close examination of his 32 anthropological propositions indicates.[19] Moreover, in keeping with his monarchian tendencies, his view of time stood in the way of gaining structural insight into developmental "psychology" (anthropology).[20]

A similar state of affairs can be observed in the writings of Jay E. Adams. His many Biblically sensitive insights are absorbed by the geneticistic monism (of the mentalistic priority type) model which he uses. As a result of the use of this conception with its underlying religious basis, man's physical functioning and his behavior are interpreted in a mechanistic, objectifying (behavioristic) manner; human sensitivity is depreciated; and man's rational and verbal functioning is elevated to the level of the primary mode for Christianly directing our behavior. Moreover, the geneticistic, monistic tendency of his thought-pattern tends to obscure the sanctifying work of God's Spirit. In the light of this tendency, it is not surprising to see that he favors traducianism over against creationism.[21]

These two examples are a reminder how much we are in need of becoming more self-conscious of the consequences of the existing models of man and the theoretical implications of the Biblical view of man. At heart we are all "synthesis" thinkers, tending to accommodate our thinking and our practice to patterns that are alien to the gospel.[22] Only if we are willing to grow in grace, also theoretically and in our professional practice, can we hope to develop a clearer Biblically founded anthropological model.

In view of this tendency of Christians to accommodate their thinking to non-Christian thought patterns, it is instructive to see what models different groups of Christians tend to use. Reformed Christians tend to use mainly the monarchian model. Evangelical Christians primarily use the spiritualistic asceticism model or the mentalistic priority model (particularly on this continent). Roman Catholics tend to make use of the

Thomistic form of the subsistence theory; Liberals can accommodate themselves to any model, although they often favor some form of geneticistic monism. These four types of Christian thought correspond directly to the four kinds of views described by Richard Niebuhr in his *Christ and Culture*.[23]

Almost all models, but particularly the ones Christians tend to use, end up depreciating man's physical, organic and sensitive ways of functioning. As a result, these dimensions of human functioning are usually regarded as man's lower nature, which is then considered to be irrational, seductive, unbridled, base, dangerous, the occasion for sin, etc., and which therefore must be controlled and directed by man's higher, rational, moral nature. Thus, these conceptions foster and keep alive strong rationalistic, moralistic and spiritualistic tendencies among Christians, and often result in an inability to cope with and integrate in a positive manner our physical, sexual functions and feelings and our emotional reactions in general. These persistent trends within orthodox Christianity give rise to strong neurotic tendencies and hinder the free acceptance of our creaturely functioning as created *very good* by God and, although subject to sin, essentially redeemed and renewed in Jesus Christ.

The contours of an alternative model

When we consider the typical models available to us and the attempts of Christian scholars to make use of these constructions, it becomes evident that the greatest challenge in developing an alternative model is to do justice to the spiritual unity and centeredness of man. Secondly, in view of the reductionistic tendencies in many models, we are in need of an alternative that can reflect the great diversity and complexity of human functioning.

The Scriptures make it abundantly clear that the whole man, in all his activities, from out of the core of his being serves God or a pseudo-god. Thus, Paul can admonish us in I Corinthians 10:31: "So, whether you eat or drink, or whatever you do, do all to the glory of God," or, as he puts it in Romans 12:1: "I appeal to you therefore, brethren, by the mercies of God, to present your bodies as a living sacrifice, holy and acceptable to God, which is your spiritual worship." In our bodies, that is, in our entire creaturely existence, we are to give expression to the allegiance of our heart. In our common day-to-day ways of functioning, like eating and drinking, we are to glorify God by obeying God's will for those dimensions of our life. Man is spirit, and his spirituality is not a separate dimension of his existence but comes to expression in all his activities.

Our challenge is to grasp and formulate *in functional terms* what the Scriptures present to us in *confessional* language.[24] Remembering how easy it is to reintroduce a separation or tension between man's spirituality and functionality, I propose that in the context of our theorizing we refer to man's spirituality only in *structural* terms. Rejecting all monistic and dualistic conceptions, we need to learn to trace more fully *the functional expression* of man's religious nature—his unity, his centeredness, his religious motivation, and his knowing and doing as religious service unto God or a pseudo-god.

In so doing, we shall not pretend that we can *functionally* fathom or grasp the depth of our being and the miracle of our God-relatedness. This mystery can only be expressed in ultimate, referential, confessional terms: "You are our God, and we are your people. Speak, Lord, for your servant hears. My Lord and my God! Abba! Father!" In the presence of our Lord, we know who we are and have our identity. Truly we are people of God—dependent creatures that can only know themselves as creatures in their relation to God.

Nevertheless, if man *is* spirit, if he is unified, centered, and motivated from within in all his knowing and doing, we shall find the functional expressions of his spirituality in all the ways man functions. In other words, man is created in such a way that *his structuration is expressive of his spirituality. His God-relatedness is constitutive for his functionality.* The ways in which man functions are not merely vehicles or instruments of man's spirit, or spheres within which man's spirit operates and provides the spiritual dynamic. Such conceptions still give some independent status to man's bodily existence. Rather, man's bodily functioning itself is expressive of his spirituality—so much is man heart, soul, mind, spirit, unity, centeredness, relation, response, service. *Thus our calling in theoretical work is to trace more consciously, more clearly, more consistently this spiritual dimension of our creaturely functioning, confessing that our very creaturely existence expresses the mystery of our relation to God.*[25] Following this guideline, we shall be helped to avoid both spiritualism and a functionalistic reductionism.

Responding to this calling, we can trace and systematically investigate man's spirituality in at least three distinct ways. First of all, we can investigate (the development of) man's sense of selfhood and identity—the fact that he is a subject. As Agnes Sutherland Ronaldson puts it in her dissertation, *The Spiritual Dimension of Personality*:

> In this field of the person, the infant needs to be seen as an active agent, a subject, a self, and not merely as a physiological organism whose biological needs require a response in a social framework. Implications of the spiritual dimension of personality for child development involve recognition by the

> adult of the infant as a person, that is, as a subject who is active on his own behalf. This perception on the adult's part requires openness of communication revealing deep sensitivity for seeing, hearing, and responding to what the infant is trying to communicate. There also needs to be given that degree of respect for the integrity of the infant even in his helplessness and immaturity which will allow the infant every opportunity to assume responsibility for his own functioning to the extent he is able.[26]

Man functions as a unified subject, able to take responsibility for his own activities, even as a small child. In the child's developing sense of identity, and in man's awareness and experience of his subjectivity, the spiritual nature of man expresses itself.

Secondly, man's religious nature can be investigated by focusing on his confessional responses. It belongs to the very structure of man's confessional way of responding to the Word of God to integrate, direct and lead all other responses. This characteristic of confessing does not make this way of functioning more spiritual—only unique. In his other ways of functioning, man equally responds as a religious creature.

And this is the third way in which we can investigate man's spiritual nature, namely, by examining his functional responses to God's order for the different dimensions of his life. When a person is *sensitive* to his environment, for example, he is responding directly to the Word of the Lord for that dimension of life. God calls man to be sensitively aware of the world and his fellow men. When he *confesses* his sensitivity, he acknowledges that being sensitive is one of the ways in which God calls him to come to know the world and to love his neighbor. By confessing, man places his being sensitive in an ultimate perspective. In both ways, however, in being sensitive and in confessing the meaning of his sensitivity, man responds directly to the different Words for man's life. In the many different ways in which man functions, the spiritual direction of his heart expresses itself.

With the heart of the matter before us, we can begin to trace the contours of an alternative model. So far we have been discussing the dimension of directionality. Before we put all the givens together, however, we must make some general comments about the dimension of modality.

Once we break more consciously with the functional reductionism of most existing anthropological models and the "hyphen" approach to a Christian alternative model (physical-psychic-spiritual unity), the way is cleared to reconsider the diversity and complexity of man's functioning. Man does not function in two or three or even four irreducible ways but in many more ways. As a working hypothesis, let us assume that man functions in about fourteen or fifteen irreducible ways.

Anyone who has difficulty with this point might consider the range of the branches of psychology or the chapter headings of child psychology books. Many child psychology books, for example, deal separately with the child's physical and motor development, his perceptual and cognitive development, his lingual development, his social development, and his moral development, often taken in the sense of fairness or awareness of values. Some will add a section on aesthetic and religious development. Although these divisions in themselves do not prove the point, I take them as indications of an awareness of the irreducibility of the distinct ways in which man functions.

In the second volume of his *A New Critique of Theoretical Thought*, Dooyeweerd has provided us with a detailed analysis of the modal dimensions of man's functioning. I find this modal theory the most fruitful part of his systematic philosophical contribution. In simplified form, his analysis can serve as a working hypothesis that has already proven to be of great heuristic value in dealing with the complexity of human behavior.

An awareness of the irreducible ways in which man functions allows us to "place" and *integrate* the insights into human behavior of non-Christian scholars in a clear cosmological and anthropological frame of reference. If we want to do justice to the insights of others and avoid a superficial eclecticism, we need a provisionally worked out alternative cosmology and anthropology. Dooyeweerd's modal theory provides us with such an alternative working model.

An important part of his modal theory is his conceptualization of the interrelation between different modes of functioning. Where we are inclined to take recourse to a hyphen, as in referring to psycho-somatic disease, Dooyeweerd provides us with a tool to come to greater clarity on this kind of interrelationship. Again, I find this part of his theory most exciting, opening up new perspectives, especially in moving away from a closed, deterministic and reductionistic view of man's physical, organic and sensitive functioning.

Much more could and needs to be said about the temporal, typical and configurational dimension of human functioning. At this point, however, It may be more useful to begin to put some of the parts together. In conceptualizing such a model and drawing diagrams, we are well advised to use as many different images as we can think of, so that we may be confronted continually by the implications and limitations of our working model.

Since man's spirituality is not a separate dimension of his life but constitutive for all of his creaturely ways of functioning, we need a theoretical construct that reflects this state of affairs. Man's spiritual dimension—or better: nature—must be conceived as "running through" all the other dimensions and not as a separate area or a connecting point. Diagrammatically, this may be difficult to picture in a two or three dimensional model, but conceptually it forces us to ask with regard to each structural dimension (modality, temporality, typicality, configuration) how man's spirituality expresses itself in that dimension.

Dooyeweerd's writings reflect a stratification model, which is popular in German thinking (Hartmann, Rothacker, Lersch, Thomae) and which is fostered by Dooyeweerd's monarchian tendencies. Although full of temptations (the tendency to give separate ontic status to the different modes), this model has its uses. It illustrates an order of dependency and increasing complexity in human functioning. The main limitation is its static character. It only provides us with a cross-cut of a person's functioning at a certain point of his development. This kind of model cannot do justice to the developmental side of human functioning.

A "stratification" or "cross-cut" kind of model obviously needs to be complemented by a developmental model which in itself requires a complex conceptualization. Such a model needs to account for the total stages of development of the person as a unity and, as part of and within those total anthropological stages, the (order of) development of the distinct modes of functioning. Next, it needs to account for the process or dynamic of development itself, for the "law" of development. Finally, it must account, in close relation to the previous point, for the formative influence of the socio-cultural environment and of parental nurturing. Without nurturing there is very little or no development, since the child is utterly dependent upon a protecting, caring and guiding environment.

Both the cross-cut and developmental model do not adequately conceptualize the fact that man is never an isolated individual but always stands in relation to fellow human beings and his environment. Both models point at it, for to develop and function socially, for example, presupposes the presence of other persons, or to react sensitively and to perceive things presupposes an environment. The subject-subject and subject-object relationships, however, need to be a more integral part of our conceptualization. Our constructs and diagrams, therefore, should always be "double" and indicate the specific nature of the relationships.

Whether one model and one diagram can do justice to this complex state of affairs remains an open question. For now, as a working model, it is perhaps sufficient to have several sketches looking at man from different angles. The important point is not whether we can develop a perfect picture in which everything fits, but whether we can develop such constructs and diagrams that will clarify, unify, suggest new relations, and lead to new investigations. Our aim is not logical perfection but the deepening of our understanding of the complexity of human behavior such that, as theorists, we may be of service to the Christian community in its different ministries and a witness to non-Christian colleagues and our society.

The different parts of the above model can be developed further, refined and modified only *in close confrontation with a great range of empirical studies*. Such development will require a team effort and much interdisciplinary study. If the history of philosophy and theology teaches us anything, it is to shy away from all speculation and the development of imposing systems of thought for the sake of systematizing. We cannot do without confessionally founded and theoretically elaborated models if we are to deepen our knowledge, but they must remain open-ended, tentative, working models if we are to be led into the Truth and, by grace and through faith, grow in our discernment of God's good order for life.

Some implications for psychotherapy

During the course of the presentation so far, the main implications for counseling of this perspective may have become evident. I shall mention only a few key points.[27]

(1) The diverse ways of human functioning can give rise to different kinds of malfunctioning, requiring special types of counseling. Problems that are rooted or have their focus in emotional malfunctioning require specific emotional therapy (psychotherapy). Other problems require a different kind of counseling. Often a combination of approaches is needed, which means that we need to be utterly sensitive to the different functional dimensions of a person's problems.

(2) Psychotherapy with regard to emotional malfunctioning needs to be guided by the norm for sensitive functioning. Man is called by God to be sensitively open to all experience and all relationships and respond appropriately to reality as it is in the light of God's Word (with joy, righteous anger, sadness, etc.). Human sensitivity is the necessary substratum of coming to know the world and of doing God's will. By sensing differences and by allowing ourselves to be moved, we come to know and put ourselves in direct contact with our surroundings. As such, human sensitivity is an inseparable aspect of responding truthfully to our world and to other persons. Sensitivity puts us "in touch"—no more, no less. But as such it is utterly essential, for as the "undercurrent" of our experience, our integrated sensitive functioning gives intensity, directness, openness, and vibrancy to all our experience. Thus the goal of psychotherapy (as a specific kind of counseling) is to help a person dissolve anxious, inappropriate reactions to his own functioning into the totality of his life.

(3) Our understanding of man's makeup as reflected in our working model allows and urges us to acknowledge freely and openly that man's physical, sexual, organic, and emotional functioning are created good and are maintained and renewed in Jesus Christ. They are not dangerous, irrational, overwhelming functions requiring constant control and vigi-

lance, always to be distrusted lest they carry us astray. On the contrary, we can trust our "lower" nature, learn more and more to give our physical functioning its rightful place in our life, the place God intended it to have from the beginning and which He gives it again in Jesus Christ, in spite of the fall. Not our physical, sexual, organic, or emotional functioning leads us astray, but what we set our heart on. With our hearts fixed on Jesus Christ, aware of His Word for our different kinds of functioning, we may abandon ourselves freely and with joy to "the pleasures of the body." "O taste and see that the Lord is good!" (Ps. 34:8) is a Biblical injunction that reminds us of this fact, and we can do so all the more freely when we know that our belly is not our god (Phil. 3:4; Rom. 16:18; I Cor. 6:13). This view of our God-created functions can provide a liberating perspective in psychotherapy, for many Christians suffer from deep anxiety created by suppressed and non-integrated bodily feelings and feelings of tenderness and aggression.

(4) This perspective also allows us to recognize fully the relative significance of human sensitivity. Emotional health and maturity is not the sum total of the Kingdom of God on earth, although it is a part of it. God's salvation is very concrete and down-to-earth. He saves and renews whole, unified persons in all their creaturely functions—not spiritual, rational, moral substances that somehow exist in distinction from or in relation to their bodily substance. Nevertheless, God's salvation in us is not yet complete. Much brokenness still remains, and sometimes much suffering. Emotional health may be sought in prayer and with great expectation in Jesus Christ, who makes all things new, beginning even now. But if some or much emotional malfunctioning remains, then we are comforted to know that our life is hid with God in Christ, and that nothing, not even the severest emotional disturbance, can separate us from the love of God in Christ Jesus. We are always more than our feelings and are called to trust this fact even in the face of the most misleading or disturbing feelings. This, too, is a liberating and comforting perspective in psychotherapy.

Conclusion

Much more can and ought to be said about the implications of this view of man for psychotherapy, for other types of counseling, and for education about the nature of therapy and the therapeutic relationship, about techniques, about responsibility, etc., but all these things deserve and must await separate treatment.

The main thing I wanted to establish in the four points above is that psychotherapy is at one and the same time utterly creaturely and utterly spiritual. *In* our sensitive malfunctioning and *in* our re-nurturing and reintegrating of our sensing, feeling and emoting, we are to seek to *obey* God's Word for this dimension of our life, *confessing* that it has its rightful but relative place. This perspective on man makes us look at and experience life much more seriously. Sin and grace have everything to do with sensitive (mal)functioning. Sin, in this context, means failing to give this dimension of life its rightful place, suppressing and denying our feelings out of anxiety; or the opposite, making an idol out of emotional health. Grace, in this context, means acknowledging and seeking to integrate our feelings, giving them the place God intended them to have in our lives. This perspective not only makes our life much more serious but also much more human, creaturely, down-to-earth. *In* our sensitivity, allegiance to God expresses itself.

We are earthly creatures—not angels or spirits—and we look forward to receiving spiritual *bodies*, on a new *earth*, with heaven as a *waiting room*, glorious, no doubt, but not the destiny of our pilgrimage. Thus, our calling is to be utterly God-related in all our creaturely ways, so help us God.

Notes

1. This paper has come about as a result of a two-year interdisciplinary seminar in theological and psychological anthropology with my colleague James H. Olthuis. Although I am solely responsible for the content of this paper, the ideas reflected here are the outcome of the stimulating and creative interaction the seminar afforded. Furthermore, the paper will evidence my indebtedness to the pioneering work of Dooyeweerd and Vollenhoven in the development of a Biblically founded cosmology and anthropology.

2. G. C. Berkouwer, *Man: The Image of God* (Grand Rapids: Eerdmans, 1962; Dutch edition, 1957), pp. 195, 196, 197.

3. Cf. the summary of the Pauline view of man in the recent book by H. N. Ridderbos, *Paul* (Grand Rapids: Eerdmans, 1975; Dutch edition, 1966), pp. 114-21; see also Tory Hoff, "The Significance of Nephesh and the Fulfillment It Receives as Psyche" (Toronto: Institute for Christian Studies, stenciled paper, 1975, 25 pp.).

4. Consider the following passages from Berkouwer's *Man: The Image of God*, p. 30: "Rather, there is justification for a theological approach only when theology deals with man as he appears in the light of the *normative* divine revelation, and then not with man in one or more of his aspects, but with the whole man.

There is a growing consensus among theologians that the Scriptural data on man do not render superfluous research directed at the various aspects of man. Or, in other words, the theological investigation of man cannot seek a solution along the lines of a scientific anthropology, or a Biblical psychology and physiology, as if the intention of Scripture were to give us information about the various *aspects* of man, or the details of the composition of man."

This kind of statement, which can be found throughout Berkouwer's writings, seems to imply that it is possible (abstractly) to study an aspect of man *apart* from his relation to God. In contrast, theology then studies the whole man as he appears in the light of revelation (cf. pp. 32ff, 139ff, 197ff). See also Berkouwer's description of the relation between the natural sciences and theology in his *General Revelation* (Grand Rapids: Eerdmans, 1955).

5. For an analysis of Dooyeweerd's conception, see Harry Fernhout, *Man, Faith and Religion in Bavinck, Kuyper and Dooyeweerd* (Toronto: Institute for Christian Studies, 1976, unpublished master's thesis, 139 pp.).

6. See Harry Fernhout, *Man: The Image and Glory of God* (Toronto: AACS, 1973, stenciled paper, 23 pp.); Paul G. Schrotenboer, *Man in God's World: The Biblical Idea of Office* (Toronto: AACS, 1967).

7. There are people who are *unable* to entrust themselves to someone or something beyond themselves. Such inability must be considered as an emotional malfunctioning in which their created ability to believe, to entrust and to confess is held down by emotional anxiety. Cf. H. C. Rumke, *Karakter en Aanleg in Verband met het Geloof* (Amsterdam: Ten Have, 1949); T. T. Ten Have, *Echt en Onecht in Geloof en Ongeloof* (Utrecht: Humanistisch Verbond, 1956); W. K. Van Dyk, "Neurosis and Religion," in: *Philosophy and Christianity: Philosophical Essays Dedicated to Herman Dooyeweerd* (Kampen: Kok, 1965). Those who call themselves atheists or agnostics upon further hearing give evidence that they, too, hold an ultimate belief, such as the autonomy of human reason. Cf. R. Bellah, *Beyond Belief: Essays on Religion in a Post-Traditional World* (New York: Harper and Row, 1970) for his notion of civic religion and the debate he evoked; and M. Marty, *The Modern Schism: Three Paths to the Secular* (New York: Harper and Row, 1969). Modern secular man is far from irreligious. More appropriate would be to say that his belief is in a stage of transition.

8. Cf. Paul G. Schrotenboer, *The Nature of Religion* (Toronto: AACS, 1964). Most modern scholars do not acknowledge that man's religion is a *response* to *God* and his *revelation*. Thus, they tend to subjectivize religion and reduce it to a mere psychic or social phenomenon, giving a functional account of religion. But since man's religious response is subject to God's law, all religions have the same universal characteristics. In responding to God's revelation, which impinges upon all people, man is bound to his God-created, religious nature. Even in his disobedience, he cannot escape God's law for his religious response.

When scholars investigate religious phenomena, therefore, they cannot but take account, in spite of their subjectivistic tendencies, of the universal features that characterize all religious expressions, regardless of their particular cultural form. The Christian religion, too, manifests these characteristics, for in their response to God's revelation, Christians, too, are subject to God's law for man's religious nature and its expressions.

Having our eyes opened again through the Scriptures to the true nature of religion as a response from the heart to God, our Maker and Redeemer, we have a criterion by which to evaluate and to distill the characteristic features from the many scholarly accounts of the nature of religion. Since every author, in spite of his subjectivistic account, focuses his attention upon some universal aspect of religious phenomena that were not so clearly noted before, our understanding of man's religious nature can be deepened by these studies.

Thus, in our evaluation of religious studies, we constantly have to ask two questions: (1) From out of what subjectivistic and reductionistic viewpoint does the author look at religious phenomena? (2) What universal characteristic of man's religious nature has the author uncovered or highlighted?

9. Cf. James H. Olthuis and Bernard Zylstra, "Confessing Christ in Education," in: *International Reformed Bulletin*, 42, (Summer 1970), pp. 36-44.

10. C. T. McIntire, *The Ongoing Task of Christian Historiography* (Toronto: Institute for Christian Studies, 1974). Cf. Jean Olthuis and Anne Tuininga, *Ways of Life* I (Toronto: Curriculum Development Centre, 1975), "Introduction"; Maarten Vrieze, *The Community Idea in Canada* (Toronto: AACS, 1966). For historical and sociological studies, the category of subgroups within a society seems most helpful. For cultural anthropology, an analysis of the dominant view of life of a society seems essential. Dooyeweerd describes the "religious ground motives" of Western civilization as very general, broad categories to describe the spiritual development of our civilization (form-matter; grace-nature; freedom-nature). It is

probably best, with C. T. McIntire, to limit and interpret his categories as an indication of the confessional view dominating an entire cultural area and historical period (like Islamic, Christian, secular humanist). Cf. Herman Dooyeweerd, *A New Critique of Theoretical Thought,* I (Amsterdam and Philadelphia: H. J. Paris, 1953), pp. 61ff; and McIntire, p. 18.

Dooyeweerd's description of religious ground motives manifests the influence of his monarchian tendencies, as a result of which the belief of non-Christians becomes problematic. True belief is a characteristic of Christians only, and yet he cannot deny full humanity, including belief, to non-Christians. He attempts a solution of the dilemma by introducing a religious dialectic for non-Christians (p. 64), since his monarchian tendencies do not allow him fully to acknowledge the function of faith in non-Christians. Cf. Fernhout, pp. 111ff.

11. Cf. R. Bijkerk, *Theories of Personality* (Grand Rapids: Calvin College, stenciled syllabus): "Ultimately it is here, in the field of personality-theory, that we see the psychologist try to *integrate* all the diversified elements of his trade and answer the question : 'What is man?' In the issues of personality theory we find the basic point of contact between fundamental religious conviction on the one hand, and scientific investigation of that was given to us for exploration on the other hand" (p. 2). "However, it becomes apparent that Rogers soon generalizes his findings from the consulting room to life and man as such. And at this point the attempt to understand and describe what is happening in certain clients changes into a philosophy of human nature, a view of man, a philosophical anthropology. It happened in Freud's development, in Adler and Jung, and it is still happening in Rogers. And might it perhaps be, that in the final analysis the view of man, the 'belief about human nature,' was always there from the start, implicitly, shaping the therapist in his own development *as a therapist*, influencing him decisively in his choice of methods and in his confidence in one approach rather than another, ultimately emerging triumphantly as a general *theory* from out of the struggle of the therapist toward scientific generalizations, emerging with a secretive or possibly even with an outspoken 'I told you so!'? To what extent is the theory sensitive to truly empirical data, especially to data *conflicting* with the theory; to what extent is the theory a formal justification of a view held already long before even the need for a theory became felt, a justification *not* sensitive to contrary empirical evidence? In other words: a particular philosophy of man, not arising out of scientific research, but an *a priori* commitment, is primary and basic, as Rogers himself appears to insist. A discussion, then, can finally be conducted only *on the level* of views of man, i.e. in terms of philosophy and metaphysics" (pp. 187ff).

12. Cf. for example, Leslie Stevenson, *Seven theories of Human Nature* (New York: Oxford University Press, 1974); S. Maddi, *Personality Theories: A Comparative Analysis* (Homewood, Ill.: Dorsey Press, 1968).

13. Cf. Duane P. Schultz, *A History of Modern Psychology* (New York: Academic Press, 1969).

14. Cf. James H. Olthuis, "The Word of God," and "The Word of God and Biblical Authority" (Toronto: Institute for Christian Studies, 1973; 1974; stenciled essays); "Needed, an Evangelical Doctrine of Creation" (an essay to be published shortly); and "God, Word, Creation: A Reply to Professor Frame," in: *Vanguard* (January-February 1975), pp. 9-11.

15. For an overview, a critical evaluation, and a bibliography of Vollenhoven's publications, see Al Wolters, "On Vollenhoven's Problem-Historical Method" (this volume); Calvin G. Seerveld, "Biblical Wisdom underneath Vollenhoven's Categories for philosophical Historiography," in: *Philosophia Reformata*, 38 (1973), pp. 127-43.

16. Cf. S. Freud, *Beyond the Pleasure Principle*, Standard Edition, Vol. XVIII, 7-64 (London: The Hogarth Press, 1955): "On the contrary, it must be an *old* state of things, an initial state from which the living entity has at one time or other departed and to which it is striving to return by the circuitous paths along which its development leads. If we are to take

it as a truth that knows no exception that everything living dies for *internal* reasons—becomes inorganic once again—then we shall be compelled to say that *'the aim of life is death'* and looking backwards, that *'inanimate things* existed before living ones.' "

"The attributes of life were at some time evoked in inanimate matter by the action of a force of whose nature we can form no conception" (p. 38).

"They [the instincts of self-preservation and self-assertion] are component instincts whose function it is to assure that the organism shall follow its own path to death, and to ward off any possible ways of returning to inorganic existence other than those which are imminent in the organism itself" (p. 39).

"The germ-cells, therefore, work against the death of the living substance and succeed in winning for it what we can only regard as potential immortality, though that may mean no more than a lengthening of the road to death" (p. 40).

"For on our hypothesis the ego instincts arise from the coming to life of inanimate matter and seek to restore the inanimate state; whereas as regards the sexual instincts, though it is true that they reproduce primitive states of the organism, what they are clearly aiming at by every possible means is the coalescence of two germ-cells which are differentiated in a particular way" (p. 44).

"Perhaps we have adopted the belief that all living substance is bound to die from internal causes because there is some comfort in it. If we are to die ourselves, and first to lose in death those who are dearest to us, it is easier to submit to a remorseless law of nature, to the sublime *Ananke* [Necessity] than to a chance which might perhaps have been escaped" (p. 45).

17. See, for example, Rousas J. Rushdoony's analysis and evaluation in his *Freud* (Philadelphia: Presbyterian and Reformed Publishing Co., 1965). Cf. also Jay E. Adams' limited analysis and negative evaluation of Freud's view in his *Competent to Counsel* (Nutley: Presbyterian and Reformed, 1972).

18. Cf. Linda R. Leenders, *The Anthropological Model in the Writings of C. G. Jung* (Toronto: Institute for Christian Studies, 1975; stenciled paper, 31 pp.).

19. H. Dooyeweerd, *The Theory of Man: Thirty-two Propositions on Anthropology* (Toronto: Institute for Christian Studies, stenciled paper, 8 pp.). Cf. Harry Fernhout's analysis of Dooyeweerd's anthropology in *Man, Faith and Religion in Bavinck, Kuyper and Dooyeweerd* (Toronto: Institute for Christian Studies, 1975, unpublished master's thesis; 139 pp.).

20. Dooyeweerd's view of time is deeply influenced by neo-Kantianism and his monarchian frame of reference. (The idea of a transcendental logical subject re-emerges in his idea of a supra-temporal heart, and the "Gegenstand" idea is maintained in his epistemology; while the structuralistic monarchianism fosters a "static" view of time.) As a result, he uses the idea of time to explain the possibility of theoretical "Gegenstand" (abstracting becomes a breaking of the temporal order of time; cf. pp. 28, 41, 92). Cf. H. Hart, "Problems of Time: An Essay," in: *Philosophia Reformata*, 38 (1973), pp. 30-42, who seeks to save certain aspects of Dooyeweerd's view of time.

With Popma, however, it seems more helpful to me to understand time as an irreducible dimension of reality rather than a "continuous order of coherence in the duration of things," or "temporality, as subjection to conditions, dependence on response to the law." Cf. K. J. Popma, *Inleiding in de Wijsbegeerte* (Kampen: Kok, 1956), pp. 59ff. There is a Word of God for functioning directionally, modally, typically, configurationally, and also temporally. Temporality has to do with beginning, development, duration and ending; with developmental stages; and with periodicity. God set a law for the length of days of different kinds of creatures. Man can obey or disobey the law for our temporality. Thus we are to know our days and redeem the time. By making these few comments, we do not pretend to have fathomed the mystery of time. Nevertheless, temporality is an obvious dimension of reality which cannot be explained in terms of any of the other dimensions, but which can yet be traced structurally and studied empirically, as for example in the developmental stages of man or the periods of history.

21. Cf. Dave Campbell and Mary Gerritsma, "I'm a Sinner . . . You're a Sinner; Nouthetic Counseling and Your Problems," in: *Vanguard* (March-April, 1974), pp. 5-8, 19-21; Mary Gerritsma, "Competent to Counsel: A Review," in: *Vanguard* (October, 1973), pp. 25-7; J. S. Hielema, *Pastoral or Christian Counseling: A Confrontation with American Pastoral Theology, in Particular Seward Hiltner and Jay E. Adams* (Utrecht: Elinkwijk, 1975; doctoral dissertation; 305 pp.), Chapter IV, "Comparison and Evaluation."

22. Cf. Al Wolters, *Our Place in the Philosophical Tradition* (Toronto: Institute for Christian studies, 1975): "To summarize: what I am saying is *first*: that Christians of whatever tradition (not excluding our own tradition at the Institute for Christian Studies) have to recognize in principle the *de facto* influence of the Western philosophical tradition in their thinking. This means that we are all to some extent *synthesis* thinkers—meaning by that term the intermingling in a single perspective of both Biblical and unbiblical patterns of thought" (p. 14). "The important thing is not whether we are synthesis thinkers, but whether we recognize it and do anything about it" (p. 15). "They [Vollenhoven and Dooyeweerd] too stand in a philosophical tradition. Does that mean they were simply a product of their times? Certainly not. The great question to ask is—what did they do with the tradition, in what direction did they bend it and how does that bending measure up to the Scriptural demands for obedience and making every thought captive to Christ?" (p. 17).

23. Cf. James H. Olthuis, "Must the Church Become Secular?" in: *Out of Concern for the Church* (Toronto: Wedge Publishing Foundation, 1970), pp. 105-25; H. Richard Niebuhr, *Christ and Culture* (New York: Harper and Row, 1956).

24. Cf. Don Sinnema, *The Uniqueness of Certitudinal Discourse, with Special Reference to the Language of Scripture* (Toronto: Institute for Christian Studies, 1975; stenciled paper, 24 pp.).

25. Agnes Sutherland Ronaldson senses the significance of this scientific task when she states in her *The Spiritual Dimension of Personality* (Philadelphia: Westminster Press, 1965): "It is assumed that spirit cannot be known empirically, but must be apprehended by faith, or through revelation. Thus, though spirit is apprehended in human experience, it is not a fact of knowledge to be ascertained by science" (p. 28).

"These human qualities [trust, autonomy, initiative, as well as relevance of faith and grace to personality development] come under scrutiny as data of subjective, personal experience as well as data which can be, to a limited extent, ascertainable by objective, scientific methods. It would seem that to gain the fullest understanding of such spiritual qualities in personality both approaches need to be employed" (p. 29).

26. Ronaldson, pp. 103, 128.

27. For some additional theses, see A. H. De Graaff, *A Christian Perspective in Psychotherapy: Some Theses* (Toronto: Institute for Christian Studies, 1972; stenciled paper, 9 pp.).

Augustine's Early Writings on a Liberal Arts Education

WENDY ELGERSMA HELLEMAN

Introduction

In the first few centuries of the existence of the Christian church, it was typical for those with greater intellectual ability to have received their formal education outside the church, prior to their conversion. The church, especially the more ascetic strains in it, tended to be suspicious of these newly won converts. But there was also an awareness that these Christians could make a real contribution; in fact, not only did the church generally welcome them, it also allowed many of them to attain positions of great authority.

For this reason it is important to study closely how educated converts such as Augustine responded to the challenge of rethinking and remolding the thought-patterns acquired in the pagan schools. They in turn greatly influenced the church, and largely determined the thinking of other Christians on political and legal, as well as cultural and educational, matters.

This was especially true in the late fourth century, when the church was beginning to discover that while the empire around it was crumbling, its own role in society had steadily increased from the time Constantine had granted it much freedom. In this very critical period of transition from "pagan" antiquity to the "Christian" Middle Ages, Augustine began his work in the church and eventually came to play a substantial role in determining the outlook of the church in many matters. His views on the subject of a program of education appropriate for Christians are of importance not only because they greatly influenced the church at that time but also in that they were determinative in deciding whether and to what degree the classical heritage of the Greco-Roman world was to survive into the Middle Ages, to be incorporated into the programs of the monastic schools.

One of the basic questions to be considered in an evaluation of Augustine's writings on education is that of the extent to which his conversion influenced his educational views. Is he indeed beginning to cast his thinking into a new mold? How does he view the relationship between God's revelation in the Scriptures and salvation in Christ Jesus, on the one hand, and whatever is good or valuable in the pagan classical tradition of which he was an intellectual heir, on the other? What place does he assign the latter in the educational edifice? Does he continue to accept it, does he reject it wholesale, or is there a middle way?

In this essay I wish to focus particular attention on the writings of the earlier period, before his ordination—in part because these are less often dealt with from the point of view of educational theories, but especially because, at Cassiciacum, Augustine was still intellectually and emotionally close to the education he had acquired, but also freshly challenged through his conversion to rethink many former assumptions. He was then still teaching a number of pupils in what may be characterized as a liberal arts program. He realized that his own education had contributed to his coming to desire the Christian faith and understand it. Yet he was already aware of the need to distantiate himself from former practices and ideas.[1]

I hope to show that Augustine's later description, in the *Retractationes,* of his intentions in dealing with education in the liberal arts in these early writings, namely, of "desiring to arrive, or to lead others, by as it were a certain number of stages, through that which is corporeal to that which is incorporeal,"[2] does indeed describe and characterize what was for Augustine a very important and central concept. Although it is more clearly present in the earlier writings, this concept was not abandoned in later times. Yet it has not always been recognized as such in the later writings, mainly because it has generally been inadequately understood in the earlier literature.

De Ordine

Of the dialogues Augustine wrote during the stay at Cassiciacum, the *De Beata Vita,* the *Contra Academicos* and the *Soliloquia* reveal a high evaluation of the liberal arts, but the *De Ordine* deals most extensively with education. Here Augustine lays the foundation for his later, more specific studies of the individual subject areas. In this dialogue he is obviously still only at the beginning of a long process of growth in understanding the Christian faith. But he does already show a real Christian concern in his struggle with problems, such as that of evil, which date from the Manichaean and Skeptic periods.

The central theme which emerges in this dialogue is that of the need to find order, both in the universe and in the propaedeutic studies necessary for dealing with more complex problems. Precepts for an upright and virtuous life must first be taken to heart and expressed in the manner of living; knowledge and understanding, however, come in a twofold manner: through authority and through reason (II 9, 26). Although authority may be an acceptable avenue to the truth for some, it has drawbacks, such as the danger of deception. Following reason, which is to be preferred, one is led through an elaborate process of ascent, from those sciences which were recognized by Aristotle as "productive," i.e. grammar, dialectics, and rhetoric (the "trivium"), through those designated as "contemplative," i.e. arithmetic, music, geometry, and astrology, which make up the "quadrivium" (II 11, 30—15, 42).

The real goal of this process is to come to an understanding of unity, for only from that pinnacle of learning and knowledge concerning the world can the vast panorama of the universe be rightly observed and can all the more complex questions of matter, time, space, good and evil, truth, the soul, and God be dealt with. Although he characterizes these problems as philosophical, and indeed these were the questions with which the philosophers traditionally busied themselves, we should not ignore their deeply religious character.[3] Augustine speaks of the process of studies in the liberal arts as a process of purification, of cultivation of the soul (I 2, 4), of healing and restoration to the light, i.e. the truth (I 8, 24), or of preparation so that one will be better equipped and more steadfast in clinging to the truth once it is found[4] (II 4, 13—5, 14).

The discussions in which we see Augustine struggle to understand God as the author and ruler of the universe do not leave one in doubt about the sincerity of the conversion and the acceptance on faith, or on "authority," of the Biblical message of salvation. However, in the attempt to lay the foundation for a rational explanation of that message, there is still much evidence of typically Platonist problematics and conceptions which will eventually prove to be incompatible with Scriptural truth. The emphasis on withdrawal from things of sense to turn inward upon oneself and gain self-knowlege (I 1, 3) calls to mind a popular theme among the Neo-Platonists.[5] The first *principium* of true philosophy and its *intellectus*, which are mentioned as the goals of understanding (II 5, 16, 9, 26), are but thinly disguised references to the Neoplatonic *to hen* (the One) and *nous* (intellect).[6] The Platonist and Pythagorean overtones are also strong in the description of that truth to which the soul is led by reason and introspection when, in quest of its immortality, it finds its power derived from number and its goal to arrive at that number by which all other numbers and all things are numbered, namely, the one, or unity.

To explain these references, we must turn to the account of the *Con-*

fessiones, for in the final period before his conversion, Augustine had found in writings of the Platonists the help he had been looking for to solve problems plaguing him from the Manichaean period. Especially the Platonist conception of the incorporeal nature of God and of evil had helped him understand and also accept the Biblical account. As a result of this, however, he also tended to explain Biblical references to body, soul, and spirit in terms of Platonist usage of these terms.[7]

It was undoubtedly because Platonist conceptions helped him in accepting the Bible that Augustine thought an understanding of these concepts was a necessary prerequisite for understanding the Bible as such. His emphasis on the importance of reason must therefore, at least in part, be attributed to the course of his own intellectual odyssey. For reason is in the *De Ordine* the guide through the studies necessary for understanding the difficult concepts. Although theoretically authority is, by itself, sufficient to lead one to the truth, and reason is the tool of the educated for understanding that same truth, in effect reason becomes much more than an alternative route. If we are really dependent on reason for an interpretation of the truth, then what Augustine is actually doing is setting up reason as a second authority, which determines the first and in effect cancels its primacy.[8] The very distinction between reason and authority, in many ways reminiscent of the Platonic distinction between sure knowledge and mere opinion, is itself unfortunate. Augustine does not seem ever to have realized fully the problems consequent upon such an illegitimate dichotomy. As matters stand at this point in his development, there is a strong suggestion that Augustine is still allowing pagan thought-patterns to dominate his thinking, certainly as it relates to education.

The evaluation of the place given to the liberal arts must be made in the light of this assessment of the role of reason. They are, as it were, the stepping stones of reason in its ascent. Their role is also reminiscent of the preparatory role of mathematics for philosophy in Plato's scheme. The value of these arts is all the more enhanced if, by passing from the simpler and lowly to the more complex and elevated of these, following reason as guide, one can be led to that truth by which an intellectually-oriented interpretation of the Bible is to be determined.

Through the liberal arts, by a progressive series of abstractions, one is to be led to a realization of the immaterial principles, especially number and numerical ratios in all things, and from there to an understanding of unity in the universe. This is to give one the vantage point from which to be able to survey all. With such a vision, many common and perplexing problems can be placed in proper perspective. The basic process for which the liberal arts are most significant, that of withdrawing from what is bodily and material toward that which is immaterial and incorporeal, is most clearly seen in the sciences of contemplation, or in the "quadrivium."

In these the soul is most clearly abstracting from evidence of sense and turning to that which is discernible by the intellect.

The process of going from what is simple to the complex, from what is bodily to immaterial truth, clearly involves and demands an ascent of the soul. This also presupposes a view of reality in which that which is corporeal or bodily is considered to be inferior, whereas that which is incorporeal—in ascending order, the soul, its reasoning powers, its intellect, and that which can be known by reason and intellect—shows a gradually increasing possession of reality, being, or truth. Only God is fully Being or Truth; the highest point to which the soul's vision can attain is a type of contemplative possession of God.[9]

Such a view of gradation in the levels of being as the basis for the ascent and mystical union of the soul does indeed give the impetus for an education in the liberal arts in Augustine's account. However, when, according to this view, the corporeal is identified with that which in the Bible is designated as carnal, i.e. as belonging to the earthly or sinful man, and the incorporeal is identified with the spiritual, or that which is of grace, a real hindrance is posed for any attempt to come to a truly Scriptural understanding of the nature of the Creator-creature relationship. It would also make such central Christian beliefs as the incarnation of Christ and the resurrection of the body problematic, and give rise to unhealthy speculation concerning the nature and origin of the soul, and about its relation to the body, to give but a few of the more obvious examples of hazards attending such a view. As for the implications of this view for the understanding of the relationship between pagan and Christian thought, it would tend to support an idea of continuity between them, rather than lead one to see a radical antithesis between Greek philosophical conceptions and Biblical truth. For Augustine this view could reinforce the high esteem in which he still held the pagan writings on the liberal arts and philosophy, considering these at the very least to have placed him on the right track toward obtaining the full truth.

We know that Augustine did take seriously the propaedeutic value of the liberal arts for the study of religious-philosophical questions. In the *Retractationes* he says that in Milan, while preparing for the Easter baptism, he began work on a very ambitious project to write a series of works on the various liberal disciplines—grammar, rhetoric, dialectics, music, geometry, arithmetic, and philosophy. Significantly, astrology, probably because of the overt pagan associations with its practice, is missing from this list. He characterizes his aim in writing on the liberal arts as "desiring to arrive, or to lead others, by as it were a certain number of stages, through that which is corporeal to that which is incorporeal."[10] Nor did he, at the end of his life, assess this attempt in a critical fashion: throughout the *Retractationes* he is quite specific in stating what he would like to see deleted or would have wished to say differently in his writings. The theme is clearly applicable to the *De Ordine*, and, as we shall see, it is also characteristic of further works on education.

All that is left to us of the large-scale project is the first part of the *De Musica*, since the second part was never written. The only work which was completed, the *De Grammatica*, was lost already in Augustine's own time.[11] A beginning was made on the *De Dialectica, De Rhetorica, De Geometria, De Arithmetica,* and *De Philosophia*. But even these he was unable to find at the time of writing the *Retractationes*.

De Musica

From the *De Musica* one may obtain some insight into how Augustine would have wished to develop the other disciplines and how in each discipline he would proceed from that which is corporeal to the incorporeal.

The first five books of the *De Musica* form a technical treatise on rhythm which differs little from the type of manual a non-Christian scholar of the period might have composed for his poetry students. It is in the sixth book that we find evidence of an attempt to proceed from the corporeal to the incorporeal (VI 2, 2), from a consideration of mutable numbers of sense perception to the incorporeal numbers of eternal truth. This book gives a more philosophical treatment of the nature of sound, of the presence of rhythm or number in sound, and of sensation in general.

In the first chapter of book six, Augustine goes to some length to explain the different character of this book and to justify what may appear to be a rather schoolbookish approach to music in the previous books. By referring to these as puerile, he wishes to indicate not only that they properly belong to the education of the child but also that in a sense they are childish or trivial. Nevertheless, his purpose was to lead young men, or whoever still clung to *carnalibus litteris*, gradually, with reason as guide, away from matters of sense experience (VI 1, 1). He spoke like the grammarians or the *poetici* for the sake of slowly weaning those too much involved with matters of the flesh. His choice was the roundabout route, not trusting his wings of faith to fly more quickly over the same road. Augustine even expresses doubt whether his own wings have yet been sufficiently nourished on the faith to be trustworthy.[12] However, he hopes that those who have taken the time to work through the first five books will find themselves rewarded in the sixth, in which they find the fruits of the earlier labors.

Augustine also specifies those for whom he had intended the work. Christians without the necessary educational background he advises not to attempt tackling the difficulties of this route, but, using well-nourished wings of faith, to fly straight to the goal. Those lacking both education and wings of piety are advised first to nourish their wings and fly to the fatherland without attempting this tortuous path. Those for whom these books were written are men who, like himself, had a good education in pagan literature and who are still attached to it. They are wasting their talents on unworthy matters by remaining with their error. Augustine wants to point out to these men that they are trapped and to show them the road they must take to escape the snares.

In the last chapter of this book, Augustine returns to this theme. He here acknowledges that his own wings have not sufficiently been purified by the flame of love, and expresses also a certain mistrust of at least some types of purification by reason. This is probably a reference to the Manichaeans, who had deceived him and others with false promises of reason and knowledge.[13] Examples of other faithful sons of the church who also used abilities acquired through childhood education to refute heretical statements encouraged him in following the tortuous path of reason to retrieve others ensnared in it.

Using a verse from Ambrose's hymn *Deus creator omnium*,[14] Augustine, in the second chapter, begins to define and organize the various types of number related to sound. Of the numbers enumerated, the *sonantes* (i.e. numbers or rhythm in sound as it is heard, also called sensuous or corporeal) are lowest. The *recordabiles* (i.e. numbers of sound in memory by which we recognize what is heard) are next, these having been caused by higher, more active numbers in the soul. Then come the *occursores* (i.e. numbers in the sense of hearing in the ear, where the soul actively receives sounding numbers). Higher again are the *progressores* (i.e. numbers of the active soul as it recites the verse and impresses number on what is corporeal). Judicial numbers, *judiciales* (i.e. those by which we judge what is heard and find delight in its sound) are at the top of this list, for they are not confined with respect to time or space nor subject to what is corporeal and mutable (VI 6, 16—7, 17).

But there are numbers which are even higher than these, numbers by which we judge the delight received through judicial numbers. These numbers reflect an appraisal by reason to determine the correctness of our prior judgment of delight (VI 9, 23-4). And reason itself is in turn directed by even more hidden and powerful numbers, because its work is done in accordance with numbers received from that realm above itself where equality, order and unity reside eternally (VI 9, 24—11, 29). We must therefore turn away from preoccupation with corporeal numbers and contemplate these highest numbers, for in them we find God's law (VI 13, 40ff).

The transition from that which is corporeal to the incorporeal, then, again forms the central theme. In the discussion of music, Augustine shows how one may use the study of rhythmics not only as one of the stepping stones in the ascent of the soul, as in the *De Ordine*, but also as, by itself, revealing all the gradations of number through which, with the help of reason and contemplation, one can pass from the sensory corporeal experiences of the soul to the incorporeal principles belonging to the eternal and unchanging wisdom of God. The ascending order of numbers in sound here corresponds to the ascent of the soul through the gradations of being as described in the *De Ordine* and the *Confessiones*.[15]

The imagery of the twofold manner of arriving at the goal of life, the fatherland, the truth, has changed. Augustine here speaks of purification by reason as the longer, more difficult and roundabout way. The flight on wings purified by faith and love here parallels the way of authority mentioned earlier. This book evidences a greater awareness of the pitfalls and snares along the path of reason, but reason is nevertheless still a very important guide in leading men from preoccupation with the carnal.[16] Platonist-Pythagorean number theories also still dominate the account to such an extent that it is very difficult to even understand what Augustine is trying to demonstrate in this book without a thorough understanding of the pagan philosophical themes.

Yet the book evidences also an increasingly deeper understanding of Biblical ideas. There is a much greater attempt to integrate the Biblical themes of creation, man's sinful nature, and the sacrificial death of Christ with the central theme in a music education, leading from the corporeal to the incorporeal.[17] The Biblical themes are still largely interpreted in terms of Platonist philosophical structures, but the fact that Augustine does begin to integrate an appeal to Biblical texts and themes is an advance, one more step in the right direction. The attempt in book six to justify his dealing with what may be looked upon as *puerilia* probably reflects a growing sensitivity to attitudes in the church towards an education in the pagan schools. A certain distantiation from *carnalibus litteris* and some types of reasoning, an almost pastoral concern for those ensnared by false promises, and an appeal to examples of other sons of the church also indicate growing maturity in the Christian faith.

Marrou, in his *St. Augustin et la fin*, pp. 580-3, has, however, concluded from such evidence in book six and especially the first chapter, that it must have been written much later, certainly after the ordination in 391. In the *Retractationes*, Augustine does say that the work was completed in Africa, but Marrou takes this to refer to the period before ordination. This view seems to find support in a letter of Memorius who had, around 406, asked Augustine for a copy of the *De Musica*. In the reply Augustine mentioned that he could not find the first five books, and was sending the sixth emended or corrected. We have no further indication from Augustine's own hand concerning the extent of the correction or emendation. If, as Marrou suggests, Augustine added the first chapter and a transitional sentence for the second chapter, he probably added the final paragraphs of the final chapter at that time as well.

Augustine does appear to demonstrate a maturity in Christian thinking in the introductory chapter and final paragraphs of book six, which is considerably advanced beyond that of the *De Ordine*. Are these differences significant enough, however, to support the conclusions of Marrou? A very basic theme in the *De Ordine*, that of the guidance of reason, and that of the need to pass on from the corporeal to the incorporeal, has remained substantially unaltered. Nor should one be surprised to find a rather extensive introduction for the sixth book, which takes an approach to the subject very different from that of the previous books of the *De Musica*. The use of a Christian hymn in the discussion would certainly be somewhat "unorthodox" to grammarians. Augustine wants his philosophical approach to music to be taken seriously by Christian colleagues as well as non-Christian ones. The smooth transition from the introduction to the rest of the sixth book does not reinforce the argument of discontinuity, nor do we have an original manuscript of the sixth book together with the other five books which Augustine could not find at the time of writing Memorius. Even if we do accept a certain lapse of time between the first five books and the sixth, Augustine does not, in the introductory remarks of that sixth book, wish to distance himself from the work of the previous books as much as to point out their peculiar value. The purpose of his work was to give others the benefit of his experience, to help those ensnared in the trap in which he had himself until recently been caught: that of a proud adherence to literary occupations for their own sake. By reintegrating philosophy with literature, he wanted to disentangle others as he had learned to disentangle himself.

I do not therefore believe that the arguments for substantial additions to the sixth book at the very late date of the correspondence with Memorius have sufficient support to lead to the conclusion of discontinuity between introductory and final remarks and the rest of the sixth book. Augustine still has a very high regard for pagan learning in the liberal arts and philosophy, and he makes use of these in providing a study of music. Though the value of such an education may be seen to apply primarily to childhood years, Augustine does go on to defend the use of his own training, both in dealing with others who have been led astray through their education and in the refutation of heretical teachings.

De Magistro

Although the *De Grammatica* was lost, as were the beginnings of the other works dealing with the liberal arts, we may still find indications of how he might have dealt with these subjects in other works. With respect to geometry, the *De Magnitudine Animae* gives an indication of how geometrical examples might be used to help in thinking more abstractly about the noncorporeal nature of the soul.[18] As for arithmetic, the number theories are explained at various places in his works, perhaps best in the second and fourth books of the *De Doctrina Christiana*, where the approach to rhetoric and dialectics also receive attention. The introductory chapters of book eight of the *De Civitate Dei* give an account of eminent philosophers, which is probably much like what Augustine would have intended in *De Philosophia*.

Much of such information is of a later date, however. To indicate how Augustine may have intended to deal with grammar, our best source is a work written only two years after his conversion, the *De Magistro*. In this discussion (with his son Adeodatus) of the role of words in learning, Augustine shows how, through an orderly succession of stages in argumentation, one may proceed from an analysis of the corporeal phenomena of words and their sounds to the incorporeal aspects of their meaning.

Of special interest is the summary of the introductory discussion on the uses of words as signs and the interrelationships of different types of signs (8,21). In a defense which may be compared to the introductory chapter of the sixth book of the *De Musica*, Augustine supports the usefulness of this discussion in terms of its preparatory nature, lest anyone think it a childish business. In leading those of weaker ability on the path to the eternal life, the pace taken and point at which one starts must be suitable for the traveler. These preliminary exercises are necessary to sharpen the mental powers, to be better equipped to endure the more intense light and heat of the realm of blessedness.[19]

In the second part of the discussion on the reality of things for which word-signs are only indicators, Augustine stresses the importance of the role of perception and understanding in knowing these things. He begins also to introduce a more abrupt distinction between things of sense perception and knowledge of intellectual concepts than was found in the *De Musica*. We need only the light of day to perceive that which we sense with our bodies, or, to use Biblical language, the carnal (12, 39). But to understand more general concepts, our reason needs the inner light of truth, to be able to discern that which is intelligible or spiritual. We must therefore listen to the truth which presides over our mind within us, our real teacher,

Christ, who dwells within the inner man, the everlasting power and wisdom of God.

Augustine has not yet by any means abandoned neo-Platonist thought-structures here. They play an important role in many of the very basic features of the discussion, such as the emphasis placed on the knowledge of intellectual concepts (as opposed to adherence to the corporeal), the illumination of the mind to behold intelligible truth, and the need to turn the will to receive illumination.[20]

Nevertheless, we see also an increasing attempt to integrate Biblical truth with philosophical statements, and in some respects Biblical ideas seem even to be getting the upper hand in determining how the basically neo-Platonist ideas are to be understood and integrated in a view of reality. Man is still considered in terms of his rational soul, but it is not reason which here leads man to an understanding of the truth by an investigation of the intellect. Augustine prays to God Himself to lead him to the goal. It is also the relative perfection of the will which determines how much of the truth is accepted through conversion or the turning of the mind to behold the truth.[21] In the very central idea of teaching intellectual concepts through the illumination of the mind, an appeal is made to the Biblical assertion that Christ is our only master and teacher, who dwells in our hearts and with His Spirit strengthens the inner man.[22]

Aside from the more general identification of what is intelligible with what is spiritual, Augustine tends to identify a basic religious knowledge of the truth in Christ with intellectual knowledge of concepts, and to interpret Christ as the *logos* (Word) illumining men's minds, in much the same way as Justin Martyr had done before him.[23] Augustine also is attempting to synthesize Biblical truth with neo-Platonic thought-structures. The Christian motivation of his thinking can hardly be doubted; yet it is still very difficult at times to determine which element is getting the upper hand. Is he using Platonist conceptions to understand a Christian view of life and reality, or is the Platonist terminology a relic, an empty shell which Christian thinking has outgrown but not yet entirely abandoned? Only subsequent developments in his thinking will clarify whether he is indeed trying to be Biblical in understanding the role of Christ as the teacher, or whether in the *De Magistro* he has basically been using Biblical ideas out of context to support previously conceived non-Biblical notions concerning education.

However, it is apparent that in the *De Magistro*, the basic ontological structure of a variety of stages on the ladder of ascent, as it is presented most clearly in the *Confessiones* VII 17, 23, remains essential to Augustine's thought. But the details of how the ascent is to proceed are beginning to change somewhat. Reason does not get as much emphasis as playing the all-important role. Reasoning about words as such, as signs, is considered in terms of dealing with that which is corporeal, and as such has only a relative value. For those who are weaker and at a lower stage of development, it can sharpen mental vision so that the mind will eventually be better able to withstand the brighter light of the realm of blessedness. Knowledge of that which is signified is more important, especially the knowledge of incorporeal concepts, which are placed above the concepts of things requiring only sense perception to be understood. Conversion, only vaguely indicated in the *De Musica*, is beginning to play a more important role in the transition from the corporeal to the incorporeal.

The role assigned in the *De Magistro* to a traditional education in a subject such as grammar, if somewhat diminished, is still a significant one. It is to help those of weaker mental abilities, or those still too much engrossed with material corporeal things to exercise their mental vision, to get them started on the road to eternal life. Augustine is no longer as enthusiastic as he was in the *De Ordine* about the essential character of these studies for understanding Biblical ideas. He refers now to the need to be attuned to the teacher within, Christ, for illumination on such matters. Without a more thoroughgoing critique of the traditionally accepted educational methods and aims, however, these changes in Augustine's thinking on education can better be characterized as shifting of emphases, for the more basic contours of the educational system remain largely undisturbed. He does not seem fully to have realized the inner connection of the concept of hierarchical gradations of being, and the concomitant ascent of the soul through a series of steps in transition from that which is corporeal to that which is incorporeal, with the more overtly pagan conception of man who, through self-purification in the sciences and philosophy, is able to perfect that which is highest in himself (his ability to reason) and so become godlike and immortal. It was the identification of what is, in Biblical terminology, carnal or sinful with what is corporeal and related to sense perception, of what is spiritual and of grace with what is noncorporeal and immaterial, which blinded Augustine to this, and also prevented him from recognizing the Biblical truth of God's love and our salvation in Christ as the very foundation of educational endeavor, not only its goal and culmination.

Although in later writings it may not be as much in the foreground, Augustine does not abandon his view of the hierarchical ordering of reality as the basis of his conception of education in terms of the ascent of the soul from the inferior levels of that which is corporeal and mutable to that which is eternal and incorporeal. Even in the *De Doctrina Christiana*, Augustine reveals a belief in the superiority of the sciences pertaining to reason over those based on bodily sense, and speaks of turning from corporeal appearances to the human mind, and to the immutable source of all things in God (II 38, 57—39, 59). Also in the *De Trinitate* Augustine still speaks of ascending from what is material under the guidance of reason to the unchangeable truth itself (XII 5, 5), going from what we have in common with animals, through a rational cognition of that which is temporal, to a cognition of that which is eternal and intelligible (XII 15, 25).

In other passages of the *De Trinitate*, Augustine also recalls some of his earlier ideas on methods to be used in education. As he explains why he began to work as he did (by seeking an image of the triune God first in the outer man, and later in the inner man, in science and wisdom), he says that the mind exercised in the lower things would be better developed to contemplate the divine Trinity, be it in obscure and shadowy form (XIII 20, 26). In the recapitulation of book fourteen, Augustine further explains that he wanted to lead those of slower understanding by external and sensible things which are more easily understood, being seen by the eyes of the flesh, to the inner power in man by which he reasons about what is temporal, beyond which is a yet greater power, by which he contemplates the things which are eternal (XIV 4, 10).

Conclusion

With respect to his thinking on the appropriate education for the Christian, Augustine revised his conceptions mainly by identifying some crucial Biblical ideas with neo-Platonic concepts, such as that of incorporeality. He does not seem to have realized fully the consequent distortion of Biblical truth this entailed. It was this distortion, basically, which allowed him to claim that the goal of a Christian education was to lead others from preoccupation with that which is corporeal to the incorporeal. He did concede that, parallel to the way of reason, the path of faith or of authority could also lead one to the truth. But for those who followed the guidance of reason, the liberal arts are of great value in helping one to abstract from matters of sense and proceed to what is incorporeal.

By thus introducing the way of reason alongside the way of faith as an alternative avenue to the same goal, Augustine was actually avoiding the vital question of the pagan nature of an education in the liberal arts and philosophy as these were typically presented in the schools of late antiquity. Such an education was aimed basically at glorifying man and cultivating that which was divine or most nearly divine in man. The conception of hierarchical gradations in the order of being, which is basic to the educational goal of proceeding from the corporeal to the incorporeal, belonged integrally to such a pagan goal for education. By continuing to use the neo-Platonic terminology, Augustine showed a lack of sensitivity to the more proper role of such terms in the original conceptions.

The fact that Augustine continued to consider the studies in the liberal arts and philosophy as having propaedeutic value[24] did have a great significance for the continued existence, in the Western world, of much of the literature from pagan antiquity—its poetry, drama, works in grammar, rhetoric, geometry, philosophy, etc. Had Augustine denied any value to these traditional subjects of education, many more literary works might have been lost, for it was largely due to Augustine's influence, through Cassiodorus, that the *trivium* and the *quadrivium* came to be the mainstay of education in the monastic schools. Such an inheritance was not to be an unmixed blessing, however; without properly discerning its pagan character, and without a more thorough critique of the aims and methods of the educational tradition to which these works originally belonged, the dangers which Augustine had failed to indicate when incorporating such studies in a Christian program remained essentially intact, only to come forward again in the Renaissance, when a renewal of pagan Humanism was easily able to remove the Christian veneer and claim these writings for its own program.

Notes

1. Cf. *Confessiones* VI 6, 9-10; IX 2, 2-4; 5, 13.

2. *Retractationes* I 5, 3: "*per corporalia cupiens ad incorporalia quibusdam quasi passibus certis vel pervenire vel ducere.*" Cf. I 3, 1.

3. We might also consider many of these problems to be theological since they also involve reasoning concerning the divine. The distinction commonly made between Augustine's earlier works as philosophical and the later as theological, as in A. Sizoo, *Augustinus' Werk over de Christelijke Wetenschap* (Delft, 1933), p. 12ff, does not accurately reflect the situation. Augustine used the term *philosophy* with its full meaning, namely, the search and love for wisdom. In the later Hellenistic period, philosophers put much emphasis on matters of a deeply religious nature, especially the theme of salvation and the process of purification. This at least partly explains why Christians referred to Biblical truth as their philosophy. Cf. *De Vera Religione*, 7, 12.

4. Compare the image of taking the roundabout way to deal with complex and difficult questions such as those of the incorporeal nature of the soul, so the mind can be accustomed to a mental vision of things which is different, more subtle than that required for everyday experience, in the *De Quantitate Animae*, 4, 6. This approach is illustrated by the process of questioning from the examples of geometry, to show the way in which that which is less corporeal can be abstracted from the corporeal; cf. *De Quant. An.* 15, 25. The roundabout way trains the mind so that it will not be dazzled by the extreme brightness of the full glory of wisdom, and it provides the mind with arguments to dispel all doubt and better establish the truth once it is found; cf. *Soliloquia* I 13, 23.

5. See the introductory chapters on self-knowledge in Proclus's commentary on the *First Alcibiades*, a dialogue often used by neo-Platonists to introduce Platonic philosophy.

6. Cf. Plotinus, *Enneads*, IV 8, 3; or V 1, 1.

7. Cf. *Confessiones* III 7, 12. Although Augustine purports to be using Biblical distinctions between the carnal and the spiritual, the explanations of the difference between the

corporeal and the incorporeal are strongly reminiscent of neo-Platonist language: the corporeal has mass, and each part is less than the whole, whereas the spiritual is everywhere complete and whole. Cf. the *Enneads*, IV 9, 5.

8. In *De Ordine* II 5, 15, Augustine seems to imply that the way of faith is the easy way out of the problems, in that he characterizes those taking this way as more sluggish and too preoccupied to take the road of reason. Cf. *De Quant. An.* 7, 12, on the problem of deception in authority; also *Contra Acad.* III 20, 43, on the need for understanding as well as belief.

9. Cf. *Confessiones* VII 17, 23, on the number of steps in the ascent to the contemplation of immutable truth. Augustine passes from what is presented to sense perception, to the power of reason and judgment, and from there to the understanding, and in a flash of vision beholds what is immutable being. Cf. the *De Quant. An.* 33, 70ff on the seven levels of the soul.

10. *Retractationes* I 5, 3; cf. note 2.

11. Various manuscripts from medieval times dealing with the topics mentioned by Augustine have been attributed to him but are evidently not authentic. It may be that some of the contents derive from epitomes made of what he did write, for we do have an epitome which seems to follow the *De Musica* quite closely. But lacking in these manuscripts are the typically Augustinian speculative philosophical discussions of the disciplines, as we find in the sixth book of the *De Musica*. Augustine's treatment of the disciplines as such, as in the first five books of the *De Musica*, is not much different from the treatment of the subjects typical of his time, in the manuals of rhetoric or grammar. To say, therefore, that the definitions and classifications of the manuscripts are like those of Augustine does not prove his authorship. Cf. H. I. Marrou, *St. Augustin et la Fin de la Culture Antique* (Paris 1938), pp. 570-9.

12. Cf. the reference to the unlearned rising to heaven more easily than those with an extensive education, *Confessiones* VIII 8, 19.

13. *Confessiones* III 6, 10ff.

14. Quoted in the *Confessiones* IX 12, 32.

15. Cf. note 9.

16. See especially *De Musica* VI 10, 25.

17. *De Musica* VI 13, 40ff. Note also the appeal to the text from Eccl. 7:26 as referring to number and wisdom, VI 4, 7. See further VI 14, 43, and 17, 56ff.

18. Cf. note 4.

19. Cf. *De Ordine* II 4, 13—5, 14.

20. Compare the discussion of the soul's descent and its return to contemplate the *nous* in Plotinus' *Enneads*, IV 8.

21. *De Magistro* 11, 38.

22. Matthew 23:8-10; Ephesians 3:16-17.

23. *Confessiones* VII 9, 13ff.

24. Cf. *De Doctrina Christiana* II 39, 58, and IV 3, 4. Such studies are, of course, here dealt with from a different point of view, being evaluated in terms of contributing to an understanding of the Bible and of Biblical truth. They are therefore organized according to a unique set of distinctions, as they deal with what is instituted by God or men, what is superstitious or non-superstitious, etc; cf. II 10, 15ff on music, history, geography, logic, rhetoric, etc. But the very basic distinction between what in corporeal and noncorporeal (or what is of reason—cf. II 31, 48) is also maintained here. And so it is that even though Augustine's influence on the Middle Ages largely derives from his later work, rather than more specifically from his earlier writings, inasmuch as the theme of the transition from the corporeal to the incorporeal continued to play its role in his thinking, one must not underestimate the importance of the earlier writings in the formation of the educational theories which were handed on.

The Problem of Time and Eternity in its Relation to the Nature-Grace Ground-motive

PETER J. STEEN

Few thinkers in Western history have penetrated to the depths of the motive power of synthesis or accommodation to non-Christian life which has characterized Christendom from its beginning to the extent that the Dutch thinker Herman Dooyeweerd has done. There are, however, some features of this ground-motive which Dooyeweerd has neglected throughout his work but which are of great importance for the understanding of this ground-motive.[1] I would like to summarize some of the results of other thinkers within the school of Calvinistic philosophy and make some suggestions of my own as to a clear path to follow with respect to these neglected features.

As Dooyeweerd (*11*) has pointed out so clearly, the accommodation of the Christian ground-motive to the form-matter motive of Greek thinking resulted in a misconceiving of the nature of the law order and the temporal order.[2] Dooyeweerd points out the effect of this accommodation on the notion of creation (*11*: 8, 85-9; *9*, 28-9, 34-40; *10*, 25-48; cf. *12*: 35, 358-81, 490) and, to some extent, on the scholastic notion of the eternity of God, the eternity of man, and the interrelation of these two to time (*10*: 2-4; *12*: 399-406; cf. *30*: 126, 145). Dooyeweerd has also laid bare the connection of the teleological, eschatological, beatific vision (*visio Dei*) of nature-grace to Aristotle's entelechy and the neo-Platonic hierarchy of being. An interesting hiatus in his treatment of the Christian synthesis scholastic ground-motive is his neglect of many of the aspects of eschatology. Consideration of this neglect of eschatology also involves the need for a more thorough investigation of the questions of time and eternity in relation to eschatology. Of great help in this regard is the impressive work of Okke Jager (*20*; cf. *45*), and especially the work of K. J. Popma. The unity of conception on these issues in nature-grace thinkers is the point that struck me as I surveyed particularly Jager's work.

A general description of these points of consensus in nature-grace thinkers will be given under three related points: (1) the eternity of God, (2) the so-called "eternity" of heaven before Judgment Day, and (3) the cessation of time or "eternity" after Judgment Day.

First, and all-controlling, is the theo-ontological[3] speculation concerning God's eternity (*33*; *39*: 98-122, 143-6; *47*; *20*; *21*: 85) in which God's eternity is conceived of as an eternal now or eternal present. The formulation of Boethius, at the conclusion of his *Consolation of Philosophy*, has played an important part in this speculation. Almost without exception, this formulation has been taken over into scholastic thinking. Reformed scholastic theology operated almost exclusively with this conception. One finds this definition in Kuyper (*39*: 122-30), Schilder, Bavinck (*1*: II, 153-4), Geerhardus Vos (*57*: I, 11, 74, 75, 79-100), and Louis Berkhof (*3*: 60, 63, 104). This definition, however, is not the exclusive property of conservative Protestant and Roman Catholic thinkers. It occurs uniformly in old Protestant liberalism, as well as in neo-orthodox thinkers like Barth and Brunner and in neo-liberals like Bultmann. Okke Jager, K. J. Popma, and H. M. Kuitert have pointed out how, via nature-grace thinking, this formulation of God's eternity influenced early rationalists such as Kant and Hegel and even an irrationalistic thinker like Kierkegaard.

Popma has traced at great length the formulation of God's eternity in which past, present and future are conceived of as compressed into an eternal present (*nunc eternum*) back beyond Boethius to the pre-Socratics. Without a doubt, this notion is present in many Greek thinkers, e.g. in the pre-Socratics generally and Parmenides specifically, and in Plato and Aristotle. Although not all Greek thinkers maintained this view of God's eternity, there is an amazing conformity.[4] The fact that the uniformity is not entirely total comes out clearly and with great importance for reformational thinking in the conception of Oscar Cullmann (*9*). The wave of influence that this book, published in 1948, had and still has for modern theology and philosophy (cf. *22*, *25*) can only appear when we see that Cullmann's conception of God's eternity as linear was in stark opposition to the power which the traditional view of God's eternity, as *nunc eternum*, had exercised on thinkers until that time. The view of God's eternity as a long line was not, however, a reformational, Biblical conception. It has, as Popma points out, a scholastic background (*38*: II, 313, 316, 331; VI, 59)[5] and can also be traced to Greek thinking.

Cullmann's alternative, which seemed to leave much more room for the redemptive historical interaction of God with Israel, brought about serious revision in many quarters. This influence can be seen in the work of G. C. Berkouwer and especially in H. M. Kuitert. Both views of the eternity of God are used by scholastic nature-grace thinkers, and both are rooted deeply and intrinsically in the theo-ontological pagan tradition. But the formulation of Boethius ruled Western thinking up until the epoch-making appearance of Cullmann's *Christus und die Zeit*, when the other line started to gain ascendency.[6]

Second, correlated with this idea of God's eternity is another idea which has exercised tremendous power on Western thinking as a whole: the idea of a heaven having the characteristic of eternity as opposed to the earth with its temporality. This speculation attributes the characteristic of successionless "eternal present" to heaven, i.e. heaven in the sense in which Scripture refers to it when it speaks of Christ in His glorified nature. This heaven is the place of the angels and departed saints, as distinguished from what Scripture calls the cloudy heavens, the starry heavens, etc.[7] It is the heaven where believers go after death when they are said in some totally mysterious way to be "with Christ" or "dead in Christ" as distinguished from their being in their graves waiting for the resurrection. Heaven in this sense can be distinguished from heaven after Judgment Day. Heaven after Judgment Day is, in some scholastic conceptions, distinguished from heaven as the place of the departed believers, the angels and Christ before Judgment Day. In this speculative position, heaven before Judgment Day is held to be eternal, i.e. non-temporal.

From this notion—tied in very closely by analogy with the idea of God's eternity as an eternal now—derive all sorts of speculation. For example, Kuyper held that dead believers with Christ have no awareness of time but have a heavenly, eternal perspective on the nearness of the *parousia* (*38*: I, 248ff; III, 36,98-9; VII, 236ff; *39*: 122-31, 278; *20*: 199-207). From this scholastic perspective, the so-called heavenly eternal perspective of God and the saints serves as a hermeneutic for interpreting all the New Testament statements about the consciousness of the Christian in respect to the nearness of the *parousia*. This speculative thinking denies the time consciousness of angels and demons (fallen angels), although Scriptural confession of the Kingdom appears to involve the opposite conclusion (*39*: 228ff; *38*: VII, 236). Since angels and demons are supposed to have inhabited the so-called eternal supra-natural heavenly world, they are thought to possess the view of eternity or what, speculatively, is often called "God's point of view." God's point of view is the point of view of His eternal present in which there is no succession from future to past, and this point of view is in an analogous fashion applied to angels, demons and departed saints (Kuyper), always, of course, in a creaturely mode (*47*: *passim*).[8]

In this conception, the important relation of heaven and earth in Scripture is radically misconstrued. In this way the Christian ground-motive of Word-revelation with respect to the whole of the creation as temporal is restricted drastically to only the earth as being temporal. The cosmic law order is not seen as enforcing, conditioning and holding for all the created—both heavenly and earthly—creatures.[9] The idea of a so-called *eternal* heaven in contradistinction to a *temporal* earth implies the acceptance of two world orders, generally also called "natural" and "supra-natural."

This conception of two orders or laws or word-ideas is completely foreign to the ground-motive of Word-revelation in regard to creation. In the Scriptural revelation concerning creation, the creative world-ordering Word of God, with its ordinances, commands and laws, embraces both the heavens and the earth, which brings with it that in creation there is a subjected, relative temporal order for all created beings (*19*: 37ff). Heaven, in Genesis 1:1, embraces all possible senses of the word *heaven* as it is further explicated and revealed in Scripture. In all of Scripture, heaven and earth and their interrelations are seen as directed by and subjected to one Word of God which orders, directs and holds as law for all that is created.[10] The creation account points to this central ground-motive of creation and gives direction and content to the theoretical ground-idea of law, which is the central hypothesis for theoretical thought. This cosmic scope of the ordinances of God can never be restricted to holding only for the *temporal earthly* cosmos. The Scriptural ground-motive of creation directs our thinking to see heaven and earth as involved in an all-embracing cosmic temporality, with one cosmic genetic unfolding process (*het grote wordingsproces*—Dooyeweerd) having one history.[11]

The influence of nature-grace thinking, in which heaven is conceived of as eternal in contrast to earthly temporal existence, is found in many places. The word *spiritual* quite often has the idea of eternity with this heavenly sense involved in it.[12] Consequently, a spiritual body came to be conceived of as a non-fleshly, heavenly-adapted eternal body,[13] sexless and unable to eat (*47*: 111; *32*: 507), "like the angels,"[14] that is, eternal, supra-natural. The most important single consequence of this view of heaven as eternal is the all-controlling direction that was exercised by this nature-grace ground-motive on the reformational ground-motive of the Word of God with respect to the Kingdom of God, the hope and joy of believers, and in eschatology or last things. Eschatology and the Kingdom of God were verticalized and supra-naturalized.[15] The constant law order and cosmic temporality with its future perspective of an everlasting new earth and new heaven were relativized, restricted, and transcended in an other-worldly, heavenly, eternal direction.

The second heavenly supra-natural world-order also transformed the Biblical ground-motive of redemption as restoration and renewal of creation. In this second unbiblical world-order, eschatology culminated in the beatific vision of God in a heavenly eternal sense. This vision could be attained immediately at death when man was to become eternal. Since eternity was reached immediately at death, this meant that the perspective of the resurrection of believers at Judgment Day tended to be regarded as an unnecessary addition to this state and thus it became secondary. The meaning and ground-motive of Word-revelation for the restorative, renewing cosmic significance of Christ's resurrection for man, the earth and heaven was lost (*34*; *31*; cf. *44*; *17*). For example, the problem which the Thomistic thinker has in relating the resurrection of the body to the beatific vision (which problem in no way eluded Protestant scholasticism) betrays this verticalizing of eschatology.

Popma has shown most convincingly how this view of creaturely eternity, as applied to the realm of heaven, filtered into the life of Christendom (e.g. in hymnology, and in cherished expressions of Christians: "He died and went to his eternal abode," or: "He died and went to eternity").[16] Popma also points out in great detail how this view of eternity always involves a depreciation of the temporality of creation. This view, in one way or another, identifies time with corruptibility and imperfection, and contrasts it with the incorruptible, angelic, changeless, and perfect eternity of heaven before Judgment Day. In this way, heaven before Judgment Day is given attributes which in no way allow for the perspective of Word-revelation in its ground-motive of redemption and restoration of the earthly creation. Eschatology is super-naturalized, spiritualized, and eternalized. Scriptural vision concerning the Kingdom, resurrection, judgment, new earth, and new heaven is reinterpreted in an almost higher critical fashion; it is mythologized, spiritualized, veiled, and made ineffective. This tendency to depreciate time and to bring it to an end in one way or another is rooted deeply in pagan antiquity.

Since succession and change, in this scholastic view, are identified with corruption and imperfection, the earth, because of its so-called temporality, is not conceived of as man's everlasting, final home. Rather, true "spirituality" and piety are to be seen only in desiring one's eternal incorruptible home. In this sense, all the references in Scripture with respect to these matters are made ineffective and are not re-forming in their direction—e.g. "laying your treasures in heaven," "citizenship in heaven" (cf. Popma, *28*). This revamping and redirecting of the Biblical ground-motive concerning the Kingdom of God and the future is of great importance for Christian philosophy and especially relates to Dooyeweerd's view of the direction of cosmic time. This leads us into a third point of the consensus which can be found in nature-grace thinking regarding eternity and time.

This third point is directly related to the eternity of God and the eternity of heaven, but it functions in different ways for different thinkers. It deals with the idea that "time is for a time," the idea that time and history will cease at the Judgment. In this view, eternity is thought to begin immediately after the Judgment. This is found almost uniformly in all nature-grace thinkers and is correlated immediately with eternity as heaven. Nature-grace accommodating thinking is here trying to reinterpret, minimize, and even do away with the ground-motive of Word-revelation which points to the present and future restoration and renewal of the whole cosmos—the earth (including the kingdoms of animals, plants, things, and man) and heaven, in all its senses. In this nature-grace thinking, the state of eternity immediately succeeding the *parousia* is identified with the state of eternity which believers have at death in heaven. After Judgment Day, all temporality has disappeared and only eternity exists.

An exception to the view that time and history cease at Judgment Day is the view that time goes on endlessly as a place of torment. This view occurs infrequently but is defended by Boethius. Boethius, in semi-mystical fashion, sees man as able to transcend time through intellectualistic contemplation to the heavens which are above the controlling bands of fate that endlessly rule time on earth. Here eschatology is completely verticalized; time is the realm of soul-less bodies in hell-like punishment.[17] This Boethian view to the effect that time goes on endlessly as a kind of hell is apparently tied to his purely cosmological, dualistic thinking, in which he seems to think of time as without beginning, as well as without end. But this conception of Boethius is not at all the view of most nature-grace thinkers. For the vast majority of them, time and history cease with Judgment Day, and created eternity continues or begins.

The eternity that is thought to begin at Judgment Day for man is often without duration and is always a successionless, eternal present. The notion of change as in the second viewpoint is here also identified with corruptibility and is therefore eliminated.[18] All historical development or unfolding of any kind is denied.[19] A world-order which is eternal in character and radically discontinuous with the present temporal world replaces the constant law order and abiding temporality of the creation. The reformational ground-motive of God's faithfulness to His creation expressed by His holding to His Word or law in the process of redemption and re-creation, despite the fall of man, is suppressed. The new earth, as in the fashion of seventeenth and eighteenth century Lutheran scholasticism, is not a restored, renewed and refined old earth but one which follows the annihilation of the old and is radically discontinuous. A good feature in some Reformed scholastics is that the term *heaven* in practice often involves the new earth, although subjected to a radically new world order having hardly any continuity with the creation and time. This feature is good because it is less of a spiritualization than is found in those conceptions in which *heaven* means *eternity*, as no longer on earth, as in the second viewpoint.[20]

Some attempts have been made by Reformed scholastics to play down the notion of a timeless, successionless, eternal existence in heaven after Judgment Day. Very recent attempts try to describe the notion of this existence as a "duration without succession." Popma has subjected this description to a devastating critique in many of his works, especially with regard to Klaas Runia (*39*: 102-38). After pointing out that duration can never occur without succession, he points to the evidence that the notion of duration without succession is very characteristic of psychotic pathological experience as uncovered by psychotherapy. It must be said, however, that it at least holds to an endless duration, although it is immediately made meaningless by the fact that it is said to be without succession.

From certain texts in Scripture, especially Revelation 10:6, where it is said that "time shall be no more," nature-grace thinkers of all varieties have inferred that cosmic time will cease. This text has no bearing on this point, but rather has reference to the fact that the time of postponement of the Judgment will be no more (cf. *58*: 290, 291; *20*: 513).

The more the futuristic dimension of the *eschaton* is emphasized, the more catastrophic is the discontinuity between history before the Judgment and existence on the new earth. The Biblical idea of sojourning and suffering is falsely emphasized, and the Kingdom with its cosmic perspective having its official inauguration day at the resurrection and ascension of Christ, and driven during this present stage of history before Judgment Day by the powerful, redirecting, life-giving Word of God, is lost.[21] Increasing stress is correspondingly laid on the scholastic view of the institutional church, giving rise to different types of tensions (*26*: 14-31). In some cases, the view of eternity as beginning on the new earth at the Judgment is put in tension with eternity as being in heaven after death, as in the second viewpoint, so that the so-called "interim" (*tussentoestand*) is practically eliminated. B. Telder, who emphasizes endless time and the unity of man in a healthy reformational fashion, in stressing the future dimension of the *eschaton*, feels compelled to deny that there is any existence of believers in heaven with Christ after death, before the Judgment. For Telder, man is one, and therefore the whole man is said to be in the grave, sleeping in Jesus, awaiting resurrection (*48*; *49*; cf. *38*: III, 191-295). The unity of heaven and earth under one cosmic law order and in one cosmic time and history is here lost sight of somewhat. Telder in general is a refreshing breeze with his stress on the reformational groundmotive of redemption in its cosmic perspective in the midst of a literal jungle of misconception. His great value is that his work in general confirms the thinking of Berkouwer, Popma, Jager, and Schoonhoven. I mention his unique emphasis on the interim state to underscore the increasing tension that arises as men break with the verticalized eschatology of

Thomistic scholasticism and stress the futuristic, more historical dimension of the *eschaton*.[22]

In general, the first, second and third viewpoints have a view of eternity in common. Reformed scholasticism, which emphasized the future idea of eternity as stated in the third viewpoint, never placed as much emphasis on the second viewpoint (eternity after death) as Roman Catholic and Lutheran scholastics did. Due to the rise of Biblical theology, by which is meant exegetical theology with a redemptive historical emphasis, increasing emphasis has been placed on eschatology. With the reexamination of eschatology, and with it the developmental, historical stress of Scripture, the view of eternity present in all three viewpoints has become suspect. It is generally recognized at present that the *eschaton* has a strong present and future aspect. This presents Reformed scholasticism, which in general stressed the third viewpoint and the future dimension, with the need for a great deal of reconstruction.[23] Where the first and second viewpoints have been emphasized, and correspondingly the present dimension of eschatology, redemptive historical considerations in exegesis have also necessitated reconstruction. In these views, eternity beginning with Judgment Day was generally conceived to be the natural continuation or completion of the eternity of heaven which man enjoyed after death in the beatific vision. This view in general is still the dominant one among the "plain folk" of Christendom. In this view, the future dimension of the *eschaton* is more spiritualized, supernaturalized, with the consequence that the new earth is for all practical purposes disregarded and heaven conceived of as a final, eternal, supra-natural home in the sky. Here the future dimension of endless eternal life on the new earth is reduced to the existential present of a supernaturalized eternity of heaven.[24] Reconstruction is being done on the future dimension of eschatology so long neglected in these views. Many questions are being raised about the view of eternity and time which lies at the basis.

In summary, we see that the idea of the Greek view of God's eternity as an eternal present penetrated the church, finding classical theo-ontological expression in Boethius' definition. It serves as a paradigm, standard and analogy from which man views his own created eternity both in heaven (second viewpoint) after death and for the final state after Judgment Day. The abiding character of the cosmos and man is therefore thought of in the time-depreciating pagan perspective of a semi-divine eternal present. In this way the law-boundary between Creator and creature is broken by theo-ontological thinking.

It is my hope that this general survey of the question of eternity and time in nature-grace thinking supplements Dooyeweerd's analysis of the nature-grace ground-motive. These supplementary considerations can only be seen in their full significance in the light of the autonomy of natural reason, its metaphysical-theo-ontological speculation concerning the being of God, its idea of the soul as a substantial, rational form, etc. The autonomy of theory as the motor behind this theo-ontological speculation and many of these latter points have been investigated thoroughly by Dooyeweerd.[25] This is necessary for seeing the background of the nature-grace views of eternity as they apply to God, man and the cosmos, as well as to time, eschatology and history.

Notes

1. Reasons for this neglect and the influence of the nature-grace motive upon Dooyeweerd's own thinking are discussed in *18, 19, 46, 50*.

2. For the background of this terminology and a discussion of Dooyeweerd's thought on these points, see *19*: 39.

3. For the meaning of the term *theo-ontology*, see *38*: VII, 408. The need for a reformational perspective concerning the relationship of theological theory to confession and for clarity as to the limits of philosophical and theological theory concerning God are of great importance to the Christian community. For the lack of such clarity among members of the Calvinistic School of Philosophy, see Begemann (*2*). For an interesting critique of the traditional idea of the spirituality of God, see *21*: 6ff. For a general survey of the influence of Greek thinking in traditional formulations of the nature of God regarding His unity and simplicity, see *27*: II, 119-83. The Reformed community needs a definitive treatment of the history of this theo-ontological speculation particularly with respect to: the will or counsel of God as composed of apriori ideas or universals in God; the use of the pagan theme of macro-microcosm in elaborating a so-called analogy between God and creation; the theme of covenant added to nature as found in the Westminster Confession (ch. VII, art. 1); and all of these themes in relation to the supposed autonomy of theory.

4. For the theme of incorruptibility or eternity of the divine and its problematics in Greek thought, see P. Meyer (*23*).

5. In *39*: 110-15 there is an interesting comparison with Cullmann in Popma's comments on the Remonstrant theologian Philippus à Limborgh. See also Mekkes (*24*), who plumbs the depths of the problematics of the autonomy of theory in its relation to "origin" and to the divine in Greek thought.

6. For the general influence of Cullmann on Berkouwer and the current scene in philosophy and theology, see *20*, *passim*.

7. For the various senses of the word *heaven* in the Bible and for a study of all the facets which have played a part in the history of scholastic theology, see *38*: VII, entries "hemel," "hemel tegenover aarde," "hemels," "hemelse dingen." See also *43*.

8. On p. 116 the idea of analogy between God and man's eternity is criticised. Stellingwerff's article is a good summary of the subject as a whole, and the footnotes introduce one to the labyrinth of questions involved.

9. This important stress in Vollenhoven has been in contradistinction to Dooyeweerd from the beginning. See *54*: 15-16, 88-90; *20*: esp. 455-578; *43 passim*; *19*: 34ff.

10. For Popma's fascinating speculation about the fall of the angels not resulting in abandonment of the work of creation, see *40*: 10ff; *41*: 7-20.

11. For this emphasis, see *38*: VII, "tijd," "paradijs," "geschiedenis," "hemel tegenover aarde"; see also *29*: *passim*.

12. Dooyeweerd makes frequent use of this term, thereby showing his closeness to

Kuyper. For a usage of the term *spiritual* as equal to *organic* or *logical*, see Vander Stelt (*50*: 183) and Fernhout (*16*). *Spiritual* is often used as synonymous with the pistical or confessional (aspect). It is used also as a synonym for *religious* where the latter has been reduced to the pistical (liturgical or confessional) aspect. The richness of the term *spiritual*, especially in the Dutch language, allows it to be used as referring also to the centrally religious, or that which moves—particularly the idea of movement, motivation orientated to the idea of "breath" or "breeze," or animal motion vs. plant. Recently a usage of *spiritual* meaning *directional, normative* is surfacing. The ambiguity and richness of such usage should be the topic of a monograph.

13. For a critique of this view and a Biblical perspective, see L. Boliek, *7*; cf. *38*; *52*: 45; *35*.

14. Matthew 22:30 has been the source of all manner of speculation in which man was viewed as being like an angel at the resurrection, rather than in the precise respect mentioned by our Lord. Nature-grace thinkers regard angels as created eternal spirits without bodies, and therefore man's body must become angel-like, "spiritual," non-fleshly at the resurrection. Cf. *38*: II, 304-8; *36*: 14-19.

15. Compare H. Hart (*19*: 41). The problem of what may be variously named "spiritualization," "verticalization," "supra-naturalization," or "confessionalization" springs from this theo-ontological speculation about divinity so characteristic of archaic pagan cultures. In this tendency the Biblical idea of office is annulled, and the force of the Biblical images and figures concerning the royal sabbath enthronement, priestly service, and prophetic praise and witness with their everlasting temporal earthly focus are overlooked. The picture of God's throne in a city on a mountain on the renewed earth after having come down from heaven after all of God's enemies are destroyed, reminiscent of God's house on earth only after David's victory over the nations in the land of Canaan, shows clearly the focus of the revelation of God; God and man on the same throne in everlasting official sabbath delight and enjoyment from the work done. In Reformed circles, election is often out of temporality and office to eternity, so that election does not serve the revelation of God as a wise, sovereign, faithful Creator. The same trouble is present in Dooyeweerd's stress on the "fullness of meaning" as a supra-temporal fullness. Dooyeweerd's idea of the "opening process" is so vitally related to this that it needs correction. On this point see *19*: 41, where Hart applies his arguments against Dooyeweerd's idea of unity and totality as supra-temporal to the idea of the fullness of creation. See also my thesis (*46*: *passim*).

16. Cf. *13*, where Dooyeweerd says: "In the midst of his work God took him away at the age of 76, without a sickbed, without a death struggle, in an almost imperceptible movement (*overglijding*) from temporal life to eternal life."

17. Popma (*39*: 116-22, 125-6); Boethius (*6*: 1-114). Vollenhoven describes Boethius as an adherent of the subsistence theory, but in *Consolation* he seems semi-mystical. This may indicate two distinct phases in the development of Boethius' thought.

18. Popma gives a survey of various Reformed scholastics who held this view (*34*; *38*: II, 309-44; *37*: 69, 241-83; *39*: 134). Also found in Jager (*20*: *passim*).

19. This view is present in Geerhardus Vos. For the influence of the later Aristotle on Vos, see *56*: ch. 6, "Heavenly Mindedness," 133-55. Here his use of the word *transcendent* shows dualistic, purely cosmological thinking. For his use of eternity and time, see *58*: 40-1, 71, ch. 12, "The Eternal State," 288-316. On p. 290 there is a good emphasis of allowing for duration and divisibility of time units, but Vos consistently eliminates all change and development from the eternal state and so runs into problems with his own good emphasis. Cf. again p. 331. In the *ISBE* (*International Standard Bible Encyclopedia*), II, p. 990, Vos' view of heaven is tied too much with his idea of the supra-natural and transcendental, and so the perspective of the new earth suffers. The tension is manifest when *heaven* primarily means *changelessness*, while he is forced to recognize eternal life as involving endless time and the

new earth. The tension between nature-grace and the reformational line comes out when he says: "The central abode of the redeemed will be in heaven, although the renewed earth will remain accessible to them as a part of the inheritance" (p. 991). In *55*: 259, the supra-natural heavenly is definitely regarded as another world-order—a sure sign of nature-grace influence: "To raise the religion of time to the plane of eternity . . . ." For a discussion of this, see Berkouwer (*5*: 266-99).

20. The guarantee for the identity of the *old* earth and the *new* earth, the first earth and the second, or the first body and the second is not to be located in anything in creation, all of which is temporal, changing, dependent, and whose abiding character does not lie "in itself." It is, rather, to be found in the Word of God, whose power causes the earth to abide. The idea of a substance that is supposed to underlie the identity of new and old is a doctrine found in purely structural thinkers and is very characteristic of Calvinists as they battled the Lutheran theory of the annihilation of the earth. See *5*: 266-99; *42*: 555-67.

21. Cf. Douma (*14*: 344-56) for a faulty limitation of sojourning.

22. For a tracing of the shifts from present to future emphasis and vice versa as they relate to the question of time and eternity, see *20*: *passim*.

23. The most dangerous attitude to be combatted is the skeptical one, which says that all thought about the future is futile. But the purpose of this article is not to offer a speculative roadmap about the future, eternity, heaven, and the new earth, but to liberate the Biblical vision of the new earth from the tangle of theo-ontological speculation which has led to skepticism. Our joy is the vision of a new age which has begun. There is no need for speculation; we can experience the power of that age to come in our lives already. Unless the human imagination is renewed and led by the faith vision of the new earth, and not by fear, the public witness to the scope of the Kingdom in an age of increasing persecution and deception cannot long endure, and accommodation and defeatism are sure to come.

24. The importance of the new earth as the everlasting horizon for God's people has been emphasized by various members of the school. Vollenhoven (*54*: 90) says: "After death, too, the soul awaits the awakening of the body, and in this respect it also differs from the angels. And the ideal of the Christian, then, is not to 'return to the fatherland of souls' but to inhabit the new earth on which righteousness dwells." Zuidema stresses that Ockham's eschatology does not allow for the Scriptural perspective of everlasting work on the new earth (*59*: 138). Van Riessen (*51*: 81) modifies *eeuwigheid* (eternity) to *oneindigheid* (infinity). The transcendental direction of cosmic time and of the faith function points to *oneindigheid* and not to *eeuwigheid*, as in Dooyeweerd. It is in striking contrast to this and to the work of Popma that Dooyeweerd never mentions the new earth in all of his works. The Kingdom of God is always the eternal and heaven. This, in the light of what we have seen, is an indication that he has not extricated himself from the nature-grace perspective on these points. O. Jager's work is here definitive, especially *20*: 459-578, where many questions relating to these three areas are treated with constant and effective Scriptural analysis. K. J. Popma has dealt with the subject all his life and has been very influential. Berkouwer (*5*: I, ch. VII) is also confirmatory and at points quite original. Schoonhoven (*43*) confirms from a somewhat different perspective. There is also a wealth of material in the old stand-by, P. Fairbairn (*15*: 328-61). By surveying these men and their writings, a staggering case can be made against the views mentioned.

25. See note 2. Cf. *8*: 41-65.

Bibliography

1. BAVINCK, H., *Gereformeerde Dogmatiek*; Kampen: J. H. Kok, 1908.

2. BEGEMANN, A. W., "Fundering voor een bijbelse anthropologie," in: *Correspondentiebladen v. d. Ver. v. Calvinistische Wijsbegeerte*, 35 (1971), pp. 21-43.

3. BERKHOF, L., *Systematic Theology*; London: Banner of Truth Trust, 1941.

4. BERKOUWER, G. C., *Dogmatische Studiën; Geloof en Rechtvaardiging*; Kampen: J. H. Kok, 1949.

5.— —. *Dogmatische Studiën; De Wederkomst van Christus*, I, II; Kampen: J. H. Kok, 1961.

6. BOETHIUS, *The Consolation of Philosophy*; Indianapolis: Bobbs-Merrill Co., 1962.

7. BOLIEK, L., *The Resurrection of the Flesh*; Amsterdam: Jacob van Campen, 1962.

8.— —. "The Integrity of Faith," in: *Philosophia Reformata*, 39 (1974), pp. 41-65.

9. CULLMANN, O., *Christus und die Zeit*; Zurich: A. G. Zollikon, 1948.

10. DOOYEWEERD, H., "Het tijdsprobleem en zijn antinomiën op het immanentie standpunt," in: *Philosophia Reformata*, 1 (1936), pp. 65-83; 4 (1939), pp. 1-28.

11 — —. "De idee der individualiteits-structuur en het Thomistisch substantiebegrip," in: *Philosophia Reformata*, 8 (1943), pp. 65-99; 9 (1944), pp. 1-41; 10 (1945), pp. 25-48; 11 (1946), pp. 22-52.

12 — —. *Reformatie en Scholastiek in de Wijsbegeerte*, I: *Het Grieksche Voorspel*; Franeker: T. Wever, 1949.

13 — —. "Ter nagedachtenis van mijn vriend Prof. Dr. Ph. Kohnstamm," in: *Mededelingen v. d. Ver. v. Calvinistische Wijsbegeerte* (Sept. 1952), p. 11.

14. DOUMA, J., *Algemene Genade*; Goes: Oosterbaan & Le Cointre, 1966.

15. FAIRBAIRN, P., *The Typology of Scripture*; Grand Rapids: Zondervan, n. d.

16. FERNHOUT, H., "Man, Faith and Religion in Bavinck, Kuyper and Dooyeweerd"; paper available from the Institute for Christian Studies, Toronto.

17. GAFFIN, R. B., *Redemption and Resurrection*; Philadelphia: Westminster Student Service, 1971.

18. GEERTSEMA, H. G., "Transcendentale openheid," in: *Philosophia Reformata*, 35 (1970), pp. 25-56; 132-55.

19. HART, H., "Problems of Time : An Essay," in: *Philosophia Reformata*, 38 (1973), pp. 30-42.

20. JAGER, O., *Het Eeuwige Leven*: Kampen: J. H. Kok, 1962.

21. KUITERT, H. M., *De Mensvormigheid Gods*; Kampen: J. H. Kok, 1962.

22. LÖWITH, K., *Meaning in History: The Theological Implications of the Philosophy of History*; Chicago: University of Chicago Press, 1949.

23. MEYER, P. A., *Socratisch Schimmenspel; Socrates' Plaats in de Griekse Wijsbegeerte* (Christelijk Perspectief 22); Amsterdam: Buijten en Schipperheijn, 1974.

24. MEKKES, J. P. A., "Knowing," in: *Jerusalem and Athens; Critical Discussions on the Philosophy and Apologetics of Cornelius Van Til* (E. R. Geehan, ed.); Philadelphia: Presbyterian and Reformed Publishing Co., 1971.

25. NIEBUHR, R. R., *Resurrection and Historical Reason*; New York: Charles Scribners Sons, 1959.

26. OLTHUIS, J. H., "Must the Church Become Secular?" in: *International Reformed Bulletin*, 10 (Jan. 1967), pp. 14-31.

27. PANNENBERG, W., *Basic Questions in Theology*; Philadelphia: Fortress Press, 1971.

28. POPMA, K. J., "Burgerschap," in: *Philosophia Reformata*, 7 (1942), pp. 98-122.

29——. *Calvinistische Geschiedsbeschouwing*; Franeker: T. Wever, 1945.

30——. "Tijd en Religie," in: *Philosophia Reformata*, 9 (1949), pp. 126-38.

31——. "Tijd en Geschiedenis," and "Geloof en Geschiedenis," in: *Correspondentie-bladen v. d. Ver. v. Calvinistische Wijsbegeerte*, 25 (March 1959) pp. 12-16; 28-31.

32——. "Maag en spijs" in: *Correspondentie-bladen v.d. Ver. v. Calvinistische Wijsbegeerte*, 20 (June 1956), pp. 5-7.

33——. "De eeuwigheid Gods volgens Boëthius," in: *Philosophia Reformata*, 22 (1957), pp. 21-51.

34——. "De zin der geschiedenis," in: *Correspondentie-bladen v. d. Ver. v. Calvinistische Wijsbegeerte*, 23 (March 1959), pp. 19-26.

35——. "Bestaat er een Bijbelse doodsproblematiek?" in: *Correspondentie bladen v. d. Ver. v. Calvinistische Wijsbegeerte*, 25 (March 1961), pp. 1-5.

36——. "Uitbreiding van het wetenschaps-'begrip,' " in: *Correspondentie-bladen v. d. Ver. v. Calvinistische Wijsbegeerte*, 25 (March 1961), pp. 14-19.

37——. *Wijsbegeerte en Anthropologie* (Christelijk Perspectief 3 and 4); Amsterdam: Buijten en Schipperheijn, 1963.

38——. *Levensbeschouwing* I-VII; Amsterdam: Buijten en Schipperheijn, 1965.

39——. *Nadenken over de Tijd* (Christelijk Perspectief 8); Amsterdam: Buijten en Schipperheijn, 1965.

40——. *Evangelie en Geschiedenis* (Christelijk Perspectief 20); Amsterdam: Buijten en Schipperheijn, 1972.

41——. *Harde Feiten*; Franeker: T. Wever, 1972.

42. RIDDERBOS, H., *Paulus; Ontwerp van zijn Theologie*; Kampen: J. H. Kok, 1966.

43. SCHOONHOVEN, Calvin R., *The Wrath of Heaven*; Grand Rapids: Eerdmans, 1966.

44. SHEPHERD, N., "The Resurrections of Revelation 20," in: *The Westminster Theological Journal*, 28 (1975), pp. 34-43.

45. STEEN, P. J., Review of O. Jager, *Het Eeuwige Leven*, in: *The Westminster Theological Journal*, 17 (Nov. 1964), pp. 60-6.

46——. *The Idea of Religious Transcendence in the Philosophy of Herman Dooyeweerd*; Ph.D. dissertation, 1970; available from University Microfilms, Ann Arbor, Michigan.

47. STELLINGWERFF, J., "Kritiek op K. Schilder als filosoferend dogmaticus," in: *Philosophia Reformata*, 17 (1962), pp. 106-25.

48. TELDER, B., *Sterven . . . en dan?* Kampen: J. H. Kok, 1960.

49——. *Sterven . . . waarom?* Kampen: J. H. Kok, 1963.

50. VANDER STELT, J. C., "Kuyper's Semi-mystical Conception," in: *Philosophia Reformata*, 38 (1973), pp. 30-42.

51. VAN RIESSEN, H., "De werkelijkheid in den toren," in: *Correspondentie-bladen v. d. Ver. v. Calvinistische Wijsbegeerte*, 6 (Dec. 1941), pp. 81-82.

52. VOLLENHOVEN, D. H. T., *Het Calvinisme en de Reformatie van de Wijsbegeerte*; Amsterdam: H. J. Paris, 1933.

53——. *Hoofdlijnen der Logica*; Kampen: J. H. Kok, 1948.

54——. *Isagoge Philosophiae; College Dictaat*; Amsterdam: THEJA, n. d.; reprint available from Filosofisch Instituut, Centrale Interfaculteit der Vrije Universiteit, Amsterdam.

55. VOS, G., "The Eschatological Aspect of the Pauline Conception of the Spirit," in: *Biblical and Theological Studies by Members of the Faculty of Princeton Theological Seminary*; New York: Charles Scribners Sons, 1912.

56——. *Grace and Glory*; Grand Rapids: The Reformed Press, 1922.

57——. *Dogmatiek*; Grand Rapids: 1910.

58——. *The Pauline Eschatology*; Grand Rapids: Eerdmans, 1953.

59. ZUIDEMA, S. U., *De Philosophie van Occam in zijn Commentaar op de Sententiën*; Hilversum: Schipper, 1936.

The *Sentences* of Peter Lombard and Medieval Philosophical Discussion

JOHN VAN DYK

Anyone who has some general acquaintance with medieval intellectual history knows that Peter Lombard's *Sentences* was the theological textbook *par excellence* of the High and Later Middle Ages. Its contents were for over 400 years the favorite object of scholastic commentary. The fact that more than 1500 of these commentaries are still extant, either in their entirety or in part,[1] testifies to its immense popularity. In fact, so popular did the *Sentences* become that Roger Bacon complained in 1267 that this work had supplanted the Bible as the source book for theology.[2] In the sixteenth century, Erasmus said that there were as many commentaries on the *Sentences* as there were theologians.[3]

To what extent did Peter Lombard's *Sentences* generate *philosophical* discussion? And to what extent does the mass of Sentence commentaries provide source material for the historian of medieval philosophy? These are important questions, especially in view of today's growing interest in the philosophical developments of the Middle Ages. It is my judgment that the Sentence literature has as yet not received the philosophical attention that it deserves. In this paper I wish to discuss this claim in some detail.

Who was Peter Lombard, and what was his remarkably successful *Book of Sentences*? Lombard was born at Novara between 1095 and 1100.[4] After initially studying at Bologna he went to France to continue his studies, first at Reims and then at Paris, where eventually he became a professor at the cathedral school of Notre Dame. During the 1140s he was known as a "celebrated theologian" and engaged in controversy, particularly with Gilbert de la Porrée, about the Trinity. By 1156 he was one of the archdeacons of Paris. In 1159 he was appointed bishop of Paris, where he died on July 20, 1160.[5]

Although Lombard composed (1) at least thirty sermons, (2) commentaries on the Psalms, and (3) Glosses (often called *Collectanea*) on the Epistles of Paul, we need to be concerned only with (4) the *Book of Sentences (Libri quatuor sententiarum)*,[6] his major and most influential work, which he completed circa 1155-58. In the prologue to the *Sentences*, Lombard explains the reason for writing the book. It is, he tells us, to promote the truth of a Church endangered by heresy and superstition. He stresses his desire to be true to the faith of the Fathers and to let the authorities speak. Humbly assuming an inferior role, he counts himself among the "unlearned."[7] For their benefit, he explains, he felt it necessary to compile in a "brief volume" the opinions (*sententiae*) of the Fathers. Thus the *Sentences* is essentially a collection of "opinions," i.e. citations from the Scriptures and the Church Fathers, brought together and harmonized into a coherent whole.

The basic principle of division of the *Sentences* is derived from Augustine, who asserts in the first book of *De Doctrina Christiana*, chapter 2, that all teaching is either "of things or of signs."[8] Lombard quotes this passage at the beginning of Distinction 1 and proposes to treat *res* first and *signa* afterwards. By "things" Lombard means God and the creation, while "signs" refer to the sacraments.

Each of the four books of the *Sentences* is subdivided into "Distinctions."[9] The first book treats of God, the Trinity, and the divine attributes. The second book is concerned with the angels, the creation, and man. Book 3 considers the incarnation and the nature of Christ, while the last book discusses the sacraments, the resurrection, and the last judgment.

Medievalists agree that Peter Lombard's *Sentences* was one of the most influential and important works produced in all of the Middle Ages. Few, if any, scholars would dispute I. C. Brady's judgment that this book influenced the shaping of scholastic thought and, even more markedly, of scholastic method throughout the later Middle Ages and into the Renaissance.[10] Nevertheless, medievalists have traditionally regarded the influence and importance of the *Sentences* as confined primarily to theology and as having only incidental interest for the history of philosophy.[11] Such a tradition, of course, is not surprising and to some extent not misplaced. Already in the thirteenth century, when the line of demarcation between theology and philosophy was sharply drawn, the *Sentences* was considered a theological textbook to be used in a theological curriculum.[12] Those who lectured and commented on the *Sentences* were theologians. The Sentence commentaries themselves were, as a result, first of all theological works. Hence both the *Sentences* and the traditions of the commentaries for centuries after are of more importance for the history of theology[13] than for the history of philosophy or of science.

This state of affairs has brought about a neglect of the *Sentences* and Sentence commentaries by many historians of medieval philosophy. For these historians, the primary sources for insight into the philosophical developments of the Middle Ages consist of avowedly logical and metaphysical treatises and commentaries on the philosophical works of Aristotle and the Arabs. At best, the Sentence literature provides a few illuminating texts for theories extracted from elsewhere. Again, to some extent this attitude is not altogether unjustified. Once the medievals became self-conscious about the difference between theology and philosophy, their more strictly philosophical work naturally became the center of the historian of philosophy's attention.[14]

Some historians of philosophy, particularly the earlier ones, have nevertheless recognized that the Sentence literature was of great importance for the development of medieval philosophy. Albert Stöckl, for example, devotes a considerable amount of attention to the *Sentences* and the commentary traditions in his *Geschichte der Philosophie des Mittelalters*, published in 1865.[15] In his "Vorbemerkungen" to his treatment of Christian philosophy from the thirteenth to the fifteenth century, he says:

> The broader development of scholastic speculation in this period attached itself closely to the books of Sentences, particularly the one of Peter Lombard. Since the theological curriculum was based on the *Sentences* of Lombard, and since it was the task of the professor to link his own further explanations and investigations to its contents, the motive was provided to compose commentaries on the *Sentences* and to deposit all of the rich content of scholastic knowledge in them. Hence it came about, as we shall see, that during the next centuries almost every one of the celebrated *coryphaei* of scholasticism wrote an extensive commentary on Lombard. An immense body of knowledge has been amassed in these commentaries.[16]

The context makes it clear that in the "immense body of knowledge" Stöckl includes philosophical knowledge. Throughout the next decades and into the twentieth century, however, relatively little attention was paid to the philosophical importance of the Sentence literature, while theological investigation of these materials flourished.[17]

In 1901 J. Espenberger published a study entitled *Die Philosophie des Petrus Lombardus und ihre Stellung im zwölften Jahrhundert*.[18] Espenberger surveys the logic and epistemology (ch. 1), ontology (ch. 2), psychology (ch. 3), theology (ch. 4), and ethics (ch. 5) contained in the works of Peter Lombard. To my knowledge, no other attempt to study and evaluate the philosophy of Lombard has ever been made.[19] As far as the Sentence commentaries are concerned, a similar situation obtains. Only here and there do we run across an extended study of some philosophical aspect of some—usually isolated—commentary.[20] Indeed, a survey of the amount of scholarship expended on the study of the philosophy of the Sentence literature could only lead one to conclude that philosophically these sources have little or nothing to offer.

The falsity of such a conclusion is readily perceived when one surveys the footnotes in recent histories of medieval philosophy. Gilson, for example, in his *History of Christian Philosophy in the Middle Ages*, repeatedly refers to Sentence commentaries to substantiate his interpretations of the medieval philosophers, even when numerous other sources are available.[21] For example, half of the footnotes to Gilson's discussion of Bonaventure involve a Sentence commentary.[22] In Copleston's *History of Philosophy*, Vol. 2: *Mediaeval Philosophy*, we find a similar state of affairs. Take as an example the chapters on Thomas Aquinas.[23] Even though the Sentence commentary of Aquinas is an early work and hence is superseded by fuller treatments in later treatises, Copleston cites the commentary in connection with the topics of philosophical anthropology,[24] a variety of metaphysical questions,[25] and the doctrine of analogy.[26] In the case where a Sentence commentary is an author's major work, such as the *Opus Oxoniense* of John Duns Scotus, the references indicate a full range of philosophical themes. From Copleston's chapters on Scotus,[27] for example, we learn that the following topics are discussed in the Sentence commentary: epistemology,[28] metaphysics,[29] natural theology,[30] philosophical anthropology,[31] and ethics.[32] With the conspicuous exception of logic, those topics cover the field of late thirteenth-century philosophy. It is quite evident, then, that the Sentence literature constitutes a very valuable source for the historians of medieval philosophy.

Thus it is that we are confronted by a paradoxical situation: on the one hand there is little scholarly evidence to indicate that the Sentence literature is important and valuable for the historian's work in medieval philosophy; on the other hand there is the large number of references to the commentaries to be found in any competent account of the history of medieval philosophy.

A closer examination of this situation reveals that historians of philosophy have used the Sentence literature primarily, if not exclusively, for purposes of interpreting individual medieval philosophers and theologians. That is, there has been little or no systematic investigation of the development of various philosophical concepts in the numerous traditions of Sentence commentaries. There is a conspicuous absence of attempts to trace such concepts through a series of commentaries.

It is my contention that the absence of philosophical research *focused* on the Sentence literature is not justified. Already I have indicated the extent to which historians such as Gilson and Copleston have used Sentence commentaries to substantiate their interpretations of various medieval philosophers. Clearly it cannot be maintained that the Sentence literature is of little or no value to historians of philosophy. Even when we look at the

Sentences itself, we see that numerous Distinctions, particularly in Books 1 and 2, are tailor-made, so to speak, for philosophical discussions. Consider, for example, the topic of philosophical anthropology. In Book 1, Distinction 3, Lombard discusses "the image and likeness of the Trinity in the human soul"; Distinction 8 examines the nature of "corporeal and spiritual creatures, and how they are compounded instead of uncompounded"; Distinctions 46 and 47 treat the question of the will. Book 2 contains, among others, Distinctions with topics such as the reason why rational creatures were created; why man is constituted as a unity of body and soul (Dist. 1); the creation of man (Dist. 16); the nature of soul and body (Dist. 17); the nature of a woman's soul (Dist. 18); the immortality of the body (Dist. 19); the free will (Dist. 25); and so on. Any commentator with a philosophical bent, working on the *Sentences*, would have plenty of opportunity to engage in anthropological discussion. It may be legitimately conjectured, meanwhile, that the success of the *Sentences* among the commentators was due, at least in part, to Lombard's knack for saying enough to inspire discussion while leaving enough unsaid to stimulate fruitful speculation.

Besides anthropology, nearly all of the other basic philosophical themes can be readily developed by commentators on the basis of the *Sentences*.[33] Do the commentators in fact do so? In a recent study I assessed the commentators' discussion of the problem of time and eternity.[34] This intriguing question itself has a history reaching back into pre-Platonic antiquity.[35] The *Sentences* of Peter Lombard again provides numerous occasions for extensive commentary. A number of Distinctions contain references to *tempus, aeternitas,* and *aevum*,[36] or employ such terms as *temporaliter* or *ex tempore*.[37] Furthermore, a variety of topics in the *Sentences*—such as the nature of God, the generation and incarnation of the Son, and the doctrine of the last things—suggest obvious connections with considerations of time and eternity.[38]

The Sentence commentators, particularly those with a propensity to philosophize, eagerly grasp the opportunity to speculate about the nature of time and eternity. Thomas Aquinas, Innocent V, John of Paris, and Giles of Rome, for example, discuss the matter in connection with Book 1, Distinction 8, where Lombard explains that God is an "essence that knows no past or future,"[39] and Distinction 19, in which the focus centers on the temporal and eternal procession of the Holy Spirit. Alexander of Hales comments extensively on Book 1, Distinction 9, which contains a chapter on the co-eternality of the Father and the Son. Particularly Distinctions 1 and 2 of Book 2 generate lengthy and interesting expositions of time and eternity. In these Distinctions, Lombard raises the issue of the creation of time itself, as well as the question regarding the point at which the angels and men came into being. Virtually all the commentators treat the problem of time in connection with these Distinctions. These commentators include most of the historically important figures, such as Albert the Great, Bonaventure, Thomas Aquinas, Innocent V, Peter John Olivi, Richard of Middleton, John of Paris, Giles of Rome, John Duns Scotus, Durandus of St. Pourçain, John Baconthorpe, William Ockham, and Gabriel Biel.

These men not only treat the philosophical issues extensively in breadth, they explore them deeply as well. That is to say, the commentators do not merely list large numbers of arguments for and against a position but enter into lengthy—and often perceptive—explanations designed to show why certain opinions are untenable or ought to be maintained. It should be remembered that the commentators were men of ability. By the time they dealt with the *Sentences*, they had survived a long and demanding university curriculum. As Sentence commentators they were, in fact, theologians trained in dialectic and philosophy,[40] competent to address themselves to the academic questions of their age. Consequently, their commentaries more often than not contain a great variety of philosophical doctrine, much of which is original, or, at least, free from a mere dull repeating of the masters. As such, the commentaries, in showing individual ingenuity and plenty of personal conviction, give us access to the medieval commentators' real opinions on numerous philosophical matters.

One final point: the commentators were well aware of the opinions of their predecessors. A goodly number of them, in fact, took pains to expound the positions of the earlier masters, in order to be able to show up their own views in clear relief. Contrasting their personal opinions with those of earlier figures is practically a matter of habit with such commentators as Thomas Aquinas, John Duns Scotus, John Baconthorpe, Willam Ockham, and others. Needless to say, this state of affairs contributes significantly to the value of the commentaries in that traditions of philosophical discussions can be laid bare by tracing a particular topic through a series of commentaries.

The evidence leading to the conclusion that the Sentence literature is fully worthy of philosophical and historical study is weighty indeed. There can be no question that an intensive and systematic examination of this vast storehouse of material[41] ought to be placed high on the agenda for historians of medieval philosophy. The time seems opportune: a steadily swelling stream of material—including newly discovered Sentence commentaries—is becoming available. At the same time, medieval studies are still in a stage of infancy; so much so, in fact, that no diligent student of the Middle Ages need be denied an opportunity for useful pioneering.

Notes

1. Catalogued by Stegmüller in his incomplete *Repertorium Commentariorum in Sententias Petri Lombardi* (Würzburg, 1947).

2. Bacon says: "The fourth sin (about the study of theology) is in that one manual (*Summa*) of a master is given preference to the text (of the Bible) in the Faculty of Theology; this is the Book of Sentences which is the glory of the theologians and (which is so weighty) that it takes a horse to carry it. And the man who has lectured on it dreams that he is already a master of theology, though he has not heard lectures on one-thirtieth of the Bible . . . . And it is strange indeed that the *Liber Sententiarum* (*Sentences*) is so strongly emphasized . . . . For it does not follow the text of the Bible closely, but wanders about vaguely outside it by means of questioning." Quoted in H. Wieruszowski, *The Medieval University* (New York, 1966), pp. 146-7.

3. "There are as many commentaries on the *Sentences* of Petrus Lombardus as there are theologians. There is no end of little *summas*, which mix up one thing with another over and over again and after the manner of apothecaries fabricate and refabricate old things from new, new from old, one from many, and many from one." From the letter to Volzius in 1518, quoted by E. Rogers, *Peter Lombard and the Sacramental System* (New York, 1917), p. 17.

4. As is the case with many other important medieval figures, the exact course of Lombard's life has not been established with any degree of certainty.

5. This brief biography of Peter Lombard is based on the *Prolegomena* to the new Quaracchi edition of the *Sentences* (1971, pp. 8-45), and on articles in the *Dictionnaire de théologie catholique* (Paris, 1909-60), the *New Catholic Encyclopedia* (New York, 1967), and the *Encyclopedia of Philosophy* (New York, 1967). I. C. Brady, who wrote the articles in the last two of these works, considerably updated the earlier versions of De Ghellinck in the first of the encyclopedias mentioned above. De Ghellinck's article in the *Dictionnaire* is generally regarded as a landmark of Lombardian scholarship. The *Prolegomena* to the Quaracchi edition probably constitutes the most up-to-date, detailed, and carefully documented account of Lombard's life available thus far.

6. The title of the *Sentences* varies from *Libri quatuor sententiarum* to *Sententiae in IV libris distinctae*. In English the work is generally called *Sentences* or *Book of Sentences*, or even *Four Books of Opinions*.

7. "*. . . multisque indoctis, inter quos etiam et mihi . . . .*"

8. "*Omnis doctrina vel rerum est vel signorum.*" In adopting the distinction between "things" and "signs," Lombard alters Augustine's meaning of these terms somewhat. Augustine calls a thing "that which is not used to signify something else, like wood, stone, cattle, and so on." In certain situations, however, these things can also function as signs and symbols. On the other hand, words are always signs. Augustine concludes that "every sign is also a thing—for that which is not a thing is nothing at all—but not every thing is also a sign." In Books 2 and 3 of *De Doctrina Christiana*, Augustine treats "signs" primarily as words.

9. Alexander of Hales (1170/80-1245) introduced the "Distinctions" (cf. I. C. Brady, "The Distinctions of Lombard's *Book of Sentences* and Alexander of Hales," *Franciscan Studies*, 25, 1965, pp. 70-116). In the earlier manuscripts of the *Sentences*, the *quaestiones* of each book follow each other without any distinctions or divisions.

10. "Not all of Lombard's opinions found acceptance: lists of his positions not commonly accepted abound in medieval manuscripts. However, this did not lessen the work's influence in shaping scholastic method and thought for four or more centuries." I. C. Brady, "Peter Lombard," *Encyclopedia of Philosophy*, Vol. 6, p. 124.

11. Consider, for example, the judgment of J. De Ghellinck, one of the greatest Lombard scholars of this century: "It is this theological work above all [i.e. *Sentences*] that made the name of Peter Lombard famous, and gives him a special place in the history of theology in the

Middle Ages" (*The Catholic Encyclopedia*, 1911, Vol. 11, p. 769). Although this statement is true, it does not do justice to the wider importance of the *Sentences*. Note, furthermore, that a general history of medieval philosophy such as Gilson's *History of Christian Philosophy in the Middle Ages* (New York, 1955) contains only incidental references to Peter Lombard.

12. Cf. H. Rashdall, *The Universities of Europe in the Middle Ages*, P. H. Powicke and A. B. Emden, eds. (Oxford, 1936), Vol. I, pp. 471-90.

13. The vast majority of studies of the Sentence literature has been produced by historians of theology, is concerned with theological aspects, and has been published in theological journals. The collection of articles in *Miscellanea Lombardiana*, published in Novara in 1957 on the occasion of the 800th anniversary of the publication of Lombard's *Sentences*, is representative of this literature. Of the 33 articles, no fewer than half deal with theological and ecclesiastical matters. The attention of the remainder is divided among mainly paleographical and historical interests. Only two articles treat a specifically philosophical topic.

14. There are exceptional cases in which a primarily theological text of the High and Later Middle Ages yields fine results for the history of medieval philosophy, e.g. Aquinas' *Summa theologiae*, a work so vast in scope that it incidentally covers a great deal of philosophical ground.

15. First published at Mainz. It was recently reprinted in Germany (Scientia Verlag Aalen, 1968). In the first of the three volumes of this work, twenty pages are devoted exclusively to Peter Lombard.

16. Vol. 2, p. 308 (translation mine).

17. See note 13. Much fruitful work was accomplished by earlier historians of theology, particularly by such pioneers as J. De Ghellinck, M. Grabmann, A. Landgraf, O. Lottin, F. Pelster, D. Vanden Eynde, and H. Weisweiler, all of them Catholic scholars.

18. This 139-page work appeared as *Heft* 5 in *Band* 3 of *Beiträge zur Geschichte der Philosophie und Theologie des Mittelalters.*

19. The nearest thing to Espenberger's work is an article by Roberto Busa, "la Filosofia di Pier Lombardo," published in *Miscellanea Lombardiana* (see note 13). This 11-page article contains an appendix of philosophical topics present in Lombard's works. It follows Espenberger's outline and is very general.

20. The work done on the Sentence commentaries (*Ordinationes*) of Duns Scotus and Ockham is an important exception.

21. This additional clause is necessary, since in a number of instances the only extant source for a medieval figure is his Sentence commentary. E.g., Innocent V, Peter Aurioli, Gregory of Rimini.

22. E. Gilson, *op. cit.*, pp. 685-7.

23. F. Copleston, *A History of Philosophy*, Vol. 2: *Mediaeval Philosophy*, Part 2 of the Doubleday Image edition (Garden City, 1962).

24. *Ibid.*, ch. 32, notes 11 and 13.

25. *Ibid.*, ch. 33, notes 3, 5; ch. 37, note 2.

26. *Ibid.*, ch. 35, note 10.

27. *Ibid.*, ch. 45-50.

28. *Ibid.*, ch. 46, majority of notes.

29. *Ibid.*, ch. 47, numerous notes.

30. *Ibid.*, ch. 48, the vast majority of notes.

31. *Ibid.*, ch. 49, majority of notes.

32. *Ibid.*, ch. 50, numerous notes.

33. Let one more example suffice: epistemological speculation can readily take off from topics such as the nature of God's knowledge and foreknowledge (Book 1, Dist. 38-39, 41), the knowledge possessed by angels (Book 2, Dist. 3, 7), and human knowledge (Book 2, Dist. 23, 26, and others).

34. See my doctoral dissertation, *The Value of the Commentaries on Peter Lombard's Sentences for the History of Medieval Philosophy: An Inquiry and an Assessment* (Cornell University, Ithaca, New York, 1975).

35. Cf. R. B. Onians, *The Origins of European Thought about the Body, the Mind, the Soul, the World, Time, and Fate* (Cambridge, 1951); M. Schofield, "Did Parmenides Discover Eternity?" *Archiv für Geschichte der Philosophie*, 52 (1970), pp. 113-35.

36. *Tempus*, time; *aeternitas*, eternity; *aevum* to the medievals was a third mode of existence, peculiar to angels and human souls, midway between eternity and time. Practically all the Sentence commentaries assume that there are three modes of existence: eternity, *aevum*, and time. For the patristic use of these three modes, cf. G. B. Ladner, *The Idea of Reform: Its Impact on Christian Thought and Action in the Age of the Fathers* (Cambridge, 1959), pp. 443-8 ("Some Patristic Distinctions Concerning Eternity, Aevum, and Time"). For an interesting discussion of *aevum* and its importance in scholasticism, see pp. 275-84 of E. H. Kantorowicz's excellent book *The King's Two Bodies: A Study of Medieval Political Theory* (Princeton, 1957). See also F. H. Brabant, *Time and Eternity in Christian Thought* (London, 1937).

37. I.e., "temporally."

38. Judging strictly from appearance, the following Distinctions count as potential candidates for discussions of time and eternity: Book 1, Distinctions 8-9, 14, 19, 22, 29-30, 35, 37-39, 41; Book 2, Distinctions 1-3, 12-15, 17, 19, 23, 25, 29; Book 3, Distinctions 2-3, 7, 10, 12, 14, 29, 32, 34; Book 4, Distinctions 15, 21, 28, 44, and 48.

39. Traditionally the notions of eternity and immutability have been closely linked.

40. The theologian-to-be completed a course in the arts before enrolling in theology. That the masters in the theology schools loved to engage in philosophical dispute is evident from Pope Gregory IX's bull of 1231, in which he admonishes the theologians "not to show themselves philosophers but to strive to become God's learned." Helen Wieruszowski, in *The Medieval University* (New York, 1966), p. 44, comments: "They [the theologians and theological students] were expected to restrict themselves to 'theology in its purity' and to dispute only on such questions as could be resolved by revelation and the writings of the Fathers. The Pope must have had good reason for so serious a warning."

41. The vast extent of Sentence literature can be gleaned by a glance at Stegmüller's *Repertorium Commentariorum in Sententias Petri Lombardi* (Würzburg, 1947).

Archibald Alexander: Inconsistent Empiricism and Theory of Scripture.*

JOHN C. VANDER STELT

Archibald Alexander's role in North American Presbyterianism has been a truly formidable one. He was not only the Founder but also for four decades the Nestor, Image, Soul, Spirit, and Symbol of Princeton Theological Seminary. Almost 2000 students received their theological training under him.[1] As a "charismatic" theologian, teacher, pastor, linguist, and philosopher, Alexander had a profound impact upon the tradition of American theology that is inseparably connected with Princeton Theological Seminary and also, to a certain extent, with Westminster Theological Seminary.

Initially, Alexander hesitated to commit his thoughts to paper. After his appointment in 1811 as Professor of Didactic and Polemic Theology at the newly established Princeton Theological Seminary, however, he managed to write, in spite of his demanding professional toil and the time-consuming ecclesiastical controversies, a number of essays and reviews for the *Biblical Repertory* and some 49 books and articles. One of his most significant publications is undoubtedly *Evidences of the Authenticity, Inspiration and Canonical Authority of the Holy Scriptures* (1836).[2]

The intent of this essay is not to indicate Alexander's ecclesiastical role, confessional stance, pastoral wisdom, or theological acumen. Rather, it is to show his basic philosophical perspective and some of the anthropological and epistemological implications of this theoretic position.

A number of salient features of Alexander's thought-pattern should become evident in our brief description of his basic views.

---

*The substance of this article is practically the same as that of my discussion of Archibald Alexander in my dissertation, see *13*: 90-114.

(1) Alexander's view of Scripture cannot be understood apart from his Common Sense anthropology and Scottish Realistic apologetics.

(2) Alexander was in a position to reject the epistemological skepticism logically implicit in Hume's radical empiricism by adding the absolute certainty, derived from the first principles of the rational voice in man's mind, to the merely relative validity of sensory knowledge.

(3) There is not only sensory evidence but also testimonial evidence. The latter has its own form of objectivity or external veracity.

(4) Having accepted the fundamental scholastic distinction between the natural and supernatural, Alexander is compelled to introduce two kinds of causes and to think of the natural as a means to an end, as something to be set aside, as something to be elevated.

(5) The distinction between natural and supernatural undermines the inherently revelatory character of the natural world.

(6) Alexander tends to reduce the meaning and scope of revelation to the soteriological role of the Scriptures.

(7) Scriptural truth consists of an inductively arrived at intellectualistic system of truths.

(8) To make room for Christianity, Alexander sought to curtail the impact of deism and empiricism. At the same time, by not being sufficiently critical, he continued to perpetuate a questionable anthropology and epistemology.

Alexander disliked liberalism, infidelity, and rationalism, but he also rejected bigotry, dogmatism, and fideism. He spent most of his life attacking these two types of errors and defending the truth of the Christian religion. In his teaching, preaching and writing, he championed the cause of Christian orthodoxy and resisted the onslaught of deism and atheism. His main weapon in this apologetic battle was the reasonable, infallible and inerrant Scriptures. To convince mitigators and opponents of the Christian religion of the fact that truth resided only with Christianity, Alexander had recourse, however, to some of the main underlying presuppositions of Scottish Common Sense philosophy.

When Hume drew the logical consequences from Locke's empiricism and opened the floodgate to epistemological relativism, a number of Scottish theologians and philosophers in Edinburgh, Glasgow and Aberdeen rushed to the defense of Christianity. In trying to stem the tide of infidelity, these men developed their own peculiar philosophy and apologetics.[3] By *modifying* radical empiricism, they believed they could keep the sea of non-teleological skepticism from inundating their "Christian" world of discourse and belief.

George Berkeley had already advanced his own unique solution to the dangers of Lockean empiricism, especially its implicit materialism and inevitable atheism. Berkeley's philosophy of *psycho-monism*, or "reduced pneumatological monarchianism,"[4] proved to be less satisfactory, however, as an answer to the philosophy of Locke and Hume than the Common Sense counteroffensive launched in Scotland a few years later.[5]

These philosophical developments in England and Scotland had a direct bearing on the theological and philosophical developments in New England. Jonathan Edwards, Sr., for example, showed much sympathy for the views—be it in modified form—of John Locke. During its initial years, the College of New Jersey in Princeton came under the influence of Berkeleyanism. With the arrival in 1768 of John Witherspoon from Scotland to become President and Professor at the College of New Jersey, Princeton became for the next century one of the main North American centers of Scottish Common Sense philosophy. Accepting the basic assumptions of Scottish Realism, John Witherspoon fervently applied its main principles in the disciplines of ethics, economics, aesthetics, jurisprudence, natural science, and theology.[6]

One of Witherspoon's many students at the Nassau Hall in Princeton was William Graham. As a frontier preacher and instructor at the Academy at Timber Ridge Meeting-House,[7] Graham exerted a strong personal and philosophical influence upon Archibald Alexander. Graham claimed that "sound principles of philosophy" would enable one to untie all sorts of knotty theological problems. Rather than deal with matters in *natural* philosophy, Graham preferred to be engaged in questions of *mental* philosophy. He acquired for his own study the works of Thomas Reid, James Beattie, and other Scottish thinkers. As instructor at the Academy, he prescribed the same textbooks in philosophy that Witherspoon had used earlier at the College of New Jersey, and he had his own students transcribe Witherspoon's lectures on *Moral Philosophy* and *Criticism*. Graham believed that even without any supernatural aid, primitive man is a morally accountable agent, a being naturally endowed with the capacity of performing his duties in a rationally respectable manner.

John Witherspoon and William Graham passed on the essential features of Scottish Common Sense philosophy to Archibald Alexander (*11*:24-5; *9*:142; *2*:366). All three theologians refused to be locked up in Lockean philosophy and to be hemmed in by Humean skepticism. They agreed with Scottish Realism that man's knowledge is not dependent merely on the givens of fragmentary, sensory experience and on the mind's subsequent inductive associating of numerous simple ideas into more and more complex ideas. Man's knowledge is dependent first of all upon general rational principles which differ essentially from the mere results of inductive reasoning. There are principles which do not *follow* thinking and knowing, but *precede*, guide and determine our logically infallible thought processes. These *first* principles, lodged in man's mind, are not acquired in a slow and gradual manner but are intuited initially and suddenly as self-evident, universally valid, and common-sensical *a priori* laws of the mind. Man's mind is more than the sum total of numerous fragmentary and sensory impressions. Man's mental self-identity transcends his psychic diversity. If this were not so, man would not be a truly moral being with a free will; instead he would be a completely sensorily determined creature. Unless they are modified, natural philosophy and sensory epistemology result in Newtonian deism and Humean atheism. To prevent this from happening, Scottish thinkers and their North American followers emphasized man's mental and moral constitution as something that is unique, independent, substantial, free, and immortal (*6*: 449, 684-5).

In his studies Archibald Alexander concentrated on three things: Scripture, doctrine, and natural religion. His peculiar views concerning the meaning of natural religion did not harmonize, however, with what he believed about Scripture and doctrine. Inasmuch as he attempted to unify his views on this score, he created an artificial synthesis of two conflicting ways of thinking. In his courses in *Mental Philosophy, Ethics* and *Natural Religion*, Alexander laid the "foundations for the scheme of revealed doctrine" (*11*: 24). He deemed studies in modified empiricistic philosophy necessary and integral to every meaningful and complete course in theological studies. To establish a reasonable system of apologetics, i.e. one in which "various schemes of argument for the being and perfections of God and the necessity and antecedent probability of revelation" (*6*: 367) must be assumed and proven at the same time, one must develop, according to Alexander, a philosophy of habit, understand the role of the inductive method, recognize the central significance of reason, and, above all, acknowledge the great importance of the intuitive principles in man's mind.

In opposition to epistemological skepticism, Alexander called attention to the central significance of mentally and morally intuited principles. For their truth character, these principles, by their very nature, do not need any evidence other than that they are intuited. This is precisely man's dignity. Man is more than his senses and feelings. Man is not determined but is free. To counteract the subjectivism of revivalistic enthusiasm, Alexander therefore advocated the significance of a rational faith, of reasonable belief that has its objectivity soundly anchored in (theo-) logically systematized Scriptural truths. To oppose the deistic tendendy to explain everything in terms of natural and rational causality, Alexander emphasized the need for a type of causality which is *super*-natural and *above*-rational. Finally, to attack the atheists' desire to think of all revelation as forms of superstition, Alexander called attention to the reasonable character of the Christian faith.

A key to the central thrust of Alexander's theory of evidences, and at the same time one of the presuppositions of his inconsistent empiricism, can be found in his philosophical stance as expressed in *Outlines of Moral Science.*[8] He defined moral philosophy as "an inquiry into the nature and grounds of moral obligation *by reason*, as *distinct from revelation*" (*4*: 376, italics mine). It is possible to have philosophy without revelation, but not religion without revelation. In connection with the relationship between philosophy and religion, Alexander rejected the idea that the two were the same: philosophy would not be needed if the two were identical. Philosophy is not superfluous, nor is it the reduction of infidelity to a system. Reason is not evil. The discoveries of reason cannot be contrary to the truth of Scripture (*4*: 376). The probability exists that reason may do much good: "There may be an illustration and confirmation of the inspired writings, from reason and observation, which will greatly add to their beauty and force" (*4*: 376). Natural and moral philosophy have not hindered the cause of religion; on the contrary, they have promoted it. From reason itself one can show the evident fallacies of the principles of infidels. What Alexander once wrote in a review of a book on apologetics can be applied to his own life and work: "While men of strong but erratic minds arise, and exert all their talents to propagate errors of the most monstrous kinds, God in mercy to the church raises up other men who, clad in the panoply of truth, are qualified to detect, and by sound reasoning and solid learning to refute, the dangerous systems of infidelity and heresy, which from time to time, the enemies of truth promulgate" (*3*: 498).[9] In any truly *intelligent* discussion about the evidences, rationality, authenticity, inspiration, and canonicity of revealed truth(s), infidels necessarily lose and Christians win.

Alexander's statements at the beginning of his *Evidences of the Authenticity, Inspiration and Canonical Authority of the Holy Scriptures* about reason, religion and revelation are fundamental for his view of apologetics and his explanation of the nature of truth. Only in the light of the anthropology there implied can we understand Alexander's subsequent discussion concerning the nature of miracles, prophecies and inspiration.

Man is endowed with a number of inherent capacities. Reason and religion are two of these mental capacities. Just as seeing requires an eye, so knowing presupposes *reason*. It is not a question of whether or not use may be made of reason, but rather whether *proper* use has been made of reason in matters of religion. Man's reason guides his religion. Reason judges the truth character of Christian evidences. "Without reason we can form no conception of a truth of any kind; and when we receive anything as true, whatever may be the evidence on which it is founded, we must view the reception of it as reasonable. Truth and reason are so intimately connected that they can never with propriety be separated, whatever be the nature of truth, or of the evidence by which it is established" (*2*: 10). While right reason is impartial, judges all truth, has self-evident principles, speaks with a clear voice, and dictates acceptance of common-sense ideas, wrong reason is blind, prejudiced, partial, perverted, and jaundiced. Reason in itself is not sinful, but only limited, weak, feeble, and insufficient. Of itself, it cannot know all truth, although all reception of truth is and must always remain reasonable. Truth and reason may not be separated from each other, nor may they be identified. Although whatever is rational is necessarily true, not everything that is true is necessarily rational: what is true can also be, as often it is, *above* or *beyond* the rational. "If a book claiming to be divine revelation," writes Alexander, "is found to contain doctrines which can in no way be reconciled to right reason, it is sure evidence that those claims have no solid foundation, and ought to be rejected. But that a revelation should contain doctrines of a mysterious and incomprehensible nature, and entirely different from all our previous conceptions, and, considered in themselves, improbable, is not repugnant to reason; on the contrary, judging from analogy, sound reason would lead us to expect such things in a revelation from God" (*2*: 10).

The distinction between Creator and creature is comparable to that between Infinite and finite, Incomprehensible and comprehensible. While the finite and the comprehensible, both of which belong essentially to man, are rational, the Infinite and Incomprehensible are *above* the rational. Though the Divine is above the rational, it is not *against* it. It is irrational, therefore, to reject the manifestations of the Infinite, and rational to accept them. Thus Alexander can argue "That sound reason would lead us to expect such things in a revelation from God" and "no doctrine can be a proper object of our faith which it is not more reasonable to receive than to reject" (*2*: 10). Whatever we chide infidels for, it should not be taken ill of them that they make use of reason. As a matter of fact, infidels proceed on the "plausible and (if rightly understood) correct principle of receiving nothing as true but that which their reason approves" (*2*: 14).

Having indicated first of all that man is a rational animal, Alexander goes on to explain that man is also a *religious* animal. Man has that inescapable religious impression, that certain feeling, that ineradicable predisposition and constitutional tendency to assent to the doctrines of orthodox Christianity (*2*: 17-20).[10]

Religion calls for revelation. In his final edition of *Evidences* (1836), Alexander added an entirely new chapter (i.e. IV) in which he discussed the meaning of revelation. Revelation is something *added* to creation. God did not have to give it. It was given to provide immediate and divinely sanctioned certainty for man's feeble mind and for the uncertain conclusions of his unassisted reason. Through this added revelation, man can again worship God. A "clear and well-attested communication from heaven" makes our religion true, rational, sober, and benevolent (*2*: 35). This super-natural (and above-rational) revelation is revealed to man such that it can be known, grasped and applied by him in his natural and rational world only through the means of miracles. The existence of miracles presupposes the presence of revelation, and vice versa. "The conjunction of these two things is reasonable: if we find the one, we may be sure the other exists also" (*2*: 64).

Alexander's semi-scholastic understanding of the relationship between Creator and creature has determined much of the North American Presbyterian debate concerning the nature of Scripture, the meaning of miracle, the role of faith, the essence of inspiration, and the relationships between revelation and creation, theology and philosophy, faith and reason. The following statement of Alexander is classic in this connection and worth quoting in full:

> Why should it be thought unreasonable, that God should sometimes depart from his common mode of acting, to answer great and valuable ends? What is there in the established course of nature so sacred and immutable, that it must never on any occasion or for any purpose be changed? The only reason why the laws of nature are uniform is, that this is for the benefit of man, but if his interest requires a departure from the regular course, what is there to render it unreasonable? The author of the universe has never bound himself to pursue one undeviating course, in the government of the world. The time may come when he may think proper to change the whole system. As he gave it a beginning, he may also give it an end. General uniformity is expedient, that men may know what to expect, and may have encouragement to use means to obtain necessary ends; but occasional and unfrequent deviations from this uniformity have no tendency to prevent the benefit arising from it. This is so evident a truth that I am almost ashamed to dwell so long upon it; but by the sophistry of infidels a strange darkness has been thrown over the subject, so that it seems to be thought there would be something immoral, or unwise and inconsistent, in contravening the laws of nature (*2*: 62-3; cf. 81-4, 86-8).

Evidences of God's revelation are miracles, prophecies, and inspiration. Prophecies and inspiration are deep down but two different manifestations of miracles. A miracle is that which truly indicates God's free power and his infinite knowledge. Anyone, therefore, who rejects miracles (and prophecies and inspiration) of necessity leaves the impression of not wanting to serve God, of doing injustice to God's incomparable power, and of detracting from the infiniteness of divine wisdom.[11] Miracles "furnish the best proof for the establishment of a revelation; they seem to be its proper seal; they are the manifestations of God. Nothing can be conceived which will more strikingly indicate his power and presence, than the visible suspension of the laws of nature. He is invisible; he must make himself known by his works, and a miracle is such a work as no other can perform" (*2*: 64-5).

Objective *proof* for true miracles is some form of reliable testimony. Hume's world of senses and observation cannot provide the proper basis for such a proof. For Hume all evidences of truth are limited to the world of *sensory* observation. Hume denied the knowability and relevance of a super-natural, i.e. super-sensory, world. Truth claims based on mere testimony are for Hume necessarily false.

Alexander differed with Hume's theory of *sensory* evidences. For Alexander a *testimonial* evidence, based on the authority of someone or something else, can have genuine validity. Rejecting Hume's denial of anything super-natural or miraculous, Alexander broadened the base of veracity and proof. While Hume believed that "facts are incredible in proportion as they are miraculous," Alexander put forward the idea that the only testimony sufficient to establish a miracle is that one the falsehood of which would be "more improbable than the fact it endeavours to establish." In other words, the burden of proof rests not on Christians but on unbelievers. Inability on the part of the latter to falsify the Christian religion is an apologetic proof that it is more reasonable to accept Christianity than it is to reject it. Evidences for the Biblical religion and for revelation are certain. That which possesses most evidence, be it natural, miraculous, or both, is most probable. "And when all evidence relating to a proposition is before the mind, THAT WHICH IS EASIEST TO BE BELIEVED IS TRUE, because it is easier to believe with evidence than against it . . . . We pledge ourselves to prove that the falsehood of the miracle of the gospel would be more improbable, and consequently more incredible, than the truth of the facts recorded in them" (*2*: 76).

Alexander's form of rationalistic apologetics, with its Pascalian use of probability, presupposes his distinction between the *natural* and *super-natural*. Alexander did maintain that the same effects will uniformly follow the same causes. The causes are not always the same, however. There are ultimately two kinds of causes, namely, natural and super-natural. A super-natural cause is extra-ordinary. It is a divine power which intervenes in our ordinary world, a superior power which interposes in nature, an unusual principle which contravenes the laws of history and nature. "Laws of nature, or mere natural causes may remain the same; and yet, by the operation of these supra-natural causes, effects entirely diverse from those that would be the sequence of natural causes, may take place" (*2*: 82). It is "absurd" and "impious" to maintain that the Great First Cause is unable to "suspend or alter the laws of nature." It is perfectly rational to believe that "all things are possible to God" and that "whatever is possible may be believed on sufficient testimony, which testimony, however, must be strong in proportion to the improbability of the event to be confirmed" (*2*: 88).

A form of circular reasoning is unavoidable at this point: to believe miracles requires acceptance of proper testimony, and proper testimony presupposes the existence of miracles. In the background of this circularity lies Alexander's inconsistent empiricistic anthropology with its principle of self-evident and intuitive rationality and its Arminian-like emphasis on the role of man's free intellectual agency. "Our conduct in the pursuit and reception of truth may be intended by our Creator to be an important part of the probation to which we are subjected; and therefore the evidence of revelation is not so great as to be irresistible, but is of such a kind, that the sincere and diligent inquirer will be in no danger of fatal mistake" (*2*: 91).[12]

Prophecies, although miraculous, differ in one important respect from general miracles. The fulfillment of prophecy can be experienced and observed in the *present*. Prophecies provide, therefore, better evidence of revelation than general miracles. As events that have happened in the *past*, general miracles recede beyond the horizon of our sensory experience, and for their proof we are compelled to rely solely on testimonial evidence. The proof of a prophecy that is fulfilled in the present is characterized by both testimonial *and* sensory evidence.

The origin of both the world and revelation is God. Both nature and Scripture are the effects of a divine power, the evidences of a supernatural impression. Especially revelation, i.e. the Bible, is "stamped with his image," both externally and internally (*2*: 189). Particularly the internal evidence, or the very content of Scripture, shows more clearly than anything else the omnipotence of its Author and proves the Bible to be the WORD OF GOD (*2*: 22).

To think meaningfully about Scripture without admitting its being inspired is impossible. Scripture and *inspiration* are two sides of one coin. Scripture's authenticity comes with its inspiration. This inspiration differs from illumination in that inspiration always entails new, infallible and inerrant revelation, while illumination merely equips man spiritually to apprehend truths already revealed. Inspiration differs also from revelation in that all inspiration is always revelation, but not all revelation is always the same as inspiration. Inspiration is the key concept in Alexander's understanding of Scripture as the Word of God. The supernatural can relate to the natural in three ways: the first is *superintendence*, i.e. the supernatural makes use of the natural to accomplish an unnatural end; the second is *suggestion*, i.e. new truths are communicated immediately, without making any use of the natural world; the third is *elevation*, i.e. the laws of nature are not merely used (superintendence) or set aside (suggestion) but are raised above and beyond the ordinary and common level of our experience. In all three forms of inspiration, the communication of divine truth is supernaturally infallible and naturally plenary.

The possibility that not the words but only the ideas have been inspired requires one to admit, sooner or later, the presence of errors in the recording of the details. Such an admission is a concession in the direction of unbelief and results in a subtle undermining of the certainty of the truths of Scripture. To claim, on the other hand, that only the words and not the ideas of Scripture have been inspired robs the Bible of its proper content and does violence to the peculiar nature of man's mind. Because of his stress on the nature and role of man's rational mind, Alexander rejected the idea that all inspiration came in the form of suggestion. Inspiration usually comes in the form of superintendence and elevation. Alexander did not think mechanistically but organically. After all, man's "natural faculties are the gift of God as much as any inspiration can be. And the clear intuitive knowledge which we possess of certain truths, may be considered as a sort of permanent inspiration" (*2*: 228).

It is in this context that Archibald Alexander has given the definition of inspiration which has played such a central role in the subsequent debates at Princeton and Westminster Theological Seminaries with respect to the nature of Scripture. Inspiration is "SUCH A DIVINE INFLUENCE UPON THE MINDS OF THE SACRED WRITERS AS RENDERED THEM EXEMPT FROM ERROR, BOTH IN REGARD TO THE IDEAS AND WORDS. This is properly called PLENARY inspiration" (*2*: 230). Rejecting this view of inspiration opens the door to the possibilities of mistakes in the Bible, detracts from the power of God, undermines the intellectual certainty of faith, evokes attacks of deists and atheists, removes the cornerstone from the building of Christian evidences, and violates the basic tenets of Common Sense philosophy, especially the inductive and intuitive theories of knowledge and truth.

Between man's reason and the design of revelation there exists a relationship of direct correspondence. Truth is first of all intellectual. The design of revelation presupposes, therefore, on the part of man, a rational essence in his soul. Truth is the WORD OF GOD, understood as a semi-empiricistic and propositionally reduced system of Biblical truths. From such a view of Truth it follows that the essence of Christian faith is seen primarily as an intellectual willing, as a rational assenting to a system of Scriptural and doctrinal truths.

There are three ways in which man can become acquainted with this rational system or design of Scripture, namely, through the intuitive truths in man's mind, through Scripture itself, and through man's rational deductions from the facts of Scripture. These three *ways* to the Truth are at the same time also the three *sources* of Truth.

Concerning the *first* way and source, Alexander went so far as to say that "to intuitive truths everything must bow. It is on the intuitive truth that all faith in a Bible, or even in God's being is pillared. The mind's intuition is the first and highest voice of God to man" (*3*: 421). It is essential for the very design of revelation to appeal to the rational mind of man. If God's mind is the sun, man's mind is the eye. Completing this analogy of nature, it is the role of man's mental reflection to scatter, not create, the received light in every direction. Alexander had no patience with the interminable controversies caused by radical empiricistic theologians who thought verbalistically and literalistically. In a natural, necessary and universal manner, man forms certain "wide gospel principles" which he uses intuitively to listen to, interpret and explain Scripture, knowing that the "instinct of the mind . . . is logical and true." Revelation, i.e. the Bible, is a "perfect rule of faith," as long as one views it "in that office for which it was given, as a guide and basis of evidence to intelligent and reasoning minds" (*3*: 422).[13]

Concerning the *third* source of our acquaintance with the design of revelation, Alexander wrote in a typically inconsistent empiricistic fashion. "The Bible reveals all truth that is necessary for us to know, virtually, but not verbally. Thought is a plane; language touches its surface only at scattered points; and all the intermediate spaces, where it fails in contact, the mind must supply . . . . The lack of this is no evil, if the mind be set to the work for which God made it; by legitimate deduction to fill up the chasms of Scripture. Revelation, in effect, includes all doctrines, that by sound reasoning are drawn from it; they were in the mind of God when he gave the parent truth from which they are deduced. The exact thought of revelation is but the framework of our thought—the seeds of things intended for the growth and increase in the soil of the mind" (*3*: 421-2).[14]

There is no doubt that, as a preacher and church leader, Archibald Alexander was opposed to the creed of Arminianism and wanted to be a confessionally orthodox Calvinist. However, as a teacher and academic, he accepted a theoretical framework of reference which seriously curtailed the theological effectiveness of his sincere intentions. His appeal to the basic tenets of Scottish Realism as an alternative to Lockean empiricism, Humean skepticism and Berkeleyan idealism and as a defense of the rationality of the Christian religion and the credibility of Biblical revelation is an example of the problems and frustrations that arise when unscriptural views in anthropology are incorporated, consciously or unconsciously, into a theology clearly intended to be Biblical.

The impact of Alexander's problematics with respect to the nature of Scripture, the essence of truth, and the role of man upon subsequent Presbyterian theology in Princeton and Westminster Theological Seminaries has been a considerable and formative one.[15] His understanding of such concepts as Scripture, truth, revelation, faith, evidences, miracle, inspiration, proposition, doctrine, and theology was to a large extent shaped by an inherently unscriptural view of reality, man, revelation, and Scripture. This situation calls for nothing less than a continued fundamental reformation of our understanding of the nature of our total existence, and specifically of the essence of theology and Biblical hermeneutics.[16]

Notes

1. For biographical information, see *6; 7; 8; 10; 11.*

2. The books and many unpublished manuscripts of Archibald Alexander are in the Speer Library of Princeton Theological Seminary; his correspondence and other materials are in the Firestone Library of Princeton University.

3. Some of the more important leaders in this school of thought were Francis Hutcheson (1694-1746), Thomas Reid (1710-96), Adam Smith (1723-90), Adam Ferguson (1723-1816), Dugald Stewart (1753-1828), Thomas Brown (1778-1820), Sir William Hamilton (1788-1856), James Fr. Ferrier (1808-64). See also H. E. Runner (*12*: 12): "The beginning of the eighteenth century was a critical time for Scotland. Since the Union with England (1707) Deism and Enlightenment ideas generally spread rapidly there . . . . This century also saw a veritable 'Scottish Renaissance,' which placed the Scottish universities in the very forefront of European culture. Sons of the Church had a great deal to do with it. But, as in other countries, a division arose in the Church between the Evangelicals . . . and the Moderates . . . . By the middle of the century the Moderates had gained possession of the universities of Glasgow, Aberdeen and Edinburgh. At this time the Scottish school of philosophy emerges."

4. This is D. H. T. Vollenhoven's philosophic description of Berkeley's conception.

5. Those philosophic conceptions which D. H. T. Vollenhoven has called "consistent empiricism" and "monarchianism" have throughout the history of Western thought always resulted in some form of heresy, while the conceptions of "inconsistent empiricism" and "semimysticism"—both of which are modifications of the previous two extreme views—have often been regarded (erroneously, of course) as being harmonizable with the Christian view of reality.

6. H. Evan Runner (*12*: 12) talks about the great impact of English and Scottish philosophy on theologians in Harvard, Yale and Princeton. John Witherspoon was the only clergyman to have signed the American Declaration of Independence in 1776.

7. Also known as Liberty Hall Academy and later as Washington and Lee College. Concerning the person and work of Rev. William Graham, see *10*: 6; *6*: 18, 83-4, 106-9, 120-1, 465; *7*: 580-3. Archibald Alexander's father had given the land for Liberty Hall. William Graham had in mind to establish a Seminary at Liberty Hall after the model of Princeton College.

8. This book appeared posthumously in 1825. Alexander tried to mediate the views of Butler, Reid and Price. Cf. *1*.

9. On the next page Alexander wrote: "While some of our strongest men are occupied in controversies about the cords and pins of the tabernacle, as though the ark itself was in no danger, we rejoice that there are those who apprehend the evils which threaten the church of God from the increase of infidelity and heresy."

10. *Ibid.*, pp. 17-20. W. J. Grier has clearly sensed Alexander's empiricistic thought pattern on this score: "There are two kinds of religious knowledge . . . . These are the knowledge of the truth as it is revealed in the Holy Scriptures, and the impression which that truth makes on the human mind when rightly apprehended. The first may be compared to the inscription

or image on a seal, the other to the impression made by the seal on the wax" (*8*: xvii; see also *9*: 141-9).

11. This explains, at least in part, why in the Princeton-Westminster tradition much of the argument for a specific view of inspiration is often couched in language of confessional admonition to avoid faithlessness.

12. Alexander refers here in a footnote to the thoughts of Pascal.

13. Alexander continues: "God meant it to bring into act every faculty of the soul, in weighing, discriminating, enlarging, balancing, in all intellectual exercise by which one truth sinks into another."

14. Against the background, Alexander explains the nature of homilies and expositions.

15. Cf. H. Evan Runner's reference to Sidney Ahlstrom's assessment of the nature of Scottish philosophy: "It is more accurate to see the Scottish philosophers as a liberal vanguard, even as theological revolutionaries, than to preserve the traditional picture of genteel conservatives bringing reason to the service of a decadent orthodoxy." This philosophy, Runner continues, "came to be adopted by Archibald Alexander, the first professor of Princeton Theological Seminary, and by Charles Hodge, his pupil, whose textbook *Systematic Theology* I still used as a main textbook in Westminster Seminary" (*12*: 21).

16. Cf. James H. Olthuis, "Towards a Certitudinal Hermeneutic," in this volume.

Bibliography

1. AHLSTROM, S. E., "The Scottish Philosophy and American Theology," in: *Church History*, 24 (1955), pp. 257-72.

2. ALEXANDER, A., *Evidences of the Authenticity, Inspiration and Canonical Authority of Holy Scriptures*; Philadelphia: Presbyterian Board of Publication, 1836. Reprinted in the *Religion in America* series.

3. ——. "Deistical Controversy in the West," in: *Princeton Review*, 16 (1844), p. 498.

4 ——. *Lectures on Moral Philosophy*; Class Lectures in original manuscript at Speer library of Princeton Theological Seminary.

5 ——. *Outlines of Moral Science*; Class Lectures published posthumously in 1852.

6. ALEXANDER, J. W., *The Life of Archibald Alexander*; New York: Charles Scribners Sons, 1854.

7. DE WITT, J., "Archibald Alexander's Preparation for his Profession," in: *Princeton Theological Review*, 3 (1905), pp. 573-94.

8. GRIER, W. J., "Biographical Introduction," in: *A. Alexander, Thoughts on Religious Experience* (1844); London: The Banner of Truth Trust, 1967, pp. vii-vx.

9. JACKSON, G. E., "Archibald Alexander's Thoughts on Religious Experience, a Critical Revisiting," in: *Journal of Presbyterian Historical Society*, 51 (1973), p. 142.

10. MACKEY, J. A., "Archibald Alexander (1772-1851)," in: *Sons of the Prophets: Leaders in Protestantism from Princeton Seminary* (ed. Hugh T. Kerr); Princeton: Princeton University Press, 1963, pp. 3-21.

11. NELSON, J. O., "Archibald Alexander, Winsome Conservative," in: *Journal of Presbyterian Historical Society*, 25 (1957), pp. 15-32.

12. RUNNER, H. E., " The Development of Calvinism in North America on the Background of its Development in Europe"; paper available from the Institute for Christian Studies, Toronto.

13. VANDER STELT, J. C., *Philosophy and Scripture: A Study in Old Princeton and Westminster Theology*; Marlton: Mack Publishing Company, 1978.

The Modern Settlement: Religion and Culture in the Early Schleiermacher

HENRY VANDER GOOT

Introduction

Schleiermacher's *Ueber die Religion: Reden an die Gebildeten unter Ihren Verächtern*[1] of 1799 is addressed to "the cultured among the despisers of religion." In the context of Schleiermacher's own immediate environment, this has a definite meaning. No doubt he had his own Romanticist friends in mind (*3*: xxxix). However, what is present in these two descriptive labels (*Gebildeten* and *Verächtern*) has a deep cultural-historical background that is the heritage of Schleiermacher's addressees. These addressees were only late eighteenth century examples of a modern attitude that had been in the making for certainly no less than 300 years. This attitude had to do with the overall relationship of religion and culture. In directing the *Reden* to these *Gebildeten* among the despisers of religion, Schleiermacher had thus directly addressed himself to the problem of the modern schism of church and state and of all that this institutional struggle symbolized. In so doing he sought to bring about a settlement that accepted as irreversible the changed historical circumstances of the modern world and yet granted to religion the autonomy he so deeply felt it demanded. In short, Schleiermacher's *Reden* is an apologetic for religion as capable of raising the life of man to its highest realization. Modern man's turn to this world (which Schleiermacher wholeheartedly applauded) had itself to be shown to be *inherently* religious and therefore even positive and good as such (*9*: 40). Schleiermacher's urge to establish this can only be understood against the background of the broad outlines of the cultural history of Europe.

At the close of the Middle Ages, the *Corpus Christianum* had begun to show signs of fundamental disintegration. For centuries it had maintained unity and concord for Western civilization. But by the fifteenth century the principles of the non-ecclesiastical order had begun to develop an autonomous life of their own, often in resistance to the hegemony of the church. In addition, the Reformation had brought onto the scene at least two religious systems that began to struggle with Rome for the allegiance of men. The European order of society, symbolized by the Holy Roman Empire, was beginning to crumble. No common European religious allegiance could be achieved, and hence a common European social order seemed unattainable.

While wars of religion raged in the sixteenth and seventeenth centuries, the efforts of the Reformation dissolved in the movement's loss of its identity. Vain attempts to re-establish a public order on a religious basis were undertaken at Augsburg in 1555 and at Westphalia in 1648. But by 1648 peace signified a stalemate. Neither Rome nor the Reformation could unite Europe. *The acceptance of this situation meant that the major questions pertaining to the unfolding of the "secular" order were to be settled by criteria other than those of religious conviction.* This situation encouraged increasing dissent and a growing rash of nationalism by the end of the seventeenth century.

The enlightened leaders of Europe (Leibniz, Herbert of Cherbury, Hugo Grotius, Malebranche, and many others) had become convinced that a new ground for a common European social order would have to be sought outside of the divisive arena of religion (*10*: 197-220). This new basis was sought in the supposed common rationality of man, that is, in Reason understood as the source and voice of self-evident truth. Religious truth (a truth that was dividing Europe) was thought to be private, individual and subjective. The ascending claim of Reason to ultimate validity was in turn denominated public and objective. It was, of course, not recognized that the appeal to Reason as a source of certainty in thought and unity in practice was itself an unexplained and, in fact, religious claim to ultimate validity. Nevertheless, once this bad bill of goods became generally acceptable to modern Enlightenment Europe, the proponents of the new religion of Reason achieved an exclusive and uncontested right to develop the public, cultural order according to their (in fact particularist and sectarian) conception of the life of man and the goals of society.

As has been indicated, for the enlightened particular religion had come to represent the private and subjective at best; superstition, war and persecution at worst. Indeed, though the Enlightenment did endorse certain universal principles of natural religion (principles, it supposed, acceptable to every rational man), the purpose of these principles was to confirm high moral standards and to sustain decent conduct. However, the enlightened were in reality repulsed by the exclusivist claims of particular, historical religions.

Thus, as embarrassed and frightened Christians became half-convinced by the new cultural leadership of Europe that European religion was certainly a narrow sectarian concern and possibly even a symptom of stupidity and backwardness, the conventional representatives of religion began to withdraw from the "public" domain and the practical tasks of life. While Enlightenment humanism had become the sole explicit culture-forming influence of modern European civilization by the middle of the seventeenth century, an intimidated and weary Christianity took to the prayer chamber and the wayside chapel. Catholicism was devitalized by a wave of Quietism. Protestantism turned to Pietism and inwardness. To the Enlightenment's deep-seated hatred of the divisiveness and persecution that religion had occasioned and of the "superstition" it had fostered in spite of the "advancement of natural knowledge," religion reacted by going inward to symbolize its own lack of confidence in its ability to effect a reorganization of natural-cultural affairs. Concern with formal institutions, structures and relationships diminished rapidly in the late seventeenth and early eighteenth centuries. These, after all, were to be constituted on standards and aims supposedly derived from the universal, rational (and therefore public) nature of man. Accordingly, concern with personal religious truth, unconditional commitment, subjective religious experience, personal development, ascetic discipline, church activities, and world missions began to increase. In this way religion had begun to accept the role of custodian of "life's little things," as Troeltsch once described them.

It was on this Pietist kind of Protestant inwardness that Friedrich Schleiermacher was raised.[2] Born in 1768, Schleiermacher was the son of Reformed, Pietist parents. Chiefly interested in Friedrich's personal faith, Schleiermacher's parents sent him off to a school of the Moravian Brethren at the age of fifteen. There Friedrich was thoroughly immersed in the life and teachings of a rigorously ascetic, discipline-oriented Pietism. In addition, he learned of inwardness first hand. Though he became increasingly uncomfortable in this setting as his rational powers increased, Friedrich had been affected in the very depths of his being by this experience. Throughout his life Schleiermacher emphatically claimed to have remained a Moravian, but then one of a "higher order."[3] Indeed, Schleiermacher's lifelong preoccupation with the inescapability of religion and his perception of it as a matter of the "heart" constitute the positive contributions of Moravian Pietism to the development of his life and thought.

By 1785 Schleiermacher had been transferred to a Moravian seminary at Barby. It was at Barby that he really began to experience the cultural narrowness of the Brethren. He longed for exposure to the cultural and intellectual world of the eighteenth century, for it buzzed with excitement all around the sheltered island of tranquility and non-involvement of the Moravians.

Hence, by 1787 Friedrich begged his father to be released from the Moravian schools and to be allowed to transfer to the rationalist University of Halle. His father reluctantly granted the young boy's request. At Halle Schleiermacher came upon the Enlightenment philosophies of Leibniz and Kant, and the conflict of this new perspective with Moravianism began to rage in his soul. In the succeeding years, Schleiermacher came to acquaint himself with the Western philosophical tradition. He cultivated a profound regard for Plato and Aristotle.

However, one philosopher more than any other out of the past attracted his attention. This figure was the unknown Spinoza of Holland. By 1789, in good Spinozistic fashion, Schleiermacher was defending determinism and writing on ethics. The problem of reconciling Kantianism and Spinozism was much on his mind, indicating his deep involvement in the problematics of modern Enlightenment philosophy. By 1796 Schleiermacher had written specifically on Spinoza and had come more and more to put much of the past out of his mind. Schleiermacher now began to substitute Christianized Enlightenment and idealistic alternatives for his Protestant heritage. Nonetheless, important dimensions of Moravianism had so taken root in his character that they were destined to factor into the composition of his early *Weltanschauung* as exemplified by the *Reden*.

In 1796 Schleiermacher came to Berlin and began to seek out its cultured society. It was there that he joined the ranks of the Romanticists, whose influence on the religious system he now began to frame was substantial. It was their Romanticized Enlightenment culture (*harmonische Ausbildung*) that Schleiermacher (in great measure) accepted and addressed in order to turn its attention (forward, as he saw it) to the value of religion for the cultural life of those who despised its past. What conception of religion this would require was presented to his enlightened friends in the *Reden*.

It is clear, then, that religion and culture had not just affected Schleiermacher negatively. They each left their positive mark on him. Schleiermacher could accept neither as they had developed up to his own time, and so he transformed the understanding of religion and accepted the new Romanticist and historicist definition of culture to effect a convergence of religion and culture that would be acceptable to the nineteenth century.

In the effort to draw the principles of religion and culture closely together, Schleiermacher, it has been indicated, drew heavily upon his own perception of religion as *Mystik*. No doubt Schleiermacher's religious appeal to religion's cultured despisers rested upon a unique conception of culture as well. However, on the culture side of the polarity Schleiermacher knew full well that he would find the most promising point of contact with his addressees, for their conception and endorsement of cultural multiformity and individuality was his no less than theirs. According to Schleiermacher and his Romanticist friends (religion's cultured despisers), the individual, individual difference and differentiation in history are positive values equal to the ideal of harmony and uniformity. It was, hence, left to Schleiermacher to show that culture and historical experience so conceived could be sanctioned and advanced by religion. *Schleiermacher accomplished this demonstration to the satisfaction of his addressees by the transformation of religion into a mysticism that sought and found its infinite object and goal in the finite itself.*[4]

My introduction must be brought to a close. I have tried to argue the following. In great measure accepting the modern Enlightenment condemnation of Christian history that inspired and encouraged the great modern schism that secularism attempted to effect, Schleiermacher sought to bring about a reconciliation of religion and culture, mysticism and individuality. This reconciliation, moreover, constituted an endorsement of progress and the unfolding of the modern world as inherently and essentially religious, and therefore even positive and good as such. Within the limits of this reconciliation, the church would henceforth have to find its place and make its home. *The cultural-historical significance of Schleiermacher's "Reden" in this context is that it effected the formal origin of this modern settlement.*[5]

A discussion of purpose and procedure

Thus far I have discussed the historical significance of Schleiermacher's *Reden* by arguing that it effected a resolution of the problem of the relation of culture and religion, or reason and faith, that became widely acceptable to Christians in the nineteenth century. Schleiermacher's resolution aimed at exhibiting an intrinsic relation between religion (understood as *Mystik*) and culture (understood as individuality). He sought, in this way, to relativize the seeming antithesis between the two that had come to characterize modern history since the Renaissance. In attempting to convince his cultured friends of the viability of this "new covenant," Schleiermacher argued two fundamental presuppositions in the *Reden*.

First, he argued that religion is an autonomous and ineradicable dimension of universal human experience. Such a view of religion was contrary to the prevailing eighteenth century reductions of religion either to assent to intellectual truths or to moral striving. By contrast, Schleiermacher argued that *Mystik* is what stands beyond both intellectual and moral life, belonging to a "third realm" independent of both science and morality. Religion so conceived is consistent with culture conceived as personal individuality and communal variety. This conception of religion is the fulcrum of Schleiermacher's apologetic and will be taken up in the next part of this essay.

Second, to convince religion's cultured despisers that religion conceived as *Mystik* fosters rather than retards the development of culture and civilization, Schleiermacher further qualifies his definition by arguing that religion is not just mystical *Anschauung* and *Gefühl* in general, but is sense and taste for the infinite in and through the finite. However, in so defining religion, Schleiermacher draws upon opposing suggestions and concepts he has found in Spinoza and Fichte. Imaginatively overcoming the tension between these two sources, Schleiermacher synthesizes from Spinoza and Fichte a new conception of mysticism as the attainment of a *visio Dei* in and through the world of concrete things. At the heart of this reworking of Spinoza and Fichte and, hence, at the heart of Schleiermacher's insight that *Selbstanschauung* is *Anschauung des Universums*, is the concept of the bi-polarity of reality in terms of infinite universality and finite particularity. This concept of the bi-polarity of reality is the basis of Schleiermacher's cultural theology. Furthermore, this same metaphysical principle constitutes the point at which Schleiermacher advances beyond the universalistic realism of Spinoza and the ethical idealism of Fichte. For these reasons I shall take up this set of relations in the final section of this essay.

The philosophical and theological fundamentals of Schleiermacher's definition of religion in the "Reden" of 1799

Schleiermacher's second speech of the *Reden* is the most important one. It constitutes the core of the whole work. Schleiermacher himself admits to Friedrich Samuel Sack that he (Sack) will discover nothing in the other speeches that cannot be found in the first two (*Briefe*, III, 107). In February of 1799, after Schleiermacher had written the first two speeches, his work was interrupted for a number of months. He had been called to Potsdam to fill in for an ailing pastor until the king could name a permanent replacement. After this break in the continuity of Schleiermacher's writing, the work began to deteriorate—at least, this was the opinion of many of Schleiermacher's friends. In any event, the substantive philosophical and theological theses of the *Reden* appear in the second speech.

In opening his second speech, Schleiermacher puzzles over why it is that religion is so misunderstood by the cultured and enlightened. In response to this problem, he observes that the peculiar development of eighteenth century culture has polluted society. Schleiermacher notes the presence of two landscapes: the cultural world and the sphere of the powers of the soul. He complains that the concord encouraged by the eighteenth century entailed the subordination of cultural distinctiveness to common rationality, and that this has impaired the soul in its capacity to see a true picture of religion. Individuality has been lost through too much cultural amalgamation. Cosmopolitanism (*harmonische Ausbildung*)

> . . . has founded such a complete and extensive sociableness in the human soul that presently among us none of its faculties in fact function in separation, however much we may conceive them as distinct. Rather, in every operation each is influenced, permeated and somewhat deflected from its course by the ready love and support of others. The result is that in this highly developed society one looks about in vain for an action or operation that could be a reliable expression of some one function of the spirit, be it sensibility, intelligence, morality, or religion (*11:* 33-4).

Hence it is necessary that a new human "Nüchternheit des Sinnes" (sobering of the senses) be cultivated to free man from old memories, preconceived notions, and the influence of culture. Schleiermacher suggests that religion's cultured despisers return to a state of sobriety unpolluted by the "wohlbekannten Bildungen" (well-known products) of Enlightenment society. Almost in the style of Rousseau and anticipating his own concept of *Anschauung*, Schleiermacher encourages a return to "the undifferentiated and incomplete state of childhood, in which everything was distinct, separated and individual" (*11*: 34).

What is sounded here, then, is a call to return to an undifferentiated state in which the form of religion is still positive, particular and individual rather than mixed, abstract and universal—a hypothetical state in which the concrete can be accepted as the standard and not as a mere example. In this way Schleiermacher voices opposition to eighteenth century developments, especially those intellectually represented by Deism (or natural religion) and the Kantian and Fichtean philosophies.

Kantian and Fichtean idealism subordinate the individual to universal structures of intelligibility. Hence, according to Schleiermacher, both lack positive content. Even Fichte's individual, finite ego is conceived as a valid, universal reality apart from individual, cultural and personal differences. In this sense Fichte separates philosophy from the concrete, according to Schleiermacher (*6*: 509). Accepting the Enlightenment reduction of religion to rational principles, both Kant and Fichte mix and confuse religion and moral striving. In addition, Deism had mixed universal, rational principles and religious faith in order to advocate a truly nonsectarian, natural religion as the basis of decent moral conduct. Against this background Schleiermacher warns his addressees about "any and every confusion of religion with that with which it is mixed and with that which here and there appears to be similar to it" (*11*: 34).

Religion is not a form of knowledge

With Kant, Schleiermacher rejects the attempt to assimilate religion to thought, especially to theoretical thought. In the conception of Schleiermacher, religion is neither speculation nor science. Though it has the same object as religion, namely, "the Universe and man's relationship to it" (*11*: 35), science or speculation deals with that object quite differently. Science, speculation, metaphysics, and transcendental philosophy are all forms of knowing. All of these forms of knowing classify the universe, divide it up into kinds of being, look for causes of what is, and deduce the necessity of the real. They have the tendency "to define Being, to get lost in an unending maze of reasons and deductions, to discover final causes, and to give utterance to eternal truths" (*11*: 36-7). Because of its very nature, knowledge cannot be appropriate to the infinite; hence, in the first edition of the *Reden*, Schleiermacher does not resist the Kantian conclusion that "thought does not take us beyond the horizons of experience and its structural conditions" (*6*: 494).

Another major dimension of Schleiermacher's denial that the absolute can be present in knowledge is his antipathy to scholastic theology and its odd reversal of the order of life and dogma (or thought) (*11*: 114-15). Schleiermacher is convinced that the divine is absent in most speculation about it. He feels deeply that religion is not an intellectual instrument of man whereby he can dispose over the divine. Because of the fundamental confusion of religion with the acceptance of ideas about its object, which had, Schleiermacher observes, destroyed the vitality and ultimate relevance of faith, Schleiermacher zealously asserts the discontinuity of religion and knowledge. In this Schleiermacher draws heavily upon Moravianism.

Religion is not a form of action

As has been noted, in his denial that religion is a form of knowing, Schleiermacher draws heavily upon the transcendentalism of Kant, the orientation of Fichte to the primacy of lived experience over thought, and the emphasis of Moravianism upon the emotional rather than rational life of man. The absolute, Schleiermacher feels, cannot be *known* but must be approached via the mediation of some non-intellectual mode of contact with reality.

Now, the Enlightenment had reduced religion to rational principles sustaining sterling virtues and confirming good moral conduct. At most the difference between religion and morality was thought to be one of perspective:religion is action based upon natural law understood as obedience to the divine will; morality is action based upon natural law considered in itself. This is exemplified in the positions of John Locke, Herbert of Cherbury, William Paley, Samuel Clarke, John Toland, and many others.

Turning to reason conceived more broadly as will, Kant and Fichte argue that human access to the absolute is attained in moral striving, regulated, according to Kant, by the postulated ideals of God, freedom and immortality. The position of Fichte, however, goes further than that of Kant. Fichte endows the free, practical ego of Kant with constitutive power. He denies that the truth is in contemplation and so transfers it to the sphere of action.

Ego is pure willing, according to Fichte. Ego projects and posits itself and the world. It is a duty-motivated operation. Being and existence, in turn, are simply functions and relationships of action, the actuation of absolute freedom. Hence the ego is nothing in itself, no substance or thing. Rather, according to Fichte, it is a task, a project, a program. Moreover, according to Fichte, the meaning of the non-ego is exhausted in its capacity to become the object of what the ego places upon itself as absolute moral obligation. Everything is the movement of reality from man outward.

It is within the context of these basic thematic principles that Fichte articulates his concept of God. Fichte's conviction is that it is in action that man achieves and grasps the infinite. Because Fichte reduces all of reality to morality, the absolute, too, can be no more than a product of the laws inherent in practical reason.

With Kant, Fichte argues that God is free of all sensible mixture. When applied to God, our concepts cannot be invested with thing-in-itself validity. And hence, with Kant, Fichte orients the idea of God to the moral sphere, that is, to the sphere of subjectivity, which is identified with faith. According to Fichte, the absolute belongs to man's system of moral actions and ideals. Insofar as the ego alone is absolute, the absolute is reducible to the compass of the subjective rationality of human action. In the language of Cornelio Fabro, Fichte's absolute is the "transcendental X, the moral order of the universe, the basis and term of human action and aspiration, rationality in selfactuation as fulfillment of man's moral perfection" (*2*: 549).

It is this Kantian and Fichtean position (conceiving religion as decent moral conduct based on rational principles, or the ultimate structure of moral striving) that Schleiermacher also rejects in his definition of religion. Morality is the exercise of feelings and thoughts, man acting upon himself and his affections. According to Schleiermacher, morality develops a system of moral duties out of the nature of man and his relationship to the universe. But, Schleiermacher insists, "Religion ought not attempt that either. It ought not deduce from the Universe certain imperatives; nor ought it construct some code of laws" (*11*: 37).

The nature of religion

Schleiermacher argues, then, that conceptual thought cannot comprehend the absolute that grounds finite being. Furthermore, moral striving is inadequate to define religious faith. Religion must be wholly other than morality and metaphysics. Religion, Schleiermacher argues,

> maintains its own domain and character by completely transcending speculation and moral praxis. Furthermore, the common sphere of human operations is only then fully rounded out when religion establishes itself alongside of science and moral action, and when human nature is completely developed also in this aspect. Religion hence reveals itself to you as a necessary and inescapable "third factor" alongside of science and morality—in short, as their equally worthy and excellent natural counterpart (*11*: 49).

Having postulated religion as a third domain alongside of metaphysics and morality, Schleiermacher argues that the absolute, which is presupposed in the finite and the partial (thought and morality, or nature and spirit), can only be *felt*. The absolute beyond both the domain of morality and the field of science discloses itself to man in the concrete through *Anschauung* and *Gefühl*, or *Sinn* and *Geschmack*.[6] Religion's essence, Schleiermacher says,

> is neither thinking nor acting but is affective perception and feeling. Religion wishes to perceive the Universe; attentively to tune itself into the representations and activities of the Universe. In childlike awe religion wishes to be gripped and filled by its immediate influences (*11*: 46-7).

Anschauung is receptive because it receives givens and is dependent upon them. Furthermore, it is immediate because it receives these givens as they are without making connections, discriminations, distinctions, separations, and associations. In addition, *Anschauung* is individual. When an individual that is given in perception is compared with other givens and so becomes the basis for the induction of general principles, it is transcended. *Anschauung* is simple, delight-filled reception of the immediately given individual thing. For Schleiermacher, the receptivity, immediacy and individuality of *Anschauung* (and religion) contrast markedly to the activism, mediacy and universalism of metaphysics amd morality.

These contrasts are sharpened and more clearly expressed as Schleiermacher adds new dimensions to his definition of religion. Religious *Anschauung* and *Gefühl* are not just *Anschauung* and *Gefühl* without further qualification. Schleiermacher observes:

> Religion also lives its entire life in nature, though in the infinite nature of the Totality, the one and the All. In quiet submission religion wishes to sense and perceive in the individual that which is uniquely its own—to perceive where everything, as well as the individual itself, desires to be driven and to reside in this eternal mixture of individual forms and beings (*11*: 48).

These constructive words of Schleiermacher once again bring into sharp focus that to which they form a contrast. *Anschauung* is repeatedly emphasized to indicate the inwardness of faith. No doubt an intellectualism is here opposed that supposes that reflection is the basis of religion. In insisting that religion is the *Anschauung* of the infinite nature of the All *in* the particular, Schleiermacher certainly seems to be struggling to overcome a mechanical and scholastic separation of God and world that makes man's cultural life and temporal abode a monumental irrelevancy. That the "universalism" of the Enlightenment and transcendental philosophy is also being chided for its failure to do justice to the concrete and to historical individuality can best be illustrated by taking a look at Schleiermacher's opposition to Fichte's first principle that no being can be posited that transcends the consciousness of the finite ego.

Schleiermacher has set out to relativize, or maybe even flatly oppose, the moral and metaphysical perspectives as they had developed, especially in the case of Fichte, in isolation from the religious point of view. This isolation has, according to Schleiermacher, yielded the belief that knowledge and moral action can derive the reality of the world and its laws from man himself. Says Schleiermacher: "Metaphysics and morality regard only man as the middlepoint of all relationships in the entire Universe. They regard him as the condition of all Being and the final cause of all becoming" (*11*: 47; cf. also *1*: 325). Here a transcendentalism (Kantian and Fichtean) is opposed that creates the infinite in the image of the finite and its limitations. Metaphysics, Schleiermacher says,

> . . . takes its starting point in the finite nature of man and wishes consciously to determine, by means of its simplest idea and with all of its power and sen-

> sitivity, what the Universe can be for it and where this must necessarily be seen . . . . Morality takes its starting point in the consciousness of freedom, whose dominion it wishes to extend into the infinite so that everything will be subordinated to it (*11*: 48).

In attempting to unfold the order of the world according to their own ideals, metaphysics and morality also lose sight of the individuality of man. Man is placed over against the universe and made a part of it. Thus Schleiermacher also assaults the logical consequence of a "universalism" that devalues historical individuality by forcing it to serve illustratively in the defense of general principles. Moreover, Schleiermacher indicts those transcendentalisms and idealisms (Kantian and Fichtean) that seek access to the absolute in moral striving, the movement of reality from man outward, and that deal with the individual finite ego only as a *universal* "individual structure of intelligibility." An "impoverished uniformity" arises, Schleiermacher complains, where religion is absent. Only abstract, general ideas and structures are recognized because the enlightened lack "a basic sense for the infinity and vitality of nature, whose symbol is multifacetedness and individuality" (*11*: 50). In Schleiermacher's view, morality and metaphysics need religion. "Everything must begin with affective perception. Those who lack the deep desire to perceive and regard the infinite have no standard—and naturally do not need any either—by which to know whether they have thought in a meaningful way about it" (*11*: 51).

Schleiermacher thus places the immediacy of *Anschauung* and *Gefühl* above the mediacy and partiality of thought and morality. Furthermore, a unique principle of individuality and concreteness is achieved and becomes metaphysically prominent in Schleiermacher's philosophy especially as he merges it with his mysticism. At this point the influence of his Romanticist acquaintances is unmistakable. They have left their mark on him. Yet Schleiermacher does not hesitate to make an appeal to them as well. After all, this is the intention of Schleiermacher's work as a whole. How can this now be seen to be so?

Schleiermacher has argued that religion is an ineradicable *a priori* of human consciousness in general. Furthermore, he has argued that in religion, many-sidedness is tolerated and even actively encouraged. In it the freedom of man to live according to his *actual* nature is affirmed against the Enlightenment attempt to subordinate religious, cultural and personal differences to some empty, common rationality that corresponds to no positive reality. *Religion, Schleiermacher appeals, makes everyone develop what is his peculiar gift, and how can the cultured (his Romanticist friends) despise this?*

The general significance of what Schleiermacher has argued thus far can now be brought into proper relief. Schleiermacher's *Reden* represents a major turning point in the modern conception of its subject. For Schleiermacher once for all fixes into the mind of modern man the truth that religion is an inerasable component of human consciousness in general. Furthermore, religion is not inconsistent with the life of man in society and culture; it is, as a matter of fact, the condition for the possibility of culture's highest realization. Once Schleiermacher's mysticism was connected with the new historical consciousness and, even further, with the general psychology and epistemology of modern philosophy, the common fundamental concepts from which it was possible to open up a way to the particular in history and society and to the concrete within the various religions were permanently established. In his *Reden* of 1799 Schleiermacher thus arranges a new covenant between religion and culture and, more specifically, founds the modern study of religion.

Fichte and/or Spinoza: The focal tension of the "Reden"

As has been shown, religion is said to be *Anschauung*—a dependent human stance (*Nüchternheit des Sinnes*) in which the spirit of religion discloses or reveals itself to man. Thus inwardness and immediacy are achieved in contrast to the externality and mediacy of thought and action. Secondly, religious receptivity is contrasted by Schleiermacher with the "activism" of metaphysics and morality and is endorsed as a proper and only means to do justice to concrete individuality.

No doubt Schleiermacher's Moravian mysticism forms a great part of the picture here. Mysticism had all along been burdened with a prominent ascetic dimension. Yet Schleiermacher tries desperately to salvage mysticism and to reconcile it with a proper involvement in the practical tasks of the modern world. And Schleiermacher in fact accomplishes this by the creation of a new mysticism that draws into itself the modern Romanticist conception of individuality (*1*: 336).

However, in the omnipresence of the idea of *Anschauung* and receptivity at almost every juncture in Schleiermacher's presentation, the blending of mysticism with the influence of a prominent figure can be discerned. This persona, always present at least in the back of Schleiermacher's mind and sometimes even unmasked and identified in the pages of his progressing argument in the *Reden*, is Spinoza.[7] Spinoza's fundamental assumption of an infinite, unknown principle underlying, sustaining and determining the coherence of known, intra-cosmic finite things and relationships makes Schleiermacher's positing of a submissive finite ego within an infinite ground intelligible. In the contrast of Spinoza and Fichte, for whom the truth that the infinite is in and through the active rational agency of the human mind unfolding itself in moral striving had become (according to Schleiermacher) too much a final rather than a relative truth, the focal tension of the *Reden* is glimpsed (*3*: xxxii).

This tension is clearly visible in a very famous and crucial passage in the *Reden*. It is in this passage that Schleiermacher proposes the idea of a "higher realism," not a relative dependence of man upon an object of ordinary knowledge, but an "absolute dependence"[8] of man upon the ground of his whole being. Praising Spinoza in superlative terms and indicating his fundamental reliance upon him, Schleiermacher says the following:

> What then shall become of the highest utterance of the speculation of our days, complete rounded idealism, if the humility of religion does not form a counterweight to it and if religion does not suggest to idealism's pride a higher realism than that which it so boldly and with such perfect right subordinates to itself? It annihilates the Universe, while it seems to aim at constructing it. It would degrade the Universe to a mere allegory, to a mere shadow of our own limitations. Offer with me reverently a tribute to the holy, rejected Spinoza. The high World Spirit pervaded him; the infinite was his beginning and his end; the Universe was his only and everlasting love. In holy innocence and in deep humility he beheld himself mirrored in the eternal world and perceived how he also was its most worthy mirror. He was full of religion, full of Holy Spirit. Wherefore, he stands there alone and unequalled; master in his art, yet without disciples and without citizenship, sublime above the profane tribe (*11*: 52).

What is this "higher realism" that Schleiermacher advocates? I would suggest at least the following. Indicating his synthesis of Spinoza and Fichte and the special complexity of his relationship to Fichte and Criticism,[9] the realism that Schleiermacher advocates could be called "higher" for a number of reasons. First, it accepts idealism; that is, it accepts the exposure of the ordinary realistic point of view as naive and uncritical, thus granting the idealistic criticism that no self-contained, self-subsistent objects exist, and that the theory of naive realism has, hence, ontologized appearance. Second, "higher realism" does *not* regard its determinant, paralleled by the independent object to which man's ideas must conform for true knowledge according to the theory of naive realism, and paralleled by Spinoza's infinite substance, as infinite *object*. Rather, "higher realism" conceives this ground as infinite *subject*, an infinite active agency or *Geist* within which a submissive finite subject is given a relative place. Third, the concern of "higher realism" is *religious* knowledge; that is, *immediate knowledge* of the *totality*. This is unlike ordinary realism, which has to do with *mediate* knowledge of the *partial*. Schleiermacher's "higher realism" is hence a theory of religious (as distinguished from empirical-sensory) knowledge and experience.

Furthermore, Schleiermacher polemicizes ". . . against the narrow arbitrariness of a worldview that places man and the world as given in man's experience in the middle of the Universe . . ." (*1*: 325). As in ordinary knowledge, the subject perceiver is dependent upon the object given, so in religion, which furnishes a total rather than partial perspective, man is dependent upon an infinite principle that discloses itself to him in mystical perception. The attempt of Spinoza to do justice to this truth is highly praised. Yet Schleiermacher accepts Fichte and idealism, though only an idealism that would subordinate itself to a "higher realism." Following Fichte, Schleiermacher concurs that the infinite cannot be immediately known and that it is therefore through the finite that we postulate the whole; that is, it is only in our minds that a world (*Universum*) is created by which and in which we unfold it. The conflict of these two perspectives, the Spinozist and the Fichtean, is a signal tension in the *Reden*.

"Selbstanschauung" as "Anschauung des Universums" ("Anschauung" of the infinite in the finite): The key to Schleiermacher's resurrection of Spinoza in a critical (Fichtean) context

As has been noted, under the influence of Spinoza Schleiermacher is committed to the necessity of not depriving the infinite of reality. As Dilthey observes, "he was firm about maintaining both the real world and the idealistic perspective" (*1*: 361). By postulating no being that transcends consciousness, Fichte, according to Schleiermacher, runs the risk of being unable to preserve the full reality of the universe and the infinite that individuates itself in the world. Nonetheless, Schleiermacher is himself a transcendentalist and idealist. He believes that the world is in some sense created by the mind (*1*: 346). In other words, Schleiermacher wishes to do justice to the full reality of the finite ego as well. But by allowing the finite to be lost in the infinite and by conceiving the infinite as object, Spinoza, according to Schleiermacher, runs the risk of being unable to preserve the full reality of individuality, finite creativity and finite active agency (*9*: 56).

In short, Schleiermacher wishes to deprive neither the finite nor the infinite of the place that each demands in the real order of things. These principles seem mutually incompatible. Yet Schleiermacher regards them as mutually indispensable. He does not believe that the finite and the infinite can be placed over against one another. In Schleiermacher's view, the infinite is not the negation of the finite but the means by which the infinite can show forth its perfection. How to justify theoretically (which to him means critically) his conviction that the finite is in the infinite and the infinite in the finite is hence Schleiermacher's problem.

Schleiermacher's attempted resolution indicates that, though he preserves the truth of Spinoza, he does so in a Fichtean, or transcendentalist and idealist, way. The Fichtean categories that Schleiermacher revises and employs in the attempted resolution of his problem by and large revolve around the ideas of intellectual *Anschauung* and *Gefühl* (*1*: 357). Fichte argues that the ego is infinite activity moving outward and inward. Through contact with a power inside of itself and opposed to it, it experiences itself as limited to finitude and as a struggle to recover the ego. Awareness of this movement and contact is, according to Fichte, *Gefühl.*

Anschauung is, however, an imaginative faculty. It is perception of that which is opposed to it and an imaginative development of that perception. Through the interaction of *Anschauung* and *Gefühl,* the objective and subjective worlds arise. The activity of the ego is thus twofold in Fichte's view: where it seeks to bring its subjectivity into correspondence with the object world, it experiences itself as a *Sich-von-ihm-bestimmen-lassen* (letting itself be determined by it); on the other hand, where subjectivity seeks to stamp the world with its impression, it experiences itself as *Handeln* or activity, which receives its clarification in practical philosophy (*6*: 504ff).

It is this general conceptuality that Schleiermacher follows. In a general philosophical sense, the ideas of *Anschauung* and *Gefühl* are borrowed from Fichte, from the idea of the activity of the ego. For Schleiermacher, however, religious *Anschauung* transcends both the active and the passive, which illustrates how Schleiermacher modifies the meaning of categories even when he borrows them in a general sense.

First, Fichte's idea of activity (*Handeln* and *Sich-von-ihm-bestimmen-lassen*) has to be deepened to an absolute "receptivity" or "passivity" beyond both the sphere of scientific knowledge and the field of moral action.[10] Second, for Schleiermacher *Selbstanschauung,* or *Anschauung* of the ego, has to be deepened to *Anschauung* of the *Individual.* In this point the Fichtean separation of the universal and the concrete can be clearly seen, according to Schleiermacher. Fichte's ego is, after all, no more than an abstract universal structure. As a Romanticist Schleiermacher is clear in his difference with Fichte on this point, and it is thus at this point that Schleiermacher makes the idea of the universal and the individual the basis of his philosophy of religion. *Anschauung* and *Gefühl* of the infinite, or the disclosure of the infinite in the finite religious soul of man, Schleiermacher regards as an activity of the self-perception of the individual (*11*: 77-8; cf. *5*: 99). Schleiermacher's notion of the intuitive self-perception of the individual is thus *Anschauung* of the infinite as it individuates and manifests itself in the individual soul of man, the highest and noblest "vehicle" through which the infinite flows into the finite. In *Selbstanschauung* as *Selbstanschauung der Individualität*, man realizes that he is part of the infinite, above space and time, and thus that individuality is the sphere and domain of eternity. What follows is presented in an attempt to clarify this important dimension of Schleiermacher's philosophy.

Schleiermacher believes that man builds up the world through *Anschauung* and *Gefühl*. Schleiermacher, moreover, assumes that the ego is an active being that reflects itself in the non-ego. "For me the Spirit," he says, "is the first and the last; for what I recognize as world is its finest product, its self-created reflection."[11] The outer is, according to Schleiermacher, created out of the inner; ". . . the Universe is reflected in the inner life and the outer is only intelligible through the inner," he remarks (*11*: 93; cf. *5*: 73). In good Fichtean style, Schleiermacher thus emphasizes that ". . . in spiritual things the origin can be created for you in no other way than if you generate it by means of an original creation in yourself and at no other moment than when you so produce it" (*11*: 43).

The highest *Anschauung*, which is the formula of religion, is *Anschauung des Universums*. "Religion perceives every individual thing as a part of the whole, every limited thing as a representation of the infinite" (*11*: 57; cf. 60-1). Schleiermacher now sets out to relate how man attains to this highest *Anschauung*. Involved is a dialectical "process" of ascending comprehensive levels of intuition deepened through experience, a great chain of *Anschauungen* through which the soul of man proceeds in its "ascent" to the highest vision of truth. At the beginning of the "process" stands *sensus* of the self; at the end *Selbstanschauung* as *Anschauung des Universums*, an *Anschauung* of oneself as being one with the infinite and yet as being a unique and individual being. The stages in between are: *Anschauungen* of others (*11*: 83), communion with nature involving the observation of orderliness and harmony in the counteraction of opposing principles (*11*: 85-7), *sensus* of humanity, *Anschauung* of love as the world's principle of organization,[12] and *Anschauung* of history, the greatest and most general revelation of the holy (*11*: 92, 109-10).

When the highest *Anschauung* is attained, man experiences the final truth in which he surrenders himself to the infinite world as a holy being. According to Schleiermacher, this experience is as it were a revelation to him. In it the distinctions of *Anschauung* and *Gefühl*, object and subject, fall away or, rather, have not yet arisen. In *Anschauung* and *Gefühl* as a unit, that is, in the first and original function of the soul (*Gemüt*),[13] man experiences himself as being one with everything that in consciousness he experiences as standing over against him. Let us now see how Schleiermacher describes his experience in this *Anschauung*.

> That first mysterious moment that appears in each sensory experience, before perception and feeling are separated—that moment in which sense

> and its object mingle and unite, then each return to their original place—I know how indescribable it is and how quickly it vanishes. Nonetheless, would that I could hold it fast and refer to it again in the higher and divine religious activity of the Soul. Would that I could and were allowed to give expression to it without desecrating it! It is fleeting and transparent as the vapor that the dew breathes on blossom and fruit; it is bashful and tender as a maiden's kiss; it is holy and fruitful as a bridal embrace. No, it is not merely like these—it is all of these themselves. Quickly and mysteriously this appearance presents itself as an occasion to form an image of the Universe. Just as this beloved and much desired apparition forms itself, it encounters my soul. I embrace it, not as a phantom but as a Holy Being. I lie directly on the bosom of the infinite world: I am in this moment its soul, for I feel all its powers and endless life as my own. In this moment it is my body for I pervade its muscles and members, and its inmost nerves are set in motion by my sense and forecasting as if they were my own. The slightest disruption shatters this holy embrace, and only now does an affective perception appear in my consciousness as a well defined *Gestalt*. I measure it and it displays itself in my open consciousness as the figure of the vanishing mistress in the opened eyes of her lover. Only now, for the first time, does feeling issue from the inmost parts, spreading itself over my whole being as the blush of shame and love over the face of the maiden. This moment is the brightest blossom of religion. If I could create it for you, I would be a god. Oh, Holy Fortune, forgive me that I have had to discover more than the Eleusian Mysteries. This moment represents the birth of everything vital in religion.[14]

Anschauung des Universums is, thus, we can say *Selbstanschauung*. In the highest religious experience, the two (the world and the self) are indistinguishable. Here, dialectically enough, the self reaches its highest individual realization by the surrender of its individuality to the infinite. *Yet religion does not cancel the self.* The world or the infinite has its being and deepest meaning in and through the self. In the highest and noblest experience of man, the all that he is and the all that he inhabits are inseparable. *Anschauung des Universums* is *Anschauung* of the infinite in the finite self, and *Anschauung* of the self is in turn *Anschauung* of that within which the infinite is perceived.

This is in effect Schleiermacher's idealistic "resolution" of the tension between Fichte and Spinoza. A relative truth is, according to Schleiermacher, the transcendentalist truth that I create the (idea of the?) infinite. Yet the truth viewed from the religious point of view, that is, from the point of view of totality, is that I am within the infinite and *therefore* can create it. Man sees his mirror reflection in the eternal world and sees the eternal world reflected in himself (cf. *11*: 52). Man can create (the idea of?) God just because God first "created"[15] man, that is, just because the finite is eternally within and a part of the infinite.[16]

Now this fact, that *Anschauung des Universums* is *Selbstanschauung*, has signal implications for the whole "process of development and ascent" that has been outlined above. The final *Anschauung*—being an *Anschauung* of the *unity* of the infinite and the finite (or *every* particular finite thing and relation)—does not merely complete the "process of ascent to the *visio Dei*," but actually invalidates the necessity or fundamentality of such a progressive ascent. Schleiermacher's conception of religious *Anschauung* is not merely *Anschauung* as the final and highest term in an order of increasing generality, but is precisely that of an *Anschauung* that is, or at least can be, present in every individual *Anschauung*; that is, an *Anschauung* of totality is possible in every *Anschauung* of every thing in every moment.

"Anschauung A" and "Anschauung B": Ambiguity in the philosophy of Schleiermacher

The material of the *Reden* having to do with the various *Anschauungen* of human experience, the highest and noblest of which is declared by Schleiermacher to be *Anschauung des Universums*, is subject to a misunderstanding that reflects a common misinterpretation of Schleiermacher's entire system. Ambiguity is abundant enough to make the suggestion of the idea that *Anschauung des Universums* is merely a final and highest term in an order of increasing generality plausible—at least at first glance. The Schleiermacher interpreter Emil Fuchs has, wittingly or unwittingly, turned to this possibility (*4*: 9-55).

However, from the point of view of Schleiermacher's "system" as a whole, Fuchs' understanding of the *Reden* indicates, in my judgment, a failure to comprehend clearly the thrust of Schleiermacher's achievement, which gropes beyond both the legacy of Spinoza and the influence of Fichte. Fuchs has failed to see that *Anschauung* of totality, the highest and noblest *Anschauung*, is only "highest" and "noblest" in a certain sense, and that this sense is certainly *not* that of its being the *top term* in a series of qualitatively similar *Anschauungen*. Fuchs has failed to see that *Anschauung des Universums* is possible in every *Anschauung* of every thing in every moment. Fuchs' failure to state this fact clearly (somewhat understandable because of the fact that Schleiermacher uses only one word—*Anschauung*—for two realities or ideas) results from his failure to distinguish sharply the two distinct conceptions of *Anschauung* that Schleiermacher works with.

Anschauung "A" is precisely that of Fichte, namely intuitions of the ego, and such intuitions can, as Fuchs has seen, be ordered in a series of increasing generality. (Schleiermacher's criticism of Fichte is exactly that he loses the individual in the highest religious *Anschauung*.) *Anschauung* "B" is Schleiermacher's addition, namely, the notion of the constant, co-present possibility of an intuition of the All in every particular intuition and in all intuitions of the manifold (*3*: xxiii).

Only as we see this distinction between two types of *Anschauungen* in Schleiermacher's thought can we properly interpret those passages in the *Reden* where Schleiermacher speaks (for pedagogical and illustrative reasons) of various *Anschauungen* that can be arranged "hierarchically" in a movement from *sensus* of the ego to *Anschauung des Universums.* It is not the case that these passages are decisive for Schleiermacher's theory of religious *Anschauung*, nor is it the case that Schleiermacher accepts the view that man must developmentally ascend from individuals to things more general and finally to God, as if the top term were in no real sense different in kind from ordinary (purely psychically qualified) *Anschauungen.*

Rather, Schleiermacher holds that the so-called top term breaks through to a *new* dimension and is, hence, *qualitatively* different from sensory perception. The "top term" is *not* highest in the sense of the *last* in an ascending series of qualitatively similar perceptions. This "top term" is *religious Anschauung*, and not just some highly developed, purely sensory-empirical, sensory-aesthetic, sensory-logical, sensory-ethical *Anschauung*. Schleiermacher holds over against this conception of *Anschauung* ("A") his own notion of an *Anschauung* "B"—the possibility of an intuition of the infinite in every *Anschauung* ("A") of a particular person or relation or thing.

Failing adequately to distinguish the two kinds of *Anschauungen* as different in kind, Fuchs has interpreted Schleiermacher's pedagogical illustrations as decisive for his overall theory. Furthermore, Fuchs has thereby blurred the decisive advance beyond Fichte that is Schleiermacher's great achievement. (This common fuzzing over of important differences is the basis for frequent accusations to the effect that Schleiermacher psychologizes religion.) *Anschauung des Universums*, dependence upon or receptivity of the infinite in the finite, and the disposition of delight have a fundamental religious meaning as total, creaturely awareness, rather than a narrow, psychically qualified meaning in the philosophy of Schleiermacher. Hence, only with the greatest caution can a "developmental process of ascending levels of intuition" be spoken of.

In every particular *Anschauung*—this is Schleiermacher's constant assertion—there is the actuality or possibility of an intuition of the infinite. In every "experience" of a finite relation or individual, there is also the possibility of an experience of the totality. Individuality is, thus, not pure determinacy, limitation or appearance, as both Spinoza and Fichte tend to assume. For Schleiermacher, an individual is any and every particular being that is viewed (perceived) in religious *Anschauung* ("B") as a finite expression of the infinite.

Conclusion

In concluding this essay, I shall briefly summarize the argument in order to specify Schleiermacher's intention and achievement as well as the point of his own unclarity, an unclarity that has led to conflicting interpretations of his philosophy. The argument of this essay is that Schleiermacher drew upon his mystical experience of religion in order to relate it to his contemporaries. It is to them that he addresses the *Reden*, and it is in the *Reden* that Schleiermacher struggles with the difficulty of arranging a new alliance between religion and culture. In forming his new definition of religion, Schleiermacher is confronted with the difficulty of how one can speak in philosophically accurate and respectable terms of the simple feeling-perception of the infinite in the finite. How can one characterize this feeling? To answer this problem Schleiermacher draws upon Spinoza's notion of the infinite in its general philosophical sense and upon the Fichtean notions of *Selbstanschauung* and *Gefühl*. But these concepts derive from signally different metaphysical outlooks and can find no easy reconciliation. The problem of reconciling them expresses the overall problematic of the *Reden*.

Schleiermacher's creative philosophical work (work that fleshes out his conviction that there is an intrinsic connection between religion and culture) is best seen in his struggling to create some new horizon within which both the truth of Spinoza and the truth of Fichte can be reconciled by being transformed. This new horizon is his "higher realism." With respect to it Schleiermacher can say with Spinoza that man is absolutely dependent upon the infinite. But unlike Spinoza, for Schleiermacher the infinite is wholly present in every individual. On the other hand, Schleiermacher agrees with Fichte that the consciousness of man is constituted by *Anschauung* and *Gefühl*, though Schleiermacher develops these in a contrasting way so that they are finally presented as the most perfect manifestations of receptivity. From this we see that Schleiermacher's program is neither eclectic nor a simple synthesis but the creative establishment of a new metaphysical horizon within which all terms must take on a new definition.

At this point the historical significance of this achievement has been, as all concede, that Schleiermacher establishes a new understanding of the locus of religion within human life and, thus, lays the foundation both for renewed consideration of the problem of the relation of religion and culture (or reason and faith) and for new intellectual methods to understand it. The modern study of the philosophy of religion, hermeneutics, comparative religions, and the theology of culture—all of these build on Schleiermacher's innovation. *To show both the historical and systematic factors that resulted in this innovation has been the goal of this essay.*

Also, in pursuing this goal it has been inevitable that we should come to understand the intrinsic difficulties of Schleiermacher's project, difficulties exposed by a certain ambiguity in Schleiermacher's terminology; for example, Schleiermacher uses only one word (*Anschauung*) for both intuition in the Fichtean sense and *Anschauung des Universums*. It is these inconsistencies and ambiguities that have led to misunderstanding (for example, the view of Fuchs).

Another internal flaw of Schleiermacher's early *Weltanschauung* is rooted in Schleiermacher's failure fully to rid his own notion of *Anschauung* of Fichtean and Romanticist overtones. This leads Schleiermacher sometimes to qualify his fundamental position that the infinite can be perceived in every individual by a recurring predilection for the view that the infinite can be best or most perceived in *Anschauung des Universums*. To employ a contemporary aphorism, we might say that Schleiermacher's view is that all religious *Anschauungen* are equal but that some are more equal than others, an ambiguity that is the material basis of an interpretation of the various *Anschauungen* of experience as ordered hierarchically. Schleiermacher seems to shift back and forth between affirming the reality of the infinite in every individual and tending to affirm a cosmic rationality of hierarchically ordered levels of perception.

These difficulties within the Schleiermachean system, far from becoming occasions for carping criticism, make us more admiring of the courage and momentous scope with which Schleiermacher undertook to unite diverse and contrary influences in an attempt to bring the church out of its Pietist inwardness and into the cultural mainstream of the nineteenth century.

Notes

1. Throughout I have used the critical edition of Bernhard Pünjer. From this point on in the essay it will be referred to as *Reden*. Also, the first edition has been used exclusively since the subsequent editions were substantially altered. The translations that appear in this essay are by and large my own. Some attention has, however, been given to the translation of John Oman, especially in case of the longer quotations. In general, most existing translations have proved to be highly inadequate to the task of substantiating the crucial metaphysical point that is argued in this essay. Only a careful reading of Schleiermacher's own language, especially as it relates to the principle of individuality, can bring to the fore a basis upon which the thesis of this essay can be built.

2. The biography of Schleiermacher is not very much disputed. The information given in the following paragraphs has been taken from *1* and *7*.

3. Quoted by Dilthey (*1*: 394) from the first volume of Schleiermacher's *Briefe*.

4. Cf. *8*: 84, for the two possible directions in which Platonism can develop itself, one being otherworldly, the other stressing very much the primacy of existence.

5. What I have called "the modern settlement" in this context Gerhard Spiegler in his excellent book has called "the covenant between faith and culture" (*12*: xv).

6. These notions have a very specific meaning just around the time of Schleiermacher. They are especially prominent in the philosophy of aesthetics and certainly, to some extent, determine the meaning of Schleiermacher's use of them. No doubt Schleiermacher uses them only as analogies to indicate that capacity of man that supplies him with a pre-sensory and para-sensory awareness of the totality in the finite. This awareness of totality is religion.

In 1725 the philosopher Hutcheson, following Locke, theorized about an inner sense and taste that almost mechanically receives from the outside the givens of empirical experience; cf. his *Inquiry into the Origin of Our Ideas of Beauty and Virtue*. In 1757 Hutcheson's disciple Hume published his *Of the Standard of Taste and Other Essays*. In this work Hume presents an essay on skepticism in which he speaks of feelings in the sense of Hutcheson. However, he adds a dimension. In addition to speaking of them as feelings of the body, Hume also speaks of feelings as sentiments of the mind. Here he introduces a new dimension to the concept of taste, namely, the idea of *mental* feelings. In the same year, Edmund Burke published a work entitled *A Philosophical Enquiry into the Origin of Our Ideas of the Sublime and Beautiful*. In a section on taste, Burke, expanding on Hume and Hutcheson, speaks of taste and feeling as "disinterested delight." More than being logically deepened feeling, feeling and taste are here also regarded as being aesthetic in character. Taste or feeling is not a simple idea, according to Burke, but involves judging, imagining and sensing all at once.

It was upon this tradition that Kant relied in his 1764 work entitled *Observations on the Feeling of the Beautiful and the Sublime*. The *Gefühlen* of *Lust* (Delight) and *Unlust* (Aversion) are spoken of not just as brute, sensuous feelings. *Gefühl* or taste, though embedded in sensation, anticipates intellectual excellence and virtuous activity. By the 1770s, Kant had begun to argue that taste has a *judgment* character.

Now, inasmuch as Schleiermacher was thoroughly familiar with Kant and inasmuch as he was deeply involved with Romanticism and its aesthetic preoccupations, the history of the terms *Gefühl* and *Geschmack* is extremely significant for understanding Schleiermacher's use of them. Certainly, by *Gefühl* and *Geschmack* Schleiermacher had in mind the aesthetic idea of a perceptive and receptive *delight*. However, the notion of *Anschauung* and *Gefühl*, or *Sinn* and *Geschmack*, as analytically and ethically deepened feeling has been eliminated. How Schleiermacher came to do this has already been demonstrated.

7. Among the idealists, a Romanticized interpretation of Spinoza came into prominence. Schleiermacher himself was introduced to such an interpretation through the *Briefe* of Jacobi. He relied heavily upon these letters because it was extremely difficult to procure Spinoza's works themselves; cf. *1*: 167, 337-52.

8. This famous phrase does not appear in Schleiermacher's works until his *Der Christliche Glaube* (*The Christian Faith*) of 1821-22.

9. The complexity of Schleiermacher's relationship to the Fichtean philosophy is especially emphasized by Hirsch (*6*): "Most complicated of all, finally, is his relationship to Fichte. Here affinity and opposition come together in a remarkable manner" (p. 500). With respect to Schleiermacher's refusal to accept that religion is either knowledge or moral activity, Hirsch remarks: "Virtually all of these theses about philosophy, life and religion are contrary to the judgments of his contemporaries" (p. 499). Also: "There are polemical passages in Schleiermacher's writing of which it cannot easily be determined whether they are aimed at just the Enlightenment and Kant or also Fichte" (p. 516). With respect to the help that Schleiermacher derived from Fichte, Hirsch notes: "Today only a few experts would deny that Fichte was Schleiermacher's philosophical destiny." Also: "There are many Fichtean formulations . . . running through the *Reden*" (p. 504).

10. The term *passivity* is not really an appropriate rendering of Schleiermacher's concept of religious *Passivität* or *Receptivität*.

11. Quoted by Dilthey (*1*: 359) from the *Monologen* (Soliloquies) of 1800. Cf. also *11*: 52.

12. Cf. also the *Soliloquies* of 1800. Its central thematic notion is that man must shape himself into an *individual*, thereby to become a representative of humanity. The means by which this is accomplished is for man to listen to his own inner nature. Cf. *11*: 120.

13. The term *Gemüt* indicates in particular openness to reality, sensitivity and receptivity, and not first of all "mind" in the sense of active intellectual agency. "Gemüt" is disposition.

14. "Jener erste geheimnisvolle Augenblick, der bei jeder sinnlichen Wahrnehmung vorkommt, ehe noch Anschauung und Gefühl sich trennen, wo der Sinn und sein Gegenstand gleichsam in einander geflossen und Eins geworden sind, ehe noch beide an ihren ursprünglichen Platz zurückkehren—ich weiss wie unbeschreiblich er ist, und wie schnell er vorübergeht, ich wollte aber, Ihr könntet ihn festhalten und auch in der höheren und göttlichen religiösen Thätigkeit des Gemüths ihn wieder erkennen. Könnte und dürfte ich ihn doch aussprechen, andeuten wenigstens, ohne ihn zu entheiligen! Flüchtig ist er und durchsichtig wie der erste Duft, womit der Thau die erwachten Blumen anhaucht, schamhaft und zart wie ein jungfräulicher Kuss, heilig und fruchtbar wie eine bräutliche Umarmung; ja nicht wie dies, sondern er ist Alles dieses selbst. Schnell und zaubrisch entwickelt sich eine Erscheinung, eine Begebenheit zu einem Bilde des Universums. So wie sie sich formt die geliebte und immer gesuchte Gestalt, flieht ihr meine Seele entgegen, ich umfange sie nicht wie einen Schatten, sondern wie das heilige Wesen selbst. Ich liege am Busen der unendlichen Welt: ich bin in diesem Augenblick ihre Seele, denn ich fühle alle ihre Kräft und ihr unendliches Leben wie mein eigenes, sie ist in diesem Augenblick mein Leib, denn ich durchdringe ihre Muskeln und ihre Glieder wie meine eigenen, und ihre innersten Nerven bewegen sich nach meinem Sinn und meiner Ahnung wie die meinigen. Die geringste Erschütterung, und es verweht die heilige Umarmung, und nun erst steht die Anschauung vor mir als eine abgesonderte Gestalt, ich messe sie, und sie spiegelt sich in der offenen Seele wie das Bild der sich entwindenden Geliebten in dem aufgeschlagenen Auge des Jünglings, und nun erst arbeitet sich das Gefühl aus dem Innern empor, und verbreitet sich wie die Röthe der Scham und der Lust auf seiner Mange. Dieser Moment ist die höchste Blüthe der Religion. Könnte ich ihn Euch schaffen, so wäre ich mehr als Eleusische Mysterien habe aufdecken müssen. Er ist die Geburtsstunde alles Lebendigen in der Religion" (*11*: 77-9).

15. I have italicized *create*, and hence use it metaphorically because Schleiermacher's philosophy is highly static, emphasizing the eternal coexistence of the infinite and the finite rather than the creation and generation of the finite by the infinite.

16. Cf. the extremely similar position of Unamuno in his *The Tragic Sense of Life*, p. 172.

Bibliography

1. DILTHEY, W., *Leben Schleiermachers 1768-1802*. Gesammelte Schriften XIII-1; Göttingen: Vandenhoeck und Ruprecht, 1970.

2. FABRO, C., *God in Exile*; New York: Newman Press, 1968.

3. FRIESS, H. L., *Schleiermacher's Soliloquies* (trans. and with an introduction by H. L. Friess); Chicago: Open Court Publishing Co., 1957

4. FUCHS, E., *Schleiermacher's Religionsbegriff und religiöse Stellung zur Zeit der ersten Ausgabe der Reden (1799-1800)*; Geissen: J. Rickersohn, 1901.

5. HERTEL, F., *Das theologische Denken Schleiermachers untersucht an der erster Auflage seiner Reden 'Ueber die Religion'*; Zurich and Stuttgart: Zwingli Verlag, 1965.

6. HIRSCH, E., *Geschichte der neueren evangelischen Theologie*, IV; Gütersloh: Gerd Mohn, 1960.

7. KATZENBACH, *F. W. Schleiermacher*; Reinbek bei Hamburg: Rowohlt Taschenbuch Verlag, 1967.

8. LOVEJOY, A., *The Great Chain of Being*; New York: Harper and Row, 1956.

9. MacINTOSH, H. R., *Types of Modern Theology*; London and Glasgow: Collins Press, Fontana Library, 1956.

10. RUNNER, H.E., *Scriptural Religion and Political Task*; Toronto: Wedge Publishing Foundation, 1974.

11. SCHLEIERMACHER, F., *Reden über die Religion* (ed. Bernhard Pünjer); Braunschweig: E. A. Schwetsche und Sohn, 1879.

12. SPIEGLER, G., *The Eternal Covenant: Schleiermacher's Experiment in Cultural Theology*; New York, Evanston, and London: Harper and Row, 1967.

Dilthey's Philosophy of the History of Philosophy

THEODORE PLANTINGA

The relation of philosophy to its own history has become an important subject of philosophical reflection during the nineteenth and twentieth centuries. Two questions or sets of questions dominate this debate. First, what is it that the historian of philosophy claims to study, and what assumptions must he make if a scientific study of philosophy's past is to be possible? Second, what is the significance of such study for philosophy itself? Does the study of philosophy's past represent a branch of historical science, or is it first and foremost a philosophical pursuit carried out by the philosophers themselves and of interest mainly to them?

Among the thinkers who have turned their attention to these matters is the German philosopher Wilhelm Dilthey (1833-1911). What Dilthey has to say is of interest not only because he was an important philosopher but also because he was a renowned historian. He possessed the personal experience in historical research and writing that would presumably entitle him to speak with authority and enable him to achieve some interesting insights into the relation between philosophy and its past.

In this essay I propose to discuss Dilthey's views on the history of philosophy, which, unfortunately, were never summed up in any single work.[1] In the process I hope to clear up some misconceptions about his approach to the history of philosophy, for his views on this subject are often confused or identified with his views on cultural and intellectual history in general.[2] In conclusion I shall offer some reasons for supposing that Dilthey's conception of the history of philosophy is to be preferred to a rival outlook whose chief exponent is Nicolai Hartmann.

I

One major reason why the study of the history of philosophy was so long neglected by the philosophers themselves is that this piece of territory had already been occupied by their enemies. Many of the earliest histories of philosophy represent the work of skeptics who hoped to warn others away from philosophy by showing that philosophers contradict one another on every conceivable topic. According to this standpoint, the history of philosophy is at best the history of opinion and at worst the history of untruth or even nonsense. To write a history of philosophy was simply to list the statements, opinions and doctrines of various philosophers. The reader would then have ample evidence to draw the desired conclusion.

The philosophers themselves, of course, were by no means oblivious to the disagreements and differences between them. Repeated attempts were made to base philosophy on an indubitable and undisputed foundation or to elevate it to a science, to use Hegel's famous phrase. And if philosophy could be made a science, there might be some hope of transforming the history of philosophy from the history of error and contradiction into the history of the truth. This occurred to Hegel, at least, and his treatment of the history of philosophy represents the first important consideration of the questions with which this essay deals. It established a framework for the discussion of these questions; virtually all subsequent debate refers explicitly or implicitly to the issues he raised and the theses he defended.

Hegel's lectures on the history of philosophy were preceded by a treatment of preliminary considerations, that is, by a philosophy of the history of philosophy. He began by disposing of the view that the history of philosophy is the history of the opinions or doctrines affirmed by various individuals. "What could be more useless and boring," he asked, "than to learn a series of mere opinions?" Philosophy, he declared, has nothing whatever to do with opinions: there is no such thing as a philosophical opinion, for an opinion is a merely contingent thought. The very term *opinion* (*Meinung*), he argued, can be derived from the possessive pronoun *mine* (*mein*).[3] As something that is merely mine, then, an opinion can make no claim to universal validity. Therefore, if the history of philosophy is to be a science, it cannot rest content with the recitation of opinions or doctrines.

The object of the history of philosophy is not opinion but truth, for philosophy is the objective science of the truth and its necessity. The truth is one, and the goal of the history of philosophy is to know the truth. Hence the study of the history of philosophy is the study of philosophy itself, which means that the history of philosophy can serve as an introduction to philosophy, i.e. to the truth. The truth, moreover, is not the product of the thinking of any one individual; the philosophy of the present, Hegel writes, contains ". . . all that has been produced by the labor of millennia; it is the final result of all that has preceded it."[4] Thus the unity of the truth and its unfolding in history must be taken into account by the historian of philosophy. What this means is that he should view the history of philosophy not first of all as the history of thinking but as the history of what has been thought. Although process and result can never be fully separated for Hegel, the emphasis definitely falls on the result. "Thus the history of philosophy is the history of thought" (*Geschichte des Gedankens*), and the historian of philosophy focuses on the "deeds of thinking reason." Although these deeds were performed in the past, that which was achieved by way of them is still with us. Hence the historian of philosophy is really concerned with something present. "Only the external, i.e. the men, their destinies, and so forth, belongs to the past," Hegel wrote, "but as far as what they have produced is concerned, it has endured."[5]

The *history* of philosophy was of special importance to Hegel because the truth develops in a progressive manner throughout the ages. The apprehension of truth made possible by our standpoint in the present enables us to discern in the history of philosophy a pattern and order that previous philosophers were not able to see. This realization must govern our approach to the history of philosophy:

> There is nothing arbitrary about the succession of philosophies; the order in which they appear is determined by necessity . . . . Each moment grasps the totality of the Idea in a one-sided way, is *aufgehoben* because of this one-sidedness, and, with its claim to finality thus refuted, joins with its opposed determination, which it lacks, thereby becoming deeper and richer. This is the dialectic of these determinations. But this movement does not end in nothingness, for the *aufgehoben* determinations are rather of an affirmative nature themselves. It is in this sense that we must deal with the history of philosophy.[6]

For Hegel, then, the history of philosophy is a unified science worthy of our attention because it traces and portrays the progressive unfolding of the truth.

II

Hegel also devoted considerable attention to the relation of philosophy to the other cultural and intellectual forms in which the Spirit manifests or expresses itself, but his remarks on this topic attracted less attention. Yet this relation was again emphasized particularly by Dilthey, despite the fact that his views on the history of philosophy represent a repudiation of Hegel's outlook. Dilthey, too, spoke of "the spirit" (*Geist*) and its expressions, but he meant the human spirit, the individual human mind that shapes the world of culture and history. Orthodox Hegelianism had collapsed not long after Hegel's death in 1831, and later thinkers who reflected on the relation between philosophy and its history abandoned Hegel's views or modified them considerably.

What strikes us first about Dilthey's work as a historian of thought is that he emphasized the personal element in philosophy, which Hegel had dismissed as secondary. Thus he took considerable interest in the lives of the philosophers he studied. The personal element, he pointed out, is important to understanding the relations between philosophy and the other cultural and intellectual manifestations of the human spirit, e.g. art, poetry and religion. Underlying such expressions of life and the spirit, he maintained, is a "worldview" (*Weltanschauung*), which forms the substance or content that a philosophical system and a work of art might have in common. The historian of culture and the intellectual world must therefore investigate worldviews as the background for understanding particular cultural expressions, including philosophical systems and ideas.

This kind of approach to cultural and intellectual history, which is known in Germany as "Geistesgeschichte,"[7] became popular and widespread during the early part of this century through Dilthey's influence. Dilthey himself led the way in his historical writings, for he insisted on understanding ideas in context, that is, in the light of their origin, their background, and the intentions of their authors. The writer of intellectual history, he declared, must concern himself (among other things) with the ". . . causal interrelations, with the origin of ideas in an earlier circle of thinkers or in the experience and contemplation of reality . . . ."[8] In an essay on the significance of archives for the study of the history of philosophy, he wrote:

> The philosophical systems have arisen out of culture as a whole and have in turn affected it. Hegel also recognized this. The task, now, is to gain knowledge of the causal interrelations and their links, i.e. the context within which this process occurs. This task Hegel did not set for himself. And its execution, i.e. placing philosophical thinkers inside the living context to which they belong, at once makes necessary a literary treatment which investigates the causal interrelations of this process on the basis of all available knowledge of the philosophers' collaborators, their opponents, and those who were influenced by them.

The philosophy of an age, he went on to explain, is the most complicated phenomenon in the historical world

> . . . insofar as this philosophy is not only to be described outwardly but is to be understood as a living power. The analysis of this phenomenon must accordingly make use of all available aids and tools and must consult all the historical remains of the process. The greater a person's life's work is, the deeper the roots of his cultural (*geistig*) labors reach into the soil of the economic system, customs and law of his time, and the more varied and living is the exchange with the surrounding air and light in which it breathes and grows.[9]

To understand philosophical ideas, then, it is often necessary to read letters, early unpublished writings and preliminary drafts of philosophical works. (Hence Dilthey argued that such materials should be preserved and made accessible in archives.) He himself demonstrated how illuminating such an approach can be by way of his book on Hegel,[10] in which the young Hegel is presented on the basis of correspondence and early writings that had not been published. This book, in which Dilthey sketched the worldview of the young Hegel, stimulated a good deal of further research on Hegel. Eventually it led to the publication of Hegel's early writings, by Dilthey's student Herman Nohl, who thereby fulfilled a wish that Dilthey had expressed in the preface to his book on Hegel.

The considerations above might appear to warrant the conclusion that Dilthey—unlike Hegel—regarded the history of philosophy as the history of thinking and then proceeded to incorporate it into cultural and intellectual history in general. But such a conclusion would be premature. Before assuming that Dilthey reduced philosophy to worldviews or the opinions of individuals, we should take note of what he did *not* say. As we have seen, he emphasized that philosophical thinking lives and grows within a larger matrix of cultural, historical and social life. Yet he did *not* argue that philosophy is totally determined by these factors, or that we can deduce a thinker's philosophical ideas from a proper knowledge of the factors that form the background of his thought. In other words, Dilthey did not maintain that philosophy is some sort of epiphenomenon hovering above the surface of life, or that the relation between life and philosophy is that of material substructure and ideological superstructure.

Furthermore, although Dilthey emphasized that the historian of philosophy who struggles to understand past philosophical ideas is dependent on the same kind of material and historical evidence that the intellectual and cultural historian uses, he did *not* declare that the history of philosophy is simply a branch of intellectual history, or that to understand philosophical ideas is simply to trace their rise and development. Here the book on Hegel has been a source of confusion. It represents a piece of intellectual history, but it was not intended by Dilthey as history of philosophy in the strict sense. Nonetheless, it is relevant to the history of philosophy—just as much of what is written in the realm of intellectual history *casts light* on the history of philosophy. Hence it is sometimes wrongly regarded as an example of history of philosophy *à la* Dilthey.

The important point to bear in mind in order to overcome this confusion is that Dilthey emphasized the importance of context to the process of understanding. Intellectual history, of course, must provide much of the context and background for understanding the philosophical ideas with which the historian of philosophy is concerned. Yet, although the latter may come to understand a difficult philosophical idea through the study of extra-philosophical factors that influenced the philosopher being examined, it is still the idea, which represents a philosophical meaning, that is the real object of interest for the historian of philosophy. In other words, neither the mental processes which the historian goes through in his efforts to understand a philosophical idea nor the mental processes which the philosopher goes through in thinking out and formulating the idea are to be equated with the meaning of the idea, for two people may arrive at an understanding of one and the same idea by entirely different routes, just as two travelers may move from point A to point B by entirely different routes.

The study of the cultural, intellectual and historical background is an aid to understanding a philosophical idea, then, but not a substitute for it. Some philosophical ideas, in fact, can be understood without such study. Dilthey expressed this confidence as early as 1870, in the foreword to his biography of Schleiermacher, which opens with the words: "We can understand the philosophy of Kant fully without concerning ourselves further with his personality and his life; Schleiermacher's meaning, his worldview, and his works require a biographical presentation if they are to be understood thoroughly."[11] Kant knew how to separate the process of thought from its results, and he learned to present the latter without the former. Schleiermacher had not learned this lesson properly, which is why extracting the philosophical results is more difficult in his case. Thus Dilthey did not intend to deny the independence of philosophical ideas.

If the meaning of a philosophical idea is not clear to us from the text in which it is presented, we must look to the background of the idea, i.e. to its origin and development, for a clarification of what the philosopher in question was trying to say. However, this does *not* mean that we are to *judge* ideas in the light of their origin, for understanding and judgment are separate operations for Dilthey. Once we have understood an idea, there still remains the philosophical task of inquiring into the grounds for its validity. Dilthey knew better than to ask whether anything good can come out of Nazareth, for he realized that the truth, like gold, is where you find it, and that gold cannot be distinguished from fool's gold at a glance.

In other words, he did not expect the truth to present itself to us armed with a pedigree.

Thus we see that Dilthey does leave room for history of philosophy as an independent discipline, even though he personally preferred to write intellectual history. He did not propose to turn the study of past philosophical ideas into the study of worldviews, opinions, or extra-philosophical factors that influence philosophical thought, and he believed that all philosophical ideas must ultimately be judged in relation to their claims to truth and validity—and not in relation to their historical origin.[12]

III

Beginning in the late nineteenth century, a reaction to the tendency to stress the connections between intellectual history and the history of philosophy set in. Philosophers of neo-Kantian background or conviction tried to limit the personal element in the history of philosophy and revive something of the Hegelian approach. In other words, the history of philosophy was to be the history of thought. More specifically, it was to be the history of the truth. This would be possible if the history of philosophy focused on philosophical problems and concepts.

The major philosophical problems, according to Wilhelm Windelband, represent "inescapable tasks for the human spirit" and give the history of philosophy the unity and continuity it needs in order to become scientific.[13] Nicolai Hartmann, in an essay of 1909, spoke of systematic philosophical problems as "transcendental conditions" for the possibility of the history of philosophy.[14] The historian of philosophy, according to this outlook, focuses on systematic problems—and not on the process of thinking or on the lives of philosophers. Because philosophical terms regularly undergo significant changes in meaning, the historian of philosophy must penetrate beyond the level of language to something more stable and abiding. Only someone who has struggled with the major philosophical problems himself is capable of this. Therefore the history of philosophy cannot be left to the historians. Like Hegel, Hartmann emphasized that it is a task to be assumed by the philosophers themselves.

But it is not enough, of course, to simply enumerate the philosophical *questions* which philosophers have faced throughout the ages. The *answers* they have given to these questions must also be dealt with. Hartmann recognized this, but he insisted that a mere "understanding" of philosophical ideas, statements and doctrines would not suffice.[15] What is of primary importance is rather what the past philosopher whom we are studying has "seen" or come to know. In other words, the history of philosophy must become the history of insights:

> Now the history of a science is in essence the history of insights and not of errors—however much the latter may slip in everywhere—at least, not of errors for their own sake. If philosophy, then, is more than mere opinion about everything under the sun, if it is science, then its real history must consist of a series of insights rather than a parade of doctrines and systems. Strictly speaking, what the latter represent—insofar as there are no latent insights behind them—is the non-philosophical element in philosophy.[16]

Moreover, the insights which the historian of philosophy seeks to trace are often separable from the philosophical systems in which they originally emerged: Hegel's writings, for example, contain various insights about the nature and structure of the world of the spirit that survived the collapse of his system.[17] Therefore we must ultimately make some sort of distinction between the "historical" and the "supra-historical" in the history of philosophy,[18] for the history of philosophy is the history of the truth alone.

This is an appealing approach to philosophy's past, for it raises the prospect of a steady accumulation of insight and wisdom. However, it rests on a basic assumption that could conceivably be called into question, namely, the impersonal character of philosophical insight or of the result of philosophical thought. Dilthey certainly rejected this assumption, and it is on this fundamental level that his outlook on the history of philosophy parts company with that of Hartmann. Dilthey was convinced that ". . . insofar as a philosophical system really contains a discovery, something of genius, it includes an aspect that arises from the depth of the person and is not subject to analysis or calculation."[19] For Dilthey, then, it is not a matter of "seeing" what some philosophical genius has "seen" before us. This would imply a greater distance between the thinker and the result of his thought than Dilthey was prepared to recognize.

To understand this claim on Dilthey's part, we must bear the problem of metaphysics in mind. Like numerous other thinkers of his time, Dilthey rejected the claim of metaphysics to scientific validity: metaphysics is impossible *as a science*. Yet he was convinced that metaphysics is by no means without value, and he refused to regard the history of metaphysics as a meaning-less chapter in the history of the human spirit. The question then became: How can we extract what is valuable in the great metaphysical systems of the past? The answer is that we must seek to understand them as much as possible as expressions of profound experiences. And since experience is more than a passive reception of sensations, since it is a lived process to which the subject's entire history contributes, we must expect the cultural and intellectual expressions that arise out of human experience to share in the uniqueness and individuality of their authors. Dilthey declared: "The true metaphysicians have lived what they write."[20] What the metaphysician has to tell us, therefore, is not something impersonal that we can "see" when he points it out; it is rather something that we must try to live through (*nacherleben*) for ourselves by transposing ourselves as much as possible into his situation and recapturing the sense of life and existence that results from his unique physical and spiritual position in the cosmos. What the history of metaphysics offers us is not a series of insights but a series of experiential possibilities through which not only our thought but our entire existence may be enriched and elevated. This is the spirit behind Dilthey's philosophy of the history of philosophy.

What applies to the history of metaphysics also applies to the history of art and the history of religion. Dilthey, who was not a Christian, insisted that the existence of man in the modern, post-Christian era could be elevated and enlarged in scope by incorporating something of the sense of life and its meaning that comes to expression in the faith of earlier ages. He illustrated this in an eloquent passage about Martin Luther, a man completely different from himself in character, temperament and outlook:

> For me as for most people today, the possibility of experiencing (*erleben*) religious states of mind in my personal existence is sharply circumscribed. But when I go through the letters and writings of Luther, the accounts of his contemporaries, the records of the religious conferences and councils, and the reports of his official contacts, I encounter a religious phenomenon of such eruptive power, of such energy, in which the issue is one of life or death, that it lies beyond the experiential possibilities of a person of our time. But I can re-live (*nacherleben*) all of this . . . . And thereby this process opens up for us a religious world in Luther and in his contemporaries in the early Reformation that enlarges our horizon by including possibilities that are available to us only in this way. Thus man, who is determined from within, can experience many other existences in imagination. Although he is limited by his circumstances, foreign beauties of the world and regions of life that he could never reach himself are laid open to him. To put it in general terms, man, bound and determined by the reality of life, is made free not only by art—which has often been pointed out—but also by the understanding of things historical.[21]

At this point we must be careful not to overlook the distinction between metaphysics, which is an illegitimate philosophical discipline, and the other branches of philosophy. When Dilthey maintains that we can inquire into the grounds supporting a philosophical idea after the idea has been understood, he does not mean to suggest that it makes sense to deal with metaphysics in this way. Because metaphysical systems purport to give us knowledge of that which transcends our experience, their claims can neither be validated nor refuted. Therefore we must either dismiss metaphysics entirely, which would be to ignore much of the history of philosophy, or devise some new approach to it. This is the dilemma underlying Dilthey's philosophy of the history of philosophy.

Dilthey's outlook differs from Hartmann's in another important respect as well. Hartmann draws a parallel between the history of philosophy and the history of science, as we saw in the quotation on p. 206 above: if philosophy is to be a science, its history, like the history of the sciences, must consist of a series of insights. Dilthey, however, sees a fundamental difference between the history of philosophy and the history of science, namely, that there is steady progress only in the latter:

> The progress of the sciences continues through all of history. This progress is steady, uninterrupted, irresistible, for what it depends on is that concepts can be handed on without loss from person to person and from age to age. In the entire realm of the understanding of expressions of life, such a transferability (*Uebertragbarkeit*) is to be found only here.[22]

It is characteristic of philosophy—and especially of metaphysics—that the personal or individual element involved in the constitution of its ideas is ineradicable. This means that philosophical ideas cannot simply be handed on unchanged from one generation to the next, for they are often altered and reinterpreted in the process of being taken over by a new generation. Hence there is no steady, cumulative progress in the history of philosophy. The three basic types of philosophical systems distinguished by Dilthey (i.e. naturalism, idealism of freedom and objective idealism) march on through history side by side, neither destroying one another nor merging in a higher synthesis. Thinkers do borrow insights from one another, and they do build on the work of their predecessors to some extent, with the result that there is a certain amount of internal development within each of the three types, but the cumulative progress that we see in the history of science will always elude philosophy.

IV

Both Hegel and Hartmann conceive of the history of philosophy essentially as the history of the truth. This is an attractive prospect, and therefore it is understandable that their views have drawn a fair amount of attention. Presumably such an outlook on the philosophy of the past could provide us with a framework or scheme for arranging and narrating the history of philosophy and could help us locate the fixed object which this discipline needs if it is to be scientific. Thus Windelband, whose position is similar to Hartmann's, maintained that the unifying factor in the history of philosophy is not what various philosophers have chosen to study nor the task they have set for themselves but what they have achieved together.[23]

Dilthey, however, could not go along with such a unified conception of the history of philosophy, and his view of philosophy's past does not include or imply the same concrete directions for the historian of philosophy that are contained in the views of Hartmann and Windelband. Yet, there is a good deal to be said for Dilthey's position over against Hartmann's, as we shall see.

Important for Hartmann, as we saw earlier, is the parallel between the history of philosophy and the history of science. In the latter history, insights derived from various thinkers are combined to form an ever more encompassing knowledge of whatever it is that the particular science studies. Something of this sort could and should be possible in philosophy as well, according to Hartmann's view. But a strong case can be made against this thesis, for nothing of this sort has in fact been achieved in twentieth century philosophy. Hartmann himself has made no serious effort to carry out such a program, despite the fact that he has written substantial books on a number of philosophical disciplines. The last major philosopher who claimed to sum up the truth as it had developed throughout the history of philosophy was Hegel. Today's philosophers feel free to reject large parts of the history of philosophy, and few of them have a thorough knowledge of philosophy's entire history. Of course they could conceivably be criticized for this, but they would be justified in replying that if Hartmann's conception of the history of philosophy is correct, someone would by now have found a way to combine the many separable insights to form a philosophical system that goes far beyond anything known to us at present in depth and comprehensiveness. In other words, once Hartmann has embarked on the path that Hegel took, it is only fair to expect him to follow it to its end.

Here the merits of the view of Dilthey, who points out the difference between the history of philosophy and the history of science, begin to become apparent, for his philosophy of the history of philosophy claims neither too much nor too little; that is to say, it explains why the history of philosophy is useful to some extent, but it also explains why it is not more useful. To take the latter point first, the usefulness of past philosophical systems and ideas is limited because a philosophical system, according to Dilthey, represents an organic unity that is by no means equivalent to the sum of its parts. The relation between part and whole is an important theme in Dilthey's writings; basic to his thinking is the view that the whole confers a meaning or significance on the part which the part simply does not have in isolation. What this means, among other things, is that a philosophical system simply cannot be resolved without loss into a series of philosophical ideas or "insights." Thus an approach to the history of philosophy that focuses on individual philosophical ideas at the expense of the systems and intellectual contexts within which these ideas were developed would fail to do justice to the philosophy of the past, to say the least. Nor do the individual ideas represent that which is of the greatest value in the history of philosophy. Underlying each philosophical or metaphysical system is a fundamental intuition, i.e. a unique point of view on the totality of reality and a deeply personal attitude toward it. "Each metaphysical system is representative only of the situation from which one soul has viewed the riddle of the world," writes Dilthey.[24] The real meaning of a particular philosophical system is to be sought in this fundamental intuition, this position vis-à-vis the riddle of life.

Because the heart of each philosophy consists of some such personal intuition, there is something essentially finite or limited about philosophical thought. The philosophical system produced by the individual thinker is always bound to his standpoint within the cosmos, that is, to the range of his experience. Thus, to embrace enthusiastically what a particular thinkers affirms is at the same time to embrace his limitations; it means excluding other fundamental intuitions that conflict with it. Unfortunately, there is no formula or method for combining these intuitions and summing up what has been achieved in the history of philosophy. Neither should the philosopher devote his attention exclusively to the history of *philosophy*, for the experience of his own generation as it comes to expression in art and literature, for example, also calls for recognition and philosophical exploration. Since philosophy, on Dilthey's view, is closely tied to experience, the value of past philosophical thought is limited by the incompleteness and inevitable one-sidedness of the experience of past philosophers. Therefore, we can make good use of the history of philosophy only if we remember that the experiential revelations it has in store for us are one-sided and incomplete.

On the other hand, once we realize the essential limitations of the history of philosophy and the fundamental difference between the history of philosophy and the history of science, we can use the philosophy of the past to combat the one-sidedness of our own experience and thinking. Because of the shortness of human life and the finitude of the human mind, certain sides of reality escape our attention unless they are disclosed to us by others whose experience includes elements and perspectives that ours does not. Because these limitations on the individual thinker are inevitable, the history of philosophy is necessary as a supplement and corrective to our own experience. If used properly, it will lead ultimately to a more balanced view of the world, for it opens up experiential possibilities outside the range of our own immediate experience, just as the study of Luther's career and writings exposes us to dimensions of religious feeling and awareness foreign to the world in which we live. The experience we gain at second hand through books is not as vivid as first-hand experience, and it does not make as deep an impression on us as it did on those who report the experiences to us, but Dilthey insisted that it is nevertheless of great value, just as accounts of travels to Africa can be of value and interest to those who have never had the opportunity of seeing Africa for themselves.[25]

V

Up to this point, I have stressed the "pedagogical" value of the history of philosophy as Dilthey viewed it. Yet, this emphasis does not bring out the full flavor and impact of his approach to this discipline. Although Dilthey never equated philosophy with its own history, he did move a long way in the direction of the view that philosophy's past provides philosophy in the present with *indispensable* material for reflection.

To understand this side of Dilthey's thought properly, we must bear in mind that he insisted on speaking of philosophy as "philosophy of life" (*Lebensphilosophie*) and liked to describe his own thinking as a "philosophy of self-reflection or of life."[26] Moreover, he identified the effort to understand "life" in terms of itself as the governing impulse in his philosophical thinking.[27] If life is to be the focus of philosophical reflection, then, how do we get at it? Dilthey's answer to this question is that we encounter life in our self-awareness, in our experience of others, in art, and in other expressions of the human spirit—including philosophy. The study of history has a central role to play in our effort to grasp life: "History is to teach us what life is," Dilthey explains.[28] Thus, one of the best ways to get at life is to study the past: "Wherever life has slipped into the past and is understood, we have history."[29] In our necessarily limited ways, we seek to grasp life's fullness as it comes to expression in culture and experience.

Such an outlook has definite implications for philosophy. Dilthey writes: "Philosophy, as a human-historical fact, must become its own object."[30] Philosophy can therefore be described as the spirit's "self-reflection."[31] For Dilthey, then, the history of philosophy is not a topic with which the philosopher concerns himself only if he is also a professor called upon to lecture on the history of his own discipline; it is a vitally important part of the material with which he wrestles in his struggle to find the proper path to the truth.

VI

In conclusion, we should note that neither Hegel nor Hartmann nor Dilthey has spoken the last word on the relation of philosophy to its own past. This complex subject demands further attention in our time. Yet, those who see some value in the philosophy of recent centuries, i.e. those who do not reject it in its totality as based on a fundamental mistake, would do well to give some attention to Dilthey's outlook on the history of philosophy. A survey of philosophy as it has developed in recent centuries would seem to support Dilthey's thesis that there is a fundamental difference between its history and the history of science—or of natural science, at least.[32] Philosophers simply do not proceed by inheriting concepts and ideas from their predecessors and then adding to them and refining them. The philosophical world is an arena of constant change, and philosophers are forced again and again to begin anew. The willingness to take this radical step, to call into question all received and accepted philosophical views, seems to be an essential ingredient of the philosophical attitude. If so, the philosopher must constantly be on the alert for ways to get beyond the confines of his own experience and the intellectual climate of his time. It is here, as Dilthey saw so clearly, that the philosophy of the past can be of great service, for it is an inexhaustible source of stimuli and thought-provoking questions. As an antidote to the provincialism of time, it deserves a place in the curriculum of every university and on the bookshelf of every thinker who hopes to become a philosopher.

Notes

1. Dilthey did write a handbook on the history of philosophy for the use of his students, but it includes no discussion of the philosophy of the history of philosophy. This handbook was later edited and published by H. G. Gadamer (*Grundriss der allgemeinen Geschichte der Philosophie*, Frankfurt am Main: Vittorio Klostermann, 1949).

2. I shall draw on my own interpretation of Dilthey's thought, which differs from any in the existing secondary literature. For the arguments in favor of my interpretation and the key passages in Dilthey on which it is based, see my book *Historical Understanding in the Thought of Wilhelm Dilthey* (Toronto and Buffalo: University of Toronto Press, 1980). The topic for this book, which is based on my Ph.D. thesis, was suggested to me by Prof. Runner.

3. *Einleitung in die Geschichte der Philosophie*, ed. Johannes Hoffmeister (Hamburg: Felix Meiner, 1959), pp. 27, 86.

4. *Ibid.*, pp. 27, 29, 35, 79, 120, 118.

5. *Ibid.*, pp. 81-2, 91, 138.

6. *Ibid.*, p. 146. I have used the characteristic Hegelian verb *aufheben* without translating it because no English verb combines the meanings which Hegel packs into this word. That which is "aufgehoben" is canceled, preserved, and raised to a higher level.

7. This term is not Dilthey's own, although he spoke of the "Geschichte der geistigen Bewegungen" and on a few occasions of the "Geschichte des Geistes." He did, of course, write the kind of history that later came to be called "Geistesgeschichte."

8. Introduction to his *Leben Schleiermachers*, reprinted in the *Gesammelte Schriften* (17 volumes, published by B. G. Teubner Verlagsgesellschaft of Stuttgart, and Vandenhoeck & Ruprecht of Göttingen), Vol. XIII-1, p. xliii.

9. "Archive der Literatur in ihrer Bedeutung für das Studium der Geschichte der Philosophie," in Vol. IV, pp. 558, 561-2.

10. *Die Jugendgeschichte Hegels* (1905), which has been reprinted in Vol. IV of the *Gesammelte Schriften.*

11. Vol. XIII-1, p. xxxiii.

12. Dilthey struggled against such misunderstandings to the very end of his life. In a letter of 1911 to Husserl, in which he responded to an attack upon him in Husserl's famous article "Philosophie als strenge Wissenschaft," he wrote that he agreed with Husserl's claim that ". . . historical conditionedness must be separated completely from validity; if the historical conditionedness of the sciences were to cancel their validity, then the idea of knowledge itself would lose its validity, and not even the statement that such an idea has no validity would remain . . . . I likewise agree that any statement from the sphere of worldviews (e.g. a religious statement) can be investigated with regard to its validity just as well as a scientific statement" (see the Dilthey-Husserl correspondence published in *Revista de Filosofia de la Universidad de Costa Rica*, Vol. I, No. 2, July-December 1957, pp. 110, 112).

13. See Windelband's *Lehrbuch der Geschichte der Philosophie*, 15th edition, ed. Heinz Heimsoeth (Tübingen: J. C. B. Mohr, 1957), pp. 8-10 and the first edition foreword.

14. See "Zur Methode der Philosophiegeschichte," reprinted in his *Kleinere Schriften*, Vol. III (Berlin: Walter de Gruyter, 1958), p. 14.

15. Hartmann's criticism of mere "understanding," in another essay on this topic, must be read as an implicit criticism of Dilthey, for whom "understanding" is central to the work of the historian. His contrast between "verstehen" and "wiedererkennen" is likewise an allusion to Dilthey and his followers. Dilthey is mentioned by name in a footnote criticizing his book on Hegel. Hartmann, who was also the author of a book on Hegel, complains: "*Die Jugendgeschichte Hegels* has taught us a great deal about this thinker as a cultural (*geistig*) figure and a great deal about the history of his times; about that which Hegel 'came to know,' what his time and the world after him could learn from him, it has taught us little" (see "Der philosophische Gedanke und seine Geschichte," in *Kleinere Schriften*, Vol. II, Berlin: Walter de Gruyter, 1957, pp. 8n, 11, 48).

16. *Ibid.*, p. 17; see also p. 5.

17. See *ibid.*, pp. 41-2.

18. See *ibid.*, p. 38.

19. "Die 3 Grundformen der Systeme in der ersten Hälfte des 19. Jahrhunderts," in Vol. IV, p. 352.

20. *Einleitung in die Geisteswissenschaften*, reprinted in Vol. I, p. 358.

21. "Plan der Fortzetzung sum Aufbau der geschichtlichen Welt in den Geisteswissenschaften," in Vol. VII, pp. 215-16.

22. "Zusätze" to *Der Aufbau der geschichtlichen Welt in den Geisteswissenschaften*, in Vol. VII, p. 346. Dilthey also dealt with the "transferability" of the contents of expressions in his unfinished continuation of *Aufbau* (see Vol. VII, pp. 205ff). On the basis of what he says in that discussion, we could conclude that philosophical systems and ideas represent what he calls "expressions of experience" (*Erlebnisausdrücke*), while scientific concepts and ideas do not.

23. See Windelband, *op. cit.*, p. 8.

24. *Einleitung in die Geisteswissenschaften*, p. 406.

25. The Africa example is Dilthey's own (see "Literaturhistorische Arbeiten über das *klassische Zeitalter unserer Dichtung*," in Vol. XI, p. 196).

26. See "Uebersicht meines Systems," in Vol. VIII, p. 178; see also *Von Deutscher Dichtung und Musik* (Leipzig and Berlin: B. G. Teubner, 1933), p. 411.

27. Preface to Vol. V of the *Gesammelte Schriften*, p. 4.

28. "Plan der Fortzetzung," in Vol. VII, p. 262.

29. *Ibid.*, p. 255.

30. "Das geschichtliche Bewusstsein und die Weltanschauungen," in Vol. VIII, p. 13.

31. See *Das Wesen der Philosophie*, in Vol. V, pp. 358, 407.

32. One might argue that the history of the historical, cultural and social sciences is subject to the same fits and starts as the history of philosophy.

On Heidegger's Early Kant Interpretation

(Kant and the Problem of Metaphysics)

JOHN KRAAY

Introduction

Heidegger gave his book *Kant and the Problem of Metaphysics* a second title. Churchill (*7a*: 9) renders it as follows: "The explication (*Auseinanderlegung*) of the idea of a fundamental ontology through the interpretation (*Auslegung*) of the *Critique of Pure Reason* as a laying of the foundation (*Grundlegung*) of metaphysics." In formulating this alternative title to his Kant book, Heidegger invites the reader to pay close attention to method.

It so happens that, on the whole, there appear to be basically two ways in which Heidegger's Kant book has been received.

(1) It is rejected by some by reason of its supposed imperialism and on account of disagreement with Heidegger's *Sein und Zeit* (*Being and Time*) philosophy. Such rejection does not exclude the possibility that these commentators may have real appreciation for specific points made by Heidegger. One could refer to the Marburger neo-Kantian Ernst Cassirer and to the Christian philosopher and lifelong adversary of neo-Kantianism Herman Dooyeweerd as typical representatives of this attitude.

(2) Among others the book is hailed as a helpful introduction to or demonstration of the *Sein und Zeit* mode of thinking (to which such authors are usually sympathetic), and the "violent interpretation" is not made a problem. This position does not seem to preclude the possibility that at least certain difficulties are admitted, especially in relation to Heidegger's subsequent development. Examples are J. W. Richardson and C. O. Schrag.

Each of these two types of evaluation is unsatisfactory, since both, through one-sidedness, cloud the issue introduced by Heidegger himself in his deliberate juxtaposition of the words *Auseinanderlegung* and *Auslegung*, mutually related by the word *durch*. T. D. Langan is surely right when he states that Heidegger is not "trying to say what Kant 'really' said" (*7a*; XII) as long as this assertion is taken in a positivistically-understood Rankean sense. Interpretation is always more than mere restatement. A balanced assessment of the Kant book should include serious consideration of lines such as those occurring toward the end of the third (and most hotly debated) chapter:

> If an interpretation merely reiterates what Kant explicitly said, it is no interpretation to start with. An interpreter's task is to make visible that which Kant, over and above the actual formulation, has brought to light in his [act of] foundation . . . . To be sure, to wrest from what the words say that which they *mean* to say, every interpretation must use *force*. Such violence, however, cannot be mere caprice. The *power* of a path-lighting idea must move and guide the interpretation (*7*: 192-4).

This statement constitutes the *pièce de résistance* of this essay; beyond and behind the issue as to how good an introduction or how bad an interpretation the Kant book is, the focus is on the method and aim of leading into *Fundamentalontologie*.

Setting and structure of Heidegger's Kant interpretation

The book has been available in translation since 1962, and Richardson's *Through Phenomenology to Thought* includes an extensive interpretative *résumé*. It will nevertheless be useful to pay special attention to the framework and background of the argument here.

The work contains four chapters, treating of the "take-off" (*Ansatz*), the execution (*Durchführung*), the originality (*Ursprünglichkeit*), and the repetition (*Wiederholung*) of Kant's founding of metaphysics respectively, preceded by a brief Preface and Introduction. Commentators tend to divide these chapters into two sets of two, such that the first two chapters are considered a serious, if misguided, interpretation of the *Critique of Pure Reason*, while chapters three and four are held to contain a concise statement on Heidegger's own philosophy as laid down in *Sein und Zeit*, Part I.

The Preface to the First Edition and the Introduction, however, point in a different direction. The Preface explicitly refers to the unpublished, second part of *Sein und Zeit* and announces that "the theme of the present investigation will [there] be treated on a broader basis," while the Introduction explains that the four chapters each treat a dimension of the one theme. What is this theme? Which the broader basis?

Heidegger has formulated the theme in the words of the second title, and paragraph 6 of *Sein und Zeit* presents a thumbnail sketch of the broader background in terms of which the idea of *Fundamentalontologie* will be brought forward in *Sein und Zeit*, Part II. He explains that in spite of all interest in "metaphysics," the question of the meaning of Being has been covered up and forgotten. If the question of the meaning of Being is to have its own history made transparent, we must "destroy" the traditional content of ontology "until we arrive at those primordial experiences in which were achieved the first ways of determining the nature of Being." This involves, Heidegger holds, not a negative rejection of tradition but rather a staking out and digging up of its positive possibilities. First the question must be raised as to whether and to what extent the interpretation of Being and the phenomenon of time have been ontologically related. "The first and only person who has gone any stretch of the way towards investigating the dimension of temporality . . . is Kant." Owing, however, to his ontological dependence on Descartes, who in turn depended via Scholasticism on Aristotle, the "Kantian account of time operates within the structures Aristotle has set forth." Part II of *Sein und Zeit* will contain a "destruction" (that is, demarcation, delimitation, definition, analysis, probing, and proving) of metaphysics in confrontation with Kant, Descartes, and Aristotle.

Hansgeorg Hoppe has pointed to what he takes to be a discrepancy:

> In view of . . . the *Sein und Zeit* Kant evaluation, it is quite astonishing that Heidegger, in his 1929 Kant book, believes that the very idea of a *Fundamentalontologie* of *Dasein*, developed in *Sein und Zeit*, may be "tested in an interpretation of the *Critique of Pure Reason* as a founding of metaphysics" (*10*: 288).

It can hardly be said that Hoppe's formulation of the problem is helpful: "The difficulty in assessing the scope of his [Heidegger's] statements is the circumstance that Heidegger is not concerned with a historico-philological interpretation—yet, in a way he is . . . . On the whole, it never becomes clear specifically to what extent Heidegger sees Kant as having progressed on the way of an inquiry uncovering the subjectivity of the subject." "We are constantly confronted with the difficulty of determining which Kant Heidegger is talking about—the historical . . . or the Heideggerian Kant." Hoppe's conclusion: the historical Kant cannot be made into a "Fundamentalontologist"—except through the use of violence! By lifting the Kant book out of its setting of the "destruction of traditional ontology," Hoppe has cut himself off from understanding the weight of the word *tested* (*bewährt*) and has failed to appreciate that Heidegger presents the Kant book as "a historical introduction to the *problematics* of Part I of *Sein und Zeit*" (italics mine), and not, as he and others suggest, as a summary of the *Sein und Zeit* solution.

As the Introduction explains, it is not this or that manifestation of *Fundamentalontologie* that is to be "tested," but the Idea. *Fundamentalontologie* is the "metaphysics of human *Dasein*" necessarily required to make metaphysics possible, or rather, to unearth the intrinsic possibility of metaphysics. To (Socratically) bring out the idea of *Fundamentalontologie* is to show the necessity of such an ontological analysis of *Dasein*, and in doing so to make clear in which respect and what manner, with what limitations and under which presuppositions it asked the concrete question "Who is man?" Since an idea witnesses to itself in its illuminating power, the idea of *Fundamentalontologie* will present and prove itself in an exposition of Kant's *Critique* as a founding of metaphysics. Kant's *Critique* is to be understood as designing the building plan, together with its specification as to on what ground and how the foundation is to be laid. Since designing the plan is itself a typical (philosophical) way of building, the very act of designing necessarily lets the bearing strength of the ground laid be operative. To the extent that a founding of metaphysics really does let the intrinsic possibility of metaphysics be possible, it merits the title of *Fundamentalontologie*.

What must Heidegger do in order to "teach" the idea of *Fundamentalontologie* by way of Kant? Over against current neo-Kantian interpretations, he must argue that Kant is not engaged in developing a theory of knowledge or of experience—at least, that Kant is not about to replace "metaphysics" with such a theory. He must show that, and how, metaphysics as a "natural disposition" (*Naturanlage*) of man is inescapable for Kant. Over against current tendencies in anthropological reflection, he must show that, and how, such metaphysics is inescapably problematic. He must demonstrate that Kant's recognition of the finitude (= temporality) of man constitutes a positive contribution towards lighting up the path that leads to a repristination of the meaningfulness of the question concerning the meaning of Being.

In view of all this, it does not seem a very good idea to divide the Kant book into two parts. When Cassirer states that in Chapter Three "Heidegger no longer speaks as commentator but as usurper," he is far too sympathetic; from his point of view, Heidegger from the very start "enters the Kantian system with force of arms, to subject it to himself and to enslave it to his own problematics."

Ansatz

Kant was confronted with a concept of metaphysics whose ambiguity bequeathed by Aristotle (*on hê on* and *timiotaton genos*) was aggravated by Scholastic dogma (*ens commune = metaphysica generalis*; theology, psychology, and cosmology = *metaphysica specialis*), and by Scholastic method (*regina scientiarum*). As queen of the sciences, metaphysics should be as stringent as the most ideal method; it should be as certain as mathematics, a "science of pure Reason." Kant adheres to this intention, demanding particularly that *metaphysica specialis* should become such a science.

For Kant the procedure of the natural scientist provides a hint: "Reason only understands that which she herself brings forth according to her design." When this hint is applied to metaphysics, the attempt at founding *metaphysica specialis* is pushed back to the question of the nature of *metaphysica generalis*; for the first time since Plato and Aristotle, ontology is made into a problem again. This is the significance of Kant's "Copernican revolution": founding metaphysics amounts to disclosing the intrinsic possibility of ontology.

In line with tradition, Kant formulates: How are synthetic judgments apriori possible? Every judgment is already synthetic in two senses: I *bring together* according to a rule that I *bring to bear*. In apriori judgments there is still another synthesis: bringing something to bear on Being which has not been derived from experience, a primordial relating oneself to Being, a "pure synthesis" which first "frames" the horizon in which Being may be experienced by the self in the empirical synthesis. An investigation concerning the nature of this "pure synthesis" Kant calls a transcendental inquiry.

Together these three paragraphs indicate why Kant's founding of metaphysics became a critique of pure reason. Recognizing the need to make the possibility of ontology into a problem, Kant inaugurates his "transcendental philosophy" in which the "ontological synthesis" is at issue.

Cassirer's objection

Cassirer's counterclaim is that for Kant, as Enlightenment thinker, metaphysics is the doctrine concerning "the first grounds of human knowledge," whereby "ground" is meant in the "harmless" sense merely of referring to the *ultimate principles* of knowledge (*2*: 24).

A decade earlier, however, his interpretation of Kant's Copernican revolution had led him to sketch bold consequences indeed. In Kant's letters to Markus Herz, Cassirer tells us in *Kants Leben und Lehre*, all the insights that Kant later used to effectuate his revolution are given. While earlier metaphysics began with the "what" of the *Gegenstand* (theoretical object), Kant starts with the "how" of judgments regarding the *Gegenstand*. In the reformulation of the question, "metaphysics" turns into "transcendental philosophy." Cassirer refers to the very text cited by Heidegger: "I entitle *transcendental* all knowledge which is occupied not so much with *Gegenstände* as with the mode of our knowledge of *Gegenstände* insofar as this mode is to be possible apriori" (B25, A 11). With this, Cassirer continues, the old, dogmatically objective ontology is left behind, while metaphysics is nevertheless maintained and deepened in the direction of the "subjective" (*1*: 164). To be sure, transcendental philosophy treats of the various forms of *Gegenständlichkeit* (objectivity); but every objective form may be grasped and understood only through the mediation of a specific form of knowledge. Thus philosophy continues to depend on the given totality of the *geistigen Kultur* as necessary starting point. Mind (*Verstand*) primarily stands for the totality called science (*Wissenschaft*), but in a broadened sense, including the various "orders" that are intellectual, ethical, or aesthetic in kind.

Certainly, if there be neo-Kantians who hold that Kant replaced metaphysics with a theory of knowledge or experience, Cassirer is not one of them without qualification. "That which in the empirical life of humanity comes to the fore piecemeal and unconnected, loaded with contingency, the transcendental critique must understand *from its first grounds* and place before us systematically" (*1*: 166). Still, Cassirer presents an appropriation of Kant's *Critique* as thoroughgoing and as far from "harmless" as the one he ascribes to Heidegger. Cassirer's criticism that Heidegger approaches Kant from a "changed spiritual climate" (*2*: 23) backfires. If Heidegger's is an existential interpretation in which Kant prefigures the phenomenology of *Dasein*, Cassirer's is a culturalistic one in which Kant instantiates the "Philosophy of Symbolic Forms" in three of its major areas.

Methodologically, Cassirer does express a great deal of agreement with Heidegger. "I would not deny that in every philosophical exposition such a [path-lighting] idea must lead and guide—indeed, I have never approached the history of philosophy except in this way" (*2*: 17). And, during the Davos seminar, he even admits that Kant "did indeed start from the sort of problem raised by Heidegger," but maintains that he went beyond it (*5*: 124), something that Heidegger in turn does not deny.

Does Cassirer really understand Heidegger's intention? It would seem not. Cassirer agrees, to some degree, that Kant started with the problem raised by Heidegger, but in the third and fourth chapters Heidegger becomes an eisegetic usurper, reading his own problem into Kant. Heidegger, however, says: "Every founding, in relation to former ones and with respect to the tradition taken up into it, is a transformation (*Verwandlung*) of its task" (7: 2). The problem of metaphysics is the problem of its intrinsic possibility, of its ground. The formulation of the problem—itself a metaphysical achievement—is necessarily tradition-bound, necessarily tradition-breaking; it necessarily depends on and consequently reveals the very ground that makes the formulation possible.

> By repetition of a foundational problem, we understand the disclosure of its original possibilities, hidden until now, so that the problem is transformed and only thus perpetuated as problem (*bewahrt in seinem Problemgehalt*) (7: 195).

Cassirer presupposes a foundation, uncritically and unproblematically. But what has Kant really done, that he should merit such trust?

The hermeneutic key

In the second chapter, Heidegger, in line with his "path-lighting" idea—testing the tensile strength of the ground laid in *Fundamentalontologie*—sets about the task of indicating Kant's specification of the ground of metaphysics. The chapter divides into two—first the hermeneutic key must be found wherewith Kant sought to gain entrance to the ground of metaphysics, secondly, Kant's steps have to be retraced. The third chapter's main concern will be to evaluate whether or not Kant has actually reached the inner *sanctum*.

This hermeneutic key is buried in obviousness, taken for granted—and therefore overlooked by most commentators. Wellspring for the founding of metaphysics is *human* pure reason. The core of the problem lies in this human-ness, that is, its finitude. At the same time, this very finitude is the secret of metaphysics' intrinsic possibility. This is because human reason is *thinking perception*; the key to an understanding of Kant's critique of the traditional *use* of reason is his understanding of the *nature* of reason or knowledge. With the aid of this recognition, the interpreter is able to reconstruct the intuitively guiding "hunch" (*Durchblick* or *Vorblick*) by which Kant proceeded and gradually came to a measure of clarity.

To get at the nature of finite knowledge, one needs a general characterization of the nature of knowledge as such, whereby the first thing one must remember is that to know is primarily to perceive ("Erkennen ist primär Anschauen"). Thought is in service of perception, which implies that there must be an intrinsic connection between them; both are of the genus of representation. Finite knowledge is non-creative. It must let the *Gegenstand* be given to us: "Perception takes place only insofar as the *Gegenstand* is given; which in turn is possible, at least for us human beings, only because it affects our mind (*Gemüt*) in a certain way" (A19, B33). With this Kant was the first to attain to a non-sensualist concept of *Sinnlichkeit*. Finite perception, in need of determination, depends on the understanding which is itself more finite still, insofar as it lacks the immediacy finite perception has. This roundaboutness (*Diskursivität*) is the most telling index of its finitude, even if a certain spontaneity accrues to it on account of its positing the form of the concept. If finite knowledge is receptive perception, then the knowable must show itself. "Appearance" refers to a being as *Gegenstand* of finite knowledge; it is in fact the very being of any "being *an sich*" which, in virtue of the finitude of finite knowledge, "appears" as *Gegenstand*. The expressions "behind the appearance" and "mere appearance" mean only that in human knowing, beings cannot be known infinitely.

Says Kant: "Our knowledge springs from two fundamental sources of the mind; the first is the capacity of receiving representations (receptivity for impressions), the second is the power of knowing a *Gegenstand* through these representations (spontaneity of concepts)" (A51, B75). But if the founding of metaphysics aims at finite knowledge as composite of two basic sources, then the original unity, the root, must announce itself. And so, indeed, both in the *Einleitung* and towards the end of the *Critique*, Kant speaks of it:

> By way of introduction or anticipation we need only say that there are two stems of human knowledge, namely, sensibility (*Sinnlichkeit*) and understanding (*Verstand*), which perhaps spring from a common, but to us unknown root (A15, B29).

> We shall content ourselves here . . . merely to outline the architectonic of all knowledge arising from pure reason; and in so doing we shall begin from the point at which the common root of our faculty of knowledge divides and throws out two stems, one of which is reason (*Vernunft*) (A835, B863).

Kant first says "perhaps," and ultimately he concludes that this common root does exist, characterizing it as "unknown." Kant's founding of metaphysics, then, does not lead to cut-and-dried principles and axioms but embarks upon and reveals the unknown. The founding of philosophy is a philosophical undertaking.

This first part of the second chapter is the crucial section of Heidegger's Kant book. Heinrich Levy, one of the earliest commentators on Heidegger's interpretation, correctly hinged the whole of his (negative) evaluation on this section. It is on account of his misunderstanding of these paragraphs mainly that Hansgeorg Hoppe is plagued by indecision ("Heidegger is not concerned with an historico-philological interpretation—yet, in a way he is"). Cassirer, too, had he but considered this *Vorblick* or *Durchblick* more seriously than he seems to have done (there is no mention of it in his article), might have been more sympathetic to the seriousness with which Heidegger insists: "If the exposition . . . is to remain interpretation, the leading idea . . . must be taken from the Kantian founding itself . . . . The thing to do is to question Kant's penetration into the dimension of the origin . . . in accordance with the leading *Vorblick*" (*6*: 119).

Dooyeweerd's objection

Herman Dooyeweerd judges that Heidegger's interpretation leads to arbitrary violence and turns the *Critique* into an introduction to *Sein und Zeit*. In support of this he presents a general maxim for interpretation: a thinker's *own* "idea of cosmic law" must guide the interpretation of his work (*3*, II: 455 = *4*, II: 523). Dooyeweerd holds that every systematic philosopher at least implicitly proceeds on the basis of a "cosmonomic idea" by which are apriorily answered the questions as to the cosmic coherence and totality of meaning, and of its origin. At the time of his consideration of Heidegger's Kant interpretation, he held that this tripartite cosmonomic idea as limiting concept is explicated philosophically by way of transcendental self-reflection upon one's subjective stance in an "Archimedean point" at which cosmic law is given (pseudo-) revelationally. Insofar as any thinker is given to self-reflection—and Kant certainly is; witness the transcendental ideas—he will, at least implicitly, reveal his "cosmonomic idea" and so provide an interpreter with the hermeneutic key to his work. Like Heidegger, Dooyeweerd arrives at the identification of the hermeneutic key on the strength of his own "path-lighting idea." Cassirer was seen to do so as well.

Both Cassirer and Dooyeweerd overlook the fact that in Heidegger's Kant-interpretation—as in their own! —the (immanent) hermeneutic key (Kant's "leading idea" or "*Vorblick*") should be distinguished sharply from the "path-lighting idea" that leads to its identification. The result is a significant misunderstanding concerning the "inner pull of the problem" to which Heidegger sees Kant respond. Cassirer held that Kant went beyond the problem of human finitude; Dooyeweerd insists on treating the one book that Heidegger dedicated to Max Scheler as dealing with theory of knowledge:

> In the "transcendental imagination," according to Heidegger, the original essential unity must be sought of the stems of knowledge (sensory perception and logical thought) that Kant had initially isolated, but which for that reason could not be fully understood (*3*, II: 456 = *4*, II: 524).

> Heidegger is confronted with the real problem of inter-functional [cognitive] synthesis and tries to solve it in his own way, though he ascribes the solution to Kant himself (*4*: 525).

To be sure, Dooyeweerd would not have "theory of knowledge" understood in a narrow, positivistic sense. He rather regards it as an organization of one's entire philosophical effort in terms of a specific theme:

> Truly transcendental theory of knowledge . . . is: theory directed to the meaning-totality of knowledge, in which our selfhood, philosophically thinking towards the limits, turns inward to itself and thus reflects on the boundaries and conditions of temporal knowledge. Viewed thus, what is philosophy other than theory of knowledge? (*3*, I: 506 = *4*, I: 543).

Good! But if these things are so, it would seem that the *Critique of Pure Reason* must, as Heidegger maintains, at least contain a hint (*Hinweis*) of the turning-inward-to-oneself which, in virtue of the very character ascribed to it by Dooyeweerd, is necessarily demanded in philosophical inquiry. An attempted characterization of the *"Rückgangsdimension"* is then legitimate, and an interpretation in terms of it is highly relevant.

The right question to ask Heidegger

The question is not whether Heidegger has correctly placed the *Critique* in the system of Kant's work as a whole. On this point Heidegger is irrelevant—in spite of the fact that in the third chapter of his Kant book he even includes "practical reason" in his considerations, or rather, just because of the way in which he does so. C. O. Schrag is on the wrong track when he assumes that on the question that divided neo-Kantians—which of the *Critiques* is the basic one? —Heidegger, for reasons of his own, sided with the Marburgers (*14*: 87). To be convinced of this, one needs only to recall that the Marburgers derive their most important prooftexts from the *second* edition. Heidegger is not concerned with how the *Critique of Pure Reason* fits in, but rather with how it stands out.

Insofar as Heidegger engages in direct battle with neo-Kantians at all, it is with positivistic neo-Kantians. His statement that the *Critique* "has nothing to do with theory of knowledge" has to be understood in that context. Kant's *Critique* is a methodological treatise tilling the ground for metaphysics. Who would deny it, save the positivist? A method is justified not by its results but by its presuppositions. Who but the positivist would object? Since the issue is metaphysics, the presuppositions are necessarily presuppositions regarding being. What is the ground—in the sense of the nature, the origin, the inner possibility? "Metaphysics is a *Naturanlage* of man," says Kant; that is, metaphysics, *specialis* and *generalis*, originates in human reason, in finite reason which lives in the unity of perception and thought. The unifying unity in human reason is at the same time none other than the intrinsic possibility of ontology. Investigation of this (*Rückgangs-*) dimension falls to a discipline for which Kant had no name. Let it be called *Fundamentalontologie*.

Now, Dooyeweerd holds that Kant does not escape the confinement subsequently declared eminent good sense among positivists, confinement, that is, to the dimension of theoretical reason. Hence Kant has cut off the possibility of a truly critical penetration of the "*Rückgangsdimension,*" and there can be no *Hinweis* at all within theoretical reason to the place from which it really begins (the "*homo noumenon*"); there is only a fixation upon a formal, Cartesian "cognito."

However, the circumstance that Kant, in the second edition, retreated before the transcendental imagination as root of reason is no reluctant "admission" on the part of Heidegger, as Dooyeweerd would have it (*3*, II: 453 = *4*, II: 521). It is his thesis. This event is the *conditio sine qua non* for Heidegger's book. Had Kant not backed away from *Fundamentalontologie*, Heidegger's self-appointed task of recovering the idea of it would be superfluous. The great Königberger's demonstration of it would forever stand as its monument. As it is, Heidegger must—amidst ubiquitous "forgetfulness of being," beginning with the second edition—bring the idea to light. There is but one way, and it must be followed out to the end. The basic tendency of Kant's *Vorblick* must be "positively appropriated" (*positieve Aneignung seiner Grundtendenz*).

It seems that the difficulty of which Hansgeorg Hoppe complained can be resolved after all. We are not confronted with a Heideggerian Kant, but rather with a Kantian Heidegger! To be sure, Heidegger is no "neo-Kantian"—positivist or idealist. He is, so to speak, a pristine Kantian, more Kantian than the Kant who retreated from *himself*. The right question to ask Heidegger is: To what extent will retracing Kant's *Vorblick* to the end really provide a *Fundamentalontogie*? Alternately formulated: Will this Socratic probing really yield the *concrete* question "Who is man?"

The fallacy of mistaken concreteness

Presupposed is that there is at least a point of connection providing justification for Heidegger's derivation of his hermeneutic key from the

Critique itself. It has been sketched in a few lines just a moment ago (metaphysics as *Naturanlage*). But Hoppe denies this connection, and in so doing involves himself in a subtle but unmistakable contradiction. His conclusion after comparing the Kant book with *Die Frage nach dem Ding* and "Kants These über das Sein" runs as follows:

> It is remarkable how, along with the development of his onto-historical (*Seinsgeschichtlichen*) thought, Heidegger's Kant interpretation becomes more "objective" and to the point—even while simultaneous work on Greek thinkers offers abundant examples of the violence (Heidegger admits it) of his interpretations . . . . However, Heidegger had appropriated Kant as prototype and co-worker in his Kant-book, and had espied in the *Critique* a founding of *Fundamentalontologie* [*sic*] which he himself had developed in *Sein und Zeit*. The "*Kehre*" in Heidegger's thought . . . means that the Kant interpretation requires revision; the leading "*Vorblick*" taken from *Sein und Zeit* [!] has "failed." The distantiation from *Sein und Zeit* leads, by way of a distantiation from the Kant book, to a distance over against Kant himself (*10*: 316).

If the Kant book is, so to speak, really a "Heidegger book," as Hoppe throughout charges, then no distantiation from it can ever index distance to Kant. Such distantiation could and did occur, however, once Heidegger "dismantled" (*auseinanderlegen*) Kant's founding of metaphysics and ultimately found it, even when carried through to the end, *not* to tend to the concrete question of man. "*Dasein*" is always an historical such or so "*sein*"; consequently, it cannot be its own ground, and is incompetent to philosophically specify any ground at all. In other words, Heidegger distantiated himself from the first-edition Kant once he distantiated himself—Heidegger would say: went beyond—the idea of *Fundamentalontologie* as envisioned prior to the "*Kehre,*" just as he abandoned the whole program of a "destruction of metaphysics" and never wrote the promised sequel to *Sein und Zeit*, Part I.

That Heidegger, while writing the Kant book, understood Kant as ascribing to the transcendental imagination a certain concreteness has already been shown; it is the very motivation of his quest, and the reason why commentators charge him with existentialist eisegesis. Only a detailed analysis of the differences between the first and second editions of the *Critique*, together with a "history of ideas" analysis of the "Archimedean point" fixed upon by Descartes, can establish whether or not Kant initially did so and subsequently backed away from it. Within the scope of this essay, just a few remarks will have to suffice.

First, one might reflect on the reasons Heidegger offers to explain Kant's retreat from the transcendental imagination as unifying unity of the two stems of knowledge. In paragraph 31 of the Kant book, Heidegger gives three considerations.

(1) Kant was quite aware of the possibility and necessity of a more original foundation, but it was not his first concern. Completion of the Subjective Deduction, though necessary, could be put off till later.

(2) There was something about the imagination itself that led Kant to turn away from it: traditionally, the imagination was considered a humble faculty in mere sensibility. To be sure, the Deduction and the Schematism pointed to a pure, transcendental imagination, but the indications were insufficiently explicit to show the totally new view of the subject actually implied. Hence Kant continued to be influenced by the view of the subjectivity of the subject in traditional anthropology and psychology. How could a lowly faculty of sense be the essence of Reason?

(3) Meanwhile, Reason had increasingly captivated him. Through his founding Kant had gained insight into the character of the "universality" of onto-metaphysical knowledge, and he put it to work in his moral philosophy.

Actually, the rationale Kant gives for not staking everything on the Subjective Deduction is very peculiar, and well worth quoting in full:

> This inquiry [the Deduction of the Pure Concepts of Understanding], which is somewhat deeply founded, has two sides. The one refers to the objects of pure understanding, and is intended to expound and render intelligible the objective validity of its apriori concepts. It is therefore essential to my purposes. The other seeks to investigate the pure understanding itself, its possibility and the cognitive faculties upon which it rests; and so deals with it in its subjective aspect. Although this latter exposition is of great importance for my chief purpose, it does not form an essential part of it. For the chief question is always simply this: —what and how much can the understanding and reason know apart from all experience? not: —how is the faculty of thought itself possible? The latter is, as it were, the search for the cause of a given effect, and to that extent is somewhat hypothetical (though, as I shall show elsewhere, it is not really so); and I would appear to be taking the liberty of simply expressing an *opinion*, in which case the reader would be free to express a different *opinion*. For that reason I must forestall the reader's criticism by pointing out that the objective deduction with which I am here chiefly concerned retains its full force even if my subjective deduction should fail to produce that complete conviction for which I hope (Axvii).

One can hardly refrain, in the light of this, from objecting to Dooyeweerd when he charges Heidegger with playing the Subjective Deduction off against the objective one. This quotation goes a long way toward justifying Heidegger in playing off the first edition against the second. On account of tradition, the founding of metaphysics must go by way of a critique of pure reason. But the "fundamental-ontological" turn inherent in the founding cannot be understood by the surrounding tradition—remember that it is precisely what constitutes the Copernican revolution. The very (supposed!) concreteness of the Subjective Deduction is Kant's reason for not, at this stage, insisting on it. In the second edition, on account of Kant's formalization of things, none of this applies any longer.

Heidegger concludes that the darkness and strangeness of the transcendental imagination and the clear power of pure Reason together conspired to close the shutters that for a moment had allowed a glimpse into the real nature of the Transcendental imagination. It is this that is the core of the often heard remark that Kant had turned from a "psychological" to a more "logical" interpretation. (Of course, it was never just "psychological," but rather transcendental.) Here, too, Heidegger would seem to have a point: Cassirer, for instance, indeed rejects Heidegger's fixation on the imagination on the ground that it is, after all, a mere "psychological" (i.e. empirical) entity (cf. *14*: 100).

Finally, a consideration of Heidegger's identification of the beneficiary of Kant's redirection is illuminating: "Kant has retreated from this unknown root. In the second edition of the *Critique*, the transcendental imagination, as it came to light in the bold strokes of the first plan, is pushed back and reinterpreted—*in favor of the understanding*" (*7*: 153). Is this what really happened? The answer must be negative. Kant dropped the transcendental imagination not in favor of the understanding but in favor of the noumenal selfhood: "Ich musste also das Wissen aufheben . . . ," he says in the Preface to the *second* edition. Under pressure of the demands of the *Critique of Practical Reason*, Kant saw himself faced with a threatening dialectic between the concrete transcendental imagination and the equally concrete noumenal selfhood—a dialectic that could be resolved only by accepting a subordination of the theoretical to the moral. Concreteness is now meant to be reserved for the noumenal only, and the transcendental imagination is degraded to a merely *formal* unity of understanding and perception.

Why is it that Heidegger does not follow Kant in this ethical turn to the concrete subject? The answer to this will have to be sought in Heidegger's response, if not reaction, to the failure of the idealist tradition. As it is, the conclusion regarding Heidegger's teaching of the idea of a *Fundamentalontologie* by way of Kant's earliest *Critique of Pure Reason* is this: it is successful only if the subjectivity of the subject is identical to man's self-consciousness, in the sense of consciousness of the self-as-consciousness. Or, to put it in terms of Descartes' image of the fulcrum (second Meditation): if the *pro*-positional, Archimedean point at which the pressure is applied ("*cogito ergo sum*")—arrived at by thought! —is at the same time the position *from* which the pressure is applied (*sum res cogitans*).

But while the merit of the quest for a *Fundamentalontologie* is questionable, primarily because it is inspired by a fatal insistence on treating the subjectivity of the subject onto-epistemologically, Heidegger's method is sound in at least one very fundamental way. His Socratic teaching is truly hermeneutic when he distinguishes between his own "path-lighting idea" and Kant's "*Durchblick.*" The relationship between these is such that the former enables him to recognize the latter as constituting the hermeneutic key. Careful observance of this basic tenet is a first step in leaving intact the subjectivity of the subject whose work is the object of interpretation. The "violence" is the spark that flies across when real contact is made, and it will occur both when "positive appropriation" is attempted and when the result is a "radical rejection."

There seems to be a difficulty. Heidegger is presented as having found a hermeneutic key true to Kant, but enabled to do so on account of his own "idea," couched in terms of an existence philosophy. The initial spark is one of sympathy. Does this not mean that even if the word *usurpation* is too strong, the word *hineininterpretieren* is applicable after all? But there is another possibility. Existence philosophy, with its concern with the subjectivity of the subject, is very well equipped to sound out responsive chords whenever the question of man is seriously at issue. It may well be that this is its specific achievement and place in the history of Western philosophical reflection, just as other schools and movements have made their unique contributions in other ways. The curious thing is that Heidegger himself was the first to learn from what he had *actually* brought to light in the Kant book. The "*Kehre,*" whether it be a conversion or a readjustment, witnesses to the problematic nature of a *Fundamentalontologie* predicated on what, after all is existentially said and done, at bottom remains a thinking thing.

Bibliography

1. CASSIRER, E., *Kants Leben und Lehre*; Berlin: Bruno Cassirer, 1919, 1921[2].

2 ——. "Kant und das Problem der Metaphysik; Bemerkungen zu Martin Heideggers Kant-Interpretation," in: *Kant-Studien*, XXXVI (1931), pp. 1-26.

3. DOOYEWEERD, H., *Wijsbegeerte der Wetsidee*, I-III; Amsterdam: H. J. Paris, 1935-36.

4 ——. *A New Critique of Theoretical Thought*; Philadelphia: Presbyterian and Reformed Publishing Co., 1953-58.

5. HAMBURG, C., "A Cassirer-Heidegger Seminar," in: *Phil. and Phen. Research*, XXV (1964), pp. 208-22 (a translation of the "Arbeitsgemeinschaft Cassirer-Heidegger" published by Guido Schneeberger, *Ergänzungen zu einer Heidegger- Bibliographie*; Bern: Suhr, 1960, pp. 17-27).

6. HEIDEGGER, M., *Sein und Zeit*; Tübingen: Niemeyer, 1972.[12]

7 ——. *Kant und das Problem der Metaphysik*; Bonn: Cohen; Frankfurt a.M.: Klostermann, 1929, 1951[2].

7a ——. Trans. J. S. Churchill, *Kant and the Problem of Metaphysics*; Bloomington, London: Indiana University Press, 1962, 1972[4].

8 ——. *Die Frage nach dem Ding: Zu Kants Lehre von den transzendentalen Grundsätzen*; Tübingen: Niemeyer, 1962.

9 ——. "Kants These über das Sein," in *Wegmarken*; Frankfurt a.M.: Klostermann, 1967, pp. 273-307.

10. HOPPE, H., "Wandlungen in der Kant-Auffassung Heideggers," in: *Durchblicke: Martin Heidegger zum 80. Geburtstag*; Frankfurt a.M.: Klostermann, 1970, pp. 284-317.

11. LEVY, H., "Heideggers Kant-Interpretation: Zu Heideggers Buch 'Kant und das Problem der Metaphysik,' " in: *Logos*, XXI (1932), pp. 1-43.

12. NADEAU, R., "Cassirer et Heidegger: histoire d'un affrontement," in: *Dialogue*, XII (1973), pp. 660-9.

13. RICHARDSON, J. W., *Heidegger: Through Phenomenology to Thought*; The Hague: Nijhoff, 1963.

14. SCHRAG, C. O., "Heidegger and Cassirer on Kant," in: *Kant-Studien*, 58 (1967), pp. 87-100.

On Vollenhoven's Problem-Historical Method[1]

ALBERT M. WOLTERS

Vollenhoven is chiefly known for his "consistent problem-historical method" (*consequent probleemhistorische methode*) in the historiography of philosophy. I believe that this is to be seen against the background of the development of the idea of *Problemgeschichte* in early twentieth-century neo-Kantianism, the philosophical movement which dominated the Dutch intellectual scene during Vollenhoven's formative years. This development, which must itself be seen as a reaction against Dilthey and the rise of historicism, finds its two most explicit spokesmen in the German philosophers Nicolai Hartmann (1882-1950) and Richard Hönigswald (1875-1947), men whose works we know were intensively studied by Vollenhoven in the early years of his development.

Characteristic of the neo-Kantian concept of *Problemgeschichte* was the subordination of historical study to systematic philosophical interests. The history of philosophy, in this view, is the story of the great thinkers' struggle to come to terms with the perennial and immutable systematic problems of philosophy. The contemporary philosopher is intensely interested in this history because he, too, is struggling with these same enduring problems and can expect to gain systematic insight from the giants who have preceded him.

It is helpful to be aware of this neo-Kantian background because it provides a context for Vollenhoven's work in the history of philosophy. One of the exasperating things about that work is that Vollenhoven seems to have an aversion to discussing the methodological presuppositions implicit in his method. The following is in large part an attempt to hunt down those presuppositions on the basis of bits of evidence scattered throughout his writings.

From his first published work, his dissertation, to his last researches,

Vollenhoven's activity as a philosopher has been dominated by that peculiar combination of systematic and historical interests which was characteristic of the idea of *Problemgeschichte*. Oddly enough, although he was acquainted from the beginning with the work of Hartmann and Hönigswald, he does not seem to have adopted the term *probleemhistorisch* until 1949[2]—in fact, he gave his method no name at all until 1948, when he spoke of "problem analysis" and "the method of philosophical analysis" to describe his approach to Plato's development (*16*: 1, 6 and *passim*). He seems to have been so absorbed with the actual task at hand that it was not until later that he realized that he had in fact been using a distinctive method all along.

From systematic priority to historical priority: a documentation

There can be no doubt, however, that the 1917 dissertation is already fully *problemgeschichtlich* in approach. Although primarily a *systematic* attempt to arrive at a specifically "theistic" philosophy of mathematics, the greater part of the work is devoted to a historical orientation of the problems involved, beginning with the pre-Socratics. The treatment of the history of philosophy proceeds from the assumption that there are basically three kinds of metaphysics: dualism, which recognizes a qualitative difference between mind and matter, and two kinds of monism, one of which reduces mind to matter (materialism), and another which reduces matter to mind (psychomonism) (*1*: 2, 3). Corresponding to these three philosophies are three basic types of mathematical theory: intuitionism (dualistic), empiricism (materialistic) and formalism (psychomonistic). On the basis of these distinctions and after an introductory chapter significantly called "A priori construction of the possible solutions of the most important problems," the history of the philosophy of mathematics is sketched in three longitudinal sections. First the "empiricistic" line is traced from Democritus and Epicurus to J. S. Mill. Then comes the "formalistic" line, including the Pythagoreans, Heraclitus, Scholasticism, and Hume. Finally "intuitionism" is pictured as beginning with Socrates and leading via Plato, Aristotle and Augustine to Kant. This takes the three basic types to the middle of the nineteenth century, the time of some important new developments (e.g. non-Euclidean geometry, symbolic logic, Meinong's *Gegenstandstheorie*). After discussing these in an intermediate chapter, Vollenhoven picks up the three lines again and brings them up to date, describing how each reacted to the new contributions. A fifth and final chapter brings his own systematic conclusions.

It is plain from this structure of the dissertation how closely allied the young Vollenhoven considered questions of systematics with their history. It is also evident that he already viewed the history of philosophy in terms of constant types reaching back to the beginning of Greek philosophy and characterized by a remarkable degree of continuity. Perhaps most striking of all is the total absence of any discussion or defense of his historiographical approach. It is simply assumed. The only reference to it is in the discussion of purposes: "in this [work] history will have to provide its ever valuable guidance" (*1*: 3).

Involuntarily, one is led to speculate on the influences which could have led the 25-year-old promovendus to assume so naturally such an unusual attitude to the history of philosophy, especially with respect to the theory of constant types. It is unlikely that his thesis supervisor, Geesink, could have contributed much towards the shaping of his views: he was an overworked pastor-turned-philosopher and had for some time been a very old man with little vigor or vision in his teaching. It is more likely that a formative influence was exercised on the young Vollenhoven by J. Woltjer, the only other member of the ten-man Free University faculty in those days who sometimes gave philosophical lectures. He was the author of a brilliant dissertation on Lucretius, the Roman materialist philosopher, and was Vollenhoven's teacher both in the Amsterdam Christian classical high school (*gymnasium*), of which he was founder and principal, and later in the university. It is certain, in any case, that Vollenhoven thought very highly of Woltjer, at one time mentioning him in one breath with Augustine, Bradwardine, Calvin, and Kuyper.[3] Perhaps it was Woltjer who first aroused in him an interest in ancient philosophy and its fundamental importance for the history of Western philosophy. Another important influence may have been Herman Bavinck, who was one of Vollenhoven's theology professors. Bavinck laid great stress in his dogmatics on thorough historical orientation, and his approach is said to have been "problem-historical."[4] Moreover, it is known that in the last years of his life (during which he had Vollenhoven as student), his interest had turned strongly to philosophical questions.[5]

Be that as it may, the fact is that Vollenhoven's subsequent work remained true to the pattern set by the dissertation: all systematic questions are set against the background of their history, and the history, in turn, is viewed in terms of systematic criteria. An especially striking example is his article (*3*) "The increase in logical consistency in recent physics," ostensibly a book review, in which he gives, within the compass of three pages, a short review of eleven chapters dealing with the history of physics. This he does by showing that history is the struggle to overcome two "dualisms," thus summing up in a nutshell both the history and the theoretical problems involved, so that it is a very easy transition to a theoretical exposition of his own systematic views.

Despite the continuity of vision, however, there is a gradual shift in Vollenhoven's development from setting systematic problems against their historical background to dealing with the history of philosophy in systematic terms. It is this shift which Vollenhoven himself calls his transition from systematic to historical studies (*22*: 97; cf. already *6*: 6), a slightly misleading representation of his development, since the historical interest was far from absent in the early period. The date of the shift is quite early—it coincides roughly with the first fundamental clarity with respect to his own systematics: the discovery of the pre-functional heart and the first elaboration of the scale of modalities in the late 1920s. In an article written in 1931, Vollenhoven writes (with reference to his own rejection of the term *theistic*): "Since that time [the author] has not ceased to be intrigued by the question of the *classification of the opponents' basic themes* in terms of his own standpoint. *In the last years* the following terminology has proven to be rather serviceable . . ." (*8:* 194—italics mine). From this it appears that the question of classifying the history of philosophy had already occupied him for some years prior to 1931. The later "consistent problem-historical method," which acquired its present general shape during or shortly after the second world war, is a lineal descendant of this early attempt specifically directed towards charting the whole history of philosophy.

There is one article in Vollenhoven's early period which does deal specifically with the historiography of philosophy and is therefore of great interest for our purposes. It is entitled (*2*) "Some methodological comments concerning Dr. T. Hoekstra's *History of Philosophy*, I"[6] and it appeared in 1922.[7] Hoekstra (born in 1880), a fellow member of the Reformed (*Gereformeerde*) Church, had written a dissertation in philosophy under the neo-Kantian Windelband in 1906 and had taught at the Theological Seminary in Kampen since 1912. His history of philosophy was intended chiefly as a non-technical survey for the benefit of interested church members, written from a Reformed point of view. The first volume, dealing with ancient philosophy, appeared in 1921. Vollenhoven's criticism came down to this, that there was too much "transcendent" and not enough "immanent" criticism (*2*: 294)[8] in the book, with the result, first, that the inner "dialectic" of the history of philosophy was not brought out (*2*: 295-9), and second, that skepticism and philosophical relativism were thereby abetted (*2*: 299-301).

This rather devastating judgment is buttressed by the following arguments. Philosophical criticism must always be both immanent and transcendent (*2*: 294),[9] but always in that order: rejection of a philosophical position from one's own standpoint (transcendent criticism) must always be based on the pointing out of an *internal* logical difficulty in the position criticized (immanent criticism). There are two kinds of immanent criticism: that which is directed against a given philosophy by its contemporaries, and that delivered by later thinkers (including historians of philosophy). Both are necessary for a well-founded transcendent criticism.

The first is necessary because it helps explain the dialectical career of philosophy. Vollenhoven writes:

> In the approaching of truth, the line which the course of human thought describes may not be a straight one, and not a zigzag either (because it is precisely the conception of a dialectic in reality which allows for other than exclusively logical oppositions); there is a line nevertheless (*2*: 296).

That is to say, the history of philosophy is concerned with *approaching truth*—a truth which is eternal and unchanging (*2*: 295)—and has *continuity*, that is, there is connection (*verband, innerlijke samenhang—2*: 296) between the succeeding systems and periods. They do not stand "in isolation from each other" (*los naast elkaar—2*: 300). This is not a continuity of *progress* (straight line), not even via temporary relapses (zigzag line), because there is more involved in philosophy than logic (namely, religious direction). Vollenhoven continues:

> And the course of this line is such that a psychologically explainable reaction to a specific point constantly allows one movement after the other to assert itself. If this reaction is not an absolute one (and where could such a reaction be found in the area of Greek-Hellenic philosophy?), but opposes the older system or prevailing culture on one or more specific points, then the recognition of this dialectic will help to explain the rise of those new schools (*2*: 296).

The continuous line of the history of philosophy, we may paraphrase, is articulated into schools and periods. These arise out of *reaction* to preceding schools and periods. Such a reaction always allows of a *psychological* explanation, that is, it is understandable as a reaction of man's *soul* (*psyche*) in the sense of the inner man, with all its more-than-logical desires and aspirations. Since that soul is always a pagan soul in Greek philosophy, that is, not guided by the light of God's Word, its reaction will always be relative and one-sided, not absolute, lacking an absolute perspective from which to judge. The faults it sees and against which it reacts will always be "out of perspective" (and give occasion to a later generation to react against *its* one-sidedness).

It is in this context that contemporary immanent criticism is important: it is the logical, specifically philosophical aspect of the reactions which shape the history of philosophy. It is the key to preserving "the intrinsic connection even in cases of great conflict" (*2*: 296) and seeing "the unity which, for all their differences, binds two periods together" (*2*: 297). As an example, Vollenhoven adduces the transition from the Hellenic to the Hellenistic period in ancient philosophy, which Hoekstra simply reports as a change from theoretical to practical interests. Vollenhoven comments: "But we look in vain for the explanation why that ethical element came to the fore so suddenly, at least, a philosophical explanation. Surely political and cultural trends are not the only ones here" (*2*: 297). What he means by such a "philosophical explanation" is illustrated in what follows: "But there is no mention of the antipathy against the earlier intellectualism, nor of the continuing effect of the pragmatic influence of the Sophists, nor of the fact that logic and ethics had come close to each other in Plato" (*2*: 297). The change in philosophical periods must thus be seen as involving a change in attitude to the philosophical issues—for or against intellectualism, pragmatism and the connection of ethics with logic. Such a change of attitude finds its expression in contemporary immanent criticism.

The other kind of immanent criticism—that given by later thinkers, including the historian—is especially important with a view to the readers. Not only does it show them how difficult and complicated the problems of philosophy are (thus fostering true scientific modesty), but it shows the philosophical position of the Christian philosopher-historian to be a positive alternative. By giving no immanent criticism, the historian presents all philosophies as standing unconnected beside each other—to which his own is then added as one more in the same loose series, with ultimately no more claim to being accepted than the others. This leads to skepticism and relativism. Instead, he must demonstrate, by pointing out the internal logical inadequacies of the systems of the past, that his own is more satisfactory.

I have dealt with this article in some detail not only because it shows how early Vollenhoven was already concerned with the methodology of the historiography of philosophy, but especially because it contains *in nuce* the principles of his own later historical work: the emphasis on the specifically philosophical, i.e. systematic, aspect; the view of the "dialectical" movement; the thesis that philosophy involves more than logical considerations; and the conviction that dealing with the history of philosophy should strengthen one's own standpoint.

The last theme is brought forward with considerable emphasis in Vollenhoven's 1926 inaugural: (*6*) *Logos and ratio: The relationship of the two in the history of Western epistemology.* At first sight one might be inclined to think that this study deals with a history of philosophical terms. Nothing could be farther from the truth: here again the systematic interest is so dominant that it is difficult to decide whether the long discourse about the history of Western epistemology should really be qualified as history. To begin with, the distinction between "logos" and "ratio" is a systematic one, taken from Vollenhoven's own epistemological investigations at that time.[10] The thinkers of the past are dealt with according to the criterion: How have they accounted for the realities which Vollenhoven calls "logos" and "ratio"? Moreover, this investigation is not interested in the history of philosophy for its own sake, but it is subservient to the goal of elaborating a positive Christian epistemology, that is, of coming to *systematic* clarity. "For my goal is not at all to bring forward particularly some recently discovered historical details, but rather, my ideal, also in the investigation of history, has been the further development of my own systematics" (*6*: 6). The conviction that such a positive working out of a specifically Christian epistemology is possible constitutes "the basis of the critique contained in the historical survey" (*6*: 66). Because this criticism is admittedly "transcendent criticism" (*6*: 6), the method he has followed is "pragmatic" (*6*: 6).

The same general point is made in Vollenhoven's first important book: (*9*) *The Necessity of a Christian Logic* (1932). Again, the title does not prepare one for the fact that more than two thirds of it is history for the sake of systematics. There are two chapters of unequal length: the first, by far the longer, is called "The struggle in the past" and deals with the history of logic from the pre-Socratics to the Reformation; the second is significantly entitled "The lesson of the past" and briefly sums up the basic systematic lines of a Christian logic. Vollenhoven introduces the systematic chapter with the words: ". . . for we do not seek knowledge concerning the past in order to show off or bother others with it, but in order to be instructed by the past" (*9*: 81).

The view is no different in the major work which followed in the next year: (*10*) *Calvinism and the Reformation of Philosophy*. Again, by far the greatest part is historical, but systematic insight is the actual goal: a Scriptural systematics must be developed.

> For that purpose we must also consult the past. A person who neglects this is like someone who had been brought blindfolded into the middle of an unknown forest, and who tries in vain to orient himself. He can easily take the wrong path. On the other hand, a person who seriously investigates the past learns from the difficulties experienced by previous generations, from the solutions which they found, and from the mistakes which they made (*10*: 314).

It would be tedious to show how this view of the relation of history to systematics is maintained in Vollenhoven's later writings. The evidence so far adduced should be sufficient to show that this relation is a reciprocal one, and that Vollenhoven's historical work was in the nature of a preparatory orientation for the sake of the actual task at hand—the working out of his own systematic conception.

Yet the slight shift of attention from systematics to history (of which he had spoken already in 1926)[11] continued. Gradually the emphasis begins to fall on the history of philosophy, not as an initial orientation for the benefit of systematics but as a goal in its own right. In the (*12*) "Provisional attempt at an ordering of philosophical conceptions" (1939), Vollenhoven writes that the goal of his historiographical work is merely "to illuminate our own times" (*12*: 4), though he does mention as a positive systematic result that the contemporary distinction between rationalism and irrationalism is relativized (*12*: 76). In his (*13*) "Guidelines for orientation in current philosophy" (1941), there is the same transitional ambivalence: on the first page he emphasizes the importance of systematics: "A provisional attempt along these lines will also, by way of side effect, prove to be fruitful for the study of the history of philosophy; yet it must follow not the historical but the systematic method" (*13*: 3). On the last pages of the same paper, however, he writes: "[May this study] be a stimulus to the study not only of systematics, but also of the history of philosophy. The latter, precisely when it is pursued in the light of Holy Scripture, has again and again yielded unexpected results" (*13*: 161-2).

When finally the *(18) History of Philosophy, I*, appears in 1950, the systematic interest has receded far into the background. Whereas he had spoken of his *Richtlijnen* (1941) as being "*by way of side effect* (*zijdelings*) fruitful also for the study of the history of philosophy," he now calls his work a "history" which "*by way of side effect* provides the indispensable criterion for the scope of one's view" ("*zijdelings* den onmisbaren toetssteen voor de breedte van eigen visie biedt" *18*: 11—italics mine). This work is now (1950) a *history* of philosophy and the method is no longer "pragmatic" (*1926*) or "systematic" (1941) but "probleem-*historisch*." In 1961 he goes so far as to say of his work on the earlier Greek thinkers: "Whatever gains for systematics may be forthcoming from the study of the earliest period accessible to us have from the beginning been of secondary importance" (*21*: 10-11).

Methodological reflections

So much for the shift in emphasis from systematics to history. We should now ask what Vollenhoven has to say about his historiographical method once his interest has turned to history in its own right, since it is then that he begins to speak specifically of *probleemhistorische methode*. He speaks of this method chiefly in two places: in the beginning of his (*18*)

History of Philosophy, I (1950), and in his article (*21*) "The consistent problem-historical method" (1961).

Every philosophical "conception" is a combination of themes. Each theme, in turn, contains implicitly a *problem* (or complex of problems—*problematiek*) and the solution given to it. With this thesis Vollenhoven begins his *History of Philosophy*, I. The immediate task at hand, therefore, was to trace the history of the chief themes of philosophy, in order to be able to sketch their various combinations against a well-illuminated background. "In this way I arrived at the problem-historical method" (*18*: 6).

Although the history of philosophy is too interesting to justify spending much time with methodological prolegomena (*18*: 14), Vollenhoven does make a few remarks under the heading "Method." The first is that the method followed in writing the history of philosophy must itself be *philosophical*. The methods of psychology or sociology are therefore necessarily inadequate.

The second remark comes to the heart of the matter. "Methode" (from the Greek word *meta-hodos*) in science always involves, besides the field of inquiry, an investigator of that field. This means that logical thinking always plays a role in the method of investigation, although it is not (except in the case of logic) the only factor. In the case of the historiography of philosophy, there is logical thinking not only on the side of the investigator (the historian), but also, in the philosophical problems and solutions of the past, on the side of the field of research. This should not lead to the conclusion, however, that the history of philosophy is a purely logical affair.

> For although the course of the history of philosophy cannot be conceived apart from the logical activity of earlier generations, yet there have appeared many other factors in that history, behind and beside the logical factors; besides religion, we can point, for example, to the influence of social life, art and politics in ancient times, and to the development of industry, technology and communications in the modern age. Consequently, there can be no question here of a purely logical process (*18*: 14).

This second "remark" on method (the third and last is about literary sources, and does not concern us in this context) merits closer study. The extremely compact text needs some elucidation. It should be realized that when Vollenhoven speaks of "method," there is in the background his early struggle against the "method-monism" of certain neo-Kantians, closely related to their discussions concerning concept formation (*Begriffsbildung*). The answer which Vollenhoven developed (and which became one of the cornerstones of his philosophy) was that a theory of scientific methodology must recognize the radical diversity of ontological *Gegenstände* corresponding to the various special sciences. Against the methodological monism of the Marburg School, a *pluralism* of method is to be maintained, which honors the unique character of each scientific field of research. The unity of the sciences lies in their *logical* character; their diversity in the variety of distinct "non-logical" fields with which this logical element is brought into synthesis. This synthesis of logical and non-logical gives rise to the various types of scientific concept formation, corresponding to the diversity of modal *Gegenstände* (fields of inquiry). The case of logic is exceptional, since here concepts are formed of a *Gegenstand* which is itself logical.[12]

Furnished with this background material, we can perhaps illuminate Vollenhoven's terse comments on his method in dealing with the history of philosophy. Scientific "method" involves an investigator (i.e. a "scientist," one who is logically busy) and a field of research (i.e. *Gegenstand*). This *Gegenstand*, except in the case of logic, is *not* logical (i.e. it is non-conceptual, *niet begripsmatig*)—at least, that is the general rule. But there is one other exception besides logic: the *Gegenstand* in the case of the historiography of thought also has a logical element, namely, the philosophical problems and solutions. But, Vollenhoven hastens to add, that does not mean that the history of philosophy does not include extra-logical factors (religion, society, art, etc.).

We are now faced with a curious problem. Vollenhoven is dealing with the "History of Philosophy" in the sense of "a complete (*volledige*) *Historia Philosophiae*" (*18*: 6). The philosophical conceptions of that history lead him to the themes which are involved in them, and these in turn lead him to the *problems* of philosophy (with their solutions). Thus he arrives at the *problem-historical* method. Now, in the discussion of this method *qua* method, we are told that the problems (and solutions) of the history of philosophy are its logical element. The problem-historical method is thus an instance, as in the case of logic, of the logical coming into a synthesis with (= forming a concept of) something which is itself also logical. The method of logic and that of the historiography of philosophy are thus in principle the same. However, we are warned at the same time that there is *more* to the history of philosophy than the logical factor. There seems to be a disparity between the historian's method (which is exclusively logical) and his *Gegenstand* (which is more than logical).

The reader who is faced with this problem can, by patient rereading of the passages in question, come to a partial solution of the difficulty, although the text does not explicitly point the way. By keeping in mind Vollenhoven's distinction between philosophy as *activity* (philosophizing) and philosophy as *result* (system, conception), a way out seems to present itself. The historian of philosophy deals with both as his *Gegenstand*: his "field of inquiry," Vollenhoven explicitly states, is "the history of philosophical thought and its results" (*18*: 14). On the basis of this distinction we could interpret Vollenhoven as saying that the problem-historical method applies to the conceptions (as *results* of philosophizing) while the extra-logical factors in the history of philosophy are restricted to the *activity* of philosophizing.

Whether this interpretation is correct or not, the initial difficulty remains: a historian is here pictured as using a method which is inadequate (or only partially adequate) to his *Gegenstand*. Even on the interpretation which distinguished conception as result from philosophizing as activity, it seems clear that the problem-historical method applies only to the first of these; another method would have to deal with that part of the historical *Gegenstand* which includes non-logical factors.

With this difficulty in mind, we may well look with expectation to the article entirely devoted to his method which Vollenhoven wrote eleven years later in *Philosophia Reformata*. After a brief sketch of how and in what philosophical climate his method arose (in which, incidentally, he denies any connection with former methodologies [*21:* 1], he mentions neither Hartmann nor Hönigswald and mentions Windelband in one breath with Ueberweg and Falckenberg [*21:* 6]), he comes to the point which interests us. Unfortunately, his remarks are again very brief: they belong to the short "preliminary considerations," preceding the "first concretization" which constitutes the body of the article, dealing with the method in action. These preliminary considerations deal with two questions regarding the delimitation of the field of inquiry. The second is of no concern to us, since it treats only the external restriction of Vollenhoven's work to Western philosophy.

It is the first question which shall have our attention here: it touches, as Vollenhoven remarks, "a fundamental point, namely, the respecting of the boundary between systematics and historical research in philosophy" (*21*: 9). Because of its importance, I shall quote the greater part *in extenso*:

> (1) The primary requirement for the delimitation of the history of philosophy as field of inquiry is clarity in regard to the mutual relationship between systematics and the study of the history of philosophy.
> This involves two questions: a methodological and an ontological one.
> (a) The methodological question touches the difference in procedure of the systematic philosopher and of the historian of philosophy. The former forms concepts which have reference (as long as he does not deal with epistemology and logic) in the first place to the non-conceptual (*het niet-begripsmatige*) in reality; the historian of philosophy, on the other hand (at least in his attempt to understand the results of previous thinkers) wants to form a concept (*zich een begrip vormen*) concerning matters which are themselves conceptual in character. Briefly put: the systematics of philosophy is concerned

with primary concepts; the study of its history, however, largely (*goeddeels*) with secondary.

(b) Here, as elsewhere, the methodological diversity is of course rooted in the ontic diversity of the fields of inquiry concerned. For systematics is the result of reflection on the structure of creatures and their ontic genesis. The study of the history of philosophy, on the other hand, deals with the genesis of a subdivision (*een onderdeel*) of human culture.

I expect it is clear that history according to this conception is not purely functional, but touches man in his totality, i.e. as body and soul (*naar lichaam en ziel*).

The question at issue is clearly the delimitation of the history of philosophy as field of inquiry: the "definition," if you like, of the *Gegenstand* of the historiography of philosophy. As in the 1950 discussion, the question is put in the general context of the methodology of science and thus involves the ideas of concept and concept formation.

To define the *Gegenstand* of the historiography of philosophy, that philosophical discipline is contrasted with another—systematics. It is of fundamental importance that these two disciplines be clearly distinguished. They are discriminated first by their differing *methods* (i.e. by the different ways in which concepts are formed in them), and then by the *ontic* difference in *Gegenstände* in which the methodological difference is rooted. The argument can be schematically represented as follows:

Philosophical Discipline

Concept Formation		Systematics	Historiography
	Primary	The structure of creatures and their genesis	
	Secondary		The genesis of a subdivision of human culture

The way the scheme stands, the distinction between the two disciplines is indeed clear and exhaustive. However, the diagram is *not* complete. There is one exception under Systematics: epistemology and logic are branches of it which deal with what is already conceptual, so that their method is typified by secondary concept formation. There is also an exception under History, although it is not named. The historian of philosophy forms concepts of what is already conceptual, "at least in his attempt to understand the results of previous thinkers" (*21*: 9). That is why his concept formation is "largely" secondary. Apparently there is a small part of his concept formation which does *not* deal with what is itself conceptual (i.e. with what is non-conceptual) and is therefore primary. In short, the neatness of the distinction between systematics and history in philosophy has been destroyed. The diagram now becomes:

Philosophical Discipline

Concept Formation		Systematics	Historiography
	Primary	The structure of creatures and their genesis, *except*:	?
	Secondary	The objects of epistemology and logic	The genesis of a subdivision of human culture at least "largely"; "at least in his attempt to understand the results . . ."

The only thing we can say about the unknown part of the historical *Gegenstand* is that it does *not* have to do with the philosophical results of the past and that it does not call for the dominant (cf. "largely") method advocated by Vollenhoven. In other words, it is that part of the *Gegenstand* which is not "conception" (result of philosophy) and is not accessible to the problem-historical method. It is, in fact, that same area for which we found the problem-historical method inadequate in our discussion of the remarks in *History of Philosophy, I*.

If we may assume that the two short passages dealing with the methodological basis of the problem-historical method, though separated by eleven years, may be interpreted in the light of each other (which we have every reason to believe), we can draw some further conclusions. The historiography of philosophy is a scientific discipline: it therefore has a specific *Gegenstand*. The method to be followed by this discipline must be adapted to its *Gegenstand*. In this case the *Gegenstand* is constituted by the activity of philosophizing ("philosophical thought," which is a "logical activity") and its result ("conceptions" which involve a combination of "problem solutions") (*18*: 5, 14). The problem is: What method is adequate for such a *Gegenstand*? That depends in the first instance on whether the *Gegenstand* is conceptual or non-conceptual (whether it is of a logical character or not). What is the case here? Are both the activity and the result of a conceptual character? It seems clear that the result (the "conception") is indeed conceptual, but is this also true of the *activity* of philosophizing? It is called a "logical activity" (*18*: 14), but can that be said to be "conceptual"? The 1950 text left us uncertain.[13] The upshot was therefore that the historical *Gegenstand* is, at least with reference to philosophy as result, of a conceptual character. The method of the historian dealing with this *Gegenstand* must thus be one geared to his forming concepts of a conceptual reality, "at least in his attempt to understand the *results* of previous thinkers" (*21*: 9—italics mine). This method, it would appear, is restricted to the *results* of philosophy in the past. The uncertainty touching this activity is thus resolved in favor of its non-conceptual character.

The following picture now emerges: the historical *Gegenstand* is constituted by two elements, i.e. activity (non-conceptual) and result (conceptual). For Vollenhoven, the latter is the major element, since the historian's method is "largely" geared to it. But that still leaves the minor element, which is treated as negligible. Very little is said about its positive character, and nothing about the method which can deal with it. Yet it is here that the actual activity of philosophizing takes place and that the extra-logical factors of the history of philosophy enter in—art and politics, commerce and society, etc. What kind of a method can deal with these? Vollenhoven, although he recognizes (in fact, emphasizes) the importance of these extra-logical factors, gives no answer to this question. The problem-historical method, which deals only with the "themes" found in "conceptions," i.e. with the conceptual result of philosophizing, is his dominant concern.

There is another point which strikes us in Vollenhoven's methodological comments. We found that the method of logic and epistemology, on the one hand, and the problem-historical method, on the other, are in principle the same:both are based on secondary concept formation. Wherein, then, do they differ, since they are referred to different disciplines? The first deals with the conceptual part of the *Gegenstand* of systematics, the second with the conceptual part of the *Gegenstand* of historiography. Wherein, then, do these *Gegenstände* differ? It is not, as one might suppose, that one views the conceptual as abstracted from time and the other in its development through time: systematics also deals with genesis. Vollenhoven distinguished their respective *Gegenstände* as follows: systematics deals with "the structure of creatures and their ontic genesis," whereas historiography of philosophy deals with "the genesis of a subdivision of human culture" (*21*: 9). It is difficult to see at first glance just where the specific difference lies: both deal with genesis, both deal with creatures (man, too, is a creature), both deal with what is ontic (he is describing the "ontic diversity of the fields of inquiry concerned") (*21*: 9). That leaves, as the distinctive difference, "structure" vs. "culture." This means, for our discussion, that the method of logic and epistemology is geared to the conceptual as *structure*, whereas the problem-historical method is geared to the conceptual as *culture*.

What does Vollenhoven mean by "structure" and "culture"? It is plain that they are mutually exclusive, and that culture is something specifically human and historical. Structure, on the other hand, is the subjective correlate of the structural law (*structuurwet*) which "is rooted in the command to exist at creation" (*wortelt in het ontstaansbevel bij de schepping—21*: 11). This gives us a clue that the answer to our question must be found in the distinction which Vollenhoven makes between "structural law" and "law for love" and their respective subjective correlates. This can be formulated briefly as follows: the structural law holds by virtue of creation and "is correlate with the structure and modal specification (*verbijzondering*) of all creatures," whereas the law of love "presupposes in the correlate creature not only creatureliness, but also a heart," and therefore holds for man (*21*: 11). *Besides* his creatureliness, man has a heart which can love or hate God and his neighbor; that is, his life is religion. That is why history, that peculiarly human phenomenon, is for Vollenhoven at bottom an affair of the heart, and all its manifestations (including culture) are fundamentally religious.

For our question this means that "structure" refers to creatureliness, "culture" (as part of history) to religion. The method of epistemology and logic therefore applies to the conceptual as structure, *that is, as creatureliness*; the problem-historical method applies to the conceptual as culture, that is, *as religion*.

It is difficult to see how this methodological distinction can be very strictly maintained. How can the concepts and judgments man forms be assigned to two different scientific studies, one of which deals with them and their development as conforming to the laws of creation, and the other with them as conforming (or not conforming) to man's basic religious task? Undoubtedly a distinction should indeed be made between structure and religious direction, also in the results of man's logical activity, but should these two moments in the conceptual be seen as the subject matter of two distinct disciplines, each with its own method? It seems odd that the systematic discipline of logic should not also deal with logical fallacies, but only with the analytical in its creatureliness, that is, apart from error. It seems, too, that the method of the historian of philosophy should differ from that of the logician in something more specific than in the added dimension of religious direction.

We may sum up our conclusions so far by saying that the problem-historical method, arising out of a systematically directed interest in the history of philosophy, deals, according to Vollenhoven's own account (so far as we have been able to piece it together), with the history of philosophy exclusively in its strictly logical or analytic aspect (and within that aspect only with that part constituted by the *result* of logical activity), and that, as method, it seems to become practically indistinguishable from that of the systematic logician and epistemologist.

The historical environment

In the light of these conclusions, it is difficult to suppress the question: What is the specifically *historical* in this "problem-historical" method, if the extra-logical factors in the history of philosophy, such as social, economic and political conditions, are deliberately excluded? With this question in mind, it will be interesting to take a glance at Vollenhoven's most recent publication dealing with questions of method in the historiography of philosophy: the article (*23*) "Methodological pitfalls in the interpretation of Parmenides." This article is a critical discussion of the Parmenides interpretation of J. Mansfeld, and goes into great detail in the discussion of the fragments involved. We are not here concerned with the philological, chronological and exegetical detail but only with the remarks on method which Vollenhoven makes in this connection.

Vollenhoven's chief and fundamental objection to the interpretation of Parmenides given by Mansfeld is that it is *anachronistic*: it does not sufficiently take into account the course of the history of philosophy both before Parmenides and after him. Both must receive due attention, since Parmenides can only be understood in the light of his philosophical *predecessors* (including contemporaries), and to do that, the exegete-historian of today must realize that he himself stands in the tradition of philosophy developed by Parmenides' *successors*. The danger of underestimating these two factors is that the historian may read into the texts of Parmenides philosophical themes which did not (in fact: *could not*) arise until much later, and therefore could not have come up in Parmenides' philosophical milieu. The result, in Mansfeld's case, is that he sees Parmenides primarily as a logician (whereas logic did not become a central concern in philosophy until Hellenism)—a logician, moreover, whose theory of logic shows a remarkable agreement with twentieth-century irrationalism. Vollenhoven's own interpretation, on the other hand, proceeds from the methodological assumption that the texts must be read *in immediate connection with the problems and solutions of their philosophical environment*. The result is that, where Mansfeld sees logic, Vollenhoven sees ontology; the crucial Fragment 2 is read by one as a disquisition on the logic of propositions (*Aussagen-logik*), by the other as a polemic against Parmenides' contemporaries.

His own interpretation, Vollenhoven sums up, demonstrates "that an approach in terms of the history of pre-Platonic ontology is considerably more fruitful for the interpretation of the fragments than an approach in terms of modern thought" (*23*: 86).

If we consider this line of argument in the light of Vollenhoven's previous remarks on the methodology of the historian of philosophy, there is one thing that stands out: his criticism of Mansfeld's method is based on *other* methodological criteria than those which he has hitherto revealed. Had he judged Mansfeld in terms of his own previously formulated rule, namely, that the historian of philosophy must be concerned exclusively with the conceptual result of a past philosopher's analytic activity, he would have had little reason to find fault with him. For Mansfeld avoids the pitfalls of a psychologizing, or Marxist, or one-sidedly philological interpretation and adopts a strictly systematic-philosophical approach, just as Vollenhoven advocates. His fault lies not in the delimitation of his *Gegenstand* but in the neglect of "the required tying of the interpretation to the historical environment" (*23*: 86).

What is the meaning of this new methodological canon? That it is of the highest importance is evident from the last pages of the article, where Vollenhoven waxes eloquent in his insistence that the exegete-historian must not rest, though it take years, until the texts become understandable in terms of the problems of their environments (*23*: 111). But what does it mean that the interpretation must at all costs be "tied" or "bound" to this environment? The answer must be sought in Vollenhoven's own interpretation of Parmenides, which places the latter squarely in the philosophical world of sixth century Greece. The ties which "bind" him to that world (and which Vollenhoven methodically seeks and finds in the texts) are the ties of philosophical kinship and dissent. The ties of kinship are those which link him with Anaximander and Xenophanes; those of dissent join him in battle with Pythagoreanism and subjectivism.

There are a number of questions which arise at this point, which it will be wise to pose and attempt to answer, since we are here at one of the half-obscured presuppositions of Vollenhoven's method. They touch his view of *verbanden* (translated as "ties," "bonds" or "connections") in the history of philosophy. Again we shall have to gather hints and clues spread throughout his writings.

I. In what sense can we speak of a "tie of dissent"? Does not the fact that Parmenides polemicized *against* subjectivism invalidate the assertion that he was "bound" to his milieu? We are reminded here of a remark made by Vollenhoven in his review of Hoekstra in 1922, with reference to the "dialectic" of history: "If we recognize it, then we are in a better position to preserve the intrinsic connection even in cases of great conflict" (*2*: 296). This is an idea which Vollenhoven has never abandoned and is, in fact, one of the mainstays of his method. Behind every philosophical difference he looks for the common ground which makes it possible. So he writes in 1961, with respect to the battle between subjectivism and objectivism in Greek thought, that we must not see this anachronistically in the light of modern philosophy, and then:

> If on the other hand we follow the problem-historical method, then there emerges, from behind the dispute which drove apart the parties involved, what both had in common, namely: first, the thesis that the law is to be found within the cosmos (and more particularly, within the correlation of subject and object), and second: the *problem*, which is understandable only in terms of this basis, whether the law lay in the subject or in the object (*21*: 13).

In other words, to use the problem-historical method means not only to limit one's investigations to the conceptual results or conceptions of the past but also to trace the *connections* between these conceptions in terms of their common framing of the problem (*probleemstelling*). Philosophical differences are not, to put it in logical terms, "contradictory" but "contrary": they always pre-suppose a common basis which makes comparison and contrast possible. This common basis is the formulation of the problem, and the comparison and contrast establishes *verbanden*.

In the case of Parmenides, one of the most important connections to be shown is that which situates him with respect to the major philosophical issue of the day—for or against subjectivism. But this is an issue which has long ago become a "dead letter" in the history of philosophy: the struggle has long since been decided in favor of subjectivism. The result is that a historian who stands in an age-old tradition of subjectivism very lightly overlooks this debate, since it no longer presents a live issue for himself. This is the mistake Mansfeld has made, in Vollenhoven's view.

To interpret Parmenides correctly, the same procedure ("method") of asking back to a shared putting of the problem must be followed for other basic philosophical issues as well, thus bringing other *verbanden* to light. Besides the question of the place of the law, which shows Parmenides, as an objectivist, to stand in a relation of kinship to Anaximander, Anaxagoras and Alcmaeon, and in a relation of dissent to the dominant tradition of subjectivists (notably Heraclitus and Xenophanes), there are three other fundamental problems which divided the philosophers of early Greece and in terms of which other *verbanden* of Parmenides to his predecessors and contemporaries are revealed. The most important of these is the question of unity-in-diversity, which sets monists against dualists. Parmenides chooses for the dualist position, and consequently sides with Xenophanes and Alcmaeon against the majority of his contemporaries. Then there is the issue for or against the view of man as a microcosm, which clashes with the traditional universalistic view. Here Parmenides chooses *for* the tradition and against such men as Alcmaeon and Anaxagoras. Finally, a whole series of bonds of sympathy and antipathy is set up with respect to the touchy issue of mythology. Here again Parmenides sides with Xenophanes, whose violent reaction pours scorn on the myths and goes to the opposite extreme of relativizing all coming-to-be in favor of a changeless structure. This affinity entails a double disagreement: both with mythologizing thinkers, who accept a certain mythological framework, and with the more moderate rejecters of mythology, who do not throw out the baby genesis with the mythological bath water.

The result of situating Parmenides in terms of these four fundamental philosophical problems of his day is that a complex of positive and negative relationships is revealed, which neatly pinpoints his position in the history of Greek philosophy until that time. It presupposes, of course, that each of his predecessors and contemporaries has been analyzed in the same way, so that their *verband* with Parmenides, with respect to each of the four problems, can be determined with a fair degree of certainty. It is the job of the historian of philosophy to track down these complicated connections: "a history of philosophy gives its author's view of the conceptions of others concerning these points [i.e. the basic problems of philosophy] *and of the connections in which these conceptions stand to one another*" (*20*: 38—italics mine).

II. The question arises: Just how *real* are these connections? Our formulation in the preceding paragraph was not strictly correct, since not the connection of Parmenides to his predecessors must be traced but those of Parmenides' *conception* to the *conceptions* of his predecessors. We must not forget the methodological restriction to the analytical result. But are the *verbanden* between conceptions more than abstract logical relations? Are they also concrete *historical* bonds? Does the fact that Parmenides was an objectivist and therefore stood in a relationship of affinity or kinship to Anaximander, the father of objectivism, mean that he knew Anaximander, or had read his writings, or had at least heard of him?

On this point, Vollenhoven is ambivalent. On the one hand, he speaks of the *verbanden* as being no more than "correspondences and differences" (*overeenkomsten en verschillen*) and clearly refers to *systematic* philosophical correspondence and difference, which is of a strictly logical character. A striking instance of this is given in his *Method* article, where he discusses some examples of wrongly construed *verbanden* in the history of philosophy. Such a misconstrued connection is the one commonly postulated between Berkeley and Hume, since in Vollenhoven's view their conceptions differed in almost every respect (*21*: 6). Yet Vollenhoven must be aware of the fact that Berkeley was, in actual history, one of the major intellectual influences on Hume. This would lead us to suppose that Vollenhoven makes a clear distinction between systematic and historical connections, and that the historian of philosophy is only concerned with the first. This conclusion is borne out by his remark, directed against Heyman's historiographical classification, that it is incorrect to suppose that psychomonism is derived from parallelism *either historically or systematically*. "Nor is materialism, in whatever sense it is taken, a one-sided derivate, *either historically or systematically*, of parallelism" (*21*: 7, 8—italics mine; cf. also *21*: 13).

On the other hand, we find the *verbanden* of which Vollenhoven speaks being presented as real historical connections. Immediately after his discussion of the relation between Berkeley and Hume (the fourth such example), he writes: "In all these cases the positing of a non-existent connection of course meant a failure to recognize the *real historical relation* and a hindrance in the inquiry after it" (*21*: 6—italics mine). This certainly seems to indicate the equivalence of *verband* and "real historical relation," which would mean that in Vollenhoven's view, there was no real historical relation between Berkeley and Hume. This must be a mistake, or else *historical* is used in a very odd sense. We are more likely to understand Vollenhoven if, at least for the moment, we stick to the purely logical meaning of *verband*.

III. Is there no difference in kinds of connection between conceptions? To find the answer to that, the following passage merits attention:

> Now there exist a great variety of such conceptions. But the history of philosophy is more than this collection. *For these conceptions all have connections with each other, and that in two ways.* In answering the question concerning the place of the law, one solution came up after the other, so that a *succession* of time-streams arose. On the other hand, from an early date different answers to the question concerning vertical structure stand *side by side* within a single time-stream. Thus succession and simultaneity here go hand in hand (*20:* 44—first italics mine).[14]

This passage is particularly illuminating, not only because it emphasizes again that the multiplicity of philosophical conceptions, rather than representing simply a disconnected collection, constitutes a *coherent* whole, but also because it makes a basic distinction of *two kinds* of coherence or *verband* among conceptions. It appears that the solutions to the basic problems of philosophy do not all have the same relation to historical time: the answer to the question about the place of the law has a special character in that it binds together an otherwise heterogenous group of conceptions into the *historical* unity of the "time-stream" (*tijdstroming*). The other answers-to-problems (here lumped together by Vollenhoven as touching the "vertical structure" of things) do not have this historical cohesive force but are relegated to co-existing *within* a given time-stream.

We now observe the following remarkable state of affairs. Whereas the answer to the problem of the law varies in each succeeding phase of philosophical history, so that as many different answers have been given as there have been different time-streams, the answers to the other basic philosophical problems are very limited in number and recur in every new historical period. The number of time-streams provisionally distinguished by Vollenhoven in 1962 was sixty-one, which entails an equal number of different solutions to the problems of the place of the law. In contrast, the problems regarding mythology and the individual have each traditionally found only three different basic solutions, and that of unity-in-diversity no more than two. There seems to be something timeless about these few last fundamental alternatives—a timelessness which contrasts sharply with the restlessness which characterizes the never-ending attempt by succeeding generations to anchor their certainty in yet another foundation. Ever since the dawn of Western philosophy, Vollenhoven writes, the battle over the place of the law "has not come to rest" (*20*: 39), whereas the basic combinations of the answers, after once having arisen, have persisted "throughout the changes of all succeeding time-streams" (*20*: 45).

The two kinds of *verband*, then, which bind together the multiplicity of philosophical conceptions into a coherent whole, are, on the one hand, the contemporaneous bond of a shared law-answer which unites the conceptions of one time-stream into a *historical* unity, and on the other hand the bond of permanence which joins specific combinations of other philosophical answers into the trans-historical *systematic* unity of continuous types.

A graphic illustration

By way of intermezzo, we shall now make an attempt to illustrate the preceding and what follows by an image of our own. We have said that Vollenhoven situates a philosophical conception according to the answers it gives to four primary ontological problems. If we leave aside one of these problems, that of the place of the law, it is possible to "place" every conception on a three-dimensional graph, of which each axis represents the scale of possible answers to one problem. Such a graph would look like this:

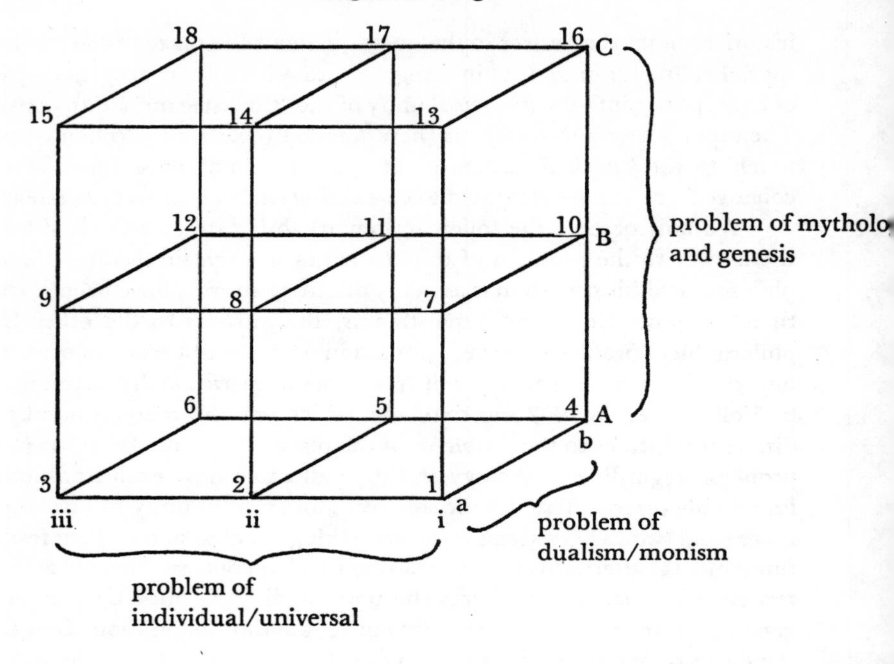

Problem of mythology and genesis
A. Mythologizing (theogono-cosmogonic)
B. Cosmogono-cosmological
C. Purely cosmological

Problem of dualism/monism
a. Dualism
b. Monism

Problem of universal/individual
i. Universalism
ii. Partial universalism
iii. Individualism

Each intersection represents one basic type of conception. The one numbered "1," for instance, is the basic type of universalistic mythologizing dualism: it is represented, according to Vollenhoven, by such disparate thinkers as Musaeus, Pythagoras, Marcion, Manichaeism, the Cabala, and Sorel, to name only a few. A less esoteric basic type is that numbered "10":

it represents the position of materialists throughout the ages, from Thales and Democritus to Holbach and Sartre.

The reason we can assign figures from such different times to the same basic position on the graph is that we have abstracted from the problem of the law, which governs the different historical periods of the history of philosophy. In the absence of a four-dimensional graph, we can include the time-streams in our pictorial representation only by repeating the framework of basic types for every one. Each graph could then be labeled according to the different answers given to the law problem. It is not until then that they could also be *dated*: the graph as it stands is trans-historical.

If we use this illustration to elucidate the argument so far, we can say the following. The primary "tie of kinship" is that which unites all the positions of a single "dated graph" (time-stream): they share a common answer to the law problem. Secondary ties of kinship unite positions on the same "plane" of the graph: the positions numbered "1" to "6," for example, are all mythologizing and thus agree in their answer to the mythology problem. As for the "ties of dissent," their binding force lies in the fact that all the positions drawn *accept the alternatives built into the scheme*: they share a common framing of the problem. In terms of the distinction between simultaneous and successive *verband*, we can say that the first refers to the unique "color" which every time-stream gives to the graph, whereas the second denotes the constant structure of the graph itself, which persists through the changes of time and "color."

Perhaps we will be forgiven if we distinguish between "boxes" (dated graphs) and the Box (the graph itself) in this connection. We can then recapitulate by saying that bonds of kinship and dissent are positive and negative forms of inter-box and intra-Box relationships (successive and simultaneous *verbanden*). Together they constitute the history of the Box.

The "problematic" and Greek philosophical origins

What in my illustration is somewhat facetiously dubbed "the Box" is referred to by Vollenhoven as "the problematic arising out of the Greek environment," which he then also calls "this thought-form" (*denkvorm*) (*21*: 32). It is this idea of a Western "thought-form" which is the key to his approach to the history of philosophy. It will serve as a guideline in the remainder of our discussion of Vollenhoven's idea of *Problemgeschichte*.

It is not without significance that Vollenhoven refers to this *denkvorm* as being characterized by its Greek origin. His thought is dominated by the fundamental maxim "As the twig is bent, so grows the tree"—or, in his own words: "The simple consideration that what is later in a historical process is shaped, if not completely, yet in great measure by what precedes" (*21*: 10). His intense concentration on early Greek philosophy and its origins is rooted in the conviction that the problems and alternatives of twentieth century philosophy received their decisive formulation in the three classical centuries of Greek civilization. We will do well to sketch briefly Vollenhoven's view of the first rise of Greek philosophy. (The following is a rather free translation of Vollenhoven's sketchy systematic account.)

The "problematic" (i.e. the theoretical universe of discourse in terms of which philosophical answers are sought) or "thought-form" of Western philosophy did not, like Minerva, spring full-grown from Zeus' head but showed a gradual development. This is why Vollenhoven begins his history of philosophy with the half-legendary figure of Musaeus, who functions as a representative of the dim mythological past out of which Greek theoretical thought developed. Though little is known about him, it can be said with a fair degree of certainty (if it were only by analogy with other primitive tribal cultures) that his thinking was subjectivistic, universalistic, mythologizing, and dualistic. It should be noted that these designations have meaning only in *opposition to* later positions which challenged these aspects of primitive thought. The first such challenge, in Vollenhoven's description of the course of events, was made by Hesiod, who is the first thinker on record to question the primary and fundamental dualism of gods and mortals: he became the first monist. With that, one dimension of the Box was established, and every succeeding thinker had to come to terms with (the tradition of) this alternative. In the century after Hesiod, the sixth before Christ (the age in which Greek philosophy is generally supposed properly to begin), new oppositions to the traditional world of thought were posited in rapid succession. Thales did Hesiod one better by not only adopting his monism but also calling into question the mythological framework of both his predecessors. So violent was his reaction against mythologizing thinking, with its emphasis on cosmogony and theogony, that he posited all coming-to-be to have but secondary importance—an extreme position which was soon moderated by his fellow Milesian and younger contemporary Anaximenes, who adopted a middle position with respect to mythology (rejecting it in itself but not the genetic element it contained), so that the three fundamental alternatives on another axis of the Box were established. At the same time, Anaximenes opened up another dimension in the thought-world of the Greeks, by making problematic a presupposition shared by all his predecessors—their universalism. He chose for the recognition of the individual as a microcosm, thus setting up the opposition universalism vs. partial universalism on the third axis of the Box. No sooner had Anaximenes opened this fundamental new perspective than a third Milesian, Anaximander, attacked an even more fundamental presupposition of all *his* predecessors: he gave a critique of their shared conviction that the law lay in the ontological *subject*. In his view, the *object* was the anchor of the constancy in the world. In other words, by revolutionizing the idea of the place of the law, he inaugurated an entirely new philosophical movement—the time-stream objectivism, in opposition to that of subjectivism.

So we see that at the very dawn of Greek philosophy, a complex system of polar alternatives has already taken shape—a system which is the prototype of the Box as we have sketched it. This prototype remains the "thought-form" of sixth century philosophers after the Milesian pioneers: the further subjectivists Heraclitus and Xenophanes, for example, as well as the objectivists Anaxagoras and Parmenides, choose for existing alternatives within the established scheme. The only exception is Pythagoras, who initiates a maverick movement within objectivism of such importance that it constitutes a new time-stream—but the rudimentary Box is left untouched.

It is in the fifth century that the existing system of alternatives is broken through—at least in one respect. The Sophists, led by Protagoras, refuse to accept the traditional alternatives universalism and partial universalism as answers to the problem of the individual. They reject both as horns of a false dilemma and choose for a third solution—individualism. With that, the basic form of the Box was complete—a form which none of the subsequent greats of Greek and Hellenistic philosophy (in spite of important innovations in other respects) ever transcended. Nor did the advent of Christianity bring any fundamental change in this regard: the conceptions of all the great Christian thinkers, both orthodox and heretical, adapted themselves to the traditional scheme of Greek thought. Each succeeding generation perpetuated and corroborated this powerful intellectual tradition, passing it on unchanged to the Middle Ages and modern times.

The preceding thumbnail sketch is of necessity oversimplified, but it gives, I believe, the basic outline of Vollenhoven's conception of the history of Western philosophy. To understand it as a product of the problem-historical method, the following should be observed.

In the first place, we must not forget the initial restriction to the conceptual: the alternatives given on each axis of the Box are *logical* alternatives, based on different *analytical* insights into the world at large (e.g. the recognition of the independent existence of individuals or objects). This means that the movement in the history of philosophy is always a matter of immanent criticism, in which only analytical considerations play a role. To take an example: if there were evidence that Anaximander, in his independent position vis-à-vis his fellow Milesians Thales and Anaximenes, was strongly motivated by ambition or jealousy, this would be irrelevant for the course of history as Vollenhoven describes it. The only thing that counts for the *problem*-historical method is the fact that Anaximander, under whatever influence or by whatever course, came to the (real and valuable) analytical insight that objects are ontically irreducible to subjects, and so introduced, by his criticism of a weak point in subjectivism, an important new theoretical option into the Greek philosophical world. This restriction to the analytical has the positive side that Vollenhoven constantly pictures new alternatives as being based on valid analytical distinctions which explain and (partially) justify a theoretical innovation. In other words, he has not forgotten his own ideal of 1922 that the continuous line of the history of philosophy should be described in terms of a "dialectic" which is explained by contemporary immanent criticism.

This brings us to the question of intellectual continuity in the history of philosophy. There is first the kind of continuity which makes it impossible, or at least highly improbable, that Anaximenes should have adopted the philosophical position he did without the preceding steps taken by Hesiod (monism) and Thales (rejection of myth). "The break of a succeeding generation with the previous one is never complete," writes Vollenhoven (*23*: 111). Few thinkers incorporate more than one philosophical revolution in their conception. In fact, the vast majority do not even have that one break with the tradition in their thought, being content to combine existing options into a new combination. This is the guiding principle of Vollenhoven's treatment of Plato's intellectual development: apart from the one great discontinuity represented by his realism (based on the valid insight that the law must be sought neither in the subject nor in the object), Plato's thought never moves outside the intellectual horizon of his predecessors, and the course of his development is circumscribed by a comparatively short trajectory within a refined version of the Box. The same applies to the development of Aristotle, in Vollenhoven's view—with one remarkable exception: midway in his career he makes a triple shift in orientation, preserving the continuity with his past only in the fact that he remained a partial universalist. But before and after this spectacular and inexplicable about-face in mid-career (Vollenhoven speaks of "a virtually complete break"—*21*: 23), the continuity of his thought is broken only by relatively minor changes.

But the question of historical continuity (in Vollenhoven's specifically *conceptual* sense) has a more striking side for the casual observer: it touches the continuity of the Greek "thought-form" itself. How is it possible that the first time-stream of Greek philosophy should already show "the six basic types of philosophy, *which govern the subsequent course of history?*" (*19*: 4—italics mine). Closely related to this question is the fact that, in Vollenhoven's view, it is in principle to be expected that each position in the Box will be "realized" in each succeeding time-stream. Though he explicitly denies that this *must* be the case in every instance (*21*: 32), in practice his method often involves not resting until it is shown that a given type has, in fact, been *uitgekristalliseerd* (*20*: 38) in a specific time-stream. Once a type of conception has arrived on the scene of history, it does not leave it again (*20*: 45; cf. *21*: 15), so that every position of the Box is likely to reappear in every generation.

Comparison and evaluation

In an attempt to understand this highly unusual view, we may compare it to the linguistic theory (as formulated by de Saussure) of *langue* as opposed to *parole*. *Langue* is the unconscious system of linguistic (phonetic, syntactic and semantic) "oppositions" which constitutes the "structure" of a particular language (e.g. Latin or French) and which is passed on by tradition from generation to generation. *Parole*, on the other hand, is the concrete speech in a language as it is actually spoken. It is as an unconscious system of oppositions perpetuated by tradition that the concept *langue* (or that of "structure" generally in contemporary structuralism) can serve as an illustration of what Vollenhoven means by the Greek "problematic" or "thought-form." It is, first of all, "unconscious," that is to say, implicit, presupposed, taken for granted, unchallenged. It is also a system of "oppositions," that is, of polar and correlative alternatives which are defined in terms of each other. For example, monism derives not only its permanence and vitality but its very meaning from its polemical relation to dualism. Thirdly, the Greek "thought-form" is quite naturally passed on through the succession of philosophical generations—that is, it is perpetuated by tradition. (Vollenhoven notes that this is partly due to the influence of philosophical "schools"—*20*: 44-5).

The Greek "mind," then, in the sense of the assumed complex of philosophical alternatives, is like a natural language which children learn unquestioningly from their parents—and which is, in fact, the condition for mutual intelligibility. This language, once learned at the beginning of Greek culture, has been spoken ever since by the thinkers of Western civilization. Seen in this light, it is not so difficult to imagine that within every historical time-stream, the latent possibilities of the shared thought-world should recur.

It bears repetition that this analogy is entirely our own:[15] it is not our intention to show that Vollenhoven has a "structuralist" approach to the history of philosophy, but only to illustrate what appears to be a basic idea in Vollenhoven's version of *Problemgeschichte*.

We should add, too, that our representation of the Box was simplified for the purpose of illustration. It represents only the basic framework of one pair and two triads of basic philosophical options, whereas a much finer differentiation is possible *within* these alternative problem solutions. There appear, for instance, to be two distinct varieties of partial universalism: one "horizontal" and one "vertical" in orientation. But the greatest differentiation is possible on the axis of monism and dualism, and it is this possible diversity which is taken by Vollenhoven as his principle of typological classification. The basic philosophical types are seen primarily as different kinds of monism or dualism, systematically discriminated and arranged according to the modal level of their primary ontological division of reality. The result of these and further refinements is that the Box of our illustration would become very complicated indeed and would have to accommodate several dozen distinct types on the monism-dualism axis. This would defeat the purpose of the illustration and cause us to lose sight of the fundamental simplicity of the "problematic" underlying the multiplicity of types. For all that, we must bear in mind that the historical development of this differentiation into sub-options ("broadening" and "unfolding of the problematic"—*19*: 7, 44; cf. *21*: 19, 33 and *24*: 71) plays an important role in Vollenhoven's view of the history of philosophy.

We come now to another very startling aspect in Vollenhoven's conception of a Greek "thought-form." It is this, that he alone has broken that spell, cast by the early Greeks, which has bewitched the philosophers of the West until this day. The reason for this is that the Greek "thought-form" is rooted in paganism, whereas Vollenhoven's philosophy is radically Scriptural. Only by subjecting itself consciously and wholeheartedly to the Word of God can philosophy escape from the pagan "problematic" of Western thought thus far.

The conclusion that Vollenhoven himself stands outside the Box appears from the fact that he does not, with one exception, accept as valid the *probleemstellingen* which determine its structure, and thus cannot choose for the existing alternatives. The choice between dualism and monism is a false dilemma which must be rejected by the Christians (*20*: 45; cf. *21*: 16; *22*: 128). The same applies to the trilemma universalism/partial universalism/individualism (*18*: 40-1, 100; cf. *19*: 3). Only in the case of the trilemma touching the myth is it legitimate to choose: the myths, being by definition paganistic, are to be rejected, as is the extreme reaction against them which relativizes all "genesis" (*20*: 45). That leaves the cosmogono-cosmological answer as the legitimate alternative.[16] As for the fourth (actually first) fundamental problem of philosophy, the question of the place of the law, the alternative solutions given by subjectivism, objectivism and realism are all to be rejected (*19*: 14; *20*: 39, 42).

To place Vollenhoven in relation to the Box would mean extending two of the axes to allow for an additional answer. It is a pity that a fourth axis, that of the law problem, cannot be included in the scheme, since it would demonstrate in an even more striking way how radical, in Vollenhoven's view, is the break of Scriptural philosophy with tradition. It would show that the most momentous decision with respect to the problem of the place of the law had been taken long before Greek philosophy began: in the primeval rejection of God's Word-revelation. All the thinkers of ancient paganism are characterized by the fact that they "hold down the Word-revelation in unrighteousness" (*18*: 18). Vollenhoven also speaks of "religious repression" in this connection (*19*: 1). The result of this deep-seated repression is that God is lost sight of, the religious law of love forgotten, and the structural law sought within the cosmos. This is first sought in the subject (subjectivism), then in the object (objectivism), and finally, with Plato and some of his disciples, outside both (realism). This development is one of *progress* within paganism (*20*: 39), although Plato's realism is still clearly un-Biblical, since his *ideai* are models, not norms (*19*: 14; *20*: 39). After this "highest point" (*19*: 18), we see in the history of philosophy "a fateful change" (*20*: 39), beginning with Aristotle. This momentous shift is the anti-realistic return to subjectivism, which has dominated philosophy ever since. The result is that modern philosophy "is the precipitate of an age-long process, in which Western European thought has moved gradually but consistently in a subjectivistic direction" (*21*: 13).

Unlike the basic answers charted in the Box, the various solutions given to the law problem do not repeat themselves in history. The classical centuries of Greek philosophy saw the comparatively brief struggle between the three chief alternative answers given in paganism, out of which subjectivism emerged victorious. The subsequent controversies which ruled the differences of later time-streams were therefore basically concerned with side issues, while they all agreed in their rejection of objectivism and realism. The conflict between rationalism and irrationalism in our own time, for example, is thus a mere tempest in a teapot—an internal skirmish among factions of the winning party, long after the crucial battle has been decided (*20:* 40-2). A radically Scriptural philosophy, which has oriented itself well in the history of philosophy, stands above such contending parties of the modern age and refuses to take sides. Only it can be truly "impartial" (*20*: 47). With the help of the problem-historical method, the Christian thinker can be rescued from the insidious influence of a long and powerful pagan tradition.

With this we have come full circle. We began and we end the discussion of Vollenhoven's idea of *Problemgeschichte* by pointing to the *systematic* interest which informs it, its subordination to the task of developing a positive philosophical systematics of his own. Though it may sometimes seem as if Vollenhoven has lost sight of his original goal and has made his problem-historical method an end in itself, his approach to history continues to bear the unmistakable mark of its systematic intent. This explains his focus on the conceptual and his interest in the first, decisive period of Western philosophy. His method is thus best understood as the tool for clearly tracing and illuminating the pagan physiognomy of European philosophy, the better to develop positively new perspectives in the light of Scripture. If his methodological restriction to the analytical aspect of history makes him the philosopher's historian of philosophy, the emphasis on the pagan "thought-form" in that history marks him as the *Calvinist* philosopher's historian of philosophy.

Notes

1. The following is substantially the central part of my *doctoraalscriptie*, "An Essay on the Idea of Problemgeschichte," written at the Free University of Amsterdam in 1970. Its first part is briefly summarized in the opening three paragraphs here. All the translations from Vollenhoven's Dutch text are my own.

2. To the best of my knowledge, his first use of the term is at *18:* 6. Since this is dated Jan. 1, 1950, we may assume that he had adopted the term in 1949.

3. Cf. *12*. Further appreciative references to Woltjer can be found in his dissertation (*1*: vii) and in 3: 136.

4. R. H. Bremmer, *Herman Bavinck als dogmaticus* (Kampen: Kok, 1961), p. 385: ". . . in this his favored approach was the problem-historical one." It is noteworthy that Bavinck's own professor in dogmatics at Leiden, J. H. Scholten, is also said by Bremmer to have had a problem-historical approach (*ibid.*, p. 389).

5. R. H. Bremmer, *Herman Bavinck en zijn tijdgenoten* (Kampen: Kok, 1966), p. 249.

6. T. Hoekstra, *Geschiedenis der Philosophie*, I (Kampen: Kok, 1921).

7. It is worthwhile seeing this article against the background of the *Gereformeerde* intellectual world of that time (of which *Stemmen des Tijds* was the journal). Hoekstra and Vollenhoven were two representatives of the small handful of young *Gereformeerde* scholars who had written dissertations in philosophy and who stood squarely in the tradition of Kuyper and Bavinck (both of whom had just died). One cannot help wondering whether there was not some jockeying for position within this new generation, especially with an eye to the chair in philosophy which would soon be vacant at the Free University: Geesink was 77 years old at that time.

8. Ironically, the title of Hoekstra's dissertation had been *Immanente Kritik zur Kantischen Religionsphilosophie* (Kampen: Kok, 1906).

9. I have not been able to discover with whom the distinction between "transcendent" and "immanent" critique originated. Both Hoekstra and Vollenhoven use the terms (as does Dooyeweerd, *suo modo*), but neither defines them. Vollenhoven speaks of "the ordinary formal requirement" that both should be applied (*ibid.*). From the context it is plain that immanent criticism is such that points out logical inconsistency or terminological confusion *within* a given philosophy, on its own premises, whereas transcendent criticism highlights errors as seen from the critic's own standpoint.

10. Cf. *4:* 388, 399; *5:* 54-9.

11. Cf. *6:* 6.

12. Cf. *4:* 5; and *17:* 14-17.

13. See above, pp. 240-1.

14. We should point out here, for the sake of clarity, that Vollenhoven's use of the words *simultaneous* and *successive* must not be taken too strictly in a merely chronological sense. Time-streams overlap to such an extent that they are sometimes practically congruent in time; such is the case in pre-Socratic subjectivism and objectivism. The result is that a particular type of conception sometimes has a representative in a "later" time-stream chronologically *before* the same type of conception is represented in the "earlier" time-stream. A striking case is that of Kierkegaard, whom Vollenhoven places as a "contemporary" of Sartre, in the time-stream "existentialism."

15. It is interesting to note, however, that Vollenhoven himself has used the image of language in this connection. With reference to the synthesis of Old Testament themes with pagan philosophy in Philo's thought, he wrote in 1933: "But when disobedient children of the covenant spoke the speech of Ashdod to such an extent, is it to be wondered at that the strangers and sojourners could not learn the language of Canaan?" (*10*: 114; with a note referring to Nehemiah 13:24).

16. Vollenhoven nowhere explicitly makes this point. Asked about it in private conversation, he agreed with the inference.

Bibliography of works by Vollenhoven

1. *De Wijsbegeerte der Wiskunde van Theïstisch Standpunt*; Amsterdam: Van Soest, 1918.

2. "Eenige Methodologische Opmerkingen Aangaande Dr. T. Hoekstra's Geschiedenis der Philosophie," in: *Stemmen des Tijds*, XI (1921/22), pp. 293-301.

3. "De Toeneming der Logische Geslotenheid in de Nieuwere Physica," in: *Stemmen des Tijds*, XI (1922), pp. III 129-43.

4. "Enkele Grondlijnen der Kentheorie," in: *Stemmen des Tijds*, XV (1926), pp. 380-401.

5. "Kentheorie en Natuurwetenschap," in: *Orgaan van de Christelijke Vereeniging van Natuur- en Geneeskundigen in Nederland* (1926), pp. 53-64, 147-97.

6. *Logos en Ratio: Beider verhouding in de Geschiedenis der Westersche Kentheorie*; Kampen: Kok, 1926.

7. "Het nominalisme van Zeno den Stoicijn," in: *Wetenschappelijke Bijdragen aangeboden door Hoogleeraren der Vrije Universiteit ter Gelegenheid van haar Vijftig-jarig Bestaan*; Amsterdam: De Standaard, 1930, pp. 175-204.

8. "De Beteekenis van het Calvinisme voor de Reformatie van de Wijsbegeerte," in: *Antirevolutionaire Staatkunde (Driemaandelijksch Orgaan)*, V (1931), pp. 180-98; 266-334 (= "The Significance of Calvinism for the Reformation of Philosophy," in: *The Evangelical Quarterly*, III, pp. 387-403; IV, pp. 128-60, 398-427.)

9. *De Noodzakelijkheid eener Christelijke Logica*; Amsterdam: Paris, 1932.

10. *Het Calvinisme en de Reformatie van de Wijsbegeerte*; Amsterdam: Paris, 1933.

11. "Schriftuurlijke Wijsbegeerte en Onderwijspraktijk," in: *Referaten-Bundel van het Vierde Nationaale Christelijk Schoolcongres*, Oct. 1936; Hoorn, 1937, pp. 200-14.

12. *Proeve eener ordening van wijsgeerige concepties,* I: *Niet-irrationalistische richtingen*; Assen: Hummelen, 1939.

13. *Richtlijnen ter Oriëntatie in de gangbare Wijsbegeerte*: Publicaties van de Reunisten-Organisatie van N.D.D.D, No. 13, 1941. (In part reprinted, with emendations and annotations, under the same title in: *Philosophia Reformata*, VI (1941), pp. 65-86; VII (1942), pp. 9-46; VIII (1943), pp. 1-33.

14. "De Waarheid in de godsdienst-wijsbegeerte," in: *Vox Theologica,* XIII (1942), pp. 113-23.

15. *Isagooge Philosophiae*; Amsterdam: Uitgave Filosofisch Instituut Vrije Universiteit, 1967 (mimeographed).

16. "The course of Plato's development," in: *Mélange Philosophique offerts en hommage aux Congressistes par l'Union des Sociétés de Philosophie des Pays Bas. Bibliothèque du Xme Congrès International de Philosophie*, Volume II; Amsterdam, 1948, pp. 1-16.

17. *Hoofdlijnen der Logica*; Kampen: Kok, 1948.

18. *Geschiedenis der Wijsbegeerte*, I; Franeker: Wever, 1950.

19. *Kort Overzicht van de Geschiedenis der Wijsbegeerte voor den Cursus Paedagogiek M.O.A.*; Amsterdam: Theja, 1956.

20. "Conservatisme en Progressiviteit in de Wijsbegeerte," in: *Conservatisme en Progressiviteit in de Wetenschap*; Kampen: Kok, 1959, pp. 35-48.

21. "De Consequent Probleem-historische Methode," in: *Philosophia Reformata*, XXVI (1961), pp. 1-34.

22. "Plato's Realisme," in: *Philosophia Reformata*, XXVIII (1963), pp. 97-133.

23. "Methode-perikelen bij de Parmenides-interpretatie," in: *Philosophia Reformata*, XXX (1965), pp. 63-112.

24. "Methodical Dangers in the Parmenides Interpretation," in: *Philosophia Reformata*, XXXI (1966), pp. 68-71.

Modal Aesthetics: Preliminary Questions with an Opening Hypothesis

CALVIN G. SEERVELD

It is a fact that aesthetics is increasingly recognized today as a special science. People who are busy with aesthetic theory or who study art as critics are by and large aware that they are not examining things as practicing psychologists or testing items as scholars in the area of linguistics. Aestheticians argue about things distinct from what physicists, sociologists and theologians argue about. Although there is heated debate about what precisely defines "aesthetic," there is a general willingness at least to not confuse the field of aesthetic investigation with matters one could circumscribe as specially and definitely "technical," "organic," or "ethical" and "legal."

This increasing recognition that there is a field of inquiry proper to aesthetics must be reckoned with. Those who contest the existence of aesthetics as a special science, perhaps because of its belated and handicapped birth in the eighteenth century supposedly at the hands of Baumgarten, or because the boundary of its supposed aesthetic domain is not clearly defined and convincingly argued, must contend with its phoenix persistence after every logical murder. And those, like myself, who believe the presence of aesthetics as a special science is a sound historical development are called upon to demonstrate the serviceability of typical aesthetic categories and to show how a method proper to aesthetic analysis affords insights that enrich our life.

My intent in this brief essay is to prospect for a path into the aesthetic woods and tentatively mark out an entrance. I should like to argue that there is an irreducible facet of human experience—better, an irreducible aspect of creaturely reality—which we may call "aesthetic," by appealing to the existence of art as a kind of cultural product which is characteristically different from other kinds of manmade things. I should like to propose further that we would do well to consider the nuclear moment of the "aesthetic" side of God-made and manmade things to be a matter of "allusiveness," and I shall try to make that a convincing hypothesis by showing how the qualifying function of art points in that direction. Although I must leave for some other occasion an account of how such an understanding of the "aesthetic" helps account for features of reality that theorists of many persuasions have wrestled with throughout history, I do wish just to hint at how an awareness of "allusiveness" might open up aesthetics as a systematic discipline, along with art theory and metacriticism, to the analysis of what I shall identify as "modal aesthetic" problems.

To be a pathfinder in the aesthetic woods is to exercise the calling of philosophical aesthetics. It is my conviction that articulation of the foundations for a modal aesthetics, which simultaneously breaks with the age-old tradition of "beauty," will encourage a Biblical reform in how men and women understand art, interpret texts, and even order a dimension of their everyday experience.

Methodological problem of definition

Since oracles are out of date, also for Christian thinkers, you face certain inescapable problems if you want to establish, rather than take for granted, that there is a definite aesthetic field of investigation. And the methodological problems seem to multiply once one admits to the historical diversity in attempts to define what gives aesthetics homogeneity as a science. Is there no way to avoid either the dogmatism of an apriori designation, perhaps derived from one's basic philosophical stance, or skepticism toward any conclusive definition, because you are really only chasing a bevy of ghosts through a viciously circular bog of language? How can one determine whether aesthetics is a special science with its own domain?

On the matter of strict definition, a neo-idealistic thinker is tempted to posit that there are certain prime realities which are ultimate and which therefore have to be accepted or denied as primary data; primes have to be immediately apprehended or they remain unknown, they are not susceptible to further logical parsing (*19*: 6, 14).* "Not at all!" says a pragmaticistic mind, especially not with respect to art. Definitions of the nature of art may be slogans for reforming critical appreciation of what is

*Italic numeral refers each time to the respective title listed in the bibliography, and the numerals after the colon refer to the pages of the reference work.

commonly called art, but to think that there is a set of sufficient and necessary conditions which things must possess to be art is the egregious, original sin of traditional aesthetics (*24*: 319, 325, 330-1). The test of whether "blanket" terms are ever justified depends upon the consistency of language and the coherence of subsequent practice when such terms are employed (*17*: 304, 310), but the existence of an (aesthetic) "essence" is simply an old philosophical pothole (*7*: 115-17).

Now, in my judgment we can learn something about the nature of definition from the stalemate between an intuitional, *ipse dixit* idealism and pragmatic operationalists, as well as get beyond the noncommittal indecision of Urmson, Weitz, Dickie, and Rader on whether "aesthetic" can cover birds of the same feather (*49*: 87-91; *52*: 31-3; *9*: 1; *33*: 5).

Idealists usually sense that the quest for philosophical definition is unlike the positive search for identifying whether so-and-so is cancer or a vitamin deficiency, and is unlike the logical exercise of specifying commonality and differentia so as to distinguish umbrellas from shotguns. Philosophical idealists normally recognize—rightly so, I think—the legitimacy of delimiting, in an open-ended way, certain irreducible features of things that cannot be conceptually determined. Although reflection on basic, irreducible aspects of things is simply not dreamt of in a philosophy which restricts language, truth and logic to matching up atomic sensa with conventionally hyphenated phonemes like "yel-low" and "sweet," idealists are on the right track, I think, in claiming that the task of "transcendental" definition (= positing discernible, categorial conditions) affords meaningful knowledge. Idealism goes wrong, however, in ascribing entitary reality to what is abstracted modal structuration—as if *modes* were *things*, which they are not.

Pragmaticistic analysis tends to undo any hypostatization of structure, whether it be Platonic *noëta*, Scholastic *essentiae*, or Kantian noumena. Pragmaticists, by and large, are also happy to functorialize entities, and by a kind of perverse, kenotic logic convert any internal, nature-defining criteria of something into various external use-relations, so that things are only what they function as. It is a markedly pragmaticistic penchant to dissolve defining typicality into circumstantial functionality. That means for philosophical definition that one can never pinpoint a centrally cohering, irreducible feature of something; it must remain permanently indeterminate, the protean object of an ongoing process of approximation. For example, Gallie maintains that art is an essentially contested concept because it is *essentially* an even expanding *complexity* (*16*: 114).[1]

Osborne sums up succinctly, with respect to aesthetics, the shortcomings of prescriptive definitions, a would-be empirical method, and the threat of a fallback, eclectic or gamesmanship position:

> Prescriptive definitions were rejected because they arbitrarily determine in the premise what purports to result in the conclusion. Empirical methods were ruled out because until the subject matter of enquiry is known and defined there can be no yardsticks by which to decide what empirical facts are relevant to it and what are irrelevant. In this situation serious doubts arose whether so admittedly diverse and disorganized a field could fruitfuly be made the subject of a unified philosophical discipline (*31*: 16).

His own statesmanlike, polemical solution is that the repudiation of definition for "aesthetic" has been premature, and if there be no validity to an artistic kind, there can be no genuinely art-critical appraisal—which is manifestly false (*31*: 16, 23).

I should like to pass through this initial thicket myself with the following observations.

(1) I believe that there are ordinances of God which hold for all kinds (and sub-sorts) of things. *That* there are various, mutually irreducible, interrelated but prime, relative structurations which order all things, events, acts, and whatever, as members of some kind (and sub-sort) or other, is an insight into creaturely reality which gives me a headstart in scientific analysis, as I see it. I believe it is the covenanting Lord God's "Let-there-be," ordaining Word which effects the real, rainbow-rich groupings of things and activities, the kindred ways creation is extant. And it is God's same cosmic limiting Word which issues the basic categorial modes of existence conditioning the many lawful patterns of order and disorder we may be busy discovering.

(2) It is the task of a philosophical definition, as I understand it, to identify *how* something is *qualified* (and perhaps founded, if you are dealing with things and events). This kind of definition, so important for orienting systematic inquiry, tries to disclose the characteristic limiting factor of what is given. So much theory and definition has made the mistake of twisting the characteristic-way-of-being-there, this question of typically-how-meaning, into a what-question. Looking for the essence, the ideal exemplar, or even minimal conditions overshoots the mark and misleads one into thinking that one must penetrate to the total being or to the causally sufficient facts of the definiendum. But definition, rightly conceived, gets at only *one*—albeit crucial—*factor* of what may be several necessary ingredients to what you are investigating, and the ontic status of the defining feature needs to be understood as an (abstract) how, not a simple what-totality.

Also, defining matters such as "aesthetic" would be less tendentious if we did not confuse the complementary heuristic and verificational stages of the process.[2] Discovery is what occurs in definition; so there is bound to be a tentative, exploratory moment. And corroboration occurs in definition; so it is normal to grow gradually in certainty about the defined characteristic. The trouble comes when verification and discovery are coalesced. Then comes the pressure to have your initial hunch certain (else it is dubious) or not to claim any reliability till there be complete enumeration of particulars (an impossibility)—hence so much conundrumic mystification surrounding definition. But tentative knowledge is normative, it seems to me, for the theoretical examination that makes up defining things—again, you are grappling not with the revealed be-all and end-all of something, but with its characteristic-how. And verified (scientific) knowledge does not result from bare logical activity; it is born of confessionally deepened analysis that takes on affirmation inexplicable as mere thought processes.

(3) It should be clear, too, that one does take a stand on a crucial meaning aspect of something in defining it. That is one reason why definitions are not won by the bread of analysis alone. It is also a reason why secular theoreticians today, still driven by an *Aufklärung* spirit of "tolerance," often display a febrile deviousness to avoid defining things, taking a stand on anything, except as a convenient handle. However, philosophical or transcendental definitions have the calling to help order our understanding of the world. Not that right definitions ensure a life of shalom while wrong definitions compromise the limiting ordinances God has set. If you define man as a "rational animal," he still functions as a human creature before God's face, although men living by pagan Aristotle's definition may try to tune their neighbor's drives and control his ratiocinative mechanism instead of loving him as a "worshiping creature." Meals may be "defined" by the packaged-food industries as an "efficient exercise in digestive health" rather than as "fellowshiping repast" (and meals still get served in God's world of TV-monitored North America): it is just our usual experience of them that may be denatured. Definitions with Christian insight would be a diaconate service of Christian theory.

So it is in this context that I should like to define "aesthetic." And it is my hunch that there is a fundamental aesthetic mode of existence, a definite, irreducible aesthetic dimension of reality, a peculiarly aesthetic side of life that we do well to recognize, understand, and obediently enact. My hunch is partially prompted by the fact that art works in our civilization comprise a kind of family of manmade things that bear a qualification irreducible to other kinds of cultural artefacts. And that qualifying characteristic of art indicates what we may call "aesthetic."

I know that this special "aesthetic" feature can be and has been denied existence, misconceived, expropriated theologically, scored mathematically, reduced to a psychological property, championed for its analogical presence in technical formation, tortured, and explained hundreds of ways, making human life the poorer, I suppose, and lamentably stunting praise of Yahweh revealed in Jesus Christ. But I should like to help straighten that out by analyzing the qualifying characteristic of art. Immediately, however, one is faced with an important complication that should first be cleared up.

Genesis of art-as-such

Art as we know it in Western civilization since the time of the so-called Renaissance and Reformation, that which you see collected in our musea built in the nineteenth century or experience at the galleries on 57th Street in New York City today, did not always exist as we understand it. Once upon a time there were no "fine arts." There was decorative ornamentation made by the skilled hands of men and women; there were specially prized stones and wrought metals kept for treaty and barter; and there have always been choreographic movements, noises, images, and incantations fashioned to celebrate the gods or victories (cf. aboriginal fertility dances, Lascaux cave paintings, Genesis 4:23-4). But drawing and sculptures, architecture and drama not bound to liturgy, fertility rites, formal tribal acts not defined by some need—art in itself for its own imaginative sake simply did not exist in human consciousness for centuries and centuries. So how can what historically comes (and goes?) like (fine) "art," for example, help us define what may be a perduring structural dimension of creation? And is it not presumptuous to assume that our Occidento-centric, secular version of "art" is normative for locating the presence of an ordinance God supposedly called "good"?

The fact that "art" was indistinct for millennia, East or West, from what we call craft today (*techné, ars*), formative control of materials and "natural" media like voice, speech and gesture, is as normal a happening as the fact that one's man or woman sexuality does not fully materialize, so to speak, until puberty. There is a cosmogonic structuring, I believe, which prompts within ordained bounds the gradual unfolding of creation's profuse, variegated richness. And the cosmogonic, structuring guidelines along which creation more or less must run occasion developments proper to the kind of creatureliness involved. Cosmogonic ordering must not be stuck with a deterministically conceived, biotic model.

For example, rock stratification and erosion or the curlicue ribbon of least resistance that continental rivers take is a cosmogonic ordering appropriate to such inanimate creation. The movement from tribal bonds to a matriarchal/patriarchal setup and later in time on to a monogamous family kind of knit is a normative process for structuring the generative-troth relatedness mankind may fully enjoy. Or again, the emergence of vocational scribal schools out of the mouth-to-mouth instruction occurring between generations, which schools later on develop into academies with libraries for reflective research, is the normal complication one expects when the critical, human activity of education is following the unfolding ordering of its particular creaturely existence. And all these quite different kinds of developments as well as the rise of sexual fertility out of one's childhood, are not just arbitrary occurrences. These developments follow the basic historical unfolding that witnesses floods, sickness, genocidal captivities, and totalitarian repression of culture: all these developments follow the basic cosmogonic law of differentiating to the primary, integrated response called for by whatever specific creaturely configuration each kind of thing or activity was given to exercise in the Lord's wisdom.

In my judgment this is a sound systematic explanation for what has in fact happened historically with the phenomenon of "art." So far back as archaeological finds presently go, there is evidence that gifted craftsmen constructed visual embellishments that were usually thoroughly meshed in ceremonial affairs. The relief modelings of pregnant animals in the caves of Altimira, Egyptian obelisks and mastabas, Etruscan wall paintings in the tombs of Tarquinii, as well as Maori face tatoos and the prows of Viking ships—all these show accomplished handicraft enveloped in a sacral, consecrated service. There was no independent "art" then—only quasi-liturgical, stylized crafting of materials.

There are many moot points, of course, as civilizations succeed one another, whether the truly cult-object nature of early Greek statuary *kouroi* (*agalmata*!) is shucked in the sculpture of fifth century Athens,or whether the pieces of Myron and Phidias, too, are not *deisidaimonesterous* props in a civic religion that embraces whole festivals of tragedies (cf. *katharsis!*). And questions about early Christian catacomb murals intent upon formulating a new iconography to identify themselves (cf. *ichthus*), the miniature ivories fashioned in the fifth century A.D. as devotional aids, and the splendid tenth century Byzantine illuminated capital letters of precious manuscripts—the question needs careful examination whether these all are wholly enclosed in the rich gymnastic of piety or breathe elements already of being somewhat indulgently on their own. But it is quite clear and has been well documented by Kristeller and others that before the 1500s, let us say, such decorative craftsmanship in the West (it was otherwise in China) was conceived, practiced and perceived as manual artistry done by artisans whose task was undifferentiated from the sort of service performed by druggists, armorers and navigators—mean, mechanical arts (*25*: 172ff). From ancient days "poetry" had always been linked, by itself, with oracular wisdom. "Rhetoric" and "music" (really, mathematicized musical theory) had been catalogued, at least since Martianus Capella (fl. 430 A.D.) among the *artes liberales*—elementary disciplines worthy of learning. But visual art was considered simply a commonplace skill, an ordinary means to varied, usually cult-related ends.

This sense of art as mere crafted artefact gradually changed. Renaissance spokesmen like Alberti wrote tracts claiming that painters, architects and sculptors were not menial tradesmen but gifted Humanists in their own right, dealing with *historia* (cf., e.g., *De Pictura*, Book 3). And architect Brunelleschi, sculptor Michelangelo and painters like Botticelli and Raphael bore out Alberti's honorific claims, winning the munificent patronage of Medici nobility and the papal rulers of Rome. Then, in 1563, Vasari founded the *Accademia del Disegno* in Florence, for the first time distinguishing institutionally the art of plastic design from the guilds of ordinary journeymen. As the gold leaf disappeared from paintings, as the allegorical emblematic side of sculpture turned this-worldly, and as ecclesiastical commissions were replaced by the secular demands of royalty, architecture became less a decoration of church buildings, vernacular poetry became less embellishment of language, and painting and sculpture became less catechetical icons, that is, less prettifying accoutrements to skillful, cleric-prescribed and liturgically confining constructions, as something distinct and worthy on its own. In fact, educated people began to think that "the arts" could only be properly appreciated if you developed the specially trained eye of a *virtuoso* (Castiglione), *connoisseur* (La Bruyère), gentry with *taste* (Shaftesbury). In this way *Il buon gusto* (the polite taste of courtiers and gentlemen) and *beaux arts* (the beautifying crafts bringing imaginative cultural refinements quite different from the "sciences"), which you could study at the many academies formed in the wake of *L'Académie Française* in the seventeenth century, gradually led to the concept of art-as-such (*25*: 193-6).

One could trace further how art-as-such firmed up in the eighteenth century of Europe, rightly becoming differentiated as something other than craft, as an activity more than competent construction and yet not just some sort of adjectival, decorative function of technique, but something deserving full-fledged attention proper to its own nature. Opening up the collections of aristocrats and the treasures of royalty for the public to see (= contemplate!) in musea, making concerts public, the developing of a reading public for witty essays and tales of adventure (Defoe's *Robinson Crusoe* was not yet called a "novel")—these societal changes formed the matrix, so to speak, in which slowly, complexly, with fits and starts, art began to come into its own as art-as-such.[3] Just as family structuring did not evolve out of the clan by legal decree, and household instruction did not turn into professional tutoring overnight (cf. the rise of sophist educators in fifth century Athens B.C., in effect making the less specialized slave-training of aristocratic children obsolete), so art as art-to-be-experienced-as-art did not get differentiated from art as hieratic craft and art as the epiphenomenal extravagance of monied privilege by a certain calendar date as a result of someone's willful decision. Art surely did not become art-as-such by theoretical fiat! Art as we more or less know it today actually did not get fully recognized as a cultural product with its own specific character, its own particularly identifying idiom and unmistakably "artistic" requirements, until the various European *l'art pour l'art* movements in the last quarter of the nineteenth century preached and practiced, dramatized it, and scandalized society by living their creed that art is something special not to be reduced to other kinds of matters, something that must be practiced, enjoyed and judged only for art's sake! To make the point that art is irreducibly different from all other cultural activities, these *l'art pour l'art* men and women denatured their humanity by *qualifying* their life *artistically*—they became "aesthetes" (*54*: xiii-xiv).

It is not apropos here to pursue the trouble that this proper historical differentiation of art suffered because it was secularistically spirited by a devil-may-care elitism. Thinkers like Huizinga, Van der Leeuw and T. S. Eliot have lamented the deracination of differentiated art and uttered pleas, in differing ways, for the remythologizing of art, for recouping the "primitive" or earlier Christianized confessional envelopment of art-as-such. Pragmaticist Dewey and absurdist Marcel Duchamp have tried, in their own way again, democratistically, to break down the peculiar cachet won by art-as-such and to dissolve art back into ordinary experience. So no art today is not subject to further development, be it normatively or anti-normatively. But from the historical sketch I have recounted, it seems to me that it cannot be gainsaid that art today has come of age. As a matter of fact, art in the twentieth century is an exceptionally good place for one to look at what characterizes art as such, since art today is not bound up definedly by other interests.

We all know that art in a pinch can serve as collateral, becomes booty, is held onto as surety, acts as pledge, is taken as an argument, or serves as conversation piece. But we also know that art is not *primarily* money, bail, safety, an ethical, logical or social object; such functions do not *characterize* a chanson, novel or painting. And I dare say it is more clear today than at any time in the cosmogonic history of "art" that if you make the *nucleus* of art, so to speak, an economic, confessional or social property, then you denature art into a matter of fashionable prestige, penance or commodity. To be sure, much art today is disgustingly a question of market, (psycho-analytic) penance or an affair of prestige. Contemporary art is pockmarked by rapacious diseases; and one must be careful when examining a sick man not to make the sickness the defining characteristic of what *men* are like. However, just as easy modern contraceptives help make more clear what marriage is in nucleus, vowed-troth-cemented-by physical-union, since the marriage relationship is not so closely embedded in bearing children (contraceptives today also permit, I know, "marriage" to be a legal contract for sexual convenience); and just as xerox machines help make more clear that teachers are not primarily for transferring notes but are "teachers" if they can bring leading insights into the habit of a new generation (copying machines also can promulgate the bookish, ivory-tower denaturing of education exemplified by the nineteenth century Germanic university); just so, art in museum and gallery today, unbeholden to anything but what is artistic, offers us a choice opportunity to probe what is characteristically art-as-such (and can condemn itself, I know, to the sterilization of an important gift God has given mankind). A differentiated cultural phenomenon in our secularized age is not the self-evident source of its definition, but it is a proper place to try the case for one's insightful identification.

A science of aesthetics

En passant it is important, I think, to agree with Tatarkiewicz and Chambers, for example, that aesthetics as a special science did not and most naturally could not exist before the eighteenth century (*47*: xix; *6*: 37-41; cf. *41*: 6-10). By a "special science" I understand systematic analysis of primary phenomena functioning in a very specific kind of way. Not until you had products like (fine) "art" historically differentiated from craft and had the specially aesthetic task of "artist" commonly recognized as distinct from that of artisan, and similar developments of peculiarly aesthetic responsibilities and authority, could one expect to have sustained, systematic analytic attention paid to an "aesthetic" zone of life and reality, giving rise to aesthetics as a distinct (special) science.

Of course men have reflected on art and artistry before it factored out, as it were. Plato's dialogic examinations of the civic service-ability of poetasters, hymn writers and pictorial conjurers (*Politeia* III, 398cl-403c8 and X, 595al-608b10; *Nomoi* III, 700al-702b3 and VII, 810e6-817e4), and Aristotle's valuable fragment dealing mostly with tragic drama as a mimetic construction of noble action in ornamented speech for the purpose of catharsis (*Peri Poiëtikês*), the maxims of Horace, and Pseudo-Longinus's manual "On Elevation in Poetry" have all contributed to a more refined knowledge of matters later found within aesthetic bounds; but these early reflections were piecemeal or were conceived as subsections of political theory (Plato), "practical" knowledge (Aristotle), techniques of rhetoric (Horace c.s.). Renaissance debates on the relative merits of different architects or on the nice relationships of poetry and music, and especially university-trained Alberti's treatises, exercised analysis on matters directly relevant to theoretical aesthetics; but Alberti, too, lacked the systematic and encyclopedic focus of probing within a delimiting category, which is what stamps inquiry as special-scientific.

I am not faulting such study about artistry for being not yet special-scientific. It is also not to the point whether one can discover who fathered aesthetics as a (special) science. There is no one "father" of scientific aesthetics. Just as art-as-such came into its own gradually, so too aesthetics as a science has had numerous historical midwives—Shaftesbury circled around and around "the fair and shapely" which "an inward eye distinguishes" like a nervous butterfly, Baumgarten schoolmasterly (mis)named the unborn child, and Kant redefined "aesthetic" out of sensation, restricted its reference, and dignified aesthetic judgment ("taste") with a critical philosophical exposition that set it firmly and distinctly within the gamut of human *Gemüt* (*39*: 8-9).[4] But at stake here is more than a technicality of dating the origination of aesthetics as a special science in the eighteenth century. At stake is recognition of the normative development and very nature of aesthetics as a discipline, as well as the Christian idea of modal aesthetics.

Voices are still raised in our day questioning: "Is the study of aesthetics a *philosophic* enterprise?" (*34*: 129f) or "Is a universal *science* of aesthetics possible?" because the nineteenth century positivist dogma defining science is still regnant, especially in North America, and frames the conceptual possibilities. The positivist model of exactly observable, experimentally verifiable science rules out scientific aesthetics except as some form of empirical psycho-social science like that long championed by Thomas Munro (*30*: 164, 186-206; cf. *22*: 260) or, for example, the funky axiology of Archie Bahm, mismatched with a hedonistic night in which all cows experience nirvana (*2*: 3-7). However, Dilthey's lifelong examination of *Geisteswissenschaft* ("human science") method and *das Verstehen* and Ernst Cassirer's incisive argument in *The Logic of the Humanities*, for example, on the irreducible difference between indeterminate "cultural concepts" and determinate "natural concepts" free aesthetics from the tyranny of the bad choice to be either an experimental fact-data kind of science or float free as speculative theory. Phenomenological aesthetics too, which recognizes the necessity of both prolegomenal philosophic aesthetic analysis and of specialized analysis that does justice to works of art as works of art (*22*: 259-60, 268-9): phenomenological aesthetics had shown beyond a doubt, it seems to me, that aesthetics as a science can be rigorously practiced without violating the special non-physical nature of its *Gegenstand*. And when "aesthetic concepts" shuck more of both logicistic and sensationalistic restrictions—that they must handle referents always as instantiations of some general class, or, to be valid, they must be governed by a set of sufficient conditions (= describable sense-causes) (*42*: 423-31)—that is, when "aesthetic concepts" gain sui generis metal and are shown still to be sound analytic coin, then we will be ready for happy advances in aesthetic science.

For anyone to oppose the development of special aesthetic science out of fear for the chill of manipulative death that secular (natural) scientism brings to knowledge of the world would be to adopt the shortsighted, antihistorical position of a reactionary. To take the alternative of dissolving aesthetics back into general philosophy, while using art for your illustrative material, would only condemn its practitioners to be viewy and "personal" in reflecting upon art and ensure that "aesthetics" remain immature. But if the "aesthetic" is a prime facet of created reality, then it is the mark of Christian wisdom to reaffirm and join in the development of aesthetics as an independent science, moving beyond the initial, philosophical definitional task, the pivotal setting of categories and methodological procedure, on into exploring, redeeming and ordering the staggering, disparate mass of aesthetic and artistic reality unearthed obliquely, devotedly and unenlightenedly by two and a half centuries of modern analysis. The Christian response to secular science is not to remain confessionally naive and insightful but to trade scholarly talents in obedience by structuring aesthetics as a relative, special science that discloses concretely the good news of our Lord.

The tradition of beauty and its demise

There is one more thicket I should like to penetrate briefly on the way to identifying, in arguing for, an irreducible "aesthetic" aspect of reality—the grand old theory of Beauty. To come to terms with Beauty vaults one immediately beyond the preliminary questions into the actual forest of systematic aesthetics. But I bring it up also to set in historical perspective the tradition of men like Abraham Kuyper, (Maritain), Dooyeweerd and Rookmaaker. Since to this day I can only reaffirm and try to strengthen the judgment I made fifteen years ago on "the curse of beauty" for understanding art and developing a sound aesthetic theory (*40*: 31-9), I should genuinely, respectfully like to engage in discussion various of my Christian colleagues who are still partial to "beauty" for thinking and speaking about art.[5]

It is no accident, I believe, that the great (European) theory of Beauty is in decline (*46*: 171-8) and that the decline began at the very time when the idea of *beaux arts* opened up the possibility for the rise of aesthetics as a science. In fact, the historical coincidence gives me the temerity to posit the thesis that the historical concept of "beauty," in all its variations, has been a concept of "order" paved with good intentions to maintain a sense of *general normativity*; therefore "beauty" had to be broken and will always have to be rejected as the kernel of art if the "aesthetic" is to be conceived in its *relative specificity*, that is, if "artistic" and "aesthetic" are to get beyond being designations of a vaguely nondescript quality.

When Plato had Socrates sparring inconclusively in the early dialogues,"beauty" was a "cosmetic" problem (in the original Greek sense of "ordered unity,"—*Gorgias* 503e4-504al) or simply "what is fitting" (*prepê—Hippias Maior* 290d5-6). Aristotle, too, let "beauty" rest as a rather unimportant quality of an overseeable unity-in-variety proportionality (*taxei—Peri Poiêtikês* 1450b36-1451a2). But mature Plato affirmed the paradigmatic reality of Beauty itself and declared that only contemplating this absolute Beauty made life worth living, making man a friend of God (e.g. *Symposium* 210el-212a7). And it is this supernality of Beauty which Plotinus mediated and Pseudo-Dionysius deified as Superbeing Beauty, the source of all that is harmony and brilliance (*to huperousion kalon . . . kai hos tês panton euarmostias kai aglaias aition—De divinis nominibus*, IV, 7), that captivated medieval Christian allegiance. Despite a more Aristotelian, hylomorphic framework, Thomas, too, anchored the traditional formulae for beauty—*proportio sive consonantia* and *claritas*—with *integritas sive perfectio* theistically, declaring them to be similar to the attributes of the Son of God (*Summa Theologica* I q. 39, a. 8 resp.).

It is difficult to determine exactly why Beauty was important to so many Scholastic thinkers. Beauty did serve to interpret, equivocally!, the sensuous, sensible world which one should flee as vain yet could recognize as a glorious epiphany, if not emanation, of God. Beauty was the erotic invitation Plato, Plotinus and Pseudo-Dionysius used to lead those who were holier than sense on and up to the ethereal realms of heavenly, sanctified light. (One should remember that the texts of Pseudo-Dionysius on Beauty carried a quasi-Biblical imprimatur until long after Thomas Aquinas, when the Humanist Laurentius Valla showed they were *not* written by Dionysius the Areopagite named in Acts 17:34.) So Beauty was at least a supple, synthetically Christian linchpin to help you have your earthly cake and eat it heavenly too.

By the time the God of heaven and hell had faded into the deity of Alexander Pope's "Universal Prayer" (1738), Beauty also had stopped trailing clouds of glory. Such a transcendental reality was no longer needed to justify the ways of man in the world to . . . Nature. But it is most telling to notice that the divine attributes of Beauty—concinnity, perfection and immediate brilliance—were assumed more or less by human sense activity, the particular sensibility of men that came to be called an "internal sense" or "taste," the kind of non-think-sensitivity immediately affected by pleasing, artful "natural Beauty."[6] That is, old Beauty diffused, as I see it, into being the heightening and validating coefficient of a subjective human sense-perceptivity that eighteenth century thinkers were trying to distinguish from ordinary sensation (cf. Kant's *das feinere Gefühl*) and gradually came to associate with a normative and certain response to *belles lettres* and *beaux arts*.[7] Human beauty-sensitivity recognized natural beauty and artful, humanly designed beauty with authority because beauty-sensitivity or taste (cf. Baumgarten's *ars pulchre cogitandi*) acted "beautifully," that is, *perfectly* (= finishedly, *ohne alles Interesse*, without any wanting interest, disinterestedly—Kant, *Kritik der Urteilskraft*, §5) and *harmoniously* (= *in bloss formalen Zweckmässigkeit im Spiele der Erkenntniskräfte des Subjekts*;—Kant, *Kritik der Urteilskraft*, §12), although not till Kant's *Critique of Judgment-ability* did anyone spell out such grounds for the authority of taste in relation to the unquestioned universal-necessary authority enjoyed by cognitive Reason. Insofar as "beauty" retained any "substantive" body, usually adjectival in nature, "beauty" meant, somewhat diffusely, architectonic wholeness and telic harmony, for which one could refer to the *edle Einheit und stille Grösse* championed by Winckelmann and find embodied in eighteenth century "neo-classical" architecture the rather bland colors and fixed contours of Raphael Anton Mengs or the paintings of David during the French Revolution through the Napoleonic Empire.

But two important events virtually destroyed the traditional concept of Beauty, on top of the secularized, subjectivized reduction it had already undergone in the seventeenth and eighteenth centuries: the fashionable rise of "the sublime," and infuential Hegel's coalescing "beauty" with "artistic" during the throes of a revolutionary, Romantic turn in the arts. And I should like to comment briefly on these two crucial developments regarding "beauty," to introduce my own thesis on the qualifying feature of art, which will afford a clue, I believe, to what we may understand as the "aesthetic" dimension of reality.

(1) When "the sublime" became understood around the middle of the eighteenth cenury as a vehement emotion filled with terror and obscurity before overpowering and immeasurable natural phenomena (Edmund Burke, *A Philosophical Enquiry into the Origin of our Ideas of the Sublime and Beautiful*, I, 7, 17-18; II, 1-8, 22), and was accepted as proper for English gentry to experience, even preferable to the pleasures of "beauty"!, then the generalizing, constrictive hold "beauty" had as the norm for (fine) art and for man's tasteful response to Nature was in principle broken. Societal adoption of "the sublime" intensified, to be sure, the humanistic subjectivizing of normativity going on (*Objects* were not sublime, only human *subjective experience* was sublime; cf. Kant, *Kritik der Urteilskraft*, §25) and helped prepare the way for a Romantic ideal of genius and originality. But this idea of "the sublime" was so important for developing our conception of "aesthetic" because it violated the very core

of Beauty which had ruled Western reflection for more than two millennia (*44*: 191-3). With "the sublime," new features and properties came into play that were diametrically opposed to the quasi-mathematical concordance (since fifth century B.C. Greek *summetria*—cf. *50*: 166-9, 175-9, 207, 253-8) and measured decorum that had always constituted the center of Beauty, especially in its current variant of Louis XIV aplomb, heroic couplets and even sunny-side-up rococo: now Burke praised Milton for his "judicious obscurity,"and distortion became a bonafide candidate for civilized taste within the flexing area of (Baumgarten's "inferior") aesthetic realm (*5*: 328). The idea of feeling "the sublime" exercised, I think, wittingly or not, a transcendental critique against the conception of "beauty" which restrictively inhibited (aesthetic) experience to the apprehension of merely unity-in-variety matters. Such unity-in-variety, integral harmony (the Great Theory of Beauty), in my view, at best points to an elemental mathematical analogy within aesthetic functioning; but "the sublime" asks one to recognize another and much deeper analogy within (aesthetic) experience, and its early proponents were reaching insightfully beyond proportional harmony in a way that opened up "aesthetic" perception more richly.

(2) Hegel explicitly restricted aesthetics to *Philosophie der schönen Kunst* (*Aesthetik*, ed. Bassenge, 2 A., 1: 13-14). In effect he relegated to the sidelines matters of natural beauty and taste, which had been in the forefront of systematic reflection starting up around "aesthetic" matters as late as Kant. Hegel focused all attention upon art, "the fine arts"—architecture, sculpture, painting, music, and poetry (as the standard lists now read)—and would have practically no place for anything like non-artistic aesthetic life; even actual art was there, believed Hegel, for the sake of the *science* of art, *Kunstwissenschaft*! (*Aesthetik*, ed. Bassenge, 1: 21-3). Hegel's enormous rationalistic, humanistic, culturalistic bias made it easy for him to absorb Beauty, and the (general, transcendent) normativity Beauty stood for, into art, so that art—better, *die schöpferische Phantasie* generating art—became its own (transcendent) norm and was declared inherently beautiful.[8] But in his most incisive remarks about *das Charakteristische* as *Kunstgesetz* for autonomous art, Hegel recognized that the ugly is "a fundamental property" of art, especially Romantic Christian art and poetry (for Hegel = e.g., medieval crucifixion altarpieces, Michelangelo, Shakespeare—*Aesthetik*, ed. Bassenge, 1: 28-31, 53-4, 160, 518). This means that for the contradictory monist Hegel, since Beauty coheres essentially in Art, and some art needs ugliness, then the ugly can also be beautiful, if in art.

Some such conceptual confusion has been with us ever since. Beauty is prescribed as the *nescio quid, flogiston* element of art. (*Flogiston* was projected by eighteenth century physical scientists as the common burning element in all things that burn.) The position that ugliness is a contrary of beauty and not unbeautiful (*43*: 72, 82) has made it possible that *anything* that can pass for artistic is beautiful. The upshot has been to alter radically the traditional meaning of Beauty and encourage utter relativity—still paired with an unquestionable normativity!—ranging all the way to André Breton's *la beauté . . . convulsive*. So the term *beauty* today has become an embarrassing catchall that one requires as canon of aesthetic judgment and uses interjectionally, but denies any substantive specificity or writes off ostensively as "what the bourgeoisie pays the artist for" (*37*: 127, 130; *23*: 166-8; *55*: 2; *32*: 331).

(3) There have been and still are serious post-Renaissance Christians who believe that Beauty has been unfairly discredited and who wish to revert to the time-honored tradition and reaffirm Beauty in all its pre-secular glory, allowing perhaps a little more flexibility in applying it to art. Abraham Kuyper's Princeton lectures of 1898 claimed as a Calvinistic confession that "art has the mystical task of reminding us in its productions of the beautiful that was lost and of anticipating its perfect coming luster" (*26*: 155). Jacques Maritain in his Mellon lectures of 1952, out of a modified Thomist perspective, adopted basically the same position, although with a much more developed philosophical theology of Beauty. He claimed that

> art struggles to surmount the distinction between aesthetic beauty and transcendental beauty and to absorb aesthetic beauty in transcendental beauty . . . . And it is by virtue of this transcendental nature of beauty . . . that all great poetry awakens in us, one way or another, the sense of our mysterious identity, and draws us toward the sources of being (*29*: 126, 127).

Gerardus van der Leeuw made *holy* the ultimate word and *beautiful* the penultimate in *Wegen en Grenzen* (1932/1955), but he confessed that whoever truly served Beauty, served God, for art and religion would connaturally merge somewhere beyond this world (*51*: 294, 306, 312, 368-71). And others, too, have sought to seek a New Orpheus, plucking the old strings of Awful Loveliness, each being faithful to thee, Beauty, in their fashion.

But it strikes me that Christians in the twentieth century who adopt Beauty in some transcendental way as the key to understanding art and human aesthetic activity are easily misled into also adopting the apologetic attitude toward art and the ontological framework in which Beauty was born. Kuyper, Maritain and Van der Leeuw on this point, each in his own way, seek divine sanction for earthly art by giving it a heavenly meaning, you could say, working with an analogical metaphysics partial to an erotic ladder of Being, amid shadows of natural theology tinctured with mysticism. And no amount of Bible quotes can rescue any similar aesthetics of Beauty with such apokatastatic paraphernalia and make it a "Christian" aesthetics.[9] Beauty is no help at all in discovering what is creaturely "aesthetic" if it only draws you into speculating about the nature of God and *per obscurius* settle down on what the answer is for creation, without any careful systematic historical examination of art, for example.

Dooyeweerd and Rookmaaker avoided any theologistic Beauty-aesthetics in positing *de schone harmonie* (beautiful fittingness) as the cohering nuclear moment of the aesthetic aspect to reality; they were more intent on the "harmony" than on the "beauty." Actually, *de schone harmonie* is an unexamined and undeveloped presupposition, replete with ancient Greek overtones (*35*: 141-2). While expositing the meaning of "harmony" in its presumably original aesthetic sense, Dooyeweerd none too carefully emphasizes the requirement of unity-in-multiplicity (which he says later himself is a mathematical analogy within aesthetic functioning—*11*: 2-346) and *mêden agan* simplicity (in his view an economic retrocipation within the typically aesthetic zone—*11*: 2-128; cf. *36*: 143, 147-8); and one is left thinking that those analogical functions are not sufficient pointers for what might be peculiarly "aesthetic," in some tradition-reforming sense.[10] So it seems to me that *de schone harmonie* should be discarded as an inadequate tradition of men that today would certainly inhibit launching an opened-up systematic aesthetics. "Beautiful fittingness" is also not helpful in that it might just happen to mislead the unwary into thinking that atonality, inscapedly complex verse, and rejection of gold-leaf background or fixed-point perspective in painting is "unfitting," and therefore aesthetically not normative.

I have no quarrel with understanding "beautiful" as describing the sacramental object-functioning of things, how rocks and zinnias, rainbows, lobsters and human sight mutely testify of God's *kabod* (*40*: 31-2), signifying and authenticating the Lord's covenanting Rule, *basileia*. But that *general*, all-encompassing Grace is not an *aesthetic* affair. And neither "beautiful" nor "harmony" (in some undefined sense) is a defining mark of art; so "beautiful fittingness" misses the modal lode we wish to mine. Secular aesthetic theorists by and large have won the war against "beauty," as I see it, but are in danger of losing the peace of aesthetic meaning because they have simultaneously excommunicated any (aesthetic) normativity other than various makeshift, subjectivist varieties. The call to *aesthetic* (and artistic) *normativity* does not, however, have to be made in the tainted name of Beauty. With art-as-such on hand and recognized as such, aesthetic theory today seems all dressed up but with no place to go theoretically. How lovely it would be if Christian theoreticians working in concert could be given the winsome grace and insight to tell secular aesthetics where to go.

Qualifying function of art

We can be less skittish about designating the qualifying function of art-as-such if we realize exactly how abstract and exactly how limited a matter it is we are trying to pinpoint. Without a doubt, whatever you designate as the characteristic limiting factor of art—or if you decide to forfeit the question—it shapes your whole aesthetics. But the typically-how-meaning of art only marks out an entrance to the aesthetic woods; it is not the whole forest. Aschenbrenner correctly observed that there are several necessary structural elements to art, all of which legitimately press important claims for theoretical analytic attention—its internally configured constitution, its (representational or not) relation to other reality, and the special bond it bears toward its human maker and beholders (*1*: 106-8). Ingarden, Wellek and Dufrenne correctly stress the multi-layered strata of painting, poetry and other art levels and moments of awareness (*22*: 266-8; *53*: 152-8; *13*: part III). No more should anyone think he must try to capture the sum total of art by one throw of the loaded theoretical dice. And if we proceed with the modesty I recommended for philosophical definition (*supra* pp. 266-7, 273), we do not need the exhaustive set of characteristics Ziff prescribed (*56*: 62-4), nor need we abandon ourselves to nominalist Dickie, who wants to institutionalize would-be definitionmongers of art—then *whatever* art musea directors nominate as art, is art (*8*: 101-8; *10*: 420-1). Instead we shall try to zero in on how art-as-such primarily, characteristically, coheres and impinges itself upon us.

How is a photograph by Ernst Haas different from a standard passport photo made to identify yourself to the police? How is my perception of a Henry Moore sculpture different from my seeing it simply as a large physical obstruction? How are the movements of Marcel Marceau on stage different from the expert movements of a high-flying trapeze "artist" somersaulting through the air? How are the sentences

> . . . the soil
> Is bare now, nor can foot feel, being shod.
> And for all this, nature is never spent . . .

different from an ordinary prayer or a weather report?

After years of careful, examining observation, my tentative answer goes like this: the decisive feature that turns photographic duplication of a face into art is allusiveness. When the reproduced lines, shadows and lighting subtly nudge into visibility character flaws or subterranean strengths of the person, for example, and portray by a quality of disciplined suggestiveness fine matters in the face that are simply neglected in photographic reproductions which merely depict so-and-so, then the result is a photographic portraiture art like that of Ernst Haas (cf. *18*: 370, 385; *21*: 42). And the modifying focus that heightens human sense-perception which recognizes a large piece of metal to be sculptural art rather than a heavy obstacle is allusiveness. When a dog notices a Henry Moore sculpture, rubs against it and urinates, or when a man looks at it simply as an expensive block in his normal corner-cutting path—you have to walk around it—both man and dog miss seeing what is really there (cf. *28*: 32); they happen to be art-blind, you could say, because they could not—or the man was not trained to be predominantly cartoonfully attentive to the intrinsic ellipticality of the compositioned spatial movement, refracted light and surface texture beaten into the cast bronze mass. Again, the quality that sets apart mime from acrobatic virtuosity is allusiveness. Pantomime and mimic theater naturally build on the extraordinary bodily control of the gymnast and demand the perfect timing and technique crucial to the tumbler, but the art of mime is of a different order (not "better," not "more valuable," but just "of another kind"), because a sheen of hinting ambiguity is built in and characterizes the performing Marceau's gesture, but that feature of ambiguity is absent or certainly not primary in the best acrobatic movement (cf. *13*: 75-9). Also, the feature that determinatively marks certain language as poetry, distinct from quotidian discourse, is allusiveness. Poetic lines emerge from the cocoon of rather straightforward English speech and show themselves an artistic butterfly when the diction, word rhythm, syntactic complexity, every semantic feature is metamorphosed into images, climaxes, overtones, into an indigenously polysemic, metaphorical kind of entity. So the nub of poetry cannot be paraphrased, and lexical and grammatical analysis is inadequate for probing through to the crux of poetic artefactuality, because its whole universe of lingual discourse has been caught—incapsulated, if you will, into a different idiom, one characterized by "allusiveness" (cf. *3*: 192-214; *12*: 196-200; *38*: 82-5).

Immediately a host of problems crowd to the fore; but most are modifying points that only emphasize how abstracted (rightly so) this real, qualifying feature of allusiveness has been conceived. For example: (1) It is important to realize that I claim "allusiveness" describes not only what typifies the excellent professional action and products of Haas, Moore, Marceau, and Hopkins but also any photography, construction, mimicking, and verse which is seriously conceived to have the vocation (to use Dufrenne's phrase) to be "allusive," which is bona fide art, no matter how threadbare or superficial its import. Of course there are fine borderlines between differing vocations, as there are between differing wave lengths, perhaps well nigh indiscernible for a given specimen; but both poor and good art is by nature characteristically allusive (cf. *21*: 52; *8*: 84).

There are many other extremely important, life-and-death type questions to ask about art, to get at its full meaning, but we have restricted our concern here only to the matter of *defining* it, discovering the primary, characteristic qualifying-how of art-as-such.

(2a) The fact that a would-be artistic entity might fail because it lacks internal, technical integration is so, but that fact does not compromise affirming "allusiveness" as the *qualifying* function of art. Every manmade thing depends upon some sort of formed, supportive base that lends instrumental viability, as it were, to however the cultured object produced is meant to be subject-activated for functioning. Without a system of organized sounds, the language of Englishmen would be undone; without a continuous pattern of felt stimuli, a man's propositional analysis founders (as in aphasia, cf. *4*: 48n.7, 161-3); without its materials meshed to telic form so that it is ready for skilled manipulation, a machine is nothing. Similarly, art-as-such, like any cultural artefact—language, analysis, or an instrument—is founded in achieved control of organized means of some sort, superintended now in the case of art by allusiveness. So without a techno-formative modal foundation, art-as-such is only a bird in the bush. But that (founding) condition (!) must not be confused with how art is defined.

(2b) It is so that a purported art work may fail to live up to its professed vocation, and it frequently happens that man and dog spectators fail to respond properly in kind to what is indeed a construction, action or event qualified artistically. It takes two, as phenomenologically oriented Ingarden and Dufrenne passionately aver, to make an "aesthetic object" appear (*22*: 262-5, 268; *13*: 218-33): it takes a human aesthetic subject in action and, in my terms, an artefact qualified by an aesthetic object-function. I do not wish to enlarge here upon this very important point except to note, first: the fact that an art product is qualified by an aesthetic *object-function*, thus needing an aesthetic subject functioning to unfold its characteristic meaning, does not lead to the conclusion that the mode of existence of an art work is "intermittent," as Margolis lucidly and subjectivistically maintained (*28*: 32; cf. rather *38*: 30-4, 59-60), for the "allusiveness" is no "second-storey" epiphenomenal ascription by occasional human subjects but is an existential, aesthetic object-functional reality binding upon all and sundry subjects. And second: the fact that art is qualified by an (aesthetic) object-function and thus, like all other kinds of cultural artefacts, is (some original subject's) objectification of certain primary-meaning givens entails that art, like all other kinds of manmade things, has what you could call a "secondary-meaning status." The (secondary) meaning of art, like that of language, argument and machines, too, must be uncovered (Margolis would say "completed,"—*28*: 32-4; cf. Soriau's "instaurative" action in *13*:223, 367), that is, activated *in kind* by subjects, with a due awareness of the (committed, original) subject-presence in the (art) object (cf. "quasi subject" in *13*: 379, 393, 398; but cf. also *15*: 115-22, 291-5). Again, these important complexities do not gainsay the very limited insight at stake, that "allusiveness" is the primary qualifying function of art-as-such.

(3) Anyone who recognizes the genetic layer within reality will not be surprised to notice that the abiding role of "allusiveness," as how art is primed, has undergone development in its historically posited concretions. The allegorical and anagogic, in between-the-lines imprint on the smile of the Notre Dame sculpture of the Virgin, for example, gave way to the *sfumato* conjuring of "atmosphere" in Da Vinci's Mona Lisa (*45*: 56); and the emblematic books which fascinated sixteenth century readers took a chiaroscuro turn in the quieting and enveloping paintings of Rembrandt. The modal imprimatur of a Phrygian or Mixolydian melody was followed later on, for example, by fugal counterpoint and then the exquisitely formal, reiterating variations within eighteenth century European music (*45*: 57-8); Baudelaire and Gauguin withdrew from the academic studio surcharge upon art, synthesized and pressed into sonnet and painterly service the pregnance of the *symbolistes* . . . . The point is: whether it was or is an allegorical, chiaroscuro, fugal, or, say, surrealist finish to the art, the nuclear moment cohering, empowering and typifying all those varieties is "allusiveness." In fact, I am inclined to press for adopting as the root meaning of STYLE as a categorial *aesthetic concept* (in contrast to decorative "stylization," a deepened, aesthetic analogical function of techno-formative activity) the positioned, historical positing of allusiveness. In its original sense, then, "style" would be the dated, particular world-and-life-view-oriented, allusive moment to human life, as it rules art in uncountable ways and as it fellow-travels functionally within dress, thought, feeling, worship, and what have you other than artistic of human activity.

(4) Art using language poses special problems for analysis. The diaphoric, connotative sublayer natural to speech and signification remains submerged until language takes on the edge of rhetorical allusiveness. Then the idiomatic felicity and straightforward, signpost-pointing transparency of language is altered, and the oratorical or poetic discourse is bound to be plurisignal, oblique, inherently ambiguous (*38*: 128-30; *12*: 199-200; *45*: 59), free to exploit especially the adherent, expressive reach proper to artistic (includes non-verbal artistic) activity. I mention this only to point up that activities which are opened up in structural dimensions that supercede the allusive (for example, the semantic and also the analytic) and have absorbed the aesthetic element into their more complex range of functioning nevertheless can still be constrained to lose their original identity, as it were, in order to regain it in an allusive

eclipse. But this involved puzzle (cf. ". . . as language, art is a semantic blasphemy"—*38*: 160) should not encourage one to make the mistake of conflating aesthetic and semantic, as Croce did, and try to develop an aesthetics on the model of a poetics.

Unless one perversely denies that such things as art objects exist, a thoughtful person should like to know what characterizes art. An advantage to the methodology I have proposed and exercised is that the court of appeal is an ongoing return to examine painting, sculpture, theater, music, and poetry (cf. *13*: lvii-lviii), *looking* for what defines that kind of cultural artefact. You avoid pulling a definitive quality out of some tall, black, speculatively theoretical or etymological hat. But I do take a stand in the push and pull of historical-systematic analysis, and I am curious whether my opening hypothesis, designating "allusiveness" as the *nuclear moment* of *how* art is *qualified*, will ring true as a starter and meet the objections of the many who have rightly doubted whether a logically exhaustive definition of some exclusive, essential generality could ever be found or built solidly out of empirical blocks (e.g. *7*: 132). The alternative to taking an informed, thetical stand is the stance of skepticism. But theoretical skepticism cannot give leadership.

"Allusiveness"

How will "allusiveness" serve as the entrance for a reforming science of systemetic aesthetics? What happens if we go that route?

I think, first, "allusiveness," like a queen's gambit, will put us in a strategic countering position in Anglo-American circles, for we shall be able to latch on, correctively, to a major development in theory of art that has been more than less shunted to the side. Along with (discredited) Hegel, the cultural philosophy of Ernst Cassirer leading to the aesthetics of Susanne K. Langer and the complementary work of Mikel Dufrenne offers a wealth of humanistic reflection still largely untapped by those who keep fussing with "the linguistic foundations" of aesthetic inquiry (cf. *14*: 1-4). The encyclopedic fabric and wide-ranging ecumenical art knowledge of Hegel, Cassirer, Langer, and Dufrenne, so foreign to structuralistic Thomism and the blanketing ontological empiricism of our day, should alone help keep one's theoretical aesthetics from becoming picky or straying too far away from reality. The baggage hidden in the trunk of their key concept of "symbolic," "expressive form" (*27*: 124-39) and "expressivity" must be critically examined, constructively related to the field work of Gombrich and Rudolf (*Visual Thinking*) Arnheim; then perhaps art as "symbolic objectification" of certain meaning-realities can become truly precise and fruitful (*40*: 39-40),[11] and we can lay to rest in a grave next to Beauty the Platonic myth of Art-as-carbon-copy-replication (cf. *18*: 313-20).

Though it sounds barbaric at this point, "symbolify," once salvaged, may well be a sound term to describe *artistic activity*. If "allusiveness" indeed indicates how art is characteristically qualified, the human activity which objectifies whatever primary meaning is lit upon, and objectifies it artistically—that human activity should be ipso-functionally, primarily "allusive"; and no concept comes closer to that kind of intensed, disciplinedly elliptical reality than "symbol" (admittedly from a German Idealist tradition that goes back at least to Kant's *ästhetische Ideen* in *Kritik der Urteilskraft*, §49; cf. René Wellek, *Discriminations: Further Concepts of Criticism* [Yale University Press, 1970], p. 126). Neo-idealist Cassirer, however, compresses mathematical science, language and myth, as well as art, into "symbolic form" (*4*: 92-5); so for Cassirer, "symbolic" lacks the specificity of "allusiveness" to which I wish to focus the term. Cassirer is probing the basic, given human capability for objectifying meaning, for constructing artefacts with a "secondary meaning" status (cf. supra [2b], pp. 282-3), for cultivating, culturating the earth, which is indeed a supportive functional base within art, language, science, societal institutions(!), and confessional worship. Just how aesthetician Langer moves beyond (or below!) Cassirer's techno-formative problematics to typify art-as-such, and how much closer than Kant's *Lustgefühl* Dufrenne's keen explications of "presence" and "expressivity" take us (or not) in precisioning "the aesthetic" (*13*: 339-40, 426-7): that is, to find out what is living and what is dead weight among these acute thinkers for helping us move towards the formation of a special science of aesthetics, needs a separate study.

I think also that "allusiveness" as the qualifying, characteristic feature of art will serve to open up the possibility of joining studies in principles of art and literary criticism, a meta-critical aesthetics like that of Beardsley (*Aesthetics: Problems in the Philosophy of Criticism*, 1958), along with Gadamer's important *Wahrheit und Methode*, 1960 (*15*), and the hermeneutical investigations of Ricoeur, Ebeling, Pannenberg, and other theologians. Once it is clear that a literary text is qualified by "allusiveness" and that it is primarily a task of philosophical aesthetics—not philosophical logic!—to forge the categories and method for interpreting literary texts, then theological hermeneutics should become a little more critical of its foundations (previously cast in relatively *ipse dixit* isolation). The special kerygmatic authority of Holy Scripture is not in any way undone by the reformation of seeing that an aesthetics with Christian insight is needed for deepening a believer's exposition of the "allusive," Truth-bearing text witnessing to the Rule of our Lord. In fact, Christian aesthetic theory has a faithful contribution to make to Biblical hermeneutics.

But most exciting for me, since precedents are scarce, will be a systematic pursuit of "allusiveness" as not just the entitary qualifying object-function of art and literature but as one kind of real, functionally coherent way-of-being-there that all creaturely things either subjectly display or objectly can be taken as. A careful exposition of the ontic irreducibility of "allusiveness," that there be this prime structural dimension of creation—call it "*suggestie-rijk*" (P. D. van der Walt), "nuanceful" (L. Zuidervaart), or "allusive"—its modal reality cannot be established frontally, as it were, by an argued deduction. Instead one will need to collate and contrast examples of affairs embedded in our normal daily experience that beg for recognition of this "aesthetic" kind of structural horizon and regional order of functioning. For example: the ubiquitous obliquity in any lingual activity cannot be accounted for, it seems to me, in strict linguistic variables, or be convincingly written off as a psychological confusion; rather, the obliquity functioning within ordinary discourse is evidence of an irreducible "allusive" layer holding analogically within the semantic ordinance for all phenomena functioning lingually. Or, for another example: the empathy certain sensitive people feel for subtle changes in a companion's mien cannot be adequately explained, it seems to me, in factors of sensory-motor alertness or by appealing merely to actually felt phenomena; rather, the empathetic dimension to human sensitivity, to which level of deepened psychic functioning human emotional life may mature, testifies to an irreducible "allusive" horizon holding analogically within the psychic ordinance for all sensitive human functioning that is opened up to such refinement. "Insensitive" people have little play to their largely sensational emotional life; they often lack "allusive" functional development to their psychic subject responses. And so on. The proof of my theoretical hypothesis on "allusiveness" will come in the pudding of concrete insights, and the concrete flesh of experiential insight should be strengthened by the backbone of theoretical ordering afforded by a (Christian) systematic aesthetic science.

"Modal aesthetic" problems include discovering the rich analogical, supportive and out-reaching structural moments of full-orbed, "allusive" functional experience. Matters that are ironic or tasteful, acts of fantasy or celebration—is this finally where "play" comes in!?—typically aesthetic events like surprise, all deserve scrutiny in a modal aesthetics. The nice, important relation sustained between artistic activity and aesthetic life experience comparable perhaps to the relation sustained between theoretical analysis and ordinary thinking, needs examination. The "allusive" element anticipatorily latent or subterraneanly operative in all other kinds of activity, and the "allusive" object-function of rocks and flowers and fish—inscape, the scapes of flouncing mackerel Hopkins saw in his boat (*20*: 55, 58), is the proper locus for all the loose reflection before Hegel on "natural

Beauty," if it would become properly "aesthetic": these are "modal aesthetic" problems.

And the fact that "allusiveness" is a real kind-of-being-there, and therefore holds the limited, ordinantial blessing and cursing power of what God said was good and needed to be responded within by his creatures—that fact takes "modal aesthetic" problems out of the realm of personal preference, dillydally trivia or adiaphora. It is in the domain of modal aesthetics to analyze the normative! moment of flirtation in ethical life, and, for example, to think through what aesthetic obedience would be for the diplomatic niceties of business or political life (rather than let the style of negotiations hang upon somebody's "personality" or having learned the techniques of "gettin' 'em drunk"). I do not expect theoretical aestheticians to speak ex cathedra for a side of human life, but it would be a mark of Christian leadership if those who are busy in modal aesthetics should occasionally issue encyclicals of ludic wisdom. If the "allusive" mode of creaturely reality is denied or neglected, or, if in reaction to the fastidious idolatry of aesthetics, one decides to live in aesthetic disobedience, the result is aesthetic closure to life. And a man or a woman's life deprived of "allusive" shalom, when school life or church life is unimaginatively dead, is a very sad, impoverished kind of closed-down creaturely existence. No less sad because it is common among Christians . . . .

But these are matters for reflection when one is actually walking in the aesthetic woods. My commitment for this article was simply to mark out an entrance with prospects for a path.

I recall the day in the spring of 1952 when Dr. Runner prompted me to go back into the stacks of the Calvin College library to look up a volume of *Philosophia Reformata*. If I wanted to know the ins and outs of Christian aesthetics, there was a place to start. The title stared up at me from the page: ONTWERP ENER AESTHETICA OP GRONDSLAG DER WIJSBEGEERTE DER WETSIDEE. I remember, it took me a long time to find the word "ENER" in the Dutch dictionary.

An incredible world of experience has come my way from the hand of our Lord since that day. So my essay in aesthetics has its own cachet of strengths and weaknesses. But I am happy to present it to the man whose teaching this volume honors, for it has been a labor of love, to thank God for having touched my life with his Grace through the formative influence of H. Evan Runner.

Notes

1. Gallie's rejection in *16*: 101 (1956) of his earlier "informed scepticism" (1948) about whether "art" "stands for any one thing" (*17*: 313) only reaffirms more decidedly his operationalistic conception of "art" and "aesthetic," although in 1956 he agrees with Passmore that "we must be able in some degree to circumscribe the field within which these probably bogus concepts have been applied" (*16*: 100n.2); and he notes "the surprising fact that almost all philosophical aestheticians (and almost [sic] the great creative critics who lie at the back of them) have sought to define art by means of one key notion or category" (*16*: 110).

2. I am indebted to Lambert Zuidervaart for the clue to some of these thoughts, which he developed in a seminar presentation on "Principles of Modal Theorization" (February 1975) as a junior member in aesthetics at the Institute for Christian Studies, Toronto.

3. In an address given at the fifth plenary session of the Fourth Congress on the Enlightenment held at Yale University, July 13-20, 1975, Meyer H. Abrams documented the changes in eighteenth century life which encouraged the evolvement of art-as-such. But Abrams described the fact only to demythologize and relativize the contemplative model holding for art since that era in the West. He exposed most perceptively how "disinterestness" before beauty (Shaftesbury, Kant) was basically a secularized version of the Platonistically conceived *agapé* common to medieval, Christianized Aristotelian theology. But Abrams did not seem to realize the historically normative feature of this development to art-as-such. For an important study of this extremely involved problem, cf. Albert Dresdner, *Die Kunstkritik, Ihre Geschichte und Theorie*, Erster Teil: *Die Enstehung der Kunstkritik* (Munich: F. Bruckmann A.G., 1915).

4. Seldom are the vagaries of etymological twists and turns so clearly documented as the influential shift Kant made on "aesthetic." In the second edition of the *Kritik der reinen Vernunft* (1787), Kant kept and corrected a footnote in the first edition (1781) on his naming analysis of the laws of sensibility, space-time *Anschauungsformen, die transzendentale Aesthetik*. In A21-22 (1781), the assumption is clearly held that "aesthetic" (1) deals with merely empiric sensation, and (2) allows only aposteriori claims. But in B35-36 (1787), Kant hedges and admits another possibility: if we use the term *aesthetic* for affairs of taste, then (1) only the *chief* origins of taste may be *bloss empirisch*—some might not be empiric?—and (2) while taste may never yield *determinative* laws, it might allow some other kind of apriori claims. Maybe, adds Kant to the footnote of 1787, as he readied the new area of Practical Reason for transcendental critique (1788), and shortly before *Kritik der Urteilskraft* was finished (1790), "aesthetic" can be taken partly in a transcendental sense and partly in a psychological sense.

5. For example: Clyde S. Kilby, *Christianity and Aesthetics* (Downers Grove: InterVarsity Press, 1961); Frank E. Gaebelein, "The Aesthetic Problem: Some Evangelical Answers," *Christianity Today*, 9 (No. 11, February 26, 1965): 3-6, and "Toward a Biblical View of Aesthetics," *Christianity Today*, 12 (No. 23, August 30, 1968): 4-6; Nicholas P. Barker, "Christians' Responsibilities in the Arts" (Paper presented for tenure at Covenant College, Tennessee, October 1969), 28 pp.; Leland Ryken, "A Christian Approach to Literature," *Christianity Today*, 13 (December 5, 1969): 10-12.

6. Cf. Francis Hutcheson (1729): "Since then there are such different Powers of Perception, where what are commonly called the *External Senses* are the same; since the most accurate Knowledge of what the External Senses discover, often does not give the Pleasure of Beauty of Harmony, which yet one of a *good Taste* will enjoy at once without much *Knowledge*; we may justly use another Name for these higher, and more delightful Perceptions of Beauty and Harmony, and call the *Power* of receiving such Impressions, an *Internal Sense*. . . . The Internal Sense is, a passive Power of receiving Ideas of Beauty from all Objects in which there is Uniformity amidst Variety" (*An Inquiry into the Origin of our Ideas of*

Beauty and Virtue, Treatise I, sect. 1 & 6). Alexander Gottlieb Baumgarten (1750): "Aesthetics finis est perfectio cognitionis sensitiuae, qua talis. Haec autem est pulchritudo . . ." (*Aesthetica*, §14). Kant (1790): ". . . sein unmittelbares Wohlgefallen an dem Gegenstande sein würde, welches . . . die wesentliche Bedingung des Urteils über Schönheit ist" (*Kritik der Urteilskraft*, §15).

7. Cf. Joseph Addison (1712): ". . . I think I may define [fine taste] to be that faculty of the soul, which discerns the beauties of an author with pleasure, and the imperfections with dislike" (*The Spectator*, §409). Abbé Charles Batteux (1747): "L'intelligence considère ce que les objets sont en eux-mêmes, selon leur essence, sans aucun rapport avec nous. Le goût au contraire ne s'occupe de ces mêmes objects que par rapport à nous. . . . Je puis définir l'intelligence: la faculté de connaître le vrai et le faux, et de les distinguer l'un de l'autre. Et le goût: la facilité de sentir le bon, le mauvais, le médiocre et de les distinguer avec certitude" (*Les beaux-arts réduits à un même principe,* quoted in W. Folkierski, *Entre le Classicisme et le Romanticisme*; [Paris: Edouard Champion, 1925], p. 40.

8. Cf. Karel Kuypers: "Dank der Romantik, die das schöpferische und ursprüngliche Element als unergründlich und an keine verstandesmässige Regel gebunden als wesentlich für alle schöne Kunst und das Kunstwerk verherrlicht und den Geniebegriff noch mehr als zuvor mit dem dichtenden und die die Wirklichkeit durch die Macht der Einbildungskraft umformenden Künstler identifiziert, verschwindet nach Hegel, der von seiner Philosophie des Geistes und der Kunst her diesser Auffassung die erforderlichen philosophische Untermauerung gab, die Notwendigkeit, der Dreiheit Kunst, Kunstwerk und Künstler zur Unterscheidung das Adjektiv 'schön' beizufügen." (*Kants Kunsttheorie und die Einheit der Kritik der Urteilskraft* [London: North-Holland Pub. Co., 1972], p. 26).

9. I am afraid most prooftexting on Beauty is a sorry, slipshod business. For example: Psalm 29:2 is as much and as little a prooftext for kneeling in church as it is for the "beauty of holiness" = ? God?! Psalm 29 is really a command more to the angels! (as in Psalm 148:2) or to heathen god worshippers! (cf. N. H. Ridderbos, *Die Psalmen* [Berlin: Walter de Gruyter, 1972], p. 219), to everything in the whole wide world! to prostrate itself ("Werft euch IHM . . hin!" translates Buber) before the Lord God Yahweh in his terribly majestic Holiness, who is speaking creationally! And Psalm 29 reverberates seven time with *qol YHWH! qol YHWH!* till one remembers Revelation 10:1-4, and any budding Christian aesthetician in his right mind who had been looking for infallible backup information on "Beauty" here would have long ago thrown away notebook, pencil, even his clothes, and full of fear and trembling be pleading like Isaiah 6.

Misuse of Scripture can be corrected passage by passage, if need be, but the trouble lies deeper. Whenever Christians of serious piety look to Scripture for help and read it presupposing (perhaps unknowingly) a gaze-on-God theology, outfitted scholastically with an assumed Substance-and-attributes philosophy, such believers, I think, are bound to go wrong.

This is not the right place to quarrel with the mixed blessing of Biblicism either, but it is wrong, in my judgment, to try to wrestle Scripture texts to the ground to pin down *artistic* and *literary* normativity. Merle Meeter exemplifies the problem in *Literature and the Gospel: Biblical Norms for Literature* (Nutley: Presbyterian and Reformed Pub. Co., 1972), stating: ". . . the inspired and inerrant Word of the True and Holy Covenant God gives the writer, the critic, and the reader much *more* than merely a general faith framework in which to evaluate a work of literature. That the most important literary principles or norms, for structure as well as content, are *also* either definitively enunciated or peerlessly illustrated in the Bible is the thesis of this book"(vii). But near the end of the book comes a last word on the normativity of the Scriptures for the basic principles of literary criticism, with a parenthesis: "(of course, the Bible is not a handbook of poetics and rhetoric, defining such formal features as simile, iambic trimeter, and metonymy) . . ." (pp. 167-8). And one rightly wonders where the *authoritative principles* of rhythm and harmony end and the *formal features* of meter and trope begin, and what happens to the Bible at the dividing line.

Somewhat differently Francis A. Schaeffer also struggles with *Art & the Bible* (Downers Grove: InterVarsity Press, 1973), and writes: "Let me say firmly that *there is no such thing as a godly style or an ungodly style*" (51), but styles do embody certain worldviews (52). Therefore, what should a Christian artist living with his Bible in our secular world do about style? ". . . as a Christian adopts and adapts various contemporary techniques, he must wrestle with the whole question, looking to the Holy Spirit for help to know when to invent, when to adopt, when to adapt and when to not use a specific style at all. This is something each artist wrestles with for a lifetime, not something he settles once and for all. In conclusion, therefore, often we will use twentieth-century art forms, but we must be careful to keep them from distorting the world view which is distinctively ours as Christians. In one way styles are completely neutral. But in another way they must not be used in an unthinking naive way" (pp. 55-6). So as I understand it, God's "propositional revelation" led the Old Testament artists of the temple while sculpting cherubim (18); in this New Testament day, however, God gives us believers the freedom to live by His Spirit, as prudent as snakes and as harmless as doves. But again, *the Bible* seems to fade away at a crucial, directing point somewhere down the line.

The only salvation from such inconclusive impasses, I believe, is for us to get together on a reorientation which sees that one must relate art *and creation* and the Bible. The only *Biblical* way to think through the nature of *art* is to examine *creaturely reality*. Examine creaturely reality as God's revelation, with eyes that are Scripturally-*directed to creaturely reality*. This article means to be continuing that approach found in *40*: 17-24.

10. Much of Dooyeweerd's intuitive, tentative brief for positing "harmony" as the nuclear moment of an irreducible "aesthetic" aspect of reality and experience is vitiated by appeal to what may be merely straightforward "economic" functioning. For example: "That primitive language also *lacks aesthetic* anticipation [which I myself doubt is so as a matter of fact—C.S.], is primarily due to the fact that here the linguistic aspect has *not yet opened* its *economic* anticipatory function" (*11*: 2-140—italics mine). The Dooyeweerdian work of H. J. van Eikema Hommes also seems to be overly glad to mention "aesthetic" in the same breath with "economic." Cf. for example, chapter 18 in *De Elementaire Grondbegrippen der Rechtswetenschap, een juridische methodologie* (Deventer: Kluwer, 1972): ". . . ligt het esthetische, evenals het economische aspect, aan het juridische ten grondslag zodat een rechtsorde, zo min zij blijvend tegen economische wetmatigheden kan ingaan, blijvend in strijd kan zijn met de eisen van de 'Aesthetik des Rechts' (Radbruch)" (p. 469). Cf. also: "Het gaat bij de juridische harmonie of evenredigheid om een juridische verevening van rechtsbelangen, alsmede om een verevening van al of niet onrechtmatige inbreuken daarop. Hier blijkt dan ook onmiddellijk de onverbrekelijke samenhang van de juridische evenredigheid met de juridische economie" (p. 473). "Bij de vraag, op welke wijze de rechtsvormer rechtsbelangen die hem binnen zijn materiële competentiegebied zijn toevertrouwd behoort te behartigen, speelt het beginsel van de juridische economie een constitutieve rol, evenals het hierna te bespreken beginsel van de juridische harmonie of evenredigheid. Ook dit laatste betreft de behartiging van rechtsbelangen, maar dan vooral in positieve zin, terwijl de juridische economie meer de negatieve kant raakt, t.w. wat de rechtsvormer daarbij niet mag doen:geen excessieve belangenbehartiging" (pp. 449-50). One suspects that "harmony" as "de evenredige verbinding en samenstemming van delen tot een schoon geheel" (p. 468) shows up in jural deliberating more as a frugal thrift-calculating-constructive moment, indeed, an opened-up economic analogical function, deemed peculiarly aesthetic only because it is needed by the systematics.

11. While I would still substantially hold to my 1962 formulation of what constitutes art, I should make one modification: "Art is the symbolical objectification of certain meaning aspects of a thing [better: "meaning-realities"—to accept a corrective comment from N. van Til], subject to the law of *allusiveness*." A. T. Kruijff signaled a discrepancy in my earlier

description: "Hoewel Seerveld de 'harmonie' als kernmoment van de kunst afwijst—op historische gronden—meen ik haar in de 'wet van samenhang (coherence) ongeschonden terug te vinden" (*Het Esthetische aspect van onze werkelijkheid*, Werkcollege Systematiek o.l.v. H. van Riessen, n.d., p. 7). As I gradually reform the ambience of "symbolical," in tandem with "allusiveness," I see that "law of *coherence*" was a redundant way of maintaining that "allusiveness" has law-norming character. For my current critical understanding of Cassirer's humanistic distortion of "symbolic form," cf. "The pedagogical strength of a christian methodology in philosophical historiography", in *Social Theory and Practice: Crosscuts and Perspectives*. J. A. L. Taljaard Festschrift (Potchefstroom, 1975).

Bibliography

1. ASCHENBRENNER, Karl, "Aesthetic Theory—Conflict and Conciliation," in: *Journal of Aesthetics and Art Criticism*, 18 (No. 1, September 1959): 90-108.

2. BAHM, Archie J., "Is a Universal Science of Aesthetics Possible?" in: *Journal of Aesthetics and Art Criticism*, 31 (No. 1, Fall 1972): 3-7.

3. BROOKS, Cleanth, *The Well Wrought Urn: Studies in the Structure of Poetry*; New York: Harvest Book HB-11, 1947.

4. CASSIRER, Ernst, *An Essay on Man: An Introduction to a Philosophy of Human Culture*; New York: Doubleday Anchor Book A3, 1944.

5. ———. *The Philosophy of the Enlightenment* (1932), trans. J. P. Pettegrove; Boston: Beacon Press, 1960.

6. CHAMBERS, Frank Pentland, *The History of Taste: An Account of the Revolutions of Art Criticism and Theory in Europe*; New York: Columbia University Press, 1932.

7. COHEN, Marshall, "Aesthetic Essence," in: *Philosophy in America*, ed. Max Black; Ithaca: Cornell University Press, 1965: 115-33.

8. DICKIE, George, *Aesthetics: An Introduction*; New York: Bobbs-Merrill Pegasus Book, 1971.

9. ———. "The Myth of the Aesthetic Attitude," in: *American Philosophical Quarterly*, 1 (No. 1, January 1964): 56-65.

10. ———. "What is Anti-art?" in: *Journal of Aesthetics and Art Criticism*, 33 (No. 4, Summer 1975): 419-21.

11. DOOYEWEERD, Herman, *A New Critique of Theoretical Thought*; Amsterdam: H. J. Paris, 1953-1957. Vol. 2: 107-40, 345-8; Vol. 3: 104-53.

12. DUFRENNE, Mikel, "Is Art Language?" in: *Philosophy Today*, 14 (Fall 1970): 190-200.

13. ———. *The Phenomenology of Aesthetic Experience* (1953), trans. Edward S. Casey et al.; Evanston: Northwestern University Press, 1973.

14. ELTON, W., ed., *Aesthetics and Language*; Oxford: Basil Blackwell, 1954.

15. GADAMER, Hans-Georg, *Wahrheit und Methode: Grundzüge einer philosophischen Hermeneutik* (1960); Tübingen: J. C. B. Mohr (Paul Siebeck), 3 A., 1972.

16. GALLIE, W. B., "Art as an Essentially Contested Concept," in: *Philosophical Quarterly*, 6 (No. 23, April 1956): 97-114.

17. — —. "The Function of Philosophical Aesthetics," in: *Mind*, 57 (No. 227, July 1948): 302-21.

18. GOMBRICH, E. H., *Art and Illusion: A Study in the Psychology of Pictorial Representation*; Princeton University Press, Bollingen series XXXV-5 (1960), 1969.

19. GREENE, Theodore Meyer, *The Arts and the Art of Criticism*; Princeton University Press, 1940.

20. HOPKINS, Gerard Manley, *A Reader*, ed. John Pick; New York: Oxford University Press, 1953.

21. HOSPERS, John, "Problems of Aesthetics," in: *The Encyclopedia of Philosophy*, ed. Paul Edwards; New York: Macmillan Co. & The Free Press, 1967; Vol. 1: 35-56.

22. INGARDEN, Roman, "Phenomenological Aesthetics: An Attempt at Defining its Range," in: *Journal of Aesthetics and Art Criticism*, 33 (No. 3, Spring 1975): 257-69.

23. JESSOP, T. E., "The Definition of Beauty," in: *Proceedings of the Aristotelian Society, New Series*, 33, 1932-33: 159-72.

24. KENNICK, William E., "Does Traditional Aesthetics Rest on a Mistake?" in: *Mind*, 67 (No. 267, June 1958): 317-34.

25. KRISTELLER, Paul Oskar, "The Modern System of Arts" (1951-1952), reprinted in: *Renaissance Thought II: Papers on Humanism and the Arts*; Harper Torchbook TB 1163, 1965: 163-227.

26. KUYPER, Abraham, "Calvinism and Art," in: *Lectures on Calvinism* (1898); Grand Rapids: Wm. B. Eerdmans, 1961: 142-70.

27. LANGER, Suzanne K., *Problems of Art*; New York: Charles Scribner's Sons, 1957.

28. MARGOLIS, Joseph, "The Mode of Existence of a Work of Art," in: *Review of Metaphysics*, 12 (No. 1, September 1958): 26-34.

29. MARITAIN, Jacques, *Creative Intuition in Art and Poetry* (1953); New York: Meridian Book M8, 1966.

30. MUNRO, Thomas, "Aesthetics as Science: Its Development in America," in: *Journal of Aesthetics and Art Criticism*, 9 (No. 3, May 1951): 161-207.

31. OSBORNE, Harold, "Definition and Evaluation in Aesthetics," in: *Philosophical Quarterly*, 23 (January 1973): 15-27.

32. PASSMORE, J. A., "The Dreariness of Aesthetics," in: *Mind*, 60 (No. 239, 1951): 318-35.

33. RADER, Melvin, "Introduction: The Meaning of Art," in: *A Modern Book of Esthetics: An Anthology*; Toronto: Holt, Rinehart & Winston, Inc., 4th edition, 1973: 1-21.

34. ROBERTS, Louise Nisbet, "Is the Study of Aesthetics a Philosophical Enterprise?" in: Tulane Studies in Philosophy, 7 (1958): 129-34.

35. ROOKMAAKER, Hans R., "Ontwerp ener Aesthetica op grondslag der Wijsbegeerte der Wetsidee," in: *Philosophia Reformata*, 11 (No. 3, 1946): 141-67, and 12 (No. 1, 1947): 1-35.

36. ———. "Wetenschap, Aesthetica, Kunst," in: *Tydskrif vir Wetenskap en Kuns* (1949): 79-100.

37. ROSS, William David, *The Right and the Good* (1930); Oxford: Clarendon Press, 1967: 116-31.

38. SAW, Ruth L., *Aesthetics: An Introduction*; New York: Anchor Book NP4, 1971.

39. —— and OSBORNE, Harold, "Aesthetics as a Branch of Philosophy," in: *The British Journal of Aesthetics*, 1 (No. 1, 1960): 8-20.

40. SEERVELD, Calvin, *A Christian Critique of Art and Literature* (1962-63); Toronto: Wedge Publishing Foundation, 1968.

41. ———. *A Turnabout in Aesthetics to Understanding*; Toronto: Institute for Christian Studies, 1974.

42. SIBLEY, Frank N., "Aesthetic Concepts," in: *Philosophical Review*, 68 (October 1959): 421-50.

43. STACE, W. T., *The Meaning of Beauty: A Theory of Aesthetics*; London: Grant Richards & Humphrey Toulmin, 1929.

44. STOLNITZ, Jerom, " 'Beauty': Some Stages in the History of an Idea," in: *Journal of the History of Ideas*, 22 (No. 2, April-June 1961): 185-204).

45. TASHIRO, Tom, "Ambiguity as Aesthetic Principle," in: *Dictionary of the History of Ideas*; New York: Charles Scribner's Sons, 1973, Vol. 1: 48-60.

46. TATARKIEWICZ, W., "The Great Theory of Beauty and Its Decline," in: *Journal of Aesthetics and Art Criticism*, 31 (No. 2, Winter 1972): 165-80.

47. ———. *Modern Aesthetics: History of Aesthetics*, Vol. 3; The Hague: Mouton, 1974.

48. TUFTS, James Hayden, "On the Genesis of the Aesthetic Categories," in: *The Decennial Publication*; University of Chicago Press, 1902, Vol. 3: 5-12.

49. URMSON, J. O., "What Makes a Situation Aesthetic?" in: *Proceedings of the Aristotelian Society, Supplement*; 31 (1957): 75-92.

50. VAN DEN BERG, D. J., *'N Kritiese Besinning op die Moontlike Invloed van die Vorm-Materie Grondmotief op die Griekse Beeldhoukuns*; Bloemfontein, 1972. Masters thesis, mimeograph.

51. VAN DER LEEUW, G., *Wegen en Grenzen: De Verhouding van Religie en Kunst* (1932/1955), 3rd edition revised by E. L. Smelik; Amsterdam: H. J. Paris, 1955.

52. WEITZ, Morris, "The Role of Theory in Aesthetics," in: *Journal of Aesthetics and Art Criticism*, 15 (No. 1, September 1956): 27-35.

53. WELLEK, René, and AUSTIN, Warren, *Theory of Literature* (1942); New York: Harcourt, Brace & Co., 1949.

54. WILLIAMS, Raymond, *Culture & Society 1780/1950* (1958); New York: Harper & Row paperback, 1966.

55. WITTGENSTEIN, Ludwig, *Lectures and Conversations on Aesthetics, Psychology and Religious Beliefs*, ed. Cyril Barrett. Los Angeles: University of California Press, 1967.

56. ZIFF, Paul, "The Task of Defining a Work of Art," in: *Philosophical Review*, 62 (No. 1, 1953): 58-78.

Counting, Number Concept and Numerosity

ANTHONY TOL

I. Introduction

In both the elementary and intuitive reflections on, and the highly specialized analysis of, the notion of number, attention is inevitably concentrated on the *natural numbers*. In everyday reckoning, computing and counting, the natural numbers are obviously central. Without some knowledge of the natural numbers, these daily operations would be quite impossible and wholly devoid of meaning. In the higher regions of number theory proper, where different types of numbers are systematically investigated and mutually interrelated, the natural numbers also play a pivotal role. Every student of mathematics knows of the various ways in which the complex numbers, real numbers, rationals, and integers can be defined as constructive systems based upon the natural numbers.[1] These systematic results are due to the efforts of many mathematicians of the latter half of the nineteenth century, of which the best known are W. R. Hamilton, L. Kronecker, K. Weierstrass, G. Cantor and R. Dedekind. Their work has also given a new poignancy to the problem of how the natural numbers are themselves to be understood. This problem will be part of the more general problem to be discussed in this essay.

The natural numbers, then, play a central role both in practice and in mathematical theory. This central role, however, must not be thought identical in both of these concerns. In reckoning, computing, etc.—which may, for convenience, be grouped together under the notion of counting, since this at least is what each practical operation involves[2]—the numbers are intimately related to the effectuation of the counting act and serve as predicates of the *judgment* into which counting issues: there are n objects here. In theoretical pursuits, however, the natural numbers may be thought of as the residue of number-theoretical analyses, as the *conception* of containing factors at all niveaux of number systems. They serve then as the building blocks for the synthetic elucidations and constructions of the diverse number systems.

These distinct roles also call up definite differences in the intellectual context in which the natural numbers are thought. Counting, with its effectuated activity and judgmatic issue, involves thought in its function of *ascertainment.* Thought is operative here in an overt way. But in theoretical pursuits, with their analysis and synthesis of number knowledge, the context is fixed by patterns of logical implication and inference. The actual operation of thought is here much more covert, involving the natural numbers, so it seems, only as terms *apperceived,* passively understood. Thus the context of the one is practical, while the other is theoretical. It may even be tempting to say that the one is of the *Vernunft*, the other of the *Verstand.* In any case, it seems that any attempt to find a common ground between these two roles and contexts of the natural numbers only lands one in confusion of thought and in an intermingling of matters that are best kept apart. Is the fact that they both involve natural numbers then only a formal agreement between them? Are natural numbers only empty symbols, as the influential formalistic school of D. Hilbert would have us believe? Must any reflection on the notion of number always presuppose a dualism like, say, that of reason and understanding? Or is a different type of contrast fundamental here?

Cardinals and ordinals

To complicate matters, an added feature which must not be neglected is that the natural numbers can be taken either as cardinals or as ordinals. Now, the arithmetics of both the (finite) cardinals and the (finite) ordinals are exactly identical, so that a formalist understanding of the natural numbers is not thereby affected. But formalists, who think of numbers only as symbols within an operative or arithmetical context, then cannot account for the distinction between cardinality and ordinality. This is more of a liability than an asset, for they thereby neglect features of the natural numbers which are evidently relevant and distinct.

Foundational thinkers of a non-formalistic stamp have generally *either* split the two features of ordinality and cardinality over the dualism of the practical and the theoretical, respectively, and then attempted a mathematical reduction of the latter from the former, *or* taken both features into account in their understanding of the number concept, but then argued that the role of number in counting is irrelevant in foundational reflection. An example of the former alternative is to be found in

H. von Helmholtz and the (so-called) intuitionists; the latter in the (so-called) logicists, G. Frege and B. Russell. On both counts a brief word.

For Von Helmholtz counting is the true beginning for foundational reflection because counting is "the foundation of the most fruitful, surest and most exact of scientific methods" (*8*: 17). Writing in a period when psychologism was in fashion, Von Helmholtz also thought that all knowledge, scientific or otherwise, required, as ultimate foundation, to be understood in how knowledge is acquired by the human subject. The *ordo essendi* follows from a psychologically conceived *ordo cognoscendi*. Number knowledge, in a systematic sense, is acquired through the process of counting. Since counting requires that consciousness retains the units of separate objects passed along in the count, essential in this process, he thought, is the sequential, time-relation of one thing following upon another, whereby one then expresses the words "first," "second," "third," etc. Counting thus delivers immediately and primarily the idea of ordinal numbers. Cardinals are *derivatives* of this process, appearing as the correlate of the last ordinal of any counting enactment. Number theory, in which the cardinals are predominant, is then a posterior development from counting with its supposedly exclusive involvement of the ordinal numbers. The systematic inadequacy of this position will become evident below.[3]

In the Frege-Russell position, Russell's is the more explicit. Thus I shall refer to him alone. In *The Principles of Mathematics* (*11*: 114, 133), Russell mentions and analyzes counting only briefly, with a view of getting it out of the way for the more relevant matters at hand. Reacting strongly to the psychologism and British idealism of his contemporaries, Russell is adamant in his rejection of any reference to "mind" in the analysis of the foundations of arithmetic (*11*: 4). He wants to base mathematical knowledge on pure thought, on universals, or on the notions of pure logic alone. His reduction of the very notion of number to logical notions is a problem in itself and will be touched on below. When Russell does analyze counting, at least the logically relevant aspect of it (*11*: 133), he finds that in the predication of number through counting, the very notion of number is presupposed rather than defined or constructed in the process. Being interested only in a logically defensible definition of number, the approach via counting is then, for him circular and thus obviously inadequate, In Russell's definition of the natural numbers, there is, however, no question of prority between cardinals and ordinals. The latter are logically more complex than the former, but each is defined independently of the other. At this point we only take note of the fact that for Russell, counting contributes nothing to the understanding of numbers, whether as cardinals or as ordinals. Their diversity is of such a nature that foundational analysis may completely reject counting as irrelevant.

The main problem of this essay can now be formulated. Given that one is after an "understanding" of the natural numbers, is the distinction between the natural numbers in counting and in their theoretical use of such a nature that one must conclude to a separation of both, either by placing counting in a position of priority to theoretical understanding or by rejecting it as irrelevant to such an understanding? If these alternatives are found to be inadequate, what is then a more adequate relation between these as involving the natural numbers, and is there a unifying "moment" about which the whole matter centers? From the point of view of exposition, it seems easiest to begin with an analysis of counting. The treatment will then, of itself, lead to the theoretical concept of number.

II. Counting

In his extensive article "Foundations of Mathematics," Charles Parsons, when coming to the discussion of number, begins with the operation of counting. He states (*10*: 194):

> In a simple case of carefully counting a collection of objects, we perhaps look at and point to each one successively, and with each of these directions of the attention we think of or pronounce one of a standard series of symbols (numerals) in its place in a standard ordering of these symbols. We are careful to reach each of these objects once and only once in the process. We thus set up a *one-to-one correspondence* between the objects and a certain segment of the series of numerals. We say that the number of objects in the collection is ________, where the blank is filled by the last numeral of the series.

This discussion, so far, is straightforward enough. However, he presupposes that when counting, there is a series of numerals available. And since counting involves setting up a one-to-one correspondence between the objects counted and these numerals, the latter become important to him. He thus continues his account:

> Before pursuing this matter further, let us examine the series of numerals itself. We have certain initial symbols and rules for constructing further symbols whose application can be iterated indefinitely. We could simplify the situation in actual language and suppose that there is one initial symbol, say "/", and a generating operation, concatenation of another "/", so that the numerals will be /, //, ///, ////, ... It is not clear, however, that it is merely a matter of "practical convenience" that ordinary numerals are, in the long run, considerably more condensed: if a string of several million

"/'s" were offered as a result of counting, one would have to count *them* to learn what the number was.

This last consideration should have put Parsons more on his guard than his vague hesitation indicates. For indeed there is something seriously amiss in his account. Not only would several million "/'s" have to be counted anew, but I think that even offered as few as nine or ten "/'s," we would require an explicit count. But what would such a count yield? According to Parsons, only another series of numerals placed in one-to-one correspondence with the given "/'s"! Parsons overlooks this threatening infinite regress and continues his account by concentrating on the one-to-one correspondence and its role in defining equivalence classes. What makes his discussion of counting so inadequate in itself is that nowhere does it appear that counting is an act of synthesis, involving, as at least Von Helmholtz stated, the conscious retention of past steps. Counting would seem at least to involve an accumulative process, otherwise the blank in the concluding statement of the count (the number of objects in the collection is ________) will never be filled.

It is quite clear from Parsons' further treatment that he was not seriously after an adequate account of counting at all. For by dwelling on the one-to-one correspondence, he finds that each numeral can be placed in one-to-one correspondence with other numerals, so that a numeral can be taken as a mark of identity for the quantity of objects or marks involved. The mark of identity identifies that *quantity*, and so introduces, as he calls it, an "abstract entity" which is the number that quantity exemplifies. Parsons' is a case of introducing numbers through counting, but in a way which leaves essential facets of counting completely out of account.

Discernible features of counting

If one reflects on the intricacies of the counting procedure, then through a careful analysis one should be able to distinguish its characteristic features as well as come to some understanding of what the unity of the procedure is. There are, I think, at least four discernible features. First of all there must be a collection of objects, mutually distinct and remaining so for the duration of the count. Secondly, since one is to pass along these objects in the course of counting, the objects must be taken in serial order. The "rule" according to which the objects are ordered can be chosen in many ways. But the rule must at least leave the objects distinct when so ordered, as well as avoid the repetition of any object of the collection. The actual passing along the objects, thirdly, requires that the objects passed by are "retained" or indexed with some mark or symbol. In practice, one usually enunciates the words "one," "two," etc. But this combines two facets of the counting act into one. The indexing procedure could just as well be done by placing marks on paper, as Parsons does, and in fact some such procedure is essential when the objects are themselves passing moments, like musical notes or the tolling of a bell. The indexing involves the establishing of a one-to-one correspondence with the objects counted and the index symbols. It is this feature which Parsons takes as being central. But there is also, fourthly, the final judgment as to "how many" objects there are. For the sake of convenience, we may call these features the collection, the rule, the indexation, and the judgment, respectively, of the counting enactment.

Collections. It is desirable to elucidate briefly each of these features. That there should be a collection of mutually distinct objects is obvious, as is also the requirement that they remain distinct. One gets nowhere in attempting to count water drops on a hot plate which evaporate before the count is finished. Nor is one likely to succeed in counting agitated mercury globules which split and coagulate continually. It is required that the objects of the collection retain their distinct being in distinction from each other. This need not be formulated with any heavy-sounding "principle of identity" which holds come what may. The requirement would be met when the distinctions between the objects hold at least for the duration of the count. A weaker "principle of differentiation" would suffice. In usual practice, differentiation in space or, if the objects are themselves on the move, as with the tolling of a bell, differentiation in time suffices. Either way, the requirement is one concerning the objects, and thus holds exclusively for what may be called the object-side of the event in which the counting act takes place.

Subject-to-object rule. The rule according to which the objects are passed along also affects the objects. But this is not grounded in the object-side. Any order will do, as long as the order followed allows no repetitions. The order chosen lies with the discretion of the person counting. This factor of order is not always expressly formulated, for the actual effectuation of the count, when passing along the objects, silently complies to an implicitly chosen order. But when explicitly expressed, it will be a rule, decided upon by the subject, such as to leave the objects distinct and without repetition. This last condition, the exemption of repetition, binds the rule to the objects. Such a rule, then, though grounded in the subject, relates the subject to the objects in a way relevant for counting. It may be said to specify a subject-to-object connection in the event of counting.

Object-to-subject indexation. The third requirement is the indexing of the objects passed by. With this feature we must take into explicit account the function of consciousness in counting and its mode of operation. In counting one must "attend" to each of the objects successively and, when passing on to the next object, retain the oneness of distinctness of the object considered and gather it together with the oneness of each successive object, likewise retained. Here memory and present, attentive consciousness supplement each other. To make the count "manageable," an indexing procedure is introduced whereby the distinctness of each object passed by is correlated one-to-one with some symbol so as to aid the synthesis. This correlation is consciousness' way not only of making the prodecure of the count manageable to itself but also of accentuating the fact that only the distinctness of the objects as composing the quantity of the collection is here relevant. Consciousness can attend to many features of the objects. But in counting, only the aspect constitutive of its quantity is relevant. Thus the transference of the distinctness of the objects into symbols, through the one-to-one correspondence, is the means whereby consciousness fixates its selective, quantitative interest.

This indexing procedure is perhaps made more clear when distinguished from two other matters with which it might easily be confused. In the first place, this indexing could be taken to be an abstraction procedure, involving the "universalization" of the selected component. But this is here not the case. The selection meant here is not so much a "drawing away"—as the word *abstraction* etymologically suggests—as expressly ignoring those features or qualities present in the objects which are irrelevant to counting. The indexing procedure remains within a *concrete context* involving the given objects, and this blocks any attempted "universalization" of the quantity in question into a number. Consciousness is here only codifying the quantitativeness of the objects involved so as to elicit just the feature of their distinctness of many-ness in disregard of whatever else they may involve. Numbers, as universals, are not laid up ready-made in the things that exemplify them, merely waiting to be drawn away and admired in themselves.[4]

This holds also for the number "one." Though we speak of a "one-to-one correspondence," this does not presuppose the number "one." The concrete context, in which this one-to-one indexing procedure is applied, here also avoids such an interpretation. The indexing, as selection procedure, presupposes both the distinctness of the objects as guaranteed by the principle of differentiation and the non-repetition of the objects as laid down by the rule. This makes it possible to refer to the objects of the collection as being merely *a* this and *a* this and *a* that, etc. The indexing procedure symbolizes this sort of (numerical) distinctness in such a way that *a* distinguished object will correspond to *a* symbol. This feature of indexing cannot be separated from the previous two features required in the counting act. But it must also not be made to be more than it is. It does not "deliver" numbers, not even the number "one." The phrase "one-to-one correspondence," therefore, though it involves the *word* "one," does not involve the *number* "one." This will become more clear when the number concept is discussed below.

A second point to be clear on is the peculiar role of consciousness in the indexing procedure. It might be thought that this involves what may be called "categorization" or the laying on of a categorial scheme, in this case, the category of quantity. But this, I think, misjudges the sort of "activity" required of consciousness at this point. The view in question is common to many forms of idealism in which the object, if recognized at all, is made completely dependent, in its structure and knowable features, upon forms of sensibility and/or forms of thought. But this is, in the first place, made irrelevant by the fact that it is not actual numbers as predicates—i.e. as things which are found in the category of quantity—that are required in the indexing procedure (including the number one). Secondly, the very notion of quantity—in distinction from the various determinate quantities—is not found laid up in the mind but is given with the fact that the world is experienced in the plural, however indefinite and changing the experienced quantities may be. We are here trying to analyze counting, and unless the world has the feature of quantity on its face, the very relevance for any counting whatsoever is non-existent. Given this presupposition, we then need to account for the fact that consciousness elicits this quantitativeness and selects it from the multivarious other features of the world. In the indexing procedure, consciousness is discriminating quantitativeness and prehends this as data in its own right precisely through the correlated indices. This procedure, though involving an "activity" of consciousness, is unintelligible unless seen as involving an initial *complying* of consciousness to the objects, whereby it then selects that feature of the objects which accords with its discriminating interest. This selective complying of consciousness to the objects is what is codified in the one-to-one indexing correspondence. Thus, in summary we may say that this third feature of counting is an object-to-subject constituent in the procedure of counting.

Judgment. The fourth feature of counting is that of judgment. Counting issues into a judgment in which the counting act is rounded off. The judgment "There are x many objects in this collection" obviously presupposes all of the other three features distinguished. But it must be understood in relation to these. Otherwise one could land in the difficulty of Parsons' account: if the judgment is merely thought of as a conjunction of the symbols by which consciousness exposes the quantitativeness of the collection, then it is all too easy to find here the requirement of a new act of counting to determine the number of the symbols, and this would lead to an infinite regress. Everything depends here on attaining an adequate insight into the nature of the judgment which results from counting.

It is common, and not incorrect, to think of judging as involving predication. This is readily understandable if there are predicates available to be predicated. It is in this vein that Parsons spoke of "a standard series of symbols (numerals)." They are, in the final analysis, the predicates involved in numerical judgments. But if this were the last word, judgment would be little more than an almost mechanical process of subjecting something—in this case, the objects of a collection—to a chosen predicate. The only responsibility which the person making the judgment would have is to choose the adequate predicate. And adequacy, one might suppose, is acquired through the procedure of applying the one-to-one correspondence between the objects to receive the predicate and the symbols which are or constitute possible predicates. The fatal fault of such reasoning lies in excluding any account of the actual knowledge acquired through counting. For we must then "know" the predicate to be applied if the judgment is to be at all relevant to our knowledge. But the symbolic character of indexation has no such "knowing" dimension about it. The symbols, even if considered as numerals, are not knowledge-laden; they only index. By pursuing this line of thought, one only lands again in the infinite regress just mentioned: to know the symbols for their quantity, one would have to actually count them!

To circumvent this difficulty, it is best to pursue an entirely different approach to understanding what is involved in the issue of a count. Accordingly, I reject the idea that predicates are here available. Only the symbols by which the objects of the collection are indexed are present. This will mean that the role of the person making the judgment is considerably greater than merely choosing an adequate predicate. One could describe the view here to be taken as one involving the constitution of a knowledge-laden predicate by means of the index symbols. The constitution is entirely the doing of the person involved in counting and thus, seen from the point of view of counting as a complex event, constitutes the subject-side of that event.

The constitution here in question is one which takes place throughout the entire act of counting. Throughout the act, one is ascertaining the quantity involved in the collection by actually passing through the manyness which the quantity involves. Having attended to the "first" object and noted it as "one," one comes to the next and notes it as a "second" "one" in relation to the first. But together—here memory prevents the first "one" from slipping into the past—they form a quantity in its own right, which is known as that quantity. Then the next "one" appears, and it is "third" with respect to the previous "ones," but together with them they constitute another distinct quantity. This process is continued through the entire collection. Each new object receives its mark—insofar the one-to-one correspondence is here involved—but it also contributes to the quantitative totality of the collection. It is precisely in understanding this contribution of each object of the collection to the latter's quantity that the mark which indexes each object as one is laden with meaning respecting the quantity of the collection as a whole.

This account may seem trivial and even circular, in view of the cardinals and ordinals used throughout. But then one must examine whether or not one still proceeds from preconceived predicates. For the words "first," "second," "third," etc. and their corresponding cardinals have here no pre-assigned meaning. Or rather, these words are here meant in their function of capturing either the differences between each object with respect to its relatedness to its predecessors or the corresponding differences in the various possible quantities, respectively. The point here is that all the words used in counting have a (functional) meaning relevant to the various phases of counting, through which one comes to the final judgment. The counting act enables one, through its execution, to become *acquainted* with these meanings, and through that acquaintance the person counting is able to ascertain, through the progressive synthesis of the marks, the predicate which "fits" the collection in question. The predicate here is but the precipitate of the intuited meanings whereby, for the person counting, the marks of the objects have been grasped knowingly into a synthesis of one meaning. That predicate, as one meaning, is the quantitative knowledge adequate for the collection in question. That predicate can then function in the final judgmatic issue of the count and embody the actual *number* of objects in the collection.

The numbers of counting and the natural numbers

This view of the judgment which counting involves has several ramifications. In the first place it becomes clear that counting, as an event with the four features here distinguished, has a unity of effectuation. For the meaning of the predicate must be ascertained while actually proceeding with the count. In that process the objects are ordered as they are passed by, and with the passing of each object attention notes it (on paper or in thought) as one, i.e. as *a* number of the group being counted, thereby correlating the object with a symbol. But these ones, in being known as one and retained in the accumulating synthesis, each contribute to the final synthesis in which the ones collectively have the meaning which expresses the quantity of the collection concerned. The four features are thus distinguishable but not separable. This also precludes the infinite regress of having to count marks which are themselves required in any counting act.

Secondly, the numbers of counting, as they appear from our analysis of counting, are neither available "entities" nor mere formal marks or symbols. They are the deposit of the mind's direct involvement. Without the actual knowing, this knowledge content would be nothing but the dead marks which index the objects. Numbers in *this* sense may be viewed—to borrow a term from "intuitionism"—as "constructions." They are a product of synthesis. But this synthesis is not the *a priori*, free mental construction of which Brouwer speaks. Here the synthesis is effectuated in the overt act of counting. Also, the synthesis is possible only with, and on the basis of, the other features of counting we have discussed. Thus it is structured and conditioned, and not the result of the free application of the will.[5]

One may wonder whether, when the number knowledge here meant has been acquired, it can then serve as making available predicates for judgment. This is undoubtedly the case. Anyone who has learned to count will use the natural numbers as the correlates to the objects of the collection being counted. But one must ask in what *sense* the natural numbers are available here. If they are merely viewed as symbols, the question recurs whether counting involves any knowledge content. If they are viewed as "abstract entities," i.e. as universals or as concepts, then one must at least admit that, when finding there are, say, fifteen marbles in a bag, one does not predicate the "fifteen itself" to the collection. At most one has found out which number concept is exemplified by the collection. But even in this sense, the predication is not purely external. For, while counting, one passes through the collection, discerning its specific quantity. Thus the number predicate which "fits" the collection is there in its role of providing the content of the known specific quantity discerned. It seems that this is the primary meaning of the numbers of counting. In what sense the predicate is more than a meaning is, *as concerns counting*—or any judging enacted or based on direct experience—an extraneous question.[6]

This last remark points out a direction for understanding the relation between counting and the natural numbers. Foundational directions in which the role of consciousness and knowing have been unduly accentuated, whether in a psychological-empiricist or a transcendental sense, have generally sought to approach the natural numbers through counting or, if considered less overtly, through an intellectual and even an *a priori* act. Such approaches have a rather odious philosophical ambiguity. They confuse, or intentionally identify, the structure of knowledge—in this case, the structure of the natural numbers—with the structure of the empirical or transcendental subjective act through which knowledge is acquired or may possibly be acquired. This latter structure is what has been analyzed in this essay so far. But we have had no indications to see in this structure any analysis of the natural numbers themselves, as *concepts* in their own right. When the two structures are identified (or confused), the structure of *what* is known is not distinguished from the procedural structure involved in *how* it is known, with the result that the "what" follows upon, and is made a direct result of, the "how."[7] With respect to the understanding of number, such an indistinction has confusing consequences. Evidently, the issue of the counting act must then involve the very essence of number itself. But since the counting act is a synthesis of sequential moments of attention, the empiricist will think that the synthesized issue has the character of the plurality he went through in the counting act. Numbers can then hardly be distinguished from the pebbles or sticks counted. Their number is there in itself, just as the pebbles and sticks are there. The idealist or transcendentalist, being more inclined to build and deduce things from out of himself rather than finding them in the world, concludes that the effectuated, structural number knowledge is, in fact, the generation or deduction of the very idea of plurality as category to which the world complied in unendingly different possible "measures" of plurality.

The confusion harbored here, so effectively criticized by G. Frege,[8] may be summarized as follows: if plurality is at once that specific numerical universal, is it then not impossible to have that plurality itself appear in the plural? If the plurality of the fingers on my right hand is the universal five itself, what about the plurality of fingers on my left hand? We require here a relation which the positions in question seem to deny, namely, that of exemplification and its converse, characterization. Any given plurality may be thought of as exemplifying its specific number, but it is not that number. It has the *character* of that number and thus, in itself, does refer beyond its own illustration to its general number. But as long as one is concerned with counting and with the given plurality of objects which a subject seeks to know, then these references to the universal number exemplified by the plurality, though implicit, are not present in consciousness when actually proceeding with counting. Even less are any idea of the numbers themselves present in counting.

This is not to minimize the relevance of counting when understanding number. Numbers, as introduced so far, are present in counting only via the mode of approach which counting is. The meaning of numbers as they appear in counting is particular—not in the sense of this particular number over against another particular number, but in the sense of expressing only the given plurality's quantity. Language also brings this to expression. The number "one," as used in counting, has the meaning of an indefinite unity; the number "two," that of "couple"; the number "three," that of "trio"; etc. These words have more evidently a particular meaning, without the universality of *the* numbers "one," "two," "three," etc. In this sense, counting gives no deduction of the universality of numbers. But it does enable us, significantly, to introduce the natural numbers as meanings entering numerical judgments, and something of the sequence of these natural numbers. If these meanings are not conceptualized in counting, that only means that one must look to different procedures for grasping the nature of a number as concept. Counting is indispensible for its immediate, intuitive knowledge of number and for its hint of exemplifying more general matters. But the latter require different modes of thought to make them appear.

This conclusion can be supported by another consideration. The elucidation of number through counting requires the introduction of the language of effectuations, of active subjects dealing with immediate objects. Are the natural numbers thus elucidated cardinal or ordinal? A first response is that this question cannot be answered, for cardinality and ordinality are hardly notions approachable in the language of effectuations. Be that as it may, one must still realize that the numbers of counting are really ordinal and cardinal in one. The very act of counting requires a *sequential* passage along the objects, but at the same time they are retained so as to constitute a *compresent* many. Both factors play their role in how the final judgment is formed, and thus also in the meaning of the number predicate of that judgment. Since counting is an effectuation, these two factors, which we earlier called the subject-to-object and object-to-subject connections, cannot come forward in their own right. They *mediate* in the procedure of counting, but place no exclusive stamp on the numerical result. To consider the numbers of counting as ordinals—recalling the position of Von Helmholtz and the intuitionists—lacks, I think, all basis when counting is at all more than superficially analyzed, and when one does not proceed *a priori* from the exclusive claim of a subjectivist method. The analysis here offered sees in counting a concentration upon concrete and immediately acquired numerical knowledge. Thus, through counting one can know the natural numbers as specific meanings, but not what numbers are generally, nor what number in general is.

Counting as event

Before proceeding to these general topics, the foregoing needs to be rounded off. Counting as event involves a subject-side and an object-side and two different types of relatedness or reference: a subject-to-object reference and an object-to-subject reference. But it was argued that this event is an actual enactment, and thus it must be more than just these structural features alone. Any description of this more than structural facet of a knowing act is bound to rely to some degree on metaphor. We shall think of this actual enactment as "spanning" these features and as giving "tension" to their mutual relevance, "holding" them together. We said already that memory is involved. This memory may here be understood in its function of retaining the objects of the collection being counted, but only in the way relevant for counting, i.e. as distinct units, indexed by the one-to-one correspondence. The objects themselves need not be recalled. Thus we have here a spanning of the object-side of the event (the objects being counted) and the object-to-subject selective compliance of consciousness through which the objects are codified with an index. Memory here is the *retention* of the objects as distinct units. Because the counting act is concrete, memory is thought to be concentrated on the objects, while the one-to-one indexation mediates the concentration.

Counting is also a forward-directed activity. This forward direction follows the sequential order of the objects, an order chosen by the subject. In following this order, the judgmatic aspect of the act is also developing in that the quantitative specificity of the predicate is thereby being formed. This forward-directedness is a kind of "*protention*"[9] which spans and brings into relevant connection the judgmatic subject-side and the subject-to-object relatedness (sequential order of the objects as chosen by the subject) of the counting event. But here the order followed is mediatory to the accumulative or synthetic development of the judgmatic subject-side. Retention and protention are, however, but facets of the kind of *attention* which spans the whole event as one enactment.

The attention which spans the whole counting enactment in its time duration is at the same time the basis for understanding the peculiar character of the counting act and the peculiar character of the number knowledge which it "produces." Attention in itself is, I think, not so terribly important. It denotes an engagement of the individual mind with whatever it is attendant upon. But this formulation makes one think too readily of a subject-object relation, which is here not intended.[10] It would be more adequate to think of attention as being a "concentration about" some point where the "tension" is "at." The whole counting enactment, with its subject-side and its object-side and concomitant memory retention and judgmatic protention is in concentration about something, and this "concentration about" may be taken in a double sense. In the first place, it concentrates about the enactor, the individual ego operative in the counting event, which may be thought of as standing under the whole event in that it makes it possible. But it is not as bare (transcendental) condition that the person—ego[11]—is present. It is *enacting*, i.e. it wishes to accomplish something which the final phase of the act, the judgmatic phase, will close off as accomplished fact. The act requires direction if the attention is to bring about a resolution which will bring the tension to rest. And that rest appears only when the judgment becomes an assertion as to the "how many" of the collection involved. Thus the whole situation seems to be that of an actual ego, alive and tensed, which proceeds *from* a state of inquiry (how many?) *to* a state of assertion (that many!). This effectuation may be thought of as led by an "epistemic concern" and is, I think, operative in any sort of engaged knowledge acquisition. But the effectuation of counting is one where the ego stands under a situation in which the tension is spanned across moments of a quantitative character. Thus the epistemic concern of the ego here resolves itself, via the counting enactment, into number knowledge. To know, says D. H. T. Vollenhoven somewhere, is to be in a situation of rest.

The numbers, which are the meaning predicates in the asserted judgment and which the enactor has acquired, may now be understood as the fitting precipitate of the tensed involvement of the inquiring ego in the quantitatively structured event. For the precipitate is itself formed through the structural features of the event. The whole event acquires its distinct character from the quantitativeness of the structural features and thus yields number knowledge. But these structural features are here but the thoroughfare for an actual, individual ego, operative within an actually given collection to be counted. The ego may claim no more than that *this* collection is understood to have *this* particular determinative quantitative extent. There is no generality to this number knowledge; there is only a qualified, engaged understanding.

The attention, then, which spans the whole counting act and brings it to a unity of accomplishment is what might be called an *ego numero*—a self which, in a quantitatively structured situation, is effectuating a count. Since the ego is clearly not bound to understand and know only in numerically qualified situations, the character of the counting situation is determined not by the ego but by the numerically qualified situation. Though I by no means wish to substantialize this character—indeed, it is the character or sustaining meaning *of an effectuation*—it could perhaps be termed "numero-sity." This notion of numerosity will be filled out in an important way in the discussion of the number concept proper.

III. Number concept[12]

The analysis of the concept of number very influential today is that given by Russell. I shall begin by sketching his view and then critically look at what it contains.

Russell has directed his analysis of number with a view to obtaining a definition of number. The details of this definition are well known.[13] Its novelty lies in first establishing a relation of similarity between classes through corresponding the elements of one class one-to-one with those of another class. Such a similarity establishes the notion of "having as many elements as." This notion does not presuppose the number concept, not even that of the number one, although the *word* "one" does occur. Its occurrence has the same meaning as discussed earlier of distinguished but indefinite unity.

A situation which exemplifies the notion "having as many elements as" is one where, at a conference, it is not known whether there are enough chairs for all the participants. One could, of course, count the people and the available chairs. But it would be simpler to have each participant occupy one chair. This establishes a one-to-one correspondence between the class of participants and the class of chairs. When all are seated, with no chairs unused, the one class then "has as many elements as" the other.

This notion of similarity, secondly, then functions as criterion for classifying classes into sets of similar classes. Thus the set of classes similar to the class consisting of the fingers on a human hand will contain the class consisting of the toes of a human foot. But it will not contain the class of fingers of both hands, since this class is not similar to that of the class of fingers on just one hand. Every possible class is then classified within some one, and only one, set of which the containing members are all mutually similar. Such a set is generally termed an equivalence class. An Equivalence class is evidently related to the number which expresses the quantity of each of the containing classes. Rather than assume that there is such an entity as the number to which each of the mutually similar classes of the equivalence class are related, Russell thought that each equivalence class in itself fulfills all the requirements demanded of numbers. Thus, the number "two" is then the class of all couples, "three," that of all trios, etc. Number in general is then simply "anything which is the number of some class" (*12*: 19).

Any understanding of this definition stands and falls with how the notions "class" and "the relation of similarity between classes" are understood. Russell tried to define these in yet more general terms which he thought were of a purely logical character. This further step, which involves a "logicistic reduction" of number, is problematic, and not everyone is agreed on its success.

But waiving for the moment the question whether Russell is indeed successful, it is easy to cast doubt upon his enterprise. For example, every married couple must fall within the class of all couples by which the number "two" is defined. But a divorce which dissolves the marriage also removes that couple from eligible membership in the class of all couples. Thus the number "two" changes with every marriage and with every divorce. It changes also with the birth of any twins. A definition which changes through such non-logical contingencies can hardly be termed purely logical.

Classes

To make headway in understanding the notion of a class, it is best to have clearly in mind reasons why some notion of a class is required in understanding the concept of number. It is tempting to think of number as derivable by a simple method of abstraction. One could then consider any given collection of things, think away its aesthetic, perceptible, physical, etc. properties and qualities, and then have its plurality remain. This will then be the number of the collection. A number is then only a "multitude composed of units."[14]

This type of argumentation presupposes that the number of a collection is a property of the collection, being of the same status as its color, weight and aesthetic appeal. But this overlooks entirely the generality which the concept of number must have, as discussed earlier. Such an abstraction of the number is not essentially different from the number knowledge gained by counting the given collection. We then know *that* collection to have *that* many elements. But we are no step closer in understanding that number as a concept. Another collection may also have that many elements. The thing here is to understand why the same number holds in both cases. Counting both collections only makes us conclude that their number is the same, not why this should be so.

Though the plurality of a collection is not the same as the number therein exemplified, it does provide a step along the way of coming to the number concept. To see this requires a more careful account of how we are to proceed from a given collection to its plurality and subsequently to its number. Some notion of a class can then be shown to be vital.

First of all, how is a collection to be thought?[15] A collection has elements, but only such elements as are eligible or theoretically possible members. Theoretically, a collection is given when a specification holds through which membership is determined. In practice such specification is most often entirely implicit. Marbles in a bag form a collection because of their being "in the bag." The books on my desk form a collection because of their being "on my desk." Men taller than six feet form a collection because of a shared characteristic as to their height. In each case, the specification of a collection is a shared feature of the elements; it is a *notio communis*. It specifies the unity of the collection, and even if the specification is such as to limit the extent of the collection, it still pertains primarily to its intensional unity.[16]

Though specification of a collection discriminates its members from its non-members, it does not discriminate between the members mutually. Also, it may be (and it is theoretically probably always the case) that more than one characteristic holds for a collection in question. A standard example of this is the collection of men as members of the human species. They may be characterized by their mortality or by the peculiarity that, of all beings, only men are featherless and two-legged. Such specifications are then said to be formally equivalent, since the elements which answer to one specification also answer to the other, and vice versa. Russell saw in this a defining feature for a class: a class is all the objects which answer to any specification, and when two or more formally equivalent specifications can be given, the class will be the common membership which they determine.[17]

But this approach towards a class, as step towards a definition of number, has a serious drawback. If numbers and collections are at all to meet, the factor of plurality is necessary. The specification for any collection gives only unity; its plurality or extent is not necessarily thereby determined. The problem which must be faced seems to me to be the following: one must seek a notion which is distinct from a class as one—hence this notion cannot be given by any specifying characteristic—but also distinct from the self-identity of the members of the collection. A mere listing of the members of a class won't do because the members, in their self-identity, are also unities in their own right, in complete disregard—at least, insofar as their self-identity is concerned—to each other. The notion needed must be distinct from these, not only because the collection as given by a specifying characteristic and the self-identity of the members remain bound to the *individualities* which they are—we require a general notion—but also because neither of these two presents us with the notion of the many-ness of the collection as a *pervasive feature* of the collection in its own right. The specifying characteristic ignores the many-ness of the collection as many, while through the self-identities of the members, each member ignores, so to speak, the other, and the collection, on this basis, is many merely because of the differentiation which differing identities call to bear. Manyness is then an inexplicable logical accident. We want a "togetherness" of the many which will preserve the many-ness but which will not atomize the many so as to lose the unification of the "togetherness." To state it in different words: we are looking for the notion of plurality as a *collective* many, not as a *distributive* many. But many it must remain. The only notion I know of which can fulfill this peculiar requirement is that of "numerical distinctness."

Numerical distinctness

Numerical distinctness cannot properly be considered a logical notion, for it involves the distinctness of something not in and for itself but *with respect to* another thing. It is the "many-ness" which this "with respect to" calls up that is important here. It involves, as I see it, a combination of one thing with another thing without any reliance upon any bond or relation which may be present. For example, were we to count some objects before us, then the actual relations holding between those objects would be of no relevance in counting them, nor need we be concerned with qualitative similarities or differences. All we need of anything when counting it is that it is capable of contributing its quantitative share in the quantity as a whole. This involves, as we can now see—since our present concern is not to actually count objects but to try and formulate why they are countable—that the objects show a distinctness with respect to each other such as would suffice to count them. It is distinctiveness in the sense of numerical presence. But this can have meaning only in conjunction (or disjunction) with other things with respect to which the numerical presence is relevant. Thus the numerical distinctness of an object involves a non-relational combination with other things, a "togetherness" which has no greater unificational effect than that of constituting what we recognize as "being many," or being "in the mode of many-ness." Each thing is then considered only in its function of contributing towards the many-ness which the many things then *collectively* are. The many-ness is then mere plurality, a numerical combination of numerically distinct things.

This "mode of numerical togetherness" is, of course, an abstract notion and is in no way separable from an actually given collection of objects, with their actual relations and qualities. But precisely because we are only after this numerical mode, our view towards the collection of objects, from which we started, is now different from the way objects are considered in a counting act. In the latter the objects are concrete and considered concretely. Now we are considering objects abstractly, where their concreteness recedes in a way which conforms to the abstractive interest we have with respect to them, which in this case is qualified as being a numerical one.

This difference is important in reminding us that the knowledge which results from this abstractive numerical interest will not have the character of that which results from the engaged activity of counting. Counting, as active effectuation, cannot be accounted *for* in theoretical terms, for that would destroy the concrete character of the effectuation which in involved. All that one can do is, to some degree, indicate or give an account *of* the complexity involved. In the final analysis, counting must be understood knowingly. But in an abstract consideration of things, which leads in the direction of theory formation, the activity of mind is not in the first place engaged knowingly but rather discerningly, that is, the activity of mind is now one of discriminating the various steps and elements which are involved in accounting *for* the separating attention given to whatever is discernible but not in itself actually separable.

It is in the context of such an accounting for that the status of a "plurality" or the "mode of numerical togetherness" becomes intelligible as theoretically separated notion and, more particularly, in what way the logical factors relate to it. The defining characteristic, the *notio communis*, which specifies which objects are to be considered as members of a class, can readily be understood as doing deputy duty for the concrete collection which would otherwise be present. But here the realization that many defining characteristics may be given for any class of members of a collection is already in itself a further step away from the concretely given collection. Any feature which singles out these elements will do. But the individual identities of the members also goes by the board. The self-identity of each member, which stands in complete disregard of any other member, prepares one for the notion of numerical extent. By disregarding the distinct intensions given with the self-identity of any member of a class, one is enabled to see these members as being only unities contributing towards numerical extension.

But numerical extent or many-ness is not deduced from the defining characteristics of a collection and the self-identities of its members. For, as argued before, the pervasiveness of numerical togetherness, which is really central in the notion of a plurality, is not thereby touched. It must be discerned for its own relevance but, being abstract, the logical procedure of specifying a defining characteristic for a collection which exemplifies some numerical extent and of indicating its separate members gives orientation to the discerning mind to find within the conditions thus specified the distinctness and combination which may be recognized as being of a numerical character. This numerical character has the intension of numerical extension. By explicitly distinguishing these logical and numerical factors, we account for how such a theoretical notion as that of a plurality is come by.[18] The next step is to understand how plurality is delimited and becomes amenable to scientific knowledge.

We have some right in identifying our plurality with the notion of a class, at least, in the sense in which Whitehead, in repudiation of its use in *Principia Mathematica*, has used it. His description of a class is that of "a composite entity arising from the togetherness of many things in symmetrical connection with each other" (*14*: 282). Furthermore, Whitehead, too, has argued that it is not sufficient to indicate a class merely by its defining characteristic alone. For each defining characteristic, "the mutual togetherness of the components issues in the unity of a composite entity which is the class in question. But some limitation, even to this assumption, is necessary" (*14*: 283). He goes on to show that the special mode of togetherness must be explicit if a vicious circle, analogous to that of Russell's paradox, is not to result immediately. The mode of togetherness which might best be considered relevant for a class is the combination indicated with the connective "or." In any case, Whitehead finds that any class needs to satisfy at least the following requisites: (i) the members of the class should be "together"; (ii) the class is the collective totality arising from that composition; (iii) in respect to membership of the class, one member is as good as another (*14*: 282). My own description satisfies these requirements. From here on the word *class* will be used synonymously with *plurality*.

At this point, before getting on with the discussion of the number concept, two remarks are in order.

(1) One should not understand this notion of a class as presupposing spatial meaning. A collection of given, physical objects will, of course, have its members spatially exterior to one another. But the collection of parliamentary statutory laws valid within any country is not spatially diverse in the sense in which these laws are numerically diverse. Nor are ideas, musical notes of a chord or temporal moments spatially diverse. Yet, in these examples the notion of a class is validly portrayed. Spatial diversity can also exemplify the sort of numerical distinctness which a class catches, but can do so only because numerical distinctness is distinct from it and irreducible to it.

(2) The distinction between collections and classes, whereby the former is always bound to concrete, distinguishable features while the latter expresses that aspect of a collection whereby it is a plurality or that mode of being in numerical distinctness, must be kept firmly in mind when speaking of collections with only one member and classes with only a single element. In both cases there is a confusing degeneracy of meaning. A collection of only a single object is not normally called a collection, nor can a single element be called a plurality. In the case of a unitary collection, the defining characteristic of the collection becomes, for all practical purposes, the mark of self-identity of its sole member. This does not abolish the general distinction between the collection as one and its members as many. It only makes it irrelevant in this particular case. However, it does remain relevant when speaking of the plurality of such a (unitary) collection. The plurality, as mode of being, comes in this case to *minimal* expression. But a case of minimal expression remains bound to the other cases of *bona fide* plurality. Thus, though here, too, there is degeneracy, it should not, as with collections, be submitted to. The degeneracy is here basically grammatical in that any singleness of composition cannot be

lingually referred to in the plural. But since conceptually this is a case of minimum plurality, it must in this way be treated as a plurality. This gives a reason for what in mathematics is maintained as an essential distinction: the class consisting of only one element must not be identified with that element.

The correspondence between classes

The notion of a class has now been elucidated. It is time to turn to the second notion which Russell introduced in explaining the number concept, namely, the one-to-one correspondence between classes. The main point of this discussion will be to investigate how the distinction between logical and numerical factors continues to hold in the one-to-one correspondence and what the immediate consequences are.

The chief use of introducing the one-to-one correspondence is for enabling a comparison between classes. Accordingly, it involves the discernment of identity or diversity between classes. Such a discernment must be seen as a *logical* discernment, by the very fact that identity and diversity are here primarily involved. But this does not exclude the numerical character of the classes being compared. For the subject matter being discerned for identity and diversity is of a numerical character. When the one-to-one correspondence holds, the logical identity thereby confirmed is one respecting the plurality of classes. The logical identity then expresses a quantitative equivalence between classes. Similarly for logical diversity: when the one-to-one correspondence does not hold, the confirmed logical diversity expresses a quantitative inequality between the classes concerned.

These two apparently harmless possibilities, which also exhaust the possibilities offered through this method, are in fact not so innocent as they seem. This becomes more clear if we keep in mind the context of this discussion and, accordingly, change the idiom. We are not comparing any given collection with another but are theoretically discerning, within the logical limits previously indicated, what results from explicating comparisons. We may say that by means of the correspondence, we are trying to relate what is theoretically posed as a numerical contrast between classes. The logical execution of this correspondence must decide upon the validity of the contrast. Logical discernment seeks to establish a relation between classes but can do so only where there is a valid contrast. Now, a relation is not itself a contrast because relations relate and don't contrast. Thus the logical process of deciding upon a relationship must not be confused with the numerical contrast, nor with the numerical outcome logically being sought.

Numerical forms. But the outcome now takes on an interesting shape. In the first place, in the case where there is a logical identity set up by the correspondence, that is, where there is quantitative equivalence, this result invalidates there being any contrast in a numerical sense between the classes. And since classes are but the theoretically discerned quantitative mode of a collection, there is no other ground available to maintain a quantitative distinction. Consequently, the supposed contrast collapses as being not numerically factually present. But through collapsing, it comfirms the equality of the quantitative extent of the classes in question, or, as it may be stated, it confirms or elicits an agreement as to the numerical *form* of that quantity. This form is universal, for any other class with that quantity will also not be capable of contrasting with the classes at hand. A definition of a natural number suggests itself immediately. *A number is the form which numerically equivalent classes are conceived to have.* It is universal in that it characterizes all classes or pluralities of that quantity; conversely, each plurality is an exemplification of the number of that form but can never be that number itself.[19]

A natural number defined in this sense should not be taken to be itself a concept. It is known or understood conceptually, in that the mind is obviously involved in conceiving it. But numbers involve, in a more essential way, pluralities or classes as a type or mode of being of things. And this, involving as it does the functioning of things in mutual numerical distinctness and combination, is not intra-mental or mind-dependent. Our conceiving is dependent on it, as referent to cogitate on. If numbers, then, are not in the mind as ready-made concepts, and if they are not in the things but only exemplified by them, what are they? They appear to be the *conditions* or *forms of definiteness* respecting the pluralities of collections; they are the forms in which the quantitativeness of pluralities are *delimited*; they are the characterization of the numerical extent of classes, of which each is constituted by "as many elements as" the other.[20]

This description of natural numbers holds for each in particular and concerns only each natural number itself. Consequently, as a group they form a rather motley bunch, with no indication of internal organization, relations or properties holding for all the numbers generally. Since arithmetic deals with such general properties and relations, it is clear that some organization principles are required to get arithmetic, as a science of numbers, off the ground; that is, we need to indicate in what way the natural numbers form a well-ordered set. For this we turn to the second possible outcome of the application of the one-to-one correspondence between classes, namely, the case of non-equivalence between classes.

Numerical contrasts. When classes or pluralities are not numerically equivalent, we get no form but rather the confirmation of a *factual* numerical contrast. This contrast elicits a numerical difference between the classes and will allow a distinction between the classes in relational terms, namely, the one will be excessive with respect to the other, and the other deficient with respect to the one. A contrast, accordingly, provides a ground for a numerical relation having a referent and relatum, in which the referent will be either "greater than" or "less than" the relatum, depending on whether the referent is taken to be excessive or deficient, respectively.

This contrast invites two different ways of development. In the first place, the pluralities standing in contrast each exemplify a number. The difference between these pluralities, which is itself a quantity in its own right, may be taken as a measure of the difference between the contrasting pluralities. But it is clear that two or more couples of contrasting pluralities may have the *same* difference without having any of the pluralities of the couples exemplifying the same number. In other words, though a contrast is itself a numerical inequality, there are inequalities of the same magnitude. Thus there will be *forms* of numerical inequality which are exemplified by diverse contrasting couples of pluralities and may be called "difference forms." These difference forms cannot be the same as those of the natural numbers because of the reference to the contrasting couples they contain.[21] Important is that these difference forms are an essential step in bringing order into the natural numbers. Important, too, is the realization that there must be a minimal value in the range of the possible difference forms. This will, of course, be that difference which is constituted by a mere unit plurality. A difference of less than a unit makes no sense here.

The second way of developing a contrast is to look to the relations definable through it. In that case we must proceed from either the excessive class or the deficient class as referent for the relations "is greater than" or "is less than," respectively. It may be expected that the difference form will have a role here, for it specifies (or "measures") the extent of the contrast which is now to be bridged. And this is indeed the case. For given that the referent class is greater than the relatum class and that an exemplification of the difference form is known, then it is clear that the referent class may be *described* in terms of the relatum and the measure of the difference in that their *sum* must give a plurality equivalent to the referent. But if the referent is taken to be the lesser of the contrasting classes, then it is clear that the referent may also be described in terms of the relatum and the exemplified difference form in that the relatum, when *diminished* by the amount of the difference, will give a plurality equivalent to the referent. It is clear that these descriptions give us the meaning of the operations of addition and subtraction.

The manner in which the term denoting the difference between the contrasting pluralities is involved in the relation, that is, whether it be added or subtracted, is clearly dependent on which of the differing pluralities is taken as referent. But this, in turn, is equivalent to taking either the relation or its converse as applied to the same referent. That is, if m and n are the natural numbers of contrasting pluralities and R^a is their relation, whereby a is the measure of their difference, and if $\overline{R}^a$ is taken as the converse of R^a, then the two propositions mR^an and $m\overline{R}^an$ express what is usually written as $m = n + a$ and $m = n - a$, respectively. Thus the difference of sign is, in fact, grounded in the difference of the "sense" (or direction) of the relation. Thus the relations R^a and $\overline{R}^a$, i.e. $+a$ and $-a$, are the positive and negative integers which, in themselves, are based on the difference forms which express the contrast between pluralities.[22] And because these relations relate natural numbers, we see how, through the injection of the integers, the natural numbers become related by a network of relations.

Natural numbers generally. The natural numbers will be optimally organized when we look to the relation which is based on the minimal difference of any two pluralities. This is the integer $+1$ (or its converse -1). Its importance is derived from the fact that when we begin with the natural number which is least—which is 1—and combine to it the integer $+1$, we get what is evidently the least but one natural number, which is 2 (since 2 with the converse of $+1$ applied to it again gives 1); and by applying $+1$ to 2 we get the "next" natural number, i.e. the least but two natural number, which is 3; etc. In this way, by an iterated application of this relation $+1$, which may be defined as the (immediate) successor relation, *any* natural number will be described if one proceeds from the number "one." On this account, we may consider this description as the characteristic to which any natural number complies. Whereas each natural number is a form of (quantitative) definiteness of a plurality, we find, upon describing each number as given by an iterated application of the relation of succession by unity starting from unity, that there is a *descriptive uniformity* in the definiteness of the number forms. This uniformity, if x denotes any natural number, is then given by the descriptive function $x+1$, whereby any natural number is related, in exactly an identical fashion, with its successor. *The iterated application of the immediate successor relation descriptively defines* (i.e. makes definite) *the whole series of the natural numbers and thus is a defining characteristic of any natural number generally.*[23]

The great importance of this defining characteristic is given with the fact that through it, a principle may be enunciated which allows one to prove the validity of many properties holding for every natural number. The principle is that of mathematical induction. It says that any property concerning the natural numbers which (i) holds for the number "one," and

(ii) holds for the (immediate) successor of any number which possesses the property, will then hold for every natural number. This principle, on the one hand, merely embodies the definition of the natural numbers generally. But on the other hand, it serves as a principle of inference, of a distinctly mathematical kind, allowing for the deduction of whatever property holds for all the natural numbers. With this principle, mathematics very literally begins. Every student of mathematics knows that to prove even the simplest properties of the natural numbers requires the application of this principle.[24]

The natural numbers and the integers completely exhaust whatever may be derived from the application of the one-to-one correspondence between pluralities. The two sorts of numbers must be clearly distinguished: the former are forms of numerical equivalence, the latter are forms of factual non-equivalence; the former have no sign, the latter are intrinsically signed. Together they make up what is *typical* of a numerical structure, as approached in the conceptualizing tendency made possible by the correspondence and the attendant notions of "contrast" and "relation."[25] With that settled, we see that mathematically this numerical structure constitutes the addition-subtraction stratum of mathematical operations (from which multiplication and exponentiation may be recursively defined).

The number concept as introduced in this section, although hemmed in by logical considerations, is itself of a non-logical nature. It has a numerical character, and the individual numbers are capable of entering into relations with each other in a systematic and lawful way, as expressed in arithmetical propositions. The arithmetical operations, as well as the definitions of the natural numbers and (finite) number generally, are all seen to be explicable in terms of the notion of a plurality and the equivalence and non-equivalence between pluralities. This explicability is not a logicist deduction from logically primitive terms and logically primitive propositions; rather, it is a justification of the concepts and basic propositions of arithmetic, including a general principle of mathematical inference, in terms of numerical states of affairs as discerned through a logically explicit methodology.

IV. Numerosity

The two topics, counting and the number concept, as discussed above, have each been developed in terms of factors and features that appear to me to be intrinsically relevant to each. It is not surprising, then, that each has gone its own way. For the one requires an analysis of effectuations, involving subjective and objective factors, caught up in events;

the other, the introduction of structurally conditioning features as apperceived within logically explicit limits. Or, to put the matter in terms of linguistic analysis, we had to become more aware of what is involved in judgments where a number word occurs as predicate, and what is involved in propositions where a number word occurs as subject term of another predicate or as term of a relation. And since it is generally recognized that a predicate actually predicated has not the independence which the content of that same predicate has when occurring as the subject of other assertions, it must be that the lingual meaning of the predicate word is different in some sense from that of the same word when an assertion is made respecting it. But since in both cases the same word occurs, one expects the two meanings at least to merge on some point, although just how this it to be understood needs to be reviewed in itself.

The double senses of number, when each was separately discussed, nowhere seemed to presuppose each other. This is, I think, the best proof one can give against those positions in the foundations of mathematics where either is placed in priority to the other, implying that the other must then be seen as derivative from the first. Although our account has not spelled out the sort of relations there are between the meaning of number as it occurs in counting and as it occurs in arithmetical propositions, at least the relation of priority cannot now hold. Since this account gives a positive analysis of the state of affairs as we see it, the onus lies with the contrary parties to adduce new counterarguments. I turn now to the problem of spelling out the relations between the two senses of number, or at least to indicate how the answer should go with respect to the question what the unified meaning of a number word might be. This may be done by examining the results of the two approaches to number each in turn.

Number concept enriched. Numbers as they occur in counting were found to consist in their being synthetic number knowledge, acquired by having passed through, so to speak, the plurality of a given collection. This number knowledge is primarily intuitive, having arisen through an actual acquaintance, in a relevant way, with the objects of the given collection. This manner of gaining number knowledge is bound to circumstances and reflects the particularity of the exemplification of that quantity. Numbers thus acquired serve as the meanings of the predicates which express the quantity of the collection at hand. Its irreducible character lies in being the *knowing* expression of the quantity involved, that is, the actual knowing of that quantity because of having gone through the numerical diversity of that quantity.

Can this knowledge now be of any relevance to the number concept, which is general and formal rather than particular and factual? This is indeed the case, and that in an essential way.

Since the number concept is acquired through the application of the logical procedure of a one-to-one correspondence between pluralities, this procedure can never itself specify the actual "how many" of any plurality but only the relative notion of the one having or not having *as many* elements as the other. Hence it indicates only the similarity or difference between the numerical diversity of pluralities. It remains, so to speak, outside of the actual numerical diversity involved. For this reason, the number concept, which signals the numerical equivalence of equipollent pluralities, can involve nothing other than a form. Not that the form is empty; it is the form of that factual plurality, the generalization of the type of exemplifications of that quantity.

If "understanding numbers" is at least to imply a material knowledge of numbers, it is clear that the internal knowledge of exemplified quantity and the more external, conceptual knowledge must exercise a mutual relevance one towards the other. That this is possible is given with the circumstance that the number forms, which are general, *characterize* the particularity of the collection counted as to its quantity; similarly, the collection counted *exemplifies* the general form of plurality it involves. Through these circumstances, the number forms must characterize the pluralities of which numerical knowledge has been acquired through the counting act, so that the "as many as," which the forms delineate, is enriched with the knowledge of the internal quantity involved. Any rejection of the relevance of counting in the face of the number concept must miss the internal acquaintance which the issue of counting infuses into the mere "as many as" of the number concept. This rapprochement of number meaning and concept not only enriches the latter but also gives to the number meanings which result from direct counting a deepened, more than intuitive definitiveness through the circumstance that the counted quantity also exemplifies the numerically delineating form. Hence, from the point of view of knowledge, any rejection of counting for "understanding" number is hereby critically rejected. We thereby dispose of the alternative of understanding number only through its conceptual-theoretical elucidation.

It is important to realize that such an acquaintance can take place only with the finite numbers. The one-to-one correspondence through which the number forms are approached is not restricted to only finite classes. Examples of such one-to-one correspondence between infinite classes are easily come by in mathematics. But the infinite cardinals and infinite ordinals which result from this procedure can never be more than forms. An "internal" understanding of these is impossible, since one can never completely "go through" the quantity involved. Accordingly, transfinite numbers cannot be referred to as numbers in a material sense.

The material understanding of the finite numbers is given extra emphasis with the "principle of mathematical induction" which, as indicated above, may be said to define number generally. Here each number form is described as an iterated unity. The principle states that each number form can be thus understood; it does not involve the actual synthesis of the unities into collective forms. The actual synthesis of the unities is, however, effectuated when counting. Thus here, too, it becomes evident how the conceptual understanding of number requires, at least in principle, the supplementation of matters which the intuitive knowledge of counting delivers.

Structure of counting act. But what about counting? Is it so complete in itself as not to refer to or require typical features of the number concept? This is plainly not the case. Granted, counting is a direct and actual involvement of subject and object, through which the subject acquires its numerical knowledge respecting the object. But our analysis of counting has yielded the result that this actual involvement is not without its own implicit mediational factors. These mediational factors are the implicit requirement of how the subject relates itself to the objects, formulated in the required ordering of the objects, and the implicit requirement of how the objects are brought in relation to the subjects, as expressed by the one-to-one indexing of the objects to symbols, which thereby marks consciousness' attention and retaining memory of the objects.

When these features are looked at in their own right, it is immediately evident that they portray the pattern required to derive both the ordinals[26] and the cardinals. The rule which orders the objects of a collection effects in fact a relational ordering of the elements of the collection as plurality, and the index-correlation is a one-to-one correspondence beteween the collection as a plurality and some class of signs, which is a plurality in its own right. In the conceptual elucidation of the ordinals and cardinals, both the ordering and the corresponding were made into *explicit* conceptual procedures in arriving at a conceptual understanding of numbers. The requisites for this procedure are in fact present already in counting, but are not logically explicit. Thus there is here no generalizing effect which such procedures bring to bear. It turns out, then, that the factual procedure of counting and the logical elucidation of the number concept are both nested in a single structural complexity. Each emphasizes different moments of this complexity and develops them in its own way, thus playing, nevertheless, distinct roles in understanding number. It seems to me, then, that to maintain either a dualism between counting and the number concept proper or a monistic subsumption of the one to the other is to seriously misconceive both counting and the number concept, whether in the analysis of their structural features or in evaluating their distinct contributions to the knowing understanding of number.

Numerosity as meaning channel

The structural complexity of the subject-to-object connection and that of the object-to-subject, which, in elucidating the number concept, became the basis of the logical procedure through which the generality of the number concept can be understood, gives a deeper insight into the meaning of numerosity as used earlier. The word was introduced as denoting the intension of the entire event which counting is. It had to catch both the type of relevance of the objects and the human subject present and operative in the event. It provides a context for the two-way reference between subject and object. Now that the structural connections through which the subject and the objects contribute their share have been made explicit, it is evident that these connections, which open up another dimension of the event, contribute their relevance to the meaning of the event. These connections make us see that that meaning has a factual side, on which the notion of a plurality or class depends, both in its cardinality and ordinality, and that it has a formal side, through which the factual side attains its definiteness.

Numbers, I suggested, whether cardinal or ordinal, are forms of definiteness which, because of their delimiting role with respect to the factual, quantitative, but unspecified givens are properly said to be forms of a mode of being of things qua many-ness. Now, modes are not properties. As a mode of being, a class or plurality is then not a property of things but a manner in which the things of the world are. Properties may change, and any particular plurality of a collection may change, but they cannot shed their plurality or many-ness, even when—as argued before—the plurality degenerates to a singularity. But if plurality is not a property of things, then *a fortiori* numbers are not. They are the forms of definiteness through which the particular pluralities may change and which differing pluralities may exemplify. These forms, whether as cardinals or as ordinals, are unending. Hence they can never be fully actualized or exemplified in experiential reality. In this sense they transcend actuality while being, at the same time, constitutive for it as to quantity. They transcend actuality only in the sense that the factual pluralities do not exhaustively exemplify their delimiting forms, in being always replete with possibility: the possibility of exemplifying again and again any actualized form, and the possibility of adducing new actualizing forms from those already actualized. This may be taken as an assertion respecting their ontological status. But it does not make them some rounded-off, metaphysical kind of actual being.

These factual and formal sides of the event of which numerosity is the intensional unity themselves constitute a meaning relationship in that facts actualize forms through exemplification and forms delimit facts in being their characterization. This is a contemporaneous kind of relationship within actuality, whereby the ontology of facts and forms is seen in its relevance for actuality. But this relationship does not remain cut off from the more subjective and judgmatic aspects as required in counting. For the *actualized* forms as exemplified in facts give conceptual-numerical content to the mind's retention of the units passed by in a count. Likewise, the numerical forms as yet *unactualized* and not characteristic of a fact give content to the mind's protensive drive to finalize the counting event. Thereby one may know that, whatever the quantity holding for the given collection, it must itself be definitive. Thus numerosity, with its retentive hindsight and protensive foresight, becomes, through the mutual reference of fact and form, a meaning channel in which counting can be effectuated as being a relevant and meaningful act.

Numerosity is itself not a concept. It is more like a transcendental condition holding for human consciousness, such that one cannot but include in one's view of the world its being a world in the plural. But it is unlike a transcendental condition in that it drives the mind in developing and deepening the understanding of plurality. This appears already in every simple counting act. Because it makes sense to *ask* with respect to some collection how many objects it contains, it makes sense to *expect* an answer. There is here a compulsion operative in our very knowing and understanding of plurality through which this expectation demands fulfillment.The compulsion is not psychological but epistemic, and the drive to understand the world also in the plural is but a species of the general compulsion of wanting to know. It is, I think, very human. But it is human because we creatures live in a reality that can be known—not in the perfect, compartmentalized way in which autonomous man would rationalize it, but in a way in which our creaturely reality moves us to seek it through *knowing* it. And through knowing *it*, we come to know what *we* don't know about it, and through realizing our doubt and bewilderment we can, by a conscious intensification of a further *directed* analysis and synthesis, go some way in resolving our partial understanding. Thus an epistemic concern is given with human life. But so are the channels which direct the understanding. Numerosity is one such channel through which the compulsion behind our numerical wonderment is directed to numerical fulfillment.

Numerosity, operative in the practice of counting, nudges man into factual involvement with the world about him. But in theorizing about the diverse forms which plurality can assume, numerosity is equally present as transcendental condition. Granted: we approach these forms through logical means. But as long as our arguments against the reduction of the notions of plurality and class to that of logic are valid, the logical methods can be understood as being but the dress which consciousness puts on in order to discern non-logical matters. The logical consciousness here provides us with the "lift" in being able to look past the factual involvement with reality and bring into focus reality's defining forms. We then conceptualize, and not merely intuit. But we conceptualize within the framework of numerical intent.

But the systematic development of the numerical forms through the logical dress of consciousness cannot do without the intuitions if the resulting conceptions are to be more than merely structural forms. Better yet: the systematizations in their own way contribute to a deepening—not to mention tremendous expansion—of our knowledge. Thus, when viewed as to containing factors, counting and the number concept do not presuppose each other. But at the same time, each requires the other in order to supplement its own deficiencies. However, when viewed as to knowledge, even the most formally considered generalizations of number theory must ultimately remain generalizations of intuited number meaning. Thus nothing supplants our everyday experiential knowledge, which arises through creaturely possibilities of coming to know. But neither is there any knowledge exempt from conceptual intensification, precision and criticism. That way we consciously search out the truth of what we have come to know.

Notes

1. There are many sources in which these definitions may be found. Particularly helpful is E. Landau (*9*), which is entirely devoted to the systematic development of number systems from the natural numbers.

2. I do not mean to suggest that operations such as computing and measuring involve no more than counting. This is certainly not the case, but it is irrelevant to this paper to work this out.

3. L. E. J. Brouwer, with his "neo-intuitionism," maintains a similar position, arguing for the priority of ordinals on the basis of a time-relation within "causal sequences." These causal sequences are, however, not merely psychological but more psycho-sociological. Causal sequences of phenomena, observed in experience—a flux of life-moments—are in science systematically catalogued in terms of natural laws, not because these laws express something lawful about "nature," but because the individual or community finds it appropriate to consider these phenomena as repeating themselves identically, and then particularly those causal sequences which can play a role in societal modes of mutual understanding (cf. *1*: 5). The notion of number is a direct extract from this view, as the following compactly formulated quotation indicates (my translation): "This neo-intuitionism views the breaking-up of life-moments into qualitatively different parts, which [being] only separated by time can again unite, as the primal occurrence in the human intellect, and [it views] the abstracting of this breaking-up of each sensational content into the intuition of bi-unity, regardless, as the primal occurrence of mathematical thinking. This intuition of bi-unity, this primal intuition of mathematics creates not only the numbers "one" and "two," but also all *finite ordinal numbers*, in that one of the elements of the bi-unity can be thought of as a new bi-unity, and this process can be repeated an arbitrary number of times" (*1*: 11-12—italics not mine). The Mar-

burg neo-Kantians, though critical of any outright psychologism, also maintained the priority of ordinal numbers to cardinals. For them "the 'essence' of numbers is completely expressed in their positions," which positions are given by serial ordering. "In this way we are finally able, by following the fixed prescribed order of the positions, to coordinate the last member of the system series with a certain ordinal number, n." "The number n, which was primarily gained as a characteristic of the last element, can thus be regarded, from another point of view, as a character of the total system: we call it the cardinal number of the system considered, and now say of the latter that it consists of n elements" (cf. E. Cassirer, *4*: 39, 41). An internal weakness of this derivation of the cardinals from the ordinals lies in the unmotivated "other point of view" required to bring cardinality into view. This breaks the logical procedure of the derivation.

4. In other words, this "selective interest" of consciousness is not a kind of "Wesensschau" which E. Husserl made popular. Consciousness' function here is better described as prehending or eliciting rather than Husserl's description of it as the intending, through its own spontaneity, of an *eidos*. The *eidos* in question would have to be a universal form somehow contained within particular givens. On Husserl's position, the (meaning-giving) tacit decision which directs the intention of consciousness at the same time makes the intended object a logical or kind of entity. In the above account, there are no "kinds of entities" but only concrete givens, whose displayed features, in this case their quantity, may be considered and codified through prehensive selection. Numerical *eide* require separate justification; cf. below.

5. Cf. note 3; in (*2*) Brouwer begins by saying (my translation): "Knowing and speaking are the forms of action whereby the lifewill [levenswil] of man and mankind maintains and imposes itself. They find their origin in the three following anthropological life-phenomena: (1) mathematical contemplation, (2) mathematical abstraction, (3) imposition of the will by means of signs, *all three of which, in extension and modality, are subject to the free will*" (italics mine).

6. Since most of us become proficient in counting already at an early age, we tend to think that we know the natural numbers independent of their application and exemplification. The sort of synthesis involved in counting is then easily made out to be one where available predicate numbers are applied to given quantities of objects or marks. Our analysis, if correct, makes this view of synthesis philosophically naive.

7. In more technical terms, this says—as mentioned in the introduction—that the *ordo cognoscendi* is prior to the *ordo essendi*. This is a dogma ubiquitous in all subjectivistic philosophy since Descartes. Cf. *13*: 75ff; also H. Caton, *The Origin of Subjectivity* (New Haven and London: Yale Univ. Press, 1973), pp. 9, 47-8.

A rather breezy objection to this whole dogma is given by Bertrand Russell: "knowing how we know is one small department of knowing what we know"; *My Philosophical Development* (London: George Allen and Unwin, 1959), p. 16. This objection has a point, but it also shows a certain lack of depth. In the first place, it overlooks the fact that when the *ordo cognoscendi* is placed first, this almost always results from ensconcing the ego within the *cogito*, so that only by cognitive, methodical reflection (from the cogito's own dynamics) can a beginning be made of dissipating the mists of ignorance and providing a vista to discern *what* there is, including that of one's own procedure. This ensconcing, however, is no part of how we know, but is a prejudice of rationalism. This Russell overlooks, and thus he does not ask the philosophically critical questions concerning the *origin* of the cogito's ability to at all proceed with methodical, reflective knowing and (related to this question) the *direction* in which this (spontaneous) dynamics of thought proceeds. Cf. also note 11.

Secondly, Russell's reply seems to imply that the two orders should be reversed as to priority. But this, too, is not without its problems. In his own early philosophy, Russell, as is well known, defended the priority of ontology. But because the immediately resulting naive realism provided no shelter against paradoxes (especially Russell's own), Russell soon tempered this ontology with a method of description which would *induce* scepticism into the robust acceptance of essences, thus producing in effect an ontological agnosticism. This agnosticism Russell in turn tempered by accepting certainties which, though never indubitable, were derived from perception (judgments of sense-data) and thought (logical premises), both of which stem from the *ordo cognoscendi*.

The relations between thinking and being easily become unruly (or even vicious?) when either is neglected or too quickly imposed upon the other. When due recognition is given to each, it seems that only then can a fruitful inquiry take place as to their relations. These relations, as the last part of this paper indicates with respect to numerical thought and numerical being, involve the difficult problem of significance and the embeddedness in the "creation dynamics."

8. G. Frege (*6*), especially the three chapters prior to his own thetical view on number, i.e. I-III.

9. This neologism occurs in E. Husserl's description of time consciousness and means "what shall be immediately conscious, though not at the moment" (*13*: 80).

10. The subject-object relation referred to here is that of knower to known. This is here avoided because, formulated as a simple dual relation, it smothers the complexity of knowing. To my mind, knowing involves at least a leading epistemic concern, which seeks fulfillment through understanding as effectuated in events which take time and take place. The knower is concerned to know, *effectuates* events, which *issue* into knowledge or the known. Precisely because of the intervention, or rather, the mediation of events—events which may be frightfully complex and variously qualified—any direct and simple knower-known relation is simply a mistake.

11. It should be clear that "ego," here understood as enacting person, is not identical with "consciousness" as used above nor with the use of "subjectivity" as indicated above with "subject-side" of an event. This use of terms, undoubtedly at first sight confusing, is nevertheless required in order to avoid simplifying pitfalls inherent in the predominantly subjectivistic tradition since Descartes. It leads too far afield to analyze this properly, so a brief indication of the distinctions will have to suffice. I would hold that the ego is the concrete person who stands in societal and communicative relations to fellow beings and in many functional relations to the situated beings of his world. A person is, however, within all these relationships, marked to be a bearer of responsibility, a responsibility which, when it is justified and accounted for, requires a supra-personal and supra-mundane source for its meaning. One of the forms which responsibility may take on is that of consciousness or, more exactly, of being sub-ject-ively conscious or aware. In this mode, the ego's relations to fellow beings and his world is characterized by understanding, an understanding which, because it is primarily an engaged concern, makes the ego a participating ingredient in the actualities and events which make up reality. Understanding, being a prerequisite for knowledge, goads the participating ego to actually acquire knowledge within and through the multi-various events of reality. This knowledge acquisition seems to involve at least a synthetic unification, which comes to expression in judgments. Here the subject, finally, in its own subjectivity, is itself actively effectuating an event involving unification. When such a unification takes place, we have the situation of thought, i.e. an *ego cogito*, an ego which *inter alia* thinks.

12. By way of transition, the word *concept* is here used for whatever is the content of the cognition of similarity—hence of indiscernibility—between things; that is, when the cognition of a thing and the cognition of another thing, or the re-cognition of the same thing, contain elements which are not discernibly different, then of that element not discernibly different one is said to have a concept or conceptual knowledge. Conceptual understanding is then different from judgmatic understanding (cf. note 11) in that the concern to know, which gives rise to actually acquired judgments, is here detoured through a patient process of comparison and repetition before issuing into a judgment (whose predicate will now have a more universal import).

13. A very readable account may be found in his *12*: Chap. 2.

14. This is Euclid's definition of number (*5*, Vol. 2, Book VII, Def. 2). When one combines this definition of number with that of "unit" (*ibid.*, Def. 1: "a unit is that in virtue of which each of the things that exist is called one"), it immediately follows that number, for him, has a distributive meaning over units, whereby there is no distinction between an indefinite unit and the number "one." This will be criticized below.

15. This question did not occur in the previous discussion of counting because there it is always given and something from which to proceed. Here I want to indicate the theoretical significance of collections and must then account for them in their own right.

16. A collection can also be given by listing its members. But such an extensional approach makes a collection unnecessarily restricted to what is effectively enumerable. But such a restriction is not principiant because every extensional list can be changed into a logically intensional one (cf. *12*: 12).

17. Russell spoke of such characterizations as "propositional functions." "A *class* is all the objects satisfying some propositional function" (*15*: 23, also 71-81, 187-99).

18. In a more technical treatise, the distinction between logical and numerical factors would have to be discussed in conjunction with Leibniz's *principium identitatis indiscernibilium* and (what is related to this principle) Russell's axiom of reducibility. Leibniz's principle states, in one of its formulations, that "no two substances are completely similar, or differ *solo numero*" (Gerhardt, ed. *Die philosophische Schriften von G. W. Leibniz*, Vol. IV, p. 433). This principle, which Leibniz deduced from his principle of sufficient reason, may well be true as concerns actual substances (things), but it hardly invalidates the possibility of distinguishing *solo numero*. E.g. separate spots of ink from a well-stirred inkwell may show the required difference in texture under a microscope, but this has nothing to do with the numerical distinctness of the spots. Or even if the spots are clearly different, say, in shape, it is not on *that* account that there is a numerical difference. The difference in predicates which descernible things must have, according to Leibniz, leads only to a distributive sense of number, and not to the collective sense as appears to be required in leading to the number concept.

Russell's axiom of reducibility is not so easily circumvented. In non-technical terms it states that any intensionally given combination or disjunction of predicates is equivalent to a single predicate (*15*: 58-9). At first sight this seems to say in terms of predicates what I have been arguing in terms of things. For if the intensionally given combination or disjunction of predicates can be interpreted as being thereby collectively given, then this given (conjunctive or disjunctive) many-ness (of predicates) is said to be equivalent to a single predicate. But there is a catch in the word *equivalent*, which is here meant in the formal sense, that is, the many given predicates can be validly applied if, and only if, the single predicate can be validly applied. This entails no actual reference of the given many predicates to the single predicate; it only specifies formal equivalence of truth-value of the propositions in which the predicates occur. This was Russell's way of *avoiding* having to speak of some sort of collectiveness in the many given predicates. But it is hard to see why the "combination or disjunction" are not already two sorts of precisely such a collective togetherness. (One must not argue that this combination and disjunction are themselves but truth-functions and accordingly imply no actual "togetherness." The truth-functions hold for propositions, not for predicates.)

19. Here the difference with Russell's definition of a number becomes evident. Lacking the logistic view of classes, in my view a class of (numerically) similar classes cannot be defined in a *numerically* relevant way. Hence our "form" is not itself a class. Nor is it, needless to say, a relation between equivalent classes. For in that case, too, there would have to be a prior numerical contrast.

The word *form* should not be associated with the word *formalism* as used in reference to

Hilbert's school. There the word has a meaning which is empty of any conceptual intension. I use the word *form* here because I need a word which delineates, is mind-dependent insofar as it can be referred to only abstractly, but is extra-mental in that it denotes an ontological definitiveness. The ontological implication here is not a concession to the metaphysical forms derived from Platonism or Aristotelianism. A form here is a structure whose chief property is to characterize whatever is so structured. It would become a kind of actual, ontic being if the conditions—logical and numerical—under which theoretical thought is here being executed were themselves made the product of thought. Thought would then be autonomous and lack the context in which to dam in an uncritical metaphysics.

20. The concept of number here elucidated is that of a cardinal number. It is exemplified in classes in disregard of any order or sequence there may be between their constituting elements. Ordinal numbers, which are exemplified in classes in which sequences are regarded, can be approached in an exactly identical fashion as the cardinals. Only, the process is slightly more complex in that, when applying the one-to-one correspondence between the ordered elements of the classes, the order of the one class must be preserved or reflected in the order of the other. The form which then arises on account of the logical identity is a "sequence number"; or, since a sequence must be given by some relation holding between the elements, it may also be called a "relation number." Ordinal numbers defined in this way do not presuppose (though they do imply) their corresponding cardinals (when they are finite, as all our numbers are here). But cardinals, as we see, in no way presuppose the ordinals. Thus neither one stands in a position of logical priority with respect to the other. Lack of space prohibits further elucidation, but the essentials are hereby given (cf. *12*: Chap. 6).

21. For example, the (absolute) difference between 17 and 12 and between 1 and 6 is the same, being 5 in both cases. When differences between contrasting couples are indistinguishable, we may speak of a "difference form." When in these difference forms one orders the containing numbers and thus distinguishes the two possible ordered couplets which result, they are then identical to what is normally called the integers, i.e. the set of numbers (. . . , -2, -1, 0, +1, +2, . . .). Cf. E. W. Beth, *The Foundations of Mathematics*; (Amsterdam: North-Holland, 1965), pp. 95-8; also I. Stewart and David Tall, *The Foundations of Mathematics*; (Oxford: University Press, 1977), pp. 177-80.

22. Cf. B. Russell, *11*: Chap. XXVII, for a more general discussion of the difference of sense of a relation and difference of sign of an arithmetical operator.

23. I take the descriptive functions of mathematics as embodying the information given by their constants and not as, in themselves, naming an entity. The constants are either terms, involving the extensional form of classes, or types of relations. When such constants are combined, we get a bundling of information, which has descriptive import for those who understand the names of the constants involved. Descriptive functions express, but do not refer. When a descriptive function involves a variable, this implies that the information contained will vary for the differing constant values of the variable.

In the definition of any natural number, the uniformity appealed to lies in the description of the natural number forms, not in the numbers themselves. Thus the definition does not hide the axiom of infinity in the cosmological sense of naming an (actual) infinity of objects. However, in a mathematical sense the axiom of infinity is involved here through the fact that the *set* of natural numbers is completely determined, in that: (a) this set exists because some specific number can be indicated (through the definition of that particular number), and (b) through the descriptive successor function, the scope of this set is fixed.

The type of arithmetic made possible by this approach is known as primitive recursive arithmetic, first developed by Thoralf Skolem, after he had studied (*15*) *Principia Mathematica* and dropped the logical quantification from the treatment of arithmetic (cf. *7*: 302-33).

24. The word *induction* is not really correct here. Historically the word came into use

because mathematicians first thought that this principle allowed one to proceed from the particular properties of some numbers to general properties of all numbers. The conclusion of the principle, as an inference, is indeed general, but is valid only if *both* the parts (i) and (ii) hold. Now, (i) is particular, but (ii) is not. The latter makes a statement about every number. Thus the inference is from a particular statement *and* a general statement to a general conclusion. This does not accord with the usual meaning of induction as found in empiricistic thought.

For the central importance of mathematical induction in mathematics, see the remarks by Jean van Heijenoort in *7*: 480-2, and also the papers referred to in these remarks.

25. H. Dooyeweerd and those who follow him in his particular view of the "numerical modality" (e.g. D. M. Stafleu and D. F. M. Strauss) also include the rational numbers in what I here call the typical numerical structure. I think there are convincing arguments against such inclusion. I agree, however, that this numerical structure can be expanded so as to anticipate spatial and physical descriptions. This expansion requires its own discussion and cannot be included here. In this paper I limit myself to a discussion of numerical states of affairs in terms of epistemological and ontological demands, which are to me philosophically justifiable.

26. Cf. note 20 above.

Bibliography

1. BROUWER, L. E. J., "Intuitionisme en Formalisme" (1912), reprinted in: *Wiskunde, Waarheid, Werkelijkheid*; Groningen: P. Noordhoff, 1919. English translation in: *Philosophy of Mathematics*, eds. P. Benacerraf and H. Putnam; Englewood Cliffs: Prentice-Hall, 1964.

2. ---. "Weten, Willen, Spreken," in: *Euclides*, 9 (1933).

3. ---. "Consciousness, Philosophy and Mathematics," in: *Proceedings of the 10th International Congress of Philosophy*, eds. E. W. Beth and H. J. Pos; Amsterdam: North-Holland, 1949.

4. CASSIRER, E., *Substance and Function*, translated by W. C. Swabey and M. C. Swabey; New York: Dover, 1953.

5. EUCLID, *Elements*, 3 vols., translated with introduction and comments by Sir Thomas L. Heath; New York: Dover, 1956.

6. FREGE, G., *The Foundations of Arithmetic/Die Grundlagen der Arithmetik* (1884), German text with English translation by J. L. Austin; Oxford: Blackwell, 1974.

7. HEIJENOORT, J. van (ed.), *From Frege to Gödel: A Source Book in Mathematical Logic, 1879-1931*; Cambridge, Mass.: Harvard University Press, 1967.

8. HELMHOLTZ, H. von, "Zählen und Messen, erkenntnisstheoretisch Betrachtet," in: *Philosophische Aufsätze, Eduard Zeller gewidmet*; Leipzig, 1887.

9. LANDAU, E., *Grundlagen der Analysis*, New York: Chelsea, 1965.

10. PARSONS, C., "Mathematics, Foundations of," in: *The Encyclopedia of Philosophy*, editor in chief Paul Edwards, Vol. 5, pp. 188-213.

11. RUSSELL, B., *The Principles of Mathematics*, 2nd ed.; London: George Allen & Unwin, 1937.

12. – –. *Introduction to Mathematical Philosophy*; London: George Allen & Unwin, 1919.

13. SON, B. H., *Science and Person: A Study on the Idea of Philosophy as Rigorous Science in Kant and Husserl*; Assen: Van Gorcum, 1972.

14. WHITEHEAD, A. N., "Indication, Classes, Number, Validation," in: *Mind*, 43 (1934), pp. 281-97; plus "Corrigenda," *idem*, p. 543.

15. WHITEHEAD, A. N. and RUSSELL, B., *Principia Mathematica*, Vol. 1, 2nd ed.; Cambridge: University Press, 1927.

Interview with Dr. H. Evan Runner

HARRY VAN DYKE
and
ALBERT M. WOLTERS

. . . so you see, if it hadn't been for the fact that I had all that Greek in high school, college and graduate school, I would not have been able to work with Vollenhoven and test the significance of what he was doing. The point I want to make is, we must not go on as Christians the way the Evangelicals generally are still doing in the United States, just suddenly trying to get into culture by going to a university and saying, "Now we'll go to a philosophy class and find out what philosophy is all about," for then you get some tradition which has been with us all these years, or in the history of philosophy you get some big textbook that has been written according to the American norm, or older books which were translations of German books from the end of the 19th century. *That's not our task!* Our task is as Christians ourselves to study those Greek texts as closely as we can as we try to understand what was going on, what they were doing *in the light of the full revelation that we have in the Scriptures.* That, to me, is a very important thing that Vollenhoven taught us, and we've only just begun to work that way—we've only just begun. And as I look back over my early years and call to mind all those apparently insignificant events, I see—well, you have to speak from out of your faith—I see that the Lord was preparing me in those simple things.

But you wanted to know about my early background. Well, I grew up in a Presbyterian church in Philadelphia. My father was Scotch-Irish and

Welsh. His great-grandfather was a Presbyterian minister who came to this country from Ulster with his congregation at the time of the potato famine in the 1840s. They established a little community in Pennsylvania—Runnersville, not too far from Oxford—and became farmers. But my grandfather—shows how short a time ago that is—he ran away from home and became a bugler in the Civil War on the Northern side. I remember him as a retired farmer; he lived to be 92 years old. My father was born in 1878, and he lived to be 84. He was a "hard-shell" Baptist until he married my mother.

My mother was English and Pennsylvania Dutch. Her father's name was Watterson; her mother's name was White. They lived in that rural area too, but they belonged to one of the more prominent churches in Oxford, the Presbyterian church. Grandfather Watterson was a schoolteacher, and as he got older he sold insurance, and then was retired. I can remember that I used to sit on his lap and pull at his long white beard. My mother worked in a dry-goods store for a number of years before she was married in 1912. I was born in 1916. My father had been married twice before, but his second wife and his only son died in the same winter, of pneumonia, and his first wife had also died. So I was the only child and a good deal of emotion was attached to me, and that probably was not good. Anyway, before I was two years old we moved to Philadelphia because, as they told me later, they wanted me to have the opportunity to study and to advance.

The church I grew up in was Westminster Presbyterian Church at 58th and Chester Avenue. Our pastor—the only one I had until I went away to college—was Warren R. Ward. He was a graduate of Princeton Seminary, but he had been a Methodist all his life. He used to organize a summer Bible school every July. It was excellent. I have never run across anything as well regulated and accoutered. The church also had a very good prayer service on Wednesday evenings. As many as 150 to 200 people would turn out. The prayer period was half the hour; and the other half was spent studying the Scriptures. The minister went through Bible books verse by verse and word by word. I remember going through Ephesians, Romans and Revelation. And we of the younger generation were encouraged in that church to memorize the Shorter Catechism. But the strangest thing, the sermonizing was Arminian! And the pastor encouraged us to attend the Keswick Conferences in New Jersey, which taught a form of perfectionism. We also had the Scofield Reference Bible recommended to us, and we heard a lot of preaching about the rapture and the millennium. And we would have men from Moody Bible Institute. But at the same time Mr. Ward would tell us about his teachers at Princeton: J.

Gresham Machen, Robert Dick Wilson, and Oswald Allis. But I'll come back to that.

What I used to read as a boy? Oh, novels having to do with the French and Indian wars, everything about the frontier, Daniel Boone—all that sort of thing. And I began to read Dickens. I just *devoured* Dickens. In the summer months you could always find me at the public library, you know, the local branch. And that's where I first started taking out philosophy books—that's right! It just comes back to me. It was in a cool, shady part of the general reading room. I would stand in front of the shelf that had books on logic and epistemology and so on, and I would take one home and leaf through it and see that I couldn't understand it and take it back later. Ha, ha! But I wanted so badly to understand what was in those books!

I went to Anna Howard Shaw Junior High School, at 54th and Warrington Avenue. It's a very bad neighborhood now, I'm told, with street gangs and stabbings sometimes taking place at night in the streets and alleys. But I have fine memories of that place! Especially the Latin teacher, Miss Catherine I. Smart. She took a great interest in her students and fired us with a desire to be able to read and work with Latin. She was an unmarried Roman Catholic lady of middle age, straight black hair, and false teeth that would regularly fall to her desk top when she burst out laughing as we, one after the other, recited *hic, haec, hoc*.

After that I went to West Philadelphia High School. It was more than a half hour's walk, but we walked in groups, picking up friends on the way. I remember I had a number of Orthodox Jewish friends, who would invite me in for just a moment while they put on their prayer caps and quickly said their prayers, saying, "Watch how I do this," and then we'd go out and walk on to school together. I remember in my last year of high school one of them invited me in and I wondered what was coming. Then he pulled out something and said: "Look, I just bought a prayer rug; I've converted from Judaism to Islam." So he would take his prayer rug to school from that day on.

Sometime during my high school years there was a "Million Dollars Testament Campaign" all across America, and I became an agent for that. I got a number of students together, and we would stand in the fire escapes (because we weren't allowed in the school building, but the fire escapes were enclosed in the building actually) and distribute New Testaments, until *that* was forbidden. And then, with the help of one of the teachers in the English department, we held a little Bible study group right after school hours, in one of the classrooms. We just felt the need of Christian fellowship, because there was no such thing. You know, our life in school and during the week was just so different from Sunday and Wednesday night at the church! We were growing up in a working-class neighborhood with many Irish Catholics and just three or four blocks from a very heavy Jewish community with a big synagogue, so you associated with *these* kids all the time. The only time you weren't with them was when you were in your own church, in the prayer meetings on Wednesday night and at young people's society and all day Sunday. So you felt the pull of two worlds very strongly. My mother never let me go to school in the morning without having me get down on my knees with her in prayer. *Every* morning. Just a short prayer for the day, you know, and for my work. And we might remember my father (he'd be off to work already) and our Korea missionaries and people that we knew and Christian work that we knew about. She had me do that every school day. Actually, when I left home for college, quite a tug was needed to pull away from that form of piety. Meanwhile, our minister was undergoing a change and started giving altar calls in the evening services. At first only three or four times a year, but gradually it became fairly regular: at the last hymn there would always be an altar call, and you could come forward and kneel in the front benches. The idea was to have your sins forgiven and to repent, that is, to expect not to engage in those sins again. But of course you did. So of course, although it was meant to be a once-for-all thing, you'd find yourself going up more than once. It has a terribly wearing and tearing effect on the emotional life of a puber. And then those sermons inviting you to give your life to the Lord, which you felt you hadn't done completely unless you volunteered to be a minister or a foreign missionary—what they called "full-time . . .*

> Young people today lack *order* or *structure* in their thinking about the Bible. That is a strange thing; for the Bible is a revelation to us of *the order of God in His creation.* And it is *the insight into this order* (proper Bible-knowledge) that gives *perspective to our life-in-the-world* (Kingdom service). The second flows out of the first. Thus it is not surprising that our young people also have no clear-cut convictions about what Kingdom service is (Rom. 12:1-2). [1963]

. . . Christian service." What I appreciate in it is that a person has to come to a point of decision, and that it is important that he make it known before the whole congregation. But whether in this way, at that moment,

*The quotations, set in a different typeface, have been selected from Dr. Runner's writings and are intended to clarify and expand on the comments he makes in the interview.

perhaps under the impression of some words you've just heard—I question whether that is good for a young person. At any rate, that's not what I would mean by "hearing and doing"!

But to get back to our pastor's interest in Princeton. Towards the end of the 1920s it was threatened with reorganization by the General Assembly, which would take away its distinctive Reformed character and make it more representative of all the movements in the church. This led in 1929 to the founding of Westminster Seminary, and our pastor was fully behind that. He would have some of these men come out and preach for us, and there would be a special offering for the new seminary. I remember hearing Robert Dick Wilson, J. Gresham Machen and Oswald Allis in this way. And I was taken by my parents to the very first opening exercises of Westminster Seminary and to its first graduation exercises. I clearly remember Robert Dick Wilson giving his final exhortation to Westminster's first graduating class.

I went to Wheaton College in the fall of 1932. That first semester my father lost his job. He was a typesetter with a firm that printed law cases and also railroad timetables and things like that. It was a very good company to work for—until the depression and the linotype machine came . . . . So here he was—unemployed at 54! He sold Fuller brushes, did anything to make a little money. It was bad. He had savings in one of the savings and loan associations, and I remember taking a long walk with him one evening—we walked to save money, that's how tight it was—to their office, and when he came out he said to me, "Well, I don't expect to see any of *that* money back." I wanted to quit school, but they insisted that I continue. How they managed to support me during those years I don't know. I myself managed to get some scholarship aid.

Right from the beginning, I chose philosophy as my major. There were always these two strains in me: my love for philosophy and a classical education—I mean the sense of the continuity of our experience of Western civilization—*and* the desire to be a missionary, to Korea first, later to China, to come to grips with that whole civilization, to make the Christian religion relate to it somehow. And that lasted right up until I was at the Free University of Amsterdam (the Netherlands), in 1946-47, where Harry Boer and I had rooms next to each other: he had been in Nigeria already, and we would sit till three or four in the morning discussing whether I should go to China. But it looked bad in China then. The northern march of the Communists was taking place: it was the demise of the Kuomintang. On the other hand, I was feeling increasingly that the

Christian base at home was eroding. And that's when I finally decided I would work here, in the West.

> Often as a child and adolescent, and indeed even later, I wondered why there were no longer any Christian martyrs. Could it be that the Spirit of Christ had conquered the world, and there was no opposition? But then I began to see that there were no struggles, no contesting of spirits, for the simple reason that the Christians had withdrawn into their own little house, the organized church, and through a spirit of gradual accommodation had abandoned the world to a spirit alien to Christ's to give form to nine-tenths of our society. [This could not but greatly affect their own spirituality.] [1967]

In my first two years at Wheaton they had only one man in philosophy. As a sophomore, I had to write a paper about values in his Medieval Philosophy course. The question was whether good was good and God was good because He participated in goodness, or whether goodness was good because God willed it so. And I felt—I think that this came from reading the Scriptures—that goodness was what it was because of the way God had made the world, that it must issue ultimately from God's creator-will. But the professor took what I would call the more platonic view, you know, that there's some kind of subsisting goodness in which God participates and is therefore good. And I got quite upset about it. So when I went home in the spring vacation, I went right down to Westminster Seminary, which was still in session, and I—I was generally quite shy when I was young, but I was determined to make this paper good—I went up to some students and asked them, "Where can I get Dr. Van Til?" And they led me to him, and I told him I was a student at Wheaton and was thinking of coming to Westminster but that I had this problem on my hands just now, and would he have any syllabuses or anything that would provide me with material for this term paper? He piled me up with stuff which I took home and tried to devour in the few days I had.

Of course, I also took Greek in college. I had had three years of it in high school, and we had read Xenophon and three books of Homer. But at Wheaton they had only one professor, a retired Methodist minister. He was about eighty-some years old, and he would just drone out a translation. But they put me in Junior Greek, and we read Herodotus the first year, and what did we read the second year? Euripides' *Alcestis*. Just one play in the whole semester. It was not good. So, mainly for that reason, in my third year I went to the University of Pennsylvania, where I took a lot of Greek with a man named Bates (a well-known editor of Sophocles). I studied hard that year and neglected a lot of other things. But that year I got much better instruction in philosophy too. I had a year course in modern philosophy from Henry Bradford Smith, one of America's best logicians. He was the one who at the end of the first lecture dared us to leave the faith of our homes behind us and follow the course with an open mind. He said: "This class is made up of all kinds of people—orthodox Protestants, liberal Protestants, Orthodox Jews, liberal Jews, Reform Jews, Roman Catholics, Greek Orthodox Christians, and unbelievers like myself. How can we possibly discuss together unless we have some common basis? And since it can't be any of those things, what else is there except that we can build up a fund of rational ideas together? And that's what modern philosophy is all about." Well, I was impressed with that. That's the day I walked home through the park and stood in front of a tree and took out my pocket knife and scratched my initials in the tree and thought: "Do I dare or don't I dare?" I finally decided I didn't dare let go of my faith. I learned from that later how important it is to grab a student in the first month—even the first week—when those fundamental decisions are being made that determine the whole direction of his life.

> At the end of the period as we were already leaving the room the professor dared us to free ourselves of our past and make a new beginning on a rational basis that would be acceptable to all reasonable persons. What would you have done? I was a serious student; I wanted more than anything else at that moment to enter into the beckoning mysteries of the history of modern philosophy. Well, I did not follow the advice of my professor, but I almost did, humanly speaking. Yet I must say this here: I did not know what was going on, and for years I was unable to say why it was not right to take the professor's "reasonable" dare. I know many Christians who took similar advice, usually with the most disastrous consequences.
>
> Permit me one more brief illustration. Many years later when I was doing graduate work in a research society at Harvard University it happened at a dinner that a professor suddenly looked up laughing into my face and asked if I could still believe that Jesus had gone "up" to heaven. He meant, of course, that with the moden scientific picture of the world that had arisen out of the work of Copernicus, Bruno, Kepler, Galileo, and others "up" could be anywhere and thus nowhere in particular. By this time I was more mature and knew something about what was going on. But the disdainful attitude still hurt; it was as if you were being cut off from any body of scholars that might be expected to do useful work.... A statement about the sunset does not refer to the earth and the sun in their mutual relations as a result of their physical motion in space; it is language which gives expression to our experience of life from out of our central (religious) human position as lords of the creation (Ps. 8). All the arguments about no longer being able to believe that man is the center of the created world and the earth the scene of the great drama of the covenantal fellowship between God and men stem from making the physical *aspect* of life the whole of life. The scientistic thinker (not, be it noted, the scientific thinker!) has identified all proper knowledge

with scientific knowledge, in particular with the mathematical methods of physics or with other areas of science that attempt to apply its methods. When we look at the earth and the sun and their mutual relations *in this particular manner*, then there is no place for a sunset. The scientistic thinker characteristically concludes that the concept "sunset" belongs to a primitive pre-scientific generation and straightway excludes it from the body of true and valid knowledge.

The same sort of thing was involved in the Harvard professor's laughing remark to me about the ascension of Christ. From the point of view of our present scientific conception of the motions of physical bodies in space it is not possible to conceive of any absolute "up"; such a concept the scientistic thinker would describe as "medieval" and "obscurantist." We need to take a slightly closer look at what is involved here. What the medieval men had done was to accommodate scriptural revelation to an old Greek science. Medieval Christians read the Greek scientific meaning back into the revelation, so that the "up" of Jesus' ascension became confused with the "up" of the Ptolemaic world-picture. But science, a human activity, has a history. And when subsequently the Ptolemaic picture was cast aside by men like Bruno and Copernicus, the effect upon the Church and upon the attitude of men towards the Word of God was disastrous. Not because science had disproved the scriptures, but because the medieval church had accommodated the supra-temporal Word of God to a time-conditioned scientific piece of work, understanding the former in the light of the latter, thus reversing the natural order. The science in the synthesis was indeed primitive.

I suppose this was in the mind of that Harvard professor that day. But, as I have already told you, there was no opportunity on that occasion to explain to him how I thought about the matter. Actually, however, his observation had no more bearing on my thought than that other half-rhetorical question once put to me by one of Harvard's most distinguished professors: "How can you believe in God in these days when space has become so vast; where do you put Him?" For all the scriptures say about the ascension is that Jesus led the disciples to a place over against Bethany and that while they looked on he was taken up, and a cloud received him out of their sight. It ought to be clear that the "up" here simply refers to the very ordinary, everyday experience of those disciples who remained standing on the earth, the place appointed by God to be man's home.

The fatal original error of scientism was to take such a word as "up" and insist that the only "true" meaning it could have was the scientific meaning that refers abstractly to relations of physical motion. In logical terms, such words were thought of as being "univocal," i.e. as having one and only one meaning.

This scientism is still essentially the faith of the men comprising the teaching staffs of our modern universities. From my observation of Christian students over a period now of slightly more than twenty-five years I am convinced that almost without exception the student is lost to *integral* Christianity not somewhere down the years of his university experiences, but at the very outset. The innocent freshman does not realize that the very *existence* of the university involves the

> philosophical problem as to its *place*, as to the *place* of science (*die Wissenschaft*) in the whole of life. [1960]

For my senior year I went back to Wheaton. I had heard that they had a new instructor for Greek, a young Ph.D. graduate of Dr. Oldfather's (University of Illinois, trained, as J. Gresham Machen had been, in Gildersleeve's classical seminar at the John Hopkins University in Baltimore, Maryland). Harriet Jamieson was her name, and she was indeed excellent. I took two courses from her. We read the *Agamemnon* of Aeschylus, and we read two books of Thucydides' *History*. I became an assistant in the department and graded papers.

I had always had seminary, particularly Westminster, in mind (as well as the idea of becoming a missionary, at first to Korea, later to China), but more and more as I got into Greek I thought about getting a doctorate in classical languages and becoming a Greek teacher. And as a matter of fact, in my senior year Miss Jamieson recommended me for a scholarship that would enable me to go to the University of Illinois to study with Dr. Oldfather. You could get a doctorate in three years. It was a strong temptation. I asked her, "How many days do I have to think it over?" And she said, "Well, I ought to have your answer in three days." So I went into my room and just thought and thought and thought, and prayed, and I decided: No, I'm not going to do it. If I do that, I'll do it *after* seminary. So I gave it up. I hated to give it up, because money was scarce in those days and I had never had much of it. In the summer following my graduation I taught a course in Plato's dialogues in the Greek department at Wheaton, and then in the fall of 1936 I began my studies at Westminster Seminary. And there I learned about the revival of the Reformed religion in the nineteenth century. And I remember in my second year there Dr. Van Til said to me: "If you want to become a Reformed thinker, you had better think about learning the Dutch language, because most of the writing in which this developing thought has been embodied will not be translated in your lifetime, if ever, and there's no way to get at it except to learn Dutch and read it well." So, right then and there, I made up my mind to learn Dutch.

> To Professor Van Til I am indebted in many ways. He first opened my eyes to the possibility of a Christian method in philosophy and from him I first heard about the serious effort being made at the Free University of Amsterdam to formulate a philosophy in the light of scriptural revelation. From him too I first learned to read the Dutch language, an accomplishment which has become a source of ever-increasing blessing and joy to me, chiefly in enabling me to follow the remarkable reformational work which the Spirit of God has wrought in the Netherlands since the days of Da Costa, Bilderdijk and Groen

> van Prinsterer. This historic movement has come to be for me what Athens was to the fourth-century Greek, the nursery of genuine *paideia.* [1951]

And then Professor Klaas Schilder of the Theological Faculty of Kampen, the Netherlands, came to Philadelphia. He had come to America at the invitation of some Christian Reformed men in New Jersey and Michigan to talk, among other things, about common grace. But at any rate, in April of 1939 Schilder stopped off at Westminster Seminary and gave three lectures. He dealt with Karl Barth's Gifford Lectures on the Scottish Confession of 1560, and he had some very critical remarks to make about how the work had been translated and interpreted. I listened very intently to those lectures, and I liked them very much. He was a blustering type of person, but I took to him, and at Dr. Van Til's suggestion I went to him to talk about my plans for the future. Since my high school days I had wanted to study at a German university. "Well," he said, "there's a high probability that there will be war very shortly, but why don't you come to Kampen for a year first? Then you can get a much better idea of what we have to offer in the Netherlands, and after a year you can decide whether you still want to go on to Germany. I can always get you references to people in Erlangen." And he tried to sum up what my expenses would be in Kampen, going into all kinds of detail about room and board, laundry, and so on . . . . Anyway, I was persuaded to go to Kampen.

I was keen on going to Europe. At this stage of my development, however, it was not to learn more about the Reformed view of life and all that; it was almost exclusively in the interest of studying theology. I wasn't thinking much beyond that. I was just an idealistic young fellow who had grown up in the American Evangelical world, and we had this distinct phenomenon of Westminster Seminary, and the struggle was to keep our Presbyterian heritage. You see, the one Presbyterian Church in the United States split during the Civil War. Afterwards the North industrialized and prospered, and the northern seminaries began to send many of their brighter students to Germany, where the Ph.D. programs had developed. They began to get their professors back newly trained under Von Harnack and people like that, and so the *religionsgeschichtliche Schule* came into the seminaries. The big battle was whether Princeton would slowly but surely be caught up in the maelstrom and undergo the same influences, or whether it would stand apart from that development as a kind of rock of traditional Scottish-American Presbyterian orthodoxy—which really meant, philosophically, as I came to see later, Scottish Realism and back to the Cambridge Platonists and the idea of reason as having its own, if not scientialistic, at least practicalistic *a priori* and all that. I didn't realize those things then. I was simply caught up in that struggle of preserving our Presbyterian heritage over against the Modernism in the church that we had till recently been part of, and I wanted to be able to work with the best theoretical-theological tools available. That was the framework. That's why I went to the Netherlands. It was part and parcel of the notion that theological science gets at the finesses of the Christian religion. It was part of that confusion that hearing the Word of God is doing and writing theology, that *there* you are closest to the Word of God and are working out its finest meaning. It was the Greek faith in *theoria*.

> In the Christian world a particularly striking example of the insidious working of the scientistic frame of mind is the confusion of the immediate awareness of the integral Truth of the Word of God in our hearts with a scientific (theological) body of propositional statements about this Truth. So much attention has been devoted to the latter that the necessary earlier possession of the former has largely been overlooked.... But the Reformation taught us that men are free from the theologians in understanding and interpreting the Word of God. Life precedes science, and in life God makes us aware of (reveals to us) the Truth .... The *terra firma* of God's truth ought not to be called theology, or we might get an unfortunate canonization, no, worse, declaration of infallibility of Berkhof or some other theologian (depending of course, on the speaker's preferences). Let us not be the cause of any theologian's becoming canon for us, or a stuffed shirt. [1960]

I sailed for Europe on August 24, 1939, the day the newspaper headlines read: *ROOSEVELT ADVISES AMERICANS TO LEAVE EUROPE*. The war broke out the day we arrived. Most of the Americans never got off the boat. They said, "We're going right back to the States," but I, a brash 23-year-old, who for so long had wanted to experience Europe and European education, finally said to myself, "I'm staying here, no matter what." I settled in Kampen (where before the war the circumstances of the nineteenth century still surrounded you on every hand and some things reminded you strongly of the Middle Ages) on September 16 to live at the Hospitium of the Theological School. Schilder appeared to have a very busy life. He published a lot, was editor of a weekly, served on a synodical committee, and during all this he would just rush into class almost out of breath and start lecturing. He never had a note in front of him, but he would talk, for example, about some dogmatics point, about when it first became a matter of articulated doctrine of the church at some medieval council or in the debates between Abelard and Bernard of Clairvaux, or something like that, and he would quote the Latin text of the decision of the Council of Soissons out of the big collection of Hefele-Leclercq from memory. He was treating the *Locus de Deo*, and he was handling the difference between *cognitio Dei insita* and *cognitio Dei acquisita* as it developed in Reformed theology in the seventeenth century, and in connection with that how Descartes and the Cartesian school dealt with the whole problem of the innate knowledge of God. Well, that was very much to the point for me, a young systematic theologian who knew something about the history of philosophy and could collate the two things. That's what attracted me to him. And although he didn't elaborate on it so explicitly, I slowly began to see in his lectures that behind that development or combined with it was this whole history of modern rationalistic philosophy and the Cartesian notion of the *a priori* which was bound up with the notion of *ratio*. And that is what made me begin to see that you can get partitioned off into theology and its history, while other people get siphoned off into philosophy and its history, and that just isn't the way to get insight into what happened, because there is some common element behind them both that causes them to run parallel. There is a parallel in the phenomena of the several sciences. It is one *Geistesentwicklung* which took place. After six months of Kampen, I returned to America when the Consulate advised us to leave Europe. It was the end of February, 1940. My immediate problem was how to continue my education. Get a doctorate . . . but in what? I was in theology and had seen these lines running parallel in modern philosophy and modern theology. So that made me want to get to know more about church history. But I had to get help somewhere, so I sent out letters to about six graduate schools. The best answer I got was from Harvard Divinity School. It offered me six hundred dollars, which was good in those days, and on that basis I decided to go there. And I thought the best thing to do was to take Philosophical Theology or Church History, and I decided on Church History because I saw that I needed a lot more historical information than I had if I was going to be precise about what I did philosophically. Also, I had seen in their catalogue that George LaPiana (formerly of the Gregorian University in Rome) was there, and I thought this man might just be a good man to work with. I went to see him as soon as I got to Cambridge and told him I wanted to become a good historian and learn all the techniques, the ancillary disciplines, and whatever else was necessary. So basically I worked with LaPiana that year.

At the end of that year I was recommended by two men of the Divinity School faculty to the Society of Fellows of Harvard University on the basis of two papers I had written—one on some aspects of Augustine's *De Trinitate* and the other on Kierkegaard's *Abschliessende unwissenschaftliche Nachschrift* (at that time not yet available in English). Well, I was appointed to the Society of Fellows. In those days I was studying Syriac. I had studied it at Westminster and was taking it at Harvard from Professor William Thomson, and I had started to read a certain man named

Ephraim Syrus, and I got the idea, in connection with my studies in philosophy, that it might be a good thing to read some of the Syrian writers about dogma and some Greek writers like the Apologists and the Anti-gnostic Fathers and see whether the structures of Greek philosophy were much less visible in the Syriac writers than in the Greek writers. That was the idea I had and that was the project I presented for the three years I would be a Junior Fellow . . . . I had an office to myself in the Widener Library near the section I would be using the most. So a lot of patristic stuff was right outside my office. And we had keys to the stacks—oh, it was an ideal set-up! As a Junior Fellow I could audit any courses I felt would be helpful. One I attended was by Edward Kennard Rand, who wrote *The Building of Eternal Rome* and *The Founders of the Middle Ages* (which has an excellent chapter on Boethius). Rand gave a course on the classical heritage of the Middle Ages, and one day he talked to me and I told him about myself and about my Syriac project. He said, "You know, a man you want to know is right upstairs—Werner Jaeger, formerly of the University of Berlin. I am going to see that you get introduced to him." So about a week later there was a note from Rand under the door of my office introducing me to Professor Jaeger.

Jaeger told me about his vow to Wilamowitz to finish the critical edition of Gregory of Nyssa, and that he had a number of people working for him and was looking for people to collate manuscripts to make a critical edition. And I said, "Oh, I would be interested in knowing a little more about that. Do you think it would be possible . . . ?" I immediately jumped at the thing because I thought if you could work with him day by day you would learn many things. Perhaps I jumped too fast giving up this other project—I just said it on the spur of the moment, actually, but I have always felt the greater desirability of being educated by an outstanding *person*. And he said, "Well, why don't you come and read for me some day?" So one day I went to his office and he gave me a page of Gregory of Nyssa to translate. Somehow I managed that, and he got up and smiled—he was always so gracious—and said, "Well, if you would like to be part of my institute, I think we could find work for you." Two days later I was up there getting photostats.

Our job was to collate manuscripts and then to determine the critical text. I was assigned a sermon of Gregory's that dealt with the resurrection. Meanwhile, Jaeger himself was continually going through catalogues of libraries in Europe, trying to find new manuscripts that might include work by Gregory and just thinking his way through manuscript history and manuscript dissemination. I learned a lot of things from Jaeger in terms of historical method, but I have had little chance to use them. I've always wanted to make an edition of something. I think it is important to get some project like this started with your students and to get an institute started. Christians ought to be doing this kind of work—in their own schools. After three years at Harvard, I taught English and Latin at a Christian high school in Paterson, New Jersey, and began working for a Th.M. degree at Westminster. I would come down to Philadelphia for a week or a long weekend and spend a lot of time there. I completed it in 1945-46 while I stayed with my parents again, and I did substitute teaching in the public school system. I concentrated on two areas: the ancient church, especially the fourth and fifth centuries, Gregory of Nyssa, the Cappadocian Fathers and the men right around there in that part of the world; and secondly, the beginning of Protestant scholasticism—Geneva, France, the men around Beza, Gomarus, Voetius, Cocceius. Also, what the differences were between the Genevan so-called decretal theology and the later covenant theology. I made big charts with hundreds of names and their writings.

Gradually, however, I was becoming a little bit skeptical about the meaning of my research projects. I was just accumulating facts, facts, facts, but my ability to unify them and to see sense in them wasn't keeping pace. And as for the relation of philosophy to the history of theology—I just felt I didn't have the key to that. And then there was the dividedness in my personal life: living in the city, attendance at public schools, voting Republican, growing up with the Shorter Catechism, the Keswick Conferences, the Scofield Bible—the dualism that characterizes so many American fundamentalists was my life too, and I began to feel I couldn't live that way any longer. My life was just a lot of bits and pieces; it wasn't pulled together. So I thought, my first task is to see my own life in a greater unity—get it all together—but I didn't know where I could get help unless it would be from that philosophical movement at the Free University. So as the war was coming to an end, I secretly in my heart longed to go back to the Netherlands.

So you see, my reason for going to the Netherlands again after the war was once more to a large extent theoretical—to gain clarity about the coherence of the history of philosophy and theology. And it wasn't until I began to study the *Wijsbegeerte der Wetsidee* more seriously that I began to sense the depth-dimension of man in the heart and the answer that a man gives and has to give to revelation. That took me years, but gradually I began to see the religious background of all human work, pre-theoretical as well as theoretical, and that our *certainties*—the problem Husserl wrestles with and the problem Heidegger wrestles with, and they haven't resolved it really: where does the apodicticity, the certainty, the universal validity, where does it come from? Husserl got it from Brentano and from

British empiricism, but if it is to arise out of our experience of sense-data and our observation of factual situations, there's no possible explanation for an absolutely universal validity. There's no way to explain that, and you fall flat on your face. But the idea that there is a *revelation*, that God's creation is of a law-order, and that that law-order somehow revelationally impinges upon us, and that our nature as religious beings in the covenant . . .

> It is difficult, Professor Vollenhoven, highly esteemed promotor, to express in words what these five years of association have meant to me. I marvel that just at the time when I threatened to succumb to the widespread pestilence of historical relativism my footsteps were directed to you. For under your tutelage the divine antidote was with remarkable skill accommodated to the peculiar symptoms of my disease. [1951]

. . . of God is to walk with Him and to know this revelation in some immediate religious confrontation with God—that began to give me a new hope, the hope that I could deal with complex factual situations and that I could rest at any given moment because my knowledge of law or of universal validity (I am using later terminology; I wasn't all that conscious of those things then) wasn't derived from or dependent upon the building up of all those facts, so that I would collapse in the accumulation of them, but there was a deeper dimension constantly at work while I was studying history—in short, it was the religious background of the *Wijsbegeerte der Wetsidee* that put solid rock under my feet. I got to Amsterdam in the fall of 1946. Holland was just pulling out of the war situation. Fuel was rationed, and so was food. I stayed in the Hospitium of the Free University on the Keizersgracht, and there I got to know Leo Oranje, and then in that winter of 1946-47 some very important things happened.

It was a very severe winter, and by February they ran out of fuel. We sat in our rooms with our overcoats on, hats on, earmuffs on, gloves—you'd take the glove off, turn the page, put the glove back on—we had boots on, and so we sat and studied! And Oranje came to my room on a Friday afternoon—it was bitter cold and I was very uncomfortable—and he said, "You can't study in this cold all weekend. I'm going to my girl's house; they'll have a little heat there. Would you like to come along?" So I said okay and I went along. And that weekend I met Elisabeth Wichers, who was to become my wife! That was in Badhoevedorp.

Later Oranje took me to Breukelen to his own family. His father was very active in all kinds of Christian causes: he was principal of a Christian day school, and he was in the Antirevolutionary Party, and he was in a Christian social organization called Patrimonium—I don't know what all. And once Leo Oranje casually remarked to me, "You take everything too theoretically!" Well, he was a law student himself, but he turned to me and said, "You take everything too theoretically. Why don't you see something of our Reformed *life* in the Netherlands?" I said, "All right, but how do I go about it?" And he said, "Why not start with a visit to the Kuyperhuis? They'll be able to tell you something about it there." So I got on the phone and it was answered by Dr. Rutgers, the one who had been governor-general of the West Indies. When they found out that there might be more students interested, they arranged a day for us. So a group of us—myself, Harry Boer, a fellow from South Africa, and a few others—we all went down to The Hague and spent a whole day with the staff of the Kuyper Foundation. And we met Dr. Gerbrandy, who had been premier in London during the war, and we met and talked with a daughter of Abraham Kuyper who was already very old. But, typically Dutch, they had three people read papers to us: Mekkes and Bruins Slot and Van Riessen all read papers, each an hour long.

As I went home and thought it all over, I began to realize that there was a broad spectrum of Reformed life, and that I had never experienced anything like this before. And I began to ask myself: Where did all this come from? There was the theology that I was used to, there was the philosophy that I was busy studying, but now I learned there was also a practical life. How were they related? I don't remember how I first got steered to Groen van Prinsterer—probably through talks with Leo at some meal or so at the girls' home—but I bought myself a copy of *Ongeloof en Revolutie* and read it. And I read about Isaac da Costa and Bilderdijk and Groen and about the differences between them. And then the problem that I originally had between philosophy and theology as two forms of scientific life got broadened out to also include pre-scientific life—what lies behind all this? And I began to sense the importance of the religious dimension of the heart and the covenant of God and what that means—that we live with God in His covenant, and that all the various aspects of our life are embraced in that, and how that openness or closedness of the heart to His revelation which impinges upon us and to which we must respond gives direction to all the various expressions of our life, whether they are scientific or pre-scientific. That began to take on some shape, but only gradually, and I don't think I got that all worked out until I had begun to teach at Calvin, really.

Early in 1948 it looked very much as if the Italians and the French would all vote Communist at the general elections that were coming up, and there was general talk that the Russian armies would just come in and march right up to the Channel. One day at the end of February, my wife and I were sitting in De Roode Leeuw across the street from De Bijenkorf drinking coffee after doing some shopping when we noticed that the man at the next table was holding a newspaper which read in big headlines: *MASARYK COMMITS SUICIDE.* I didn't believe it. I thought he had been forced to do that, so I said, "It's time for us to get out of here." We left Europe somewhere early in March.

For a year we lived in Philadelphia, and then rented a cottage in Pella, Iowa, at the suggestion of Glenn Andreas, who lived there. Glenn and I have been close friends ever since we met at Wheaton, and he has been a source of encouragement to me in many ways all these years. I had all my Aristotle books with me and worked on my thesis. In March, 1950, we were back in the Netherlands to get the dissertation finished and approved and to receive my degree. I worked very closely with Vollenhoven. He was himself working on the development of Aristotle at this time and was preparing something for publication because I had to be able to refer to it in my thesis.

> The work of Vollenhoven makes claim to have penetrated far beyond the present insight into the nature and relations among the philosophical results of individuals and "schools" in antiquity . . . . Can the promise which the method of Vollenhoven holds for getting Aristotelian research out of the impasse into which it has fallen indeed be realized? May we now look forward to the possibility of getting an interpretation of the Aristotelian corpus more in accordance with historical fact? It was such questions as these that induced me to undertake the present study . . . . In sharp contrast to the opinions [of Nuyens and Jaeger] is the view of Vollenhoven, according to which almost every phase of Aristotle's development is represented in various parts of the *Physics*. Here is room, apparently, for more thorough textual analysis than has hitherto been forthcoming. [1951]

I tried to meet S. G. De Graaf this time, and I was very disappointed to hear that it was no longer possible because of his condition. You see, by this time I had begun to realize the importance of men like Sikkel and De Graaf and of that new covenantal preaching which had arisen and which was really the religious setting of the development of the *Wijsbegeerte der Wetsidee*. Also, I again participated in a series of gatherings at the Kuyperhuis for foreign students. I was doing a lot of thinking that year, and it involved my background. Knowing that Calvinism in America had generally meant Puritanism, I began to think: "How do I distinguish what I have come to see—how I've come to read the Scriptures and understand them—from the Puritanism which the word *Calvinism* had always meant to me?" And I made notes of important points that I would want to get across to students once I was back in the States and teaching. There were something like fifteen to twenty points, and when I rediscovered those . . .

> We must distantiate ourselves from the Pilgrims and Calvinists of New England, as well as from previous attempts to erect a "Christian political party" on this continent. (Cf. Schlesinger, *Age of Jackson*, p. 56.) We are not conservatives. Conservatives are one wing of the humanistic bloc, which, as times get increasingly severe, loses to the liberals or radicals. Train young college students to think of these things, and awaken through them the Christian people. [1950]

. . . notes years later and looked down that list, I saw that practically every one of those points had already been met in some way or other by the work that had been done in the meantime in the Groen Club. But we'll get to that in a moment.

I began teaching at Calvin College in the fall of 1951. For my course in Greek philosophy I chose one of the standard textbooks. But I thought to myself: "I am a beginning teacher. If I use the book to group our class discussions around, I will come more and more into that American way of talking and putting the problem, and that will be the end of *me*." So immediately I started making a syllabus. I used to sit up till two in the morning writing it out, and the next day I would dictate the few pages that I had ready.

> We confess that God created us men and that He deals with us by way of covenant (Westminster Confession of Faith, ch. VII). Since the Fall, however, men are in two different ways related to God by way of covenant: some, by virtue of the gracious restorative work of God the Spirit in their hearts . . . are once again in principle obedient to God, submissive to Him and His sovereignly declared will . . . ; others are in a state of active revolt against God and His rule . . . . These latter, though they cannot escape Him in this world of His creation, confronted as they are on every side with His works and working, make every effort of which their created nature is capable to demonstrate that the world is self-sufficient, i.e. capable of sustaining (ontology) and explaining (epistemology) itself. This dual relation in which men stand to God has always had, and of necessity must have, much to do with their *philosophizing*. It has always affected their—thus also our—study of the *history of philosophy*. In the sequel this will become increasingly clear and meaningful. For the present we shall merely say that it is because of the radical (from the Latin "radix," root) influence of our confession upon our philosophical work that this syllabus is a necessity. We do not, nor may we, feel at home in the philosophical studies of non-Christians. [1952]

Then in my second year at Calvin, in the Christmas holidays, one evening after dinner three men came to my door. They were Mr. Steven Harkema, Mr. Peter Boonstra, and Mr. Jacob VanderWilp. And they wanted me to speak for a group. It seemed that there was in Grand Rapids a group of immigrants who had formed a choir which met regularly, and these men wanted to deepen the meaning of the thing by getting conversations going in this group about the dangers of humanism in American public life. They thought that out of the membership of the choir there could be set up a Calvinistic Culture Association, and they asked me if I would speak for them at a public meeting to inaugurate such an Association. I agreed to do it. *And that's how it all got started!* In my speech I said basically that to start this separate Christian organization for cultural action was to throw the rudder over and launch out in a new direction. And I attacked the prevailing notion of common grace as though it could form a basis for cooperation in existing organizations inspired by humanism. Well, some of my colleagues who were present didn't like that at all! But some of the students who were present came to me later that spring and asked me if we couldn't get together regularly to discuss these issues.

> The meeting was held on the evening of February 5, 1953, in the Franklin Street Christian Reformed Church and the title of my address that evening was "Het roer om!" (which, I have been informed, should be translated into English as "Rudder Hard Over"). A number of Calvin professors were present, and several of them, unfortunately, were made exceedingly angry. There had also been a very good number of students present . . . . Almost at once discussion, heated and persistent, began. To be sure, everything did not happen at once. But there must have been a great deal of talk among the Canadian students and Dutch immigrant students of the United States. Finally, I think early in March, Jan Kunst and Bernie Zylstra, who were together in my afternoon logic class, came to me one afternoon after class . . . and asked me if I would be willing to give one evening out of every fourteen days to some students who felt the need of discussion of such matters as Christianity and culture, and particularly the necessity of Christian cultural organization. I accepted immediately, before they had a chance to think twice . . . . [1963]

That summer I drew up a program of study. It has never been completely worked out yet. It involved the question of who the Puritans were, the meaning of the Enlightenment, its influence in America, the basic ideas of the Declaration of Independence and the Constitution, the nature of Scholasticism, particularly as manifested in Reformed theology, the concept of natural law, the religious ground-motives that have successively given order to the experience of Western man, the origins of capitalism, the rise of the labor movement, and so on and so forth. And I had it divided according to topics: there were something like eight, but we started with about five, since there were around twelve or fifteen students who joined the club, and so two or three fellows started working on each of these topics. And then we would have meetings together. We would read the Scriptures and pray together and talk about our academic life and the meaning of it all, and then we would have a report on what work was being done in each of these groups. That's what we originally did. And gradually out of these study groups came fuller and fuller reports. But then the students wanted to so something more on their own. And just at that time Mr. Harkema—he and I had talked a great deal at the beginning—and Mr. Boonstra had a painting business together. He hadn't had much formal education himself, but he kept saying, "We've got to form a group of students!" So when I was approached by these students, I must have told Harkema almost immediately, and shortly after that he brought me a whole set of folders which had been published by the Antirevolutionary Party for their leadership courses. (Each folder contained 15 to 20 lessons on a certain topic.) I took a quick look at the set and saw that most of them were not helpful (they were full of details about the Dutch political system and party history), but the first one was what came to be referred to as the Groen Club syllabus: *The Bible and the Life of the Christian*. I showed that one to these students at board meetings during that first year, and we came to the conclusion that we needed something like that in English, and then we decided to translate it. So that's how that got started. Now let's . . .

> The following lessons have been translated and adapted by students of Calvin College and Seminary under my general supervision in the Groen van Prinsterer Society. After we had twice used them ourselves we felt so enthusiastic about them that we decided to make them more generally available. *They have helped us greatly*, and we feel confident they will help many others . . . *Do* books of human words ever help here unless the Divine Word—singular, thus a *structure*!—gets through, which alone is the POWER that can grip a human heart, draw it together in one and give it direction? In how many of our books, sermons, catechism classes, etc. does that happen? Or do we too often get lost in unrelated facts, individual persons in the Bible about whom we can moralize, etc.? No wonder so many of our words are POWERless! They do not convey the WORD!
>
> The thing to do in the circumstances is not to fume and fuss but to *provide the insight* for which our young people are unwittingly hungering and thirsting, and for lack of which they will surely utterly lose their bearings. That is exactly what we think these lessons will do. [1963]

. . . see, oh yes, I was also persuaded that we needed to get into Groen van Prinsterer's *Ongeloof en Revolutie*, so I assigned it chapter by chapter, and we had just begun it when I also decided that we ought to try our hand at translating it, to get more deeply into the work and into the meaning of it. That all happened in those early years, and although I myself only half knew where it would take us, we soon felt sure in our hearts that we were working in the right direction.

And then in 1956, in Toronto, the Association for Reformed Scientific Studies was founded—by ministers like the Reverend Henry Venema and the Reverend François Guillaume, and by Mr. Peter Speelman and Mr. Vande Riet, who were booksellers, and by a number of other men. Their second public meeting was held that fall, and Steven Harkema and I attended on behalf of the Calvinistic Culture Association. I remember, we drove over one Friday evening in Harkema's car. It was pouring rain as we crossed the Canadian border. Several fellows of the Groen Club came along—can't remember who . . . Henk Hart, John Vander Stelt, Jan Kunst, Jan Groen, John Van Dyk (big John), Bernie Zylstra, Albert Huls (now deceased)—about five of those fellows. Well, it became quite apparent at this meeting, to me at least, that their ultimate aim, goal, was to establish a Reformed university in North America, but that they didn't really, apart from possessing a general vision, know how to go about it—I mean, they had only a very vague notion of what that meant and what it involved: a Reformed university, higher education that could be called Reformed. And there was opposition from some of the American home missionaries in Ontario, who felt that their experience and guidance needed to be consulted more and who may have felt that this thing would mean competition for Calvin College. The Canadian men wanted to provide guidance for their Christian schoolteachers. They were thinking of making a night school out of it. So plans were discussed to give evening courses in a Toronto church basement. I got up at one point and said some things about, you know, the true significance of the Reformation, and its decline, and its revival in the nineteenth century, and the need to make this a *national* movement, bringing in the western Canadian provinces.

> Every effort, anywhere in the world, at building Reformed Christian (institutions of) higher education is doomed to certain failure if, before it assembles large faculties from this or that trusted church denomination and builds appropriate buildings, it does not possess *insight into the inner point of connection* between God's revelation of Himself in Jesus Christ and the materials of the several areas of theoretical investigation and cultural forming. [1965]

There won't be time to go into how the Unionville Conferences came to be organized, starting with 1959—three days of lectures for our college and university students. These gave the A.A.C.S. (then still called the A.R.S.S.) a tremendous momentum . . . .

> This Study Conference ... is designed ... also to call attention to the really desperate need that exists here in Canada for *a center of scholarly research and university instruction of our own*, where we can, above all, just *be ourselves*, where, I mean to say, we can quite naturally and happily go from Scripture to our field of research and back again, glorying in our God and Father, Who is above all and blessed forever. [1959]
>
> Mr. Chairman, for the third successive year I have the honour of being one of your lecturers here at the Unionville Conference. I alone, of your speakers, have had the wonderful privilege of seeing this Conference grow to what, in the brief span of these three years, it has already become .... The experiences I have had at these conferences I count among the most precious of my life. God has been pleased in our midst to perform a mighty work. In these conferences we are experiencing a recovery of the Word of God in its integral meaning as directing Principle of our *whole* life, of our "walk" in life, that is, of our life-dynamics. Specifically, as students we have been brought to view the whole of the scientific enterprise as a "moment" of our religion .... And what is this blessed thing that we have been experiencing here at this place if not a re-discovery of the Biblical "hearing and doing" ... ? [1961]
>
> There is a tempo in human affairs. We cannot keep attracting students with mere *promises* of development and brief suggestions with respect to it. The *development* will have to come. There must be produced in our midst *a body of scripturally directed scientific knowledge.* This is what our students are waiting for. [1962]

After many years of hard work it was finally possible in 1967 to open the Institute for Christian Studies in Toronto. I was invited to give the opening address and for four years (1970-74) I had the privilege of . . .

> We come today introducing into the life of this nation and of this continent a new institution. More weighty is the fact that for the English-speaking world it is even a new, an unheard of, kind of institution. The emergence of this new thing means that a new concentration of forces is taking shape. It signifies a re-organization of our human and material resources to accomplish a task not yet undertaken. There is a re-alignment with the avowed purpose of carrying out the Christian Mission in higher education in a manner and to a degree never hitherto attempted on our continent. This is a radical Christian proposal for radical times. [1967]
>
> We do not put our confidence in rituals and liturgies, in our denominational histories or our theological systems. That is not to deny the relative importance of any or all of these when they are themselves scripture-directed. But our confidence is in the life-producing, life-sustaining, life-developing Word of our God ... in the Word of God

alone. The God who came near in Jesus Christ is our strength; His Word is our life. Mindful of our calling to be agents of reconciliation, our hearts cry out in the words of an Old Testament prophet: O earth, earth, earth, hear the Word of God and *live*. [1967]

. . . teaching a number of courses there on alternate weekends. At first we rented a classroom on the University of Toronto campus on Saturday mornings. I shall never forget that first session when I was introduced to my first class there by Bernard Zylstra. There must have been close to 100 persons present. Now I am a Fellow of the Institute, which for a young struggling institution has proven thus far largely to be an honorary position.

Meanwhile, the outlook for a greater penetration of North American culture and civilization by the Gospel as understood in the spirit of Calvin's Reformation has grown significantly brighter in recent years. For besides the Institute for Christian Studies in Toronto, we have the King's College opening in western Canada (Alberta), and in the state of Iowa Dordt College continues to take on distinctive coloring. In addition to all that, a renewed effort to find distinctive Biblically-reformed answers to crucial questions of our time, both theoretical and practical (and these in their relation to each other) is seen in a number of new undertakings at my own college—for example, the Calvin Center for Christian Scholarship. And then there is, in the political sector, what appears to me to be a most significant movement in the United States, the Association for Public Justice (A.P.J.).

You know what we need in Christian circles? Leaders, courageous and daring leaders for new and untried areas of scholarship, men who have been given very careful guidance and training for a period of some ten years or more. Thus also the means for such training. What you have to do is get promising young people who are wholly committed to serving Jesus Christ, get them when they are about 18 or 19 years of age and start them on various programs of education. We sorely need some kind of a private program to see to this training of leaders in crucial and new areas of scholarship. It's a question, first, of religion, just as a commitment to life service as a missionary to a particular country is. For the young person may be asked to commit himself to an area of scholarship for which the need isn't even generally recognized in his circles yet, which means, among other things, that he cannot foresee job possibilities. I have myself been involved in such situations, as when I advised Bernard Zylstra not to go on, as was the custom in those days, to prepare for the gospel ministry but to become an opening wedge in a reformational study of the law sciences, and when I suggested to Richard Van Houten that he make use of his Vietnam language experience to at last enter upon a study of the history of Chinese thought from a reformational point of view. In neither case were there jobs that could be promised. We had to expect everything from our Lord, but we *had* to venture out. The Lord, we knew, is always faithful and will open up the possibilities just in the nick of time, often to our own surprise.

I have been very much concerned about our realizing our world mission. We are very far from doing what Reformed Christians *ought* to be doing in this regard. What I'd *like* to do is get hold of such a committed, bright young man with a feeling for languages and say to him, "Learn Arabic and (modern) Hebrew, or Russian and Slavic languages, or Chinese and Japanese, or Sanskrit and a couple of modern languages of India. Become as authoritative as you can in the language, literature, history, and thought of the people who are united in their language, and when you are we'll set you up in a chair or department somewhere." You see, in our large universities there has grown up, around the traditional center, that is, the various departments, another kind of life, that of institutes. And that is my idea, that around a traditional center we erect an Institute for Slavic Language Area Studies, an Institute for Sinic Language Area Studies, an Institute for the study of Hebrew and Arabic and Middle Eastern Studies, a Center for Hispanic Language Area Studies, and a Center of the study of India and its languages. And then you've covered most of the great cultural areas of the globe. (Indonesia and Africa are missing.) If, to begin with, we could get just one well-trained man in each institute, why, within ten years, think of the tens of people that would be in the process of being trained in that way, out of which further teaching staff would surely come.

This is of the essence if we are going to realize our world mission. If we do not develop that *world* calling, I think that what will happen to us is that we will become increasingly restricted and we'll say we only must try to hold on to what we've got (whatever that is) in our Anglo-Saxon civilization or in our Western European civilization, and then we will lose even this. One must always be pushing outward into the variety of cultures and peoples that have providentially emerged in history. Because revelation comes to all of them: the world that envelopes them is revelational—their own very beings are, but they suppress that truth in their unrighteousness, and only the Gospel can break through that.

> And what of the philosophies of China and ancient India in this ecumenical age when not only dialogue among adherents of the world's "higher" religions is being sought but we are at the same time being confronted with the irrelevance, and consequent impotence, of our Christian Mission to the proud cultures of Asia? [1965]

I've known enough missionaries, missionaries to Asia, for example, to feel that we aren't doing at all what ought to be done. I think that we ought to take those peoples very seriously, and the cultural and historical influences that molded them and made them what they are and in the midst of which they live as individuals and by which they are being influenced all their lives. We ought to try to understand from a Scriptural standpoint what fundamental distortions of creational revelation on the part of their predecessors have given form to their lifestyle and their institutions. But we aren't training our missionaries to do that sort of thing. What we need are places where they could be prepared for that. I really do think that we should begin with the major centers of culture and make an effort to understand their history and their literatures, the images with which they think and after which they model themselves, and their institutions. We should try, by the light of the Scriptures, to understand in what way men were giving response (however faulty) to that ultimate revelation of God to which they must respond, and in what way all that, in obedience to Christ, has got to be reformed by the light of the Word of God. In that sense you deal integrally with them. You allow them to stand in their full dignity, as they say, but a dignity which takes account of the fact that they are radically fallen from fellowship with God. Only then are you able in a meaningful way to lead to the reformation of what is there without destroying the sense, the religious sense, that they were, in what Paul calls the blindness of their hearts, responding to the ultimate religious conditions of our whole existence.

You know, I once had a Navaho student in my class in Greek philosophy. He told me over a cup of coffee: "Your missionaries came to my people and they—they're known as the People with the Book—they came and just threw that book into our laps, as it were, and told us that this was the Book of God and that we had to believe this. They never asked a question about how we thought, or what our religious ideas were, or why we lived as we did." I could tell that he resented it. Then he said to me: "I never knew that there was another way of relationship between us and you people until I sat in this class. But when you talked of all these concepts—universalism and partial universalism and individualism, about the theme of macrocosm and microcosm, about Realism and objectivism and dualism and monism—then I began to realize that here were many of the themes of my own people. And then I began to see how those things could be related to what the Scriptures present. I had never seen that before—how the real thoughts of my people were related to the fundamental themes of the Scriptures as (aberrational) responses to revelation."

So that's what I mean, you see, that revelation is a reality and that man everywhere must respond and that that is why we can talk together. Once you've seen that all the scientific and pre-scientific work is given direction by a person's religious stance in the heart with respect to God's revelation, then you really begin to work with people in the creational fullness of their life and your life and the life of culture. Then you get a true encounter, then you have true dialogue. Even if there is an antithesis of direction with respect to that ultimate revelation, you *meet* each other in the notion that these positions, these views, are both there because we've got to answer some kind of a revelational impingement on our lives. And both of us are called to order in that situation by the Word of God. God has given an order for human life, and that order is revelation which addresses us inescapably and calls us to obedience, to acceptance, to walking in its light, and so to blessedness.

> In suggesting the incompatibility of Christianity and humanism I do not wish to be misunderstood. Not for a moment do I believe that . . . Christian and humanist have nothing to say to each other or must have no dealings with each other. The two can always in this life talk together, and they may repeatedly find ways of working together. But that talk and that practical cooperation will surely not be possible, as has so often been claimed, because the two faiths down deep somewhere share a common foundation before they diverge to two distinct and opposed movements . . . but solely—I speak from the Christian point of view (one must speak from a definite point of view)—solely because of the overwhelming, convincing testimony of the revelational creation-ordinances of God. The humanist, like the Christian, lives in the world God created, the world that is upheld and driven onward by His Word and by His Spirit . . . . *All* men respond to the *one* law-order. Right here every man, just in this central capacity of *homo respondens*, is more than his own subjective systematizing of the moment. There is an element of *resisting*, which speaks of more than is contained in the positive systematic position that is being developed. Men do, after all, have to account for the structure of the creation as it is taken up in their experience, and until they adequately account for it they are restless, driven on to new modifications or to still deeper turnings of thought. [1968]

Well, I can see why you got me to say some of these things again here, because it has been central to what I've tried to say all these years to my students: it is the Word of God that orders our thinking and makes things fall into place. No, I wouldn't want to say just the Bible. The Bible is part of revelation: we can no longer understand creational revelation apart from God's gracious redeeming revelation of Jesus Christ—that's the coming of the Mediator. And Scripture—what has been inscripturated—is part of that, part of the whole coming of the renewing Word of God. But we—we guard Article 2 of the Belgic Confession,* and we say the words, but we're not living as though revelation is real. I don't mean a *doctrine* of revelation, or a *theory* of revelation; I don't even mean a statement of fact about revelation. I mean that we live in a world whose very reality is revelation. We are living constantly in revelational light. I don't think we live and work in that realization. *And at this crucial point things are getting worse!* I think we're losing, under several influences. In the hands of men around Barth—*Zwischen den Zeiten*, Gogarten—creational revelation or general revelation got to be *Schöpfungsordnungen*, a kind of theoretical vindication of existing society. So there came a reaction against any talk about creation ordinances. And then there is historicism, which has been developing for a long time, and the influence of which I find is overwhelming now, just overwhelming. And then finally you have the traditional scholasticism—Scriptural revelation gets to be propositional statements—and that's very strong at many of our seminaries today.

Thus a good deal of distrust arises whenever you talk about God's Word as Power. Yet, that is simple Scripture, and it's at this point that we've got to start if we're going to recover a vital Christian faith. All I've been concerned to do is to preserve the idea of revelation as God's sovereign Address to us, His Word that goes forth from His mouth into the world to do His will. I think, for instance, of Isaiah 55:11: "So is my word that goes out from my mouth: it will not return to me empty but will accomplish what I desire and achieve the purpose for which I sent it." And then there's Hebrews 4:12-13. The Word of God—whether that means the preached Word or that portion which came to be inscripturated makes no difference—is, as the very Address to us of the sovereign God, living, full of activity and power to accomplish. God is active in it to bring salvation or judgment. It penetrates with divine efficacy to the innermost being of man, commanding a response. Thus we can understand I Peter 1:23, that we "have been born anew . . . through the living and abiding word of God." In its codified form, that Word, like the incarnate Son of God, becomes the object of our perception and analysis, but the Word of God itself is never object (and never subject, for that matter) but always *LAW-WORD*, a word that commands our life. It is usually the working in the

---

*Article 2 of the Belgic Confession reads as follows: "We know Him by two means: First, by the creation, preservation, and government of the universe; which is before our eyes as a most elegant book, wherein all creatures, great and small, are as so many characters leading us to *see clearly the invisible things of God*, even *his everlasting power and divinity*, as the apostle Paul says (Rom. 1:20). All which things are sufficient to convince men and leave them without excuse. Second, He makes Himself more clearly and fully known to us by His holy and divine Word, that is to say, as far as is necessary for us to know in this life, to His glory and our salvation."

background of the thinker's mind of a philosophy that does not comport with Scriptural revelation, a philosophy which leads Christians to think of Biblical revelation in terms of "propositions" to which the "mind" gives "assent." The anti-Christian philosophy of positivism has given us a view of "facts" which underlies much of the present discussion on the subject of Scriptural infallibility. And it is usually the anti-Christian philosophy known as phenomenology, or perhaps existentialistic phenomenology (Heidegger), that has brought historicism to the fore.

The solution is to allow the Scriptures themselves to speak to us again. The Word of God pierces to the very heart with its truth. That's why my wife and I have been translating S. G. De Graaf's work *Verbondsgeschiedenis* (English title: *Promise and Deliverance*, Paideia Press, St. Catharines, Ontario, Canada). We really have great hopes that these four volumes will penetrate the whole Evangelical world, will draw worldwide attention, and will accompany our outreach to all the world's cultures. Already more than 25,000 copies have been sold, and now the work is being translated into Spanish and Chinese. We hope to see the day when it will be translated into Japanese, Korean, Arabic, French, and German. I just hope everyone will *read* this work, and that the covenantal structure of Biblical religion will get across. With Bavinck, I believe that the covenant relationship is the essence of the Christian religion, and that it explains the phenomenon of the world's religions.

There's another thing that concerns me very much, namely, that Christians must face up to the obvious collapse of our political system, and to the meaninglessness of the two-party system we now have in the United States, or even of the party structure as it is in Canada. What I think about this can be found in my little book *Scriptural Religion and Political Task*. I'm encouraged by the direction taken recently by the Association for Public Justice (A.P.J.) in the United States. What about the political forming of the minds of the people in between the presidential election years? There is, you might say, none. And that is because the parties don't really stand for anything. In the mad rush for votes they tend to become parties of the center, or comprehensive parties that welcome all viewpoints, thus standing for none. How can we form the minds of the people politically in a Christian way? How will we handle the political education of our Christian youth? Until you have a party that *stands* for something, and candidates of such a party, you can't tell what kind of political forming of the mind you've got to engage in. Our present system is nihilistic. We *need* Christian political organization and action.

... the real powers in life, the mainsprings and directors of cultural life and development, are convictions of faith. If the American parties wish to become significant as directors of *political* life, they will have to embrace clear-cut *political* points of view, a *political* creed. [1961]

Dealing with this little fact or that little sin, kicking out the liquor bosses, ridding the streets of men engaged in illegal businesses, voting to keep a divorced person out of the White House—these matters, pressure groups, which have to work within existing organizations and concentrate only on individual problems—none of these get at the *root* of the matter. None of them deal with the problem. For the problem is *to array principle over against principle.* Liberalism is a religious *direction* in political matters. The two-party system, putting conservatism over against liberalism, or liberalism over against socialism, does not *realize* in American life the real struggle between the Gospel, the direction of life, and all these movements together as representing the humanistic direction of death. [1956]

So there's lots of work to be done! I still hope to do some of that work myself. I want to write especially for my Evangelical people—about the task in philosophy and why *this* type of Christian philosophy, and what *we mean* by a Christian philosophy. I want to explain all that very simply—prolegomena. And then I'd like to write on Greek philosophy, and on phenomenology . . . .

Grand Rapids, Michigan, 18 June 1976

Badhoevedorp, The Netherlands, 6 September 1976

Select List of Publications
by
Dr. H. Evan Runner

Books and Articles

The Development of Aristotle Illustrated from the Earliest Books of the Physics. Kampen: Kok, 1951. Ph.D. dissertation, Free University of Amsterdam.

The Relation of the Bible to Learning (The Unionville Lectures for 1959 and 1960). Toronto: Wedge, 1974.

Scriptural Religion and Political Task (The Unionville Lectures for 1961). Toronto: Wedge, 1974.

"ARSS and Its Reorganization," in *Calvinist-Contact* (January 26, 1962), pp. 5-7.

"Place and Task of an Institute of Reformed Scientific Studies." Hamilton, Ontario: Association for Reformed Scientific Studies, 1965.

"Some Observations on the Condition of Calvin College at the Celebration of Its Centennial," in *Prism 1976*, ed. Bernhard VanderWilp. Grand Rapids, Michigan, 1976, pp. 30-39.

"Dooyeweerd's Passing: An Appreciation," in *The Banner* (April 22, 1977), pp. 20-23.

Book Reviews in the Westminster Theological Journal

May 1941, pp. 209-212. Douglas Clyde MacIntosh: *The Problem of Religious Knowledge* (New York, 1940).

November 1941, pp. 31-38. Etienne Gilson: *God and Philosophy* (New Haven, Connecticut, 1941).

November 1942, pp. 73-80. Nels F. S. Ferré: *The Christian Faith: An Inquiry into Its Adequacy as Man's Ultimate Religion* (New York, 1942).

November 1944, pp. 82-84. Matthew Spinka: *John Amos Comenius, That Incomparable Moravian* (Chicago, 1943).

May 1946, pp. 201-206. Erich Frank: *Philosophical Understanding and Religious Truth* (New York, 1945).

November 1948, pp. 63-67. Herman Dooyeweerd: *Transcendental Problems of Philosophic Thought* (Grand Rapids, Michigan, 1948).

May 1949, pp. 201-208. J. D. Dengerink: *Critisch-historisch onderzoek naar de sociologische ontwikkeling van het beginsel der "Souvereiniteit in eigen Kring" in de 19e en 20e eeuw* (Kampen, 1948).

November 1957, pp. 71-77. Richard Kroner: *Speculation in Pre-Christian Philosophy* (Philadelphia, 1956).

November 1958, pp. 127-132. Herman Dooyeweerd: *A New Critique of Theoretical Thought*, 4 volumes (Philadelphia, 1953-58).

Published Addresses

"Het Roer Om!" An Address delivered on February 5, 1953 in Grand Rapids, Michigan under the sponsorship of the Calvinistic Culture Association. An English text appears in *Torch and Trumpet* (April-May, 1953), pp. 1-4.

"Cui Bono? (To What End Men's Societies?)" An address delivered on September 15, 1953 in Grand Rapids, Michigan to the Fall Mass Meeting of the Grand Rapids League of Reformed Men's Societies. Published in *Torch and Trumpet* (October-November, 1953), pp. 1-6.

"The Christian and the World: An Historical Introduction to a Christian Theory of Culture." A paper read at the Faculty-Board Conference of Calvin College and Seminary held near Holland, Michigan on September 9-10, 1953. Published in *Torch and Trumpet* (April, May, July, September, October, 1955).

"Year of Decision: One Faith or Two?" A public lecture given on November 14, 1956 in Grand Rapids, Michigan under the sponsorship of the Groen van Prinsterer Society on the eve of the centennial of the Christian Reformed Church. Mimeographed.

"The Development of Calvinism in North America on the Background of Its Development in Europe." A speech delivered on November 9, 1957 in Calgary, Alberta at the Study Conference of the Calvinistic Action Association. Mimeographed.

"Can Canada Tolerate the CLAC? The Achilles' Heel of a Humanistic Society." An address delivered on April 29, 1967 in Toronto at the Fifteenth Anniversary Convention of the Christian Labour Association of Canada. Published by the Christian Labour Association of Canada (Rexdale, Ontario: no date). Republished in *A Christian Union in Labour's Wasteland*, ed. Edward Vanderkloet. Toronto: Wedge, 1979, pp. 71-106.

"Point Counter Point." An address delivered on October 7, 1967 in Toronto on the occasion of the opening of the Institute for Christian Studies. Offset.

"Christianity and Humanism (A Re-Thinking of the Supposed Affinity of their Fundamental Principles)." An address delivered on April 24, 1968 at the annual meeting of the Christian Freedom Foundation in the International Year for Human Rights. Published by the Institute for Christian Studies (Toronto: no date).

"On Being Anti-Revolutionary and Christian-Historical at the Cutting Edge of History, 1979-1980." Presented at the Centennial Symposium of the Anti-Revolutionary Party in the Netherlands on April 2-6, 1979. Forthcoming.

Contributors

Hugh Cook teaches English at Dordt College (Sioux Center, Iowa). He received an M.A. from Simon Fraser University and an M.F.A. from the Writers' Workshop at the University of Iowa. His fiction, poetry and criticism have appeared in such journals as *The Malahat Review, The University of Windsor Review*, and *Studies in Canadian Literature*.

Arnold H. De Graaff lectured for four years on psychology at Trinity Christian College, Palos Heights, Illinois. In 1970 he joined the Institute for Christian Studies in Toronto, where he concentrates on theory of personality, theory of emotions and sensations, and theory of learning. He has been a counselor for many years and has served as a director of the Curriculum Development Centre in Toronto. His publications include *The Educational Ministry of the Church* (1966), *Joy in Learning* (1973), and articles on psychological themes.

Hendrik Hart teaches systematic philosophy at the Institute for Christian Studies in Toronto. Before that he was head of the Philosophical Institute of the Free University of Amsterdam, where he studied with D. H. T. Vollenhoven. The focal point of his work in the last fifteen years has been the area of problems surrounding the question of the relation of Christian commitment to the academic enterprise, especially epistemology and philosophy of science. His publications include *Communal Certainty and Authorized Truth: An Examination of John Dewey's Philosophy of Verification* (1966) and *The Challenge of Our Age* (1968). At present he is preparing a major work on theory of knowledge.

Wendy Elgersma Helleman received an M.A. in classics at the University of Toronto, after which she continued her studies in classical languages at the Free University of Amsterdam. At present she is working on a doctoral dissertation on Plotinus. She also teaches New Testament Greek at the Christian Reformed Seminary and Bible College in Bacolod, the Philippines, where, together with her husband, the Reverend Art Helleman, she serves as a missionary teacher for the Christian Reformed World Missions.

John N. Kraay is an instructor in modern philosophy at the Free University of Amsterdam. His interests are primarily focused on continental philosophy, especially existentialism.

Edward A. Langerak is Associate Professor of Philosophy at St. Olaf College (Northfield, Minnesota). He completed the M.A. requirements at the University of Michigan and received a Ph.D. at Princeton University. He has published articles in the areas of ethics and philosophy of religion.

James H. Olthuis joined the Institute for Christian Studies in Toronto in 1968. He concentrates on theological anthropology, hermeneutics, philosophy of revelation, and ethics. His publications include *Facts, Values and Ethics: A confrontation with twentieth century British moral philosophy, in particular G. E. Moore* (1968), and *I Pledge You My Troth: A Christian view of marriage, family, friendship* (1975).

Theodore Plantinga studied at the Johns Hopkins University (Baltimore, Maryland), the University of Freiburg (West Germany), and the University of Toronto, where in 1975 he received a Ph.D. degree in philosophy. His book on Dilthey will be published by the University of Toronto Press in 1980. He has taught elementary school and philosophy on the college level. At present he is a free-lance editor and translator.

Calvin Seerveld was born in West Sayville, New York in 1930. In 1953 he received an M.A. in English literature and classics from the University of Michigan, after which he studied with D. H. T. Vollenhoven at the Free University of Amsterdam. At present he teaches philosophical aesthetics at the Institute for Christian Studies in Toronto. Among his numerous and wide-ranging publications are *Benedetto Croce's Earlier Aesthetic Theories and Literary Criticism* (1958), *The Greatest Song: In Critique of Solomon* (1967), and *For God's Sake Run with Joy* (1972). His recent writings deal with the philosophy and theory of art and art history.

Peter J. Steen completed a Th.D. at Westminster Theological Seminary in 1970. He also took courses at Temple University (Philadelphia), Villanova University, and the Free University of Amsterdam. His teaching experience includes philosophy at Trinity Christian College (Palos Heights, Illinois), philosophy at Geneva College (Beaver Falls, Pennsylvania), and lectures and courses for the Coalition for Christian Outreach (Pittsburgh). Since 1974 he has served as Field Director for Christian Educational Services (Pittsburgh), an organization offering Christian scholarship and teaching to many college campuses. His doctoral dissertation deals with "Religious Transcendence in the Philosophy of Herman Dooyeweerd."

Anthony Tol lectures in modern philosophy at the Free University of Amsterdam. His major interests lie in the history and theory of mathematics. He is preparing a dissertation on Bertrand Russell.

Henry Vander Goot received an M.Div. from Princeton Theological Seminary and a Ph.D. from St. Michael's College of the University of Toronto. Since 1976 he has been teaching theology at Calvin College. He is the editor of Gustav Wingren's *Creation and Gospel: The New Situation in European Theology* (1979).

John C. Vander Stelt studied philosophy and theology at the Free University of Amsterdam and Calvin Theological Seminary (Grand Rapids, Michigan). From 1965 to 1967 he was a pastor in the Christian Reformed Church in Canada. Since 1968 he has been teaching at Dordt College (Sioux Center, Iowa) in the areas of theology and philosophy. He is the author of *Philosophy and Scripture: A Study in Old Princeton and Westminster Theology* (1978).

John Van Dyk is Professor of Philosophy at Dordt College (Sioux Center, Iowa). He received an M.A. from the University of Michigan and a Ph.D. from Cornell University. His doctoral dissertation focused on the value of Sentence commentaries for the history of medieval philosophy. The interplay of theology, philosophy and science in the Middle Ages is his specific area of research. He has published articles and speeches in various periodicals and books.

Harry van Dyke is an instructor in philosophy of history at the Free University of Amsterdam. He has been engaged in numerous editorial projects, such as S. U. Zuidema's *Communication and Confrontation: A Philosophical Appraisal and Critique of Modern Society and Contemporary Thought* (Toronto: Wedge, 1972) and Guillaume Groen van Prinsterer, *Unbelief and Revolution*, Lectures VIII and IX and Lecture XI (Amsterdam: Groen van Prinsterer Fund, 1973 and 1975).

Albert M. Wolters has taught history of philosophy at the Institute for Christian Studies in Toronto since 1974. He studied philosophy at the Free University of Amsterdam from 1964 to 1972. He has written a doctoral dissertation on Plotinus which is being prepared for publication.

Bernard Zylstra is Principal of the Institute for Christian Studies in Toronto, where he has taught political theory since 1968. He is especially interested in the relation between religion, culture, and the political realm. His publications have focused on representatives of significant political theories in the modern period, such as John Locke, Karl Marx, Harold Laski, Herman Dooyeweerd, Eric Voegelin, and George Grant. He received an LL.B. from the University of Michigan and an S.J.D. from the Free University of Amsterdam, where he studied with Herman Dooyeweerd. His publications include *From Pluralism to Collectivism: The Development of Harold Laski's Political Thought* (1968). He was coeditor of L. Kalsbeek's *Contours of a Christian Philosophy: An Introduction to Herman Dooyeweerd's Thought* (1975), and final editor of Herman Dooyeweerd, *Roots of Western Culture: Pagan, Secular, and Christian Options* (Toronto: Wedge, 1979).

Index of Persons